Point Reyes Teen Graphic
Novel
Teen Graphic Novel Johns
Johns, Geoff, 1973-
Green Lantern. Volume 1,
Sinestro
31111032521211   6/12

P9-CRL-176

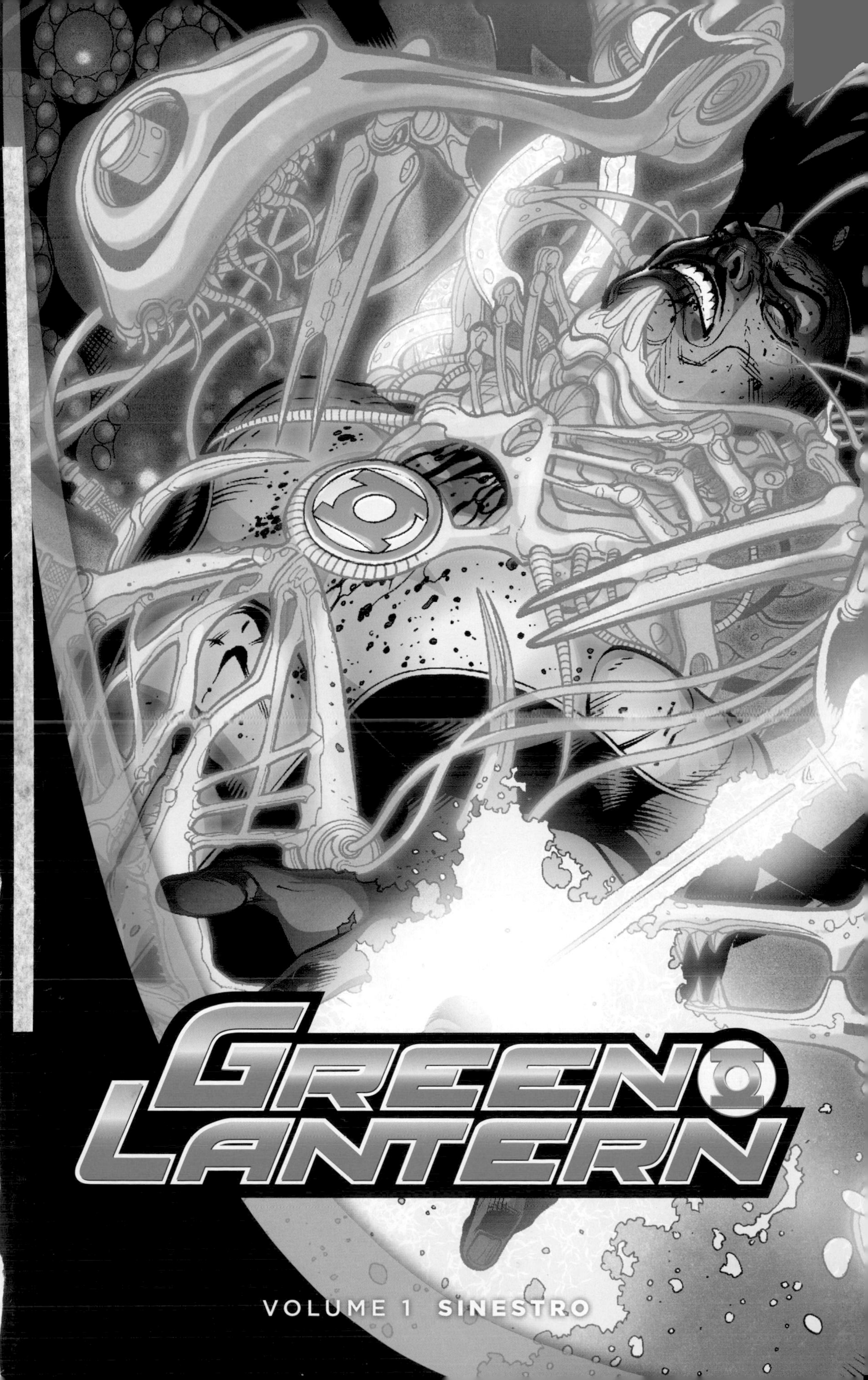

GREEN LANTERN

VOLUME 1 SINESTRO

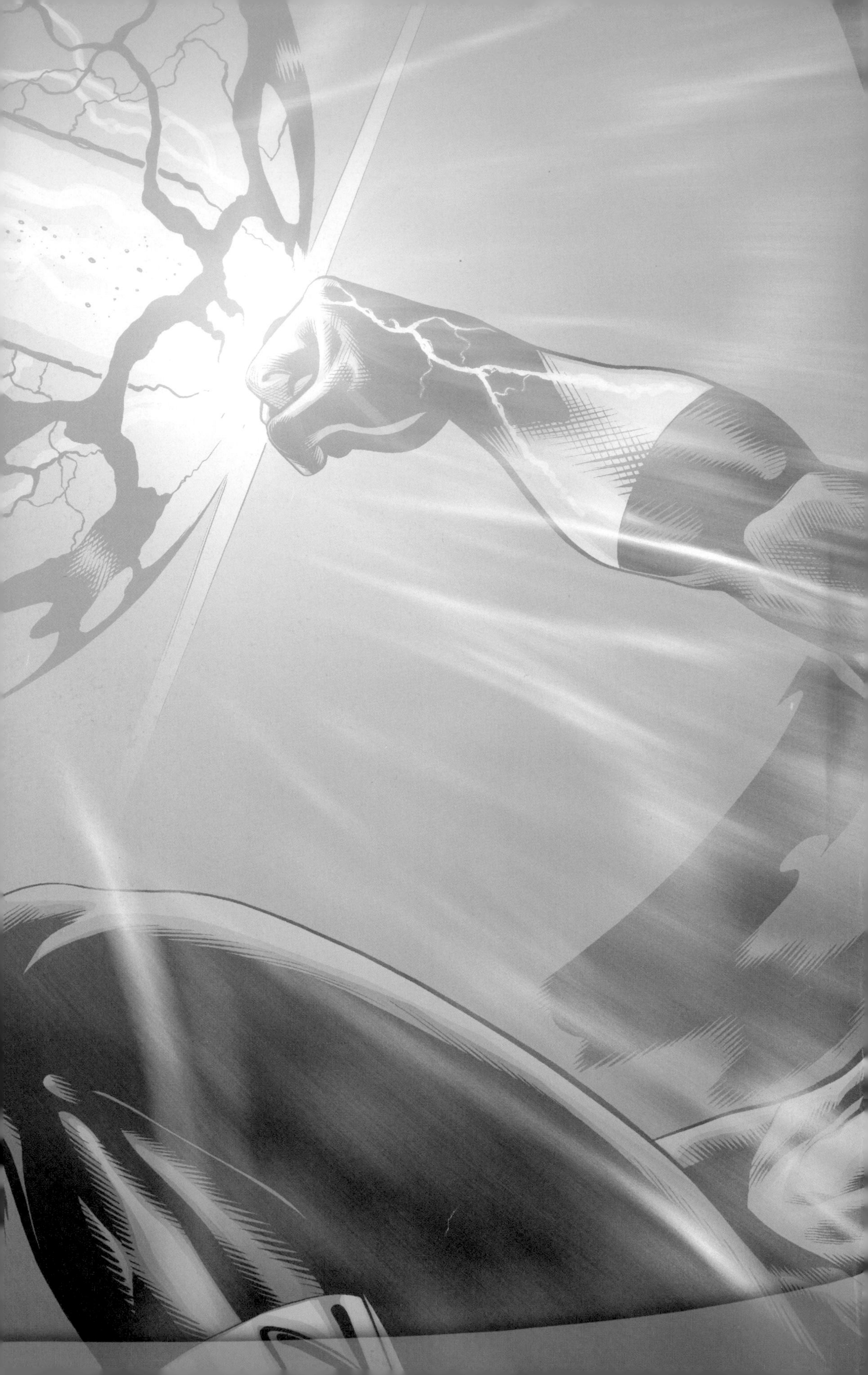

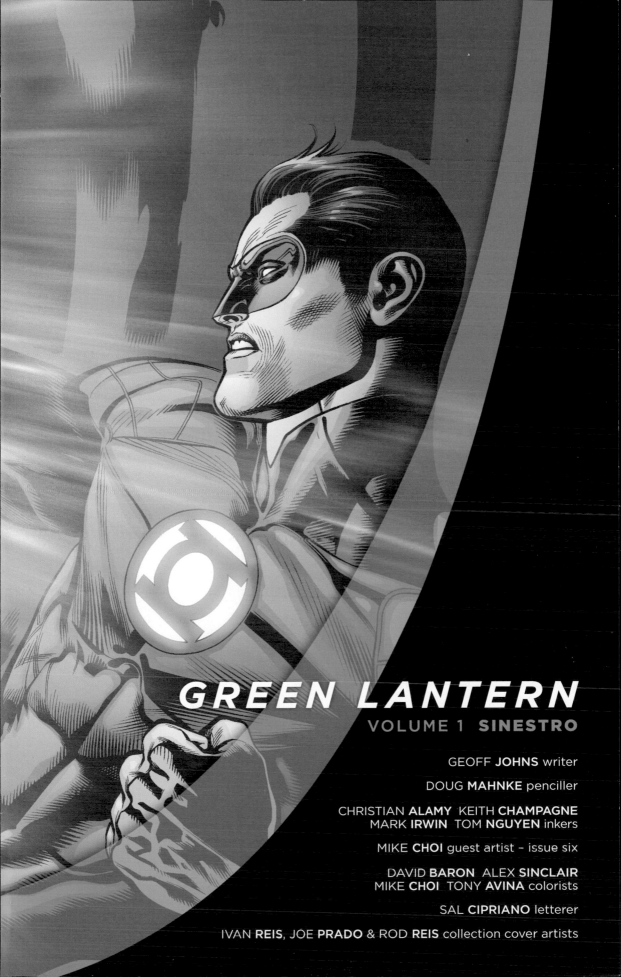

GREEN LANTERN
VOLUME 1 SINESTRO

GEOFF **JOHNS** writer

DOUG **MAHNKE** penciller

CHRISTIAN **ALAMY** KEITH **CHAMPAGNE**
MARK **IRWIN** TOM **NGUYEN** inkers

MIKE **CHOI** guest artist – issue six

DAVID **BARON** ALEX **SINCLAIR**
MIKE **CHOI** TONY **AVINA** colorists

SAL **CIPRIANO** letterer

IVAN **REIS**, JOE **PRADO** & ROD **REIS** collection cover artists

BRIAN CUNNINGHAM Editor – Original Series DARREN SHAN Assistant Editor – Original Series
PETER HAMBOUSSI Editor ROBBIN BROSTERMAN Design Director – Books
ROBBIE BIEDERMAN Publication Design

EDDIE BERGANZA Executive Editor
BOB HARRAS VP – Editor-in-Chief

DIANE NELSON President DAN DIDIO and JIM LEE Co-Publishers
GEOFF JOHNS Chief Creative Officer
JOHN ROOD Executive VP – Sales, Marketing and Business Development
AMY GENKINS Senior VP – Business and Legal Affairs NAIRI GARDINER Senior VP – Finance
JEFF BOISON VP – Publishing Operations MARK CHIARELLO VP – Art Direction and Design
JOHN CUNNINGHAM VP – Marketing TERRI CUNNINGHAM VP – Talent Relations and Services
ALISON GILL Senior VP – Manufacturing and Operations DAVID HYDE VP – Publicity
HANK KANALZ Senior VP – Digital JAY KOGAN VP – Business and Legal Affairs, Publishing
JACK MAHAN VP – Business Affairs, Talent NICK NAPOLITANO VP – Manufacturing Administration
SUE POHJA VP – Book Sales COURTNEY SIMMONS Senior VP – Publicity
BOB WAYNE Senior VP – Sales

GREEN LANTERN VOLUME 1: SINESTRO

Published by DC Comics. Cover and compilation Copyright © 2012 DC Comics.
All Rights Reserved.

Originally published in single magazine form in GREEN LANTERN 1-6. Copyright © 2011, 2012 DC Comics.
All Rights Reserved. All characters, their distinctive likenesses and related elements
featured in this publication are trademarks of DC Comics. The stories, characters and incidents featured in this
publication are entirely fictional. DC Comics does not read or accept unsolicited
submissions of ideas, stories or artwork.

DC Comics, 1700 Broadway, New York, NY 10019
A Warner Bros. Entertainment Company
Printed by RR Donnelley, Salem, VA, USA. 4/13/12. First Printing.
HC ISBN: 978-1-4012-3454-6
SC ISBN: 978-1-4012-3455-3

SUSTAINABLE
FORESTRY
INITIATIVE

Certified Chain of Custody
At Least 25% Certified Forest Content
www.sfiprogram.org
SFI-01042
APPLIES TO TEXT STOCK ONLY

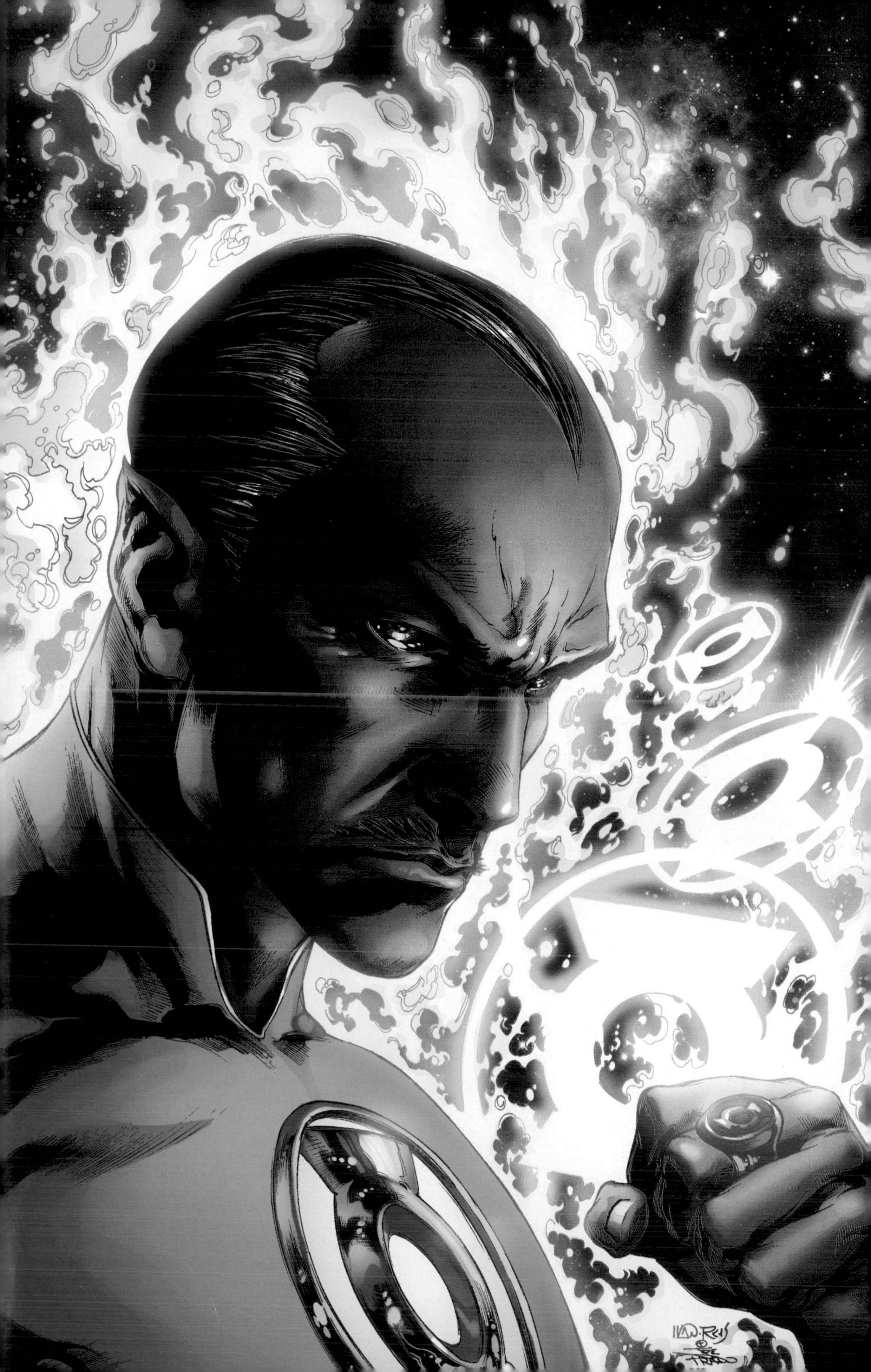

Ivan Reis, Joe Prado & Rod Reis

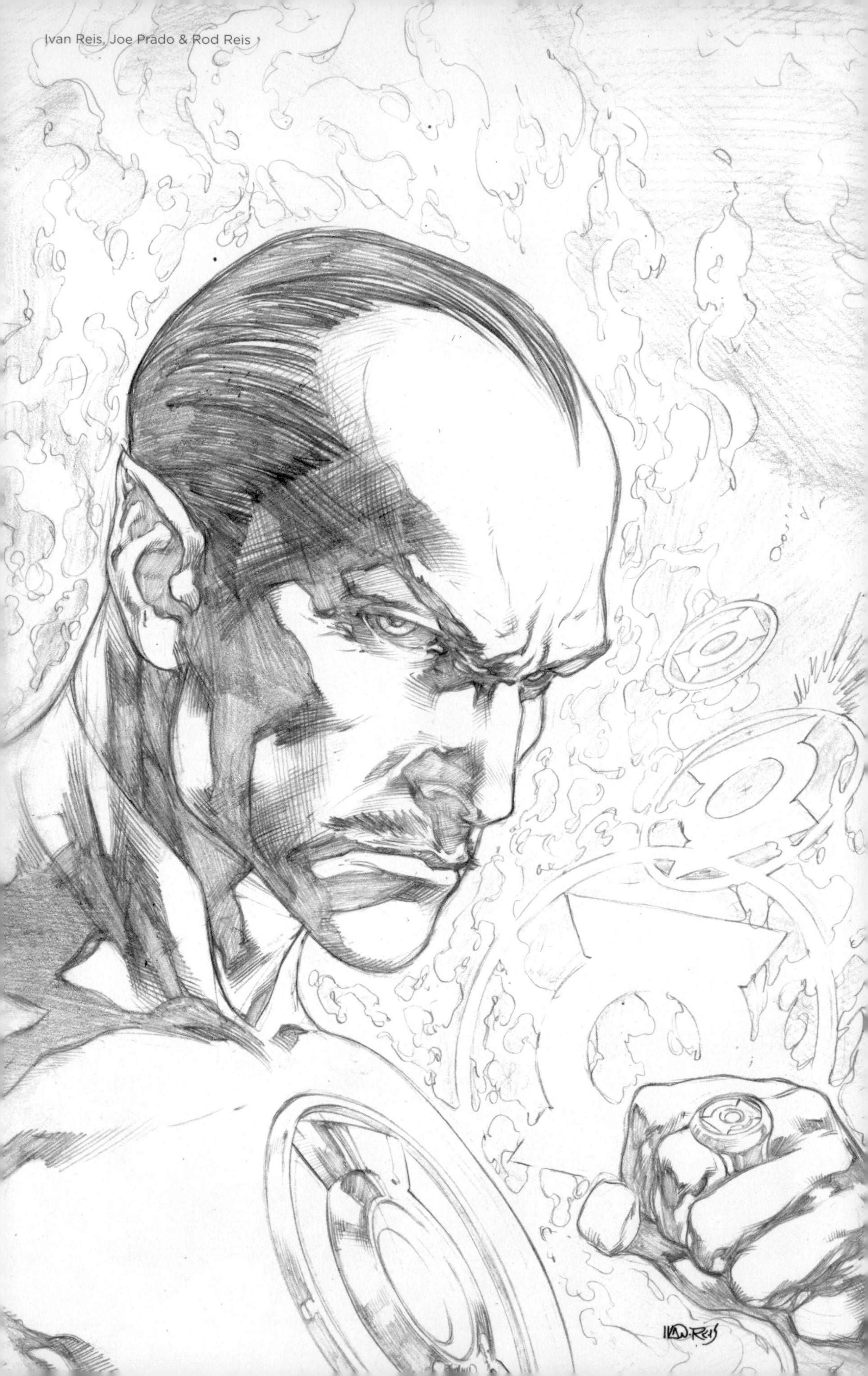

IN... BRIGHTEST DAY... IN BLACKEST NIGHT
NO EVIL SHALL ESCAPE MY SIGHT
LET THOSE...WHO WORSHIP EVIL'S MIGHT
BEWARE MY POWER

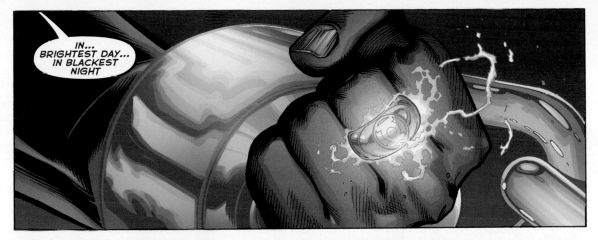

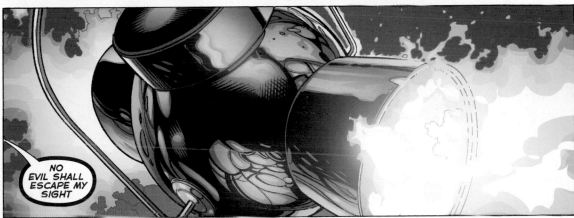

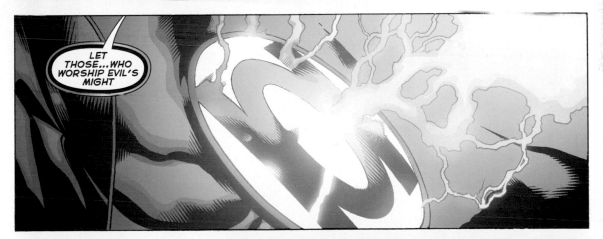

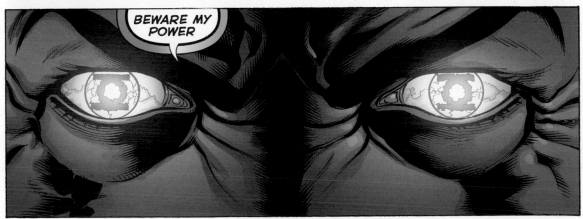

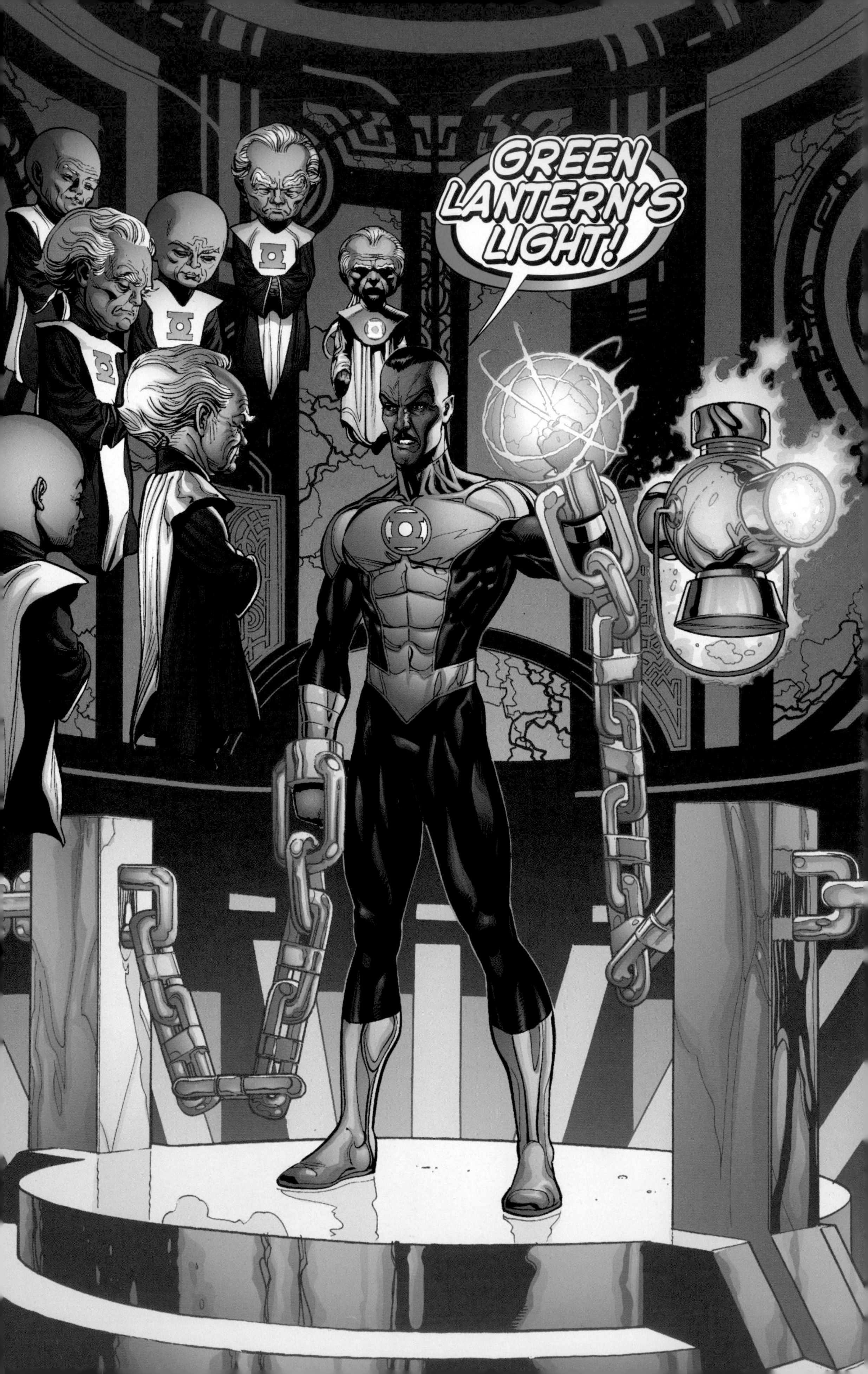
GREEN LANTERN'S LIGHT!

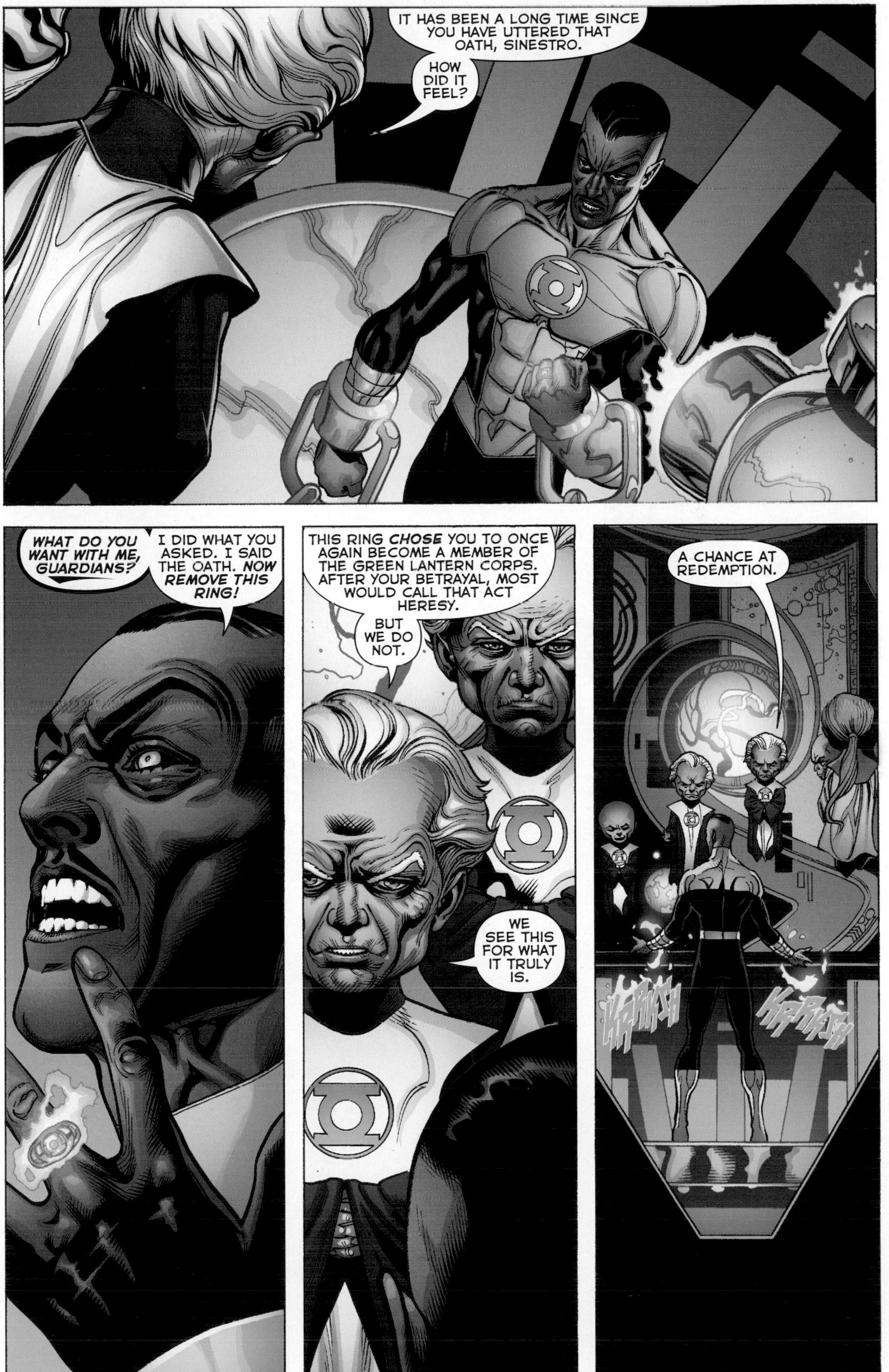

IT HAS BEEN A LONG TIME SINCE YOU HAVE UTTERED THAT OATH, SINESTRO.
HOW DID IT FEEL?
WHAT DO YOU WANT WITH ME, GUARDIANS?
I DID WHAT YOU ASKED. I SAID THE OATH. ***NOW REMOVE THIS RING!***
THIS RING ***CHOSE*** YOU TO ONCE AGAIN BECOME A MEMBER OF THE GREEN LANTERN CORPS. AFTER YOUR BETRAYAL, MOST WOULD CALL THAT ACT HERESY.
BUT WE DO NOT.
WE SEE THIS FOR WHAT IT TRULY IS.
A CHANCE AT REDEMPTION.
KRAKSH
KRAKSH

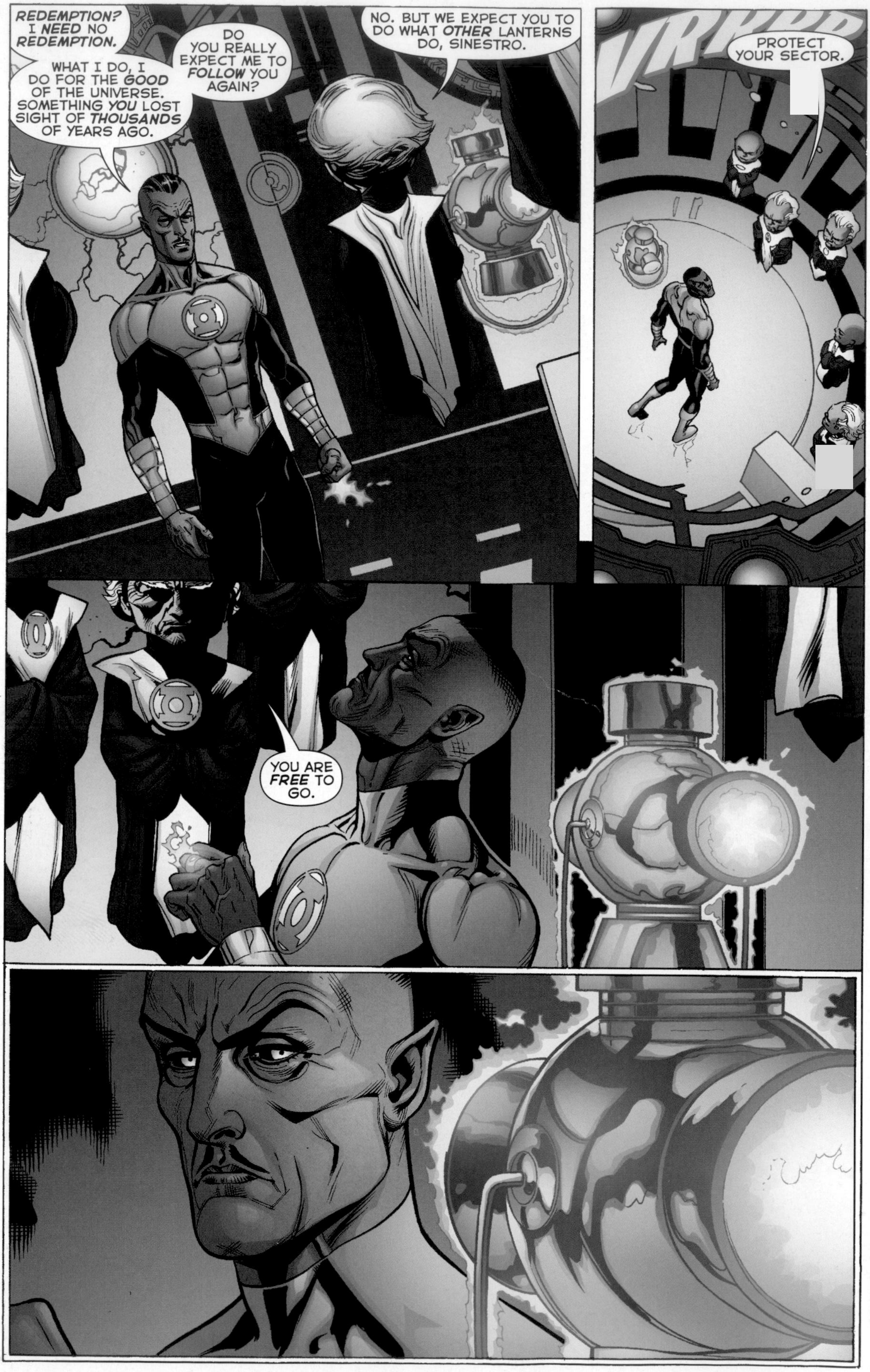
REDEMPTION? I NEED NO REDEMPTION.
WHAT I DO, I DO FOR THE GOOD OF THE UNIVERSE. SOMETHING YOU LOST SIGHT OF THOUSANDS OF YEARS AGO.
DO YOU REALLY EXPECT ME TO FOLLOW YOU AGAIN?
NO. BUT WE EXPECT YOU TO DO WHAT OTHER LANTERNS DO, SINESTRO.
PROTECT YOUR SECTOR.
YOU ARE FREE TO GO.

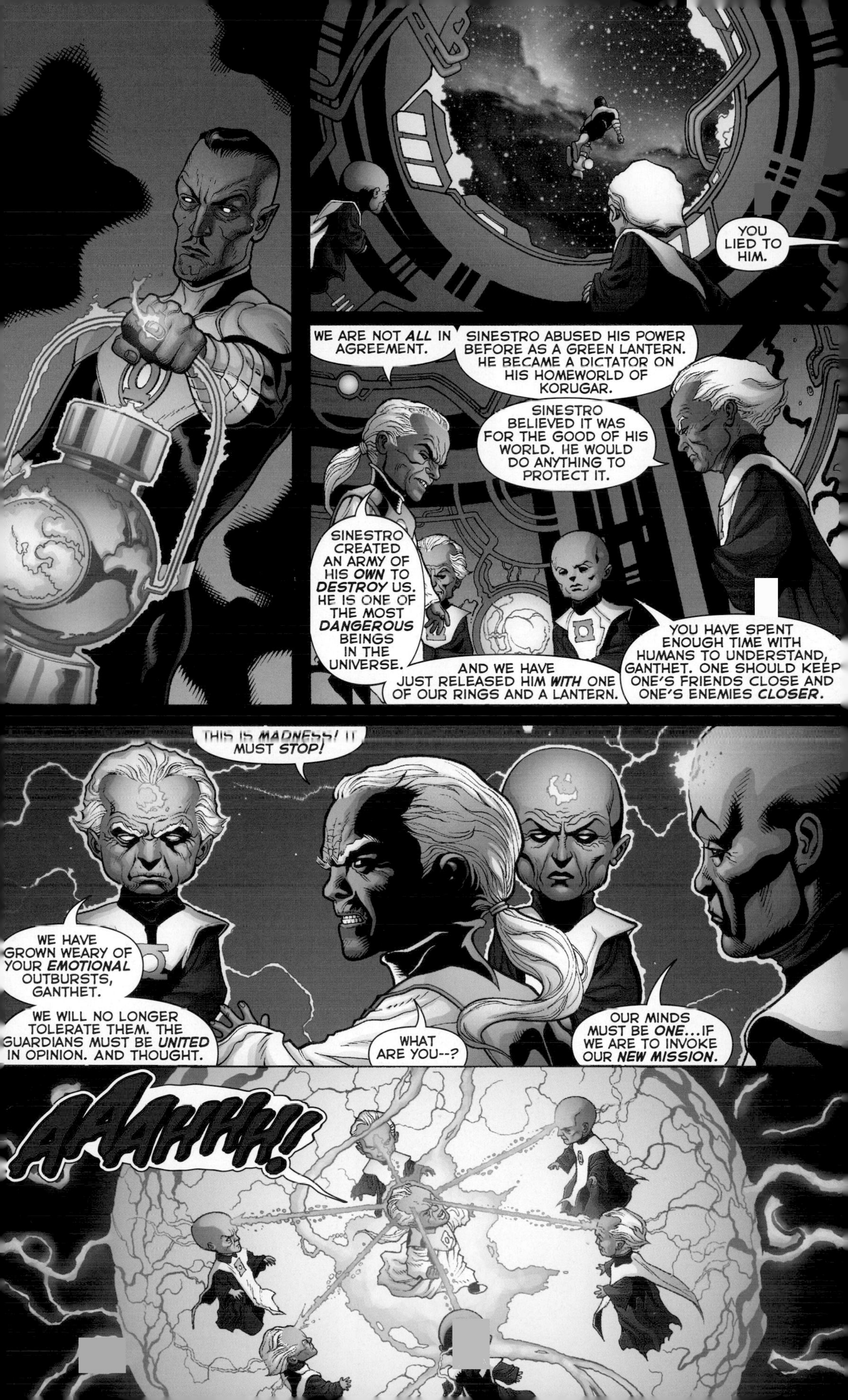
YOU LIED TO HIM.
WE ARE NOT ALL IN AGREEMENT.
SINESTRO ABUSED HIS POWER BEFORE AS A GREEN LANTERN. HE BECAME A DICTATOR ON HIS HOMEWORLD OF KORUGAR.
SINESTRO BELIEVED IT WAS FOR THE GOOD OF HIS WORLD. HE WOULD DO ANYTHING TO PROTECT IT.
SINESTRO CREATED AN ARMY OF HIS OWN TO DESTROY US. HE IS ONE OF THE MOST DANGEROUS BEINGS IN THE UNIVERSE.
AND WE HAVE JUST RELEASED HIM WITH ONE OF OUR RINGS AND A LANTERN.
YOU HAVE SPENT ENOUGH TIME WITH HUMANS TO UNDERSTAND, GANTHET. ONE SHOULD KEEP ONE'S FRIENDS CLOSE AND ONE'S ENEMIES CLOSER.
THIS IS MADNESS! IT MUST STOP!
WE HAVE GROWN WEARY OF YOUR EMOTIONAL OUTBURSTS, GANTHET.
WE WILL NO LONGER TOLERATE THEM. THE GUARDIANS MUST BE UNITED IN OPINION. AND THOUGHT.
WHAT ARE YOU--?
OUR MINDS MUST BE ONE...IF WE ARE TO INVOKE OUR NEW MISSION.
AAAHHHH!

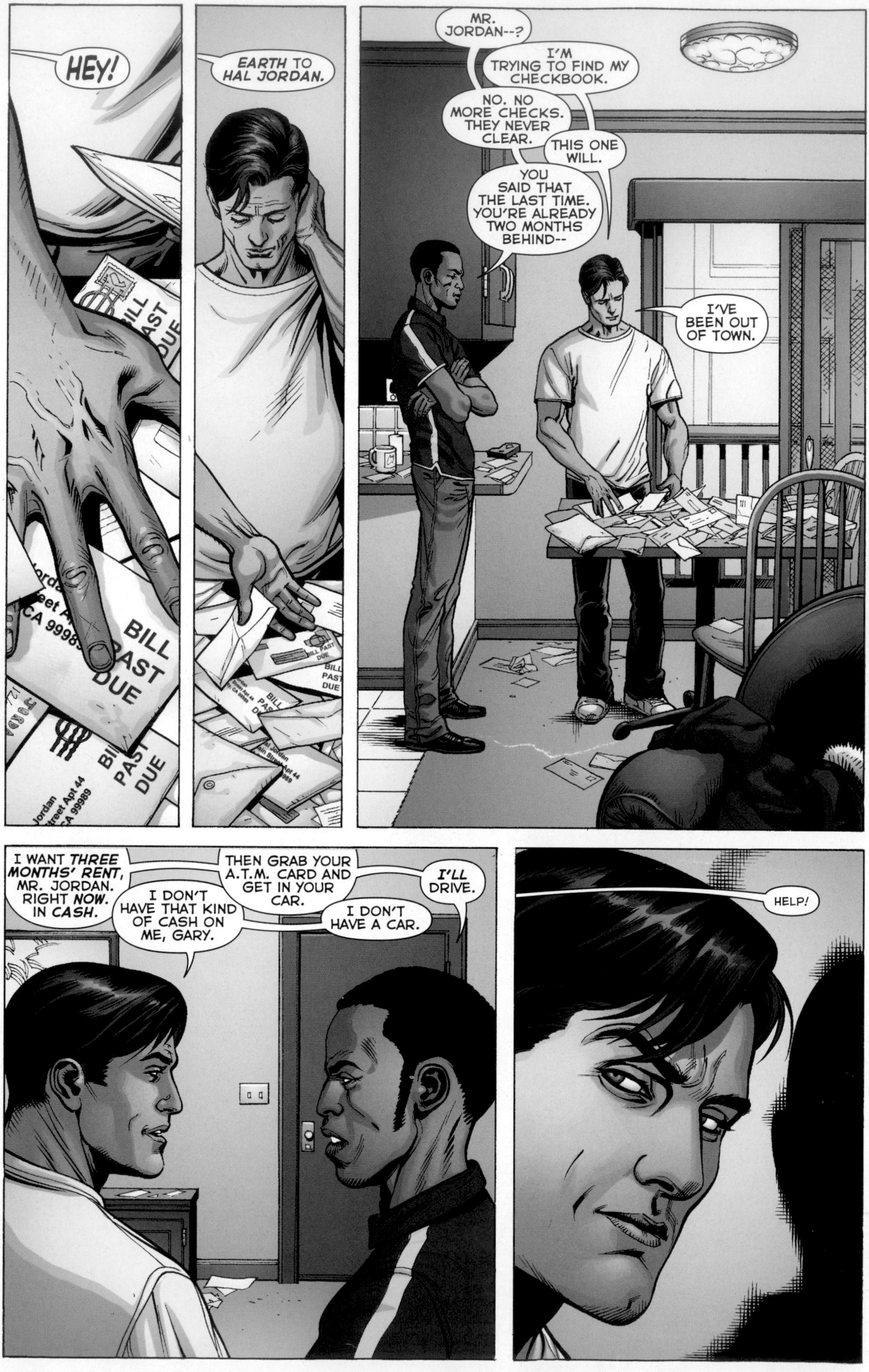
HEY!
EARTH TO HAL JORDAN.
BILL PAST DUE
MR. JORDAN--?
I'M TRYING TO FIND MY CHECKBOOK.
NO. NO MORE CHECKS. THEY NEVER CLEAR.
THIS ONE WILL.
YOU SAID THAT THE LAST TIME. YOU'RE ALREADY TWO MONTHS BEHIND--
I'VE BEEN OUT OF TOWN.
I WANT *THREE MONTHS' RENT*, MR. JORDAN. RIGHT *NOW*. IN *CASH*.
I DON'T HAVE THAT KIND OF CASH ON ME, GARY.
THEN GRAB YOUR A.T.M. CARD AND GET IN YOUR CAR.
I DON'T HAVE A CAR.
I'LL DRIVE.
HELP!

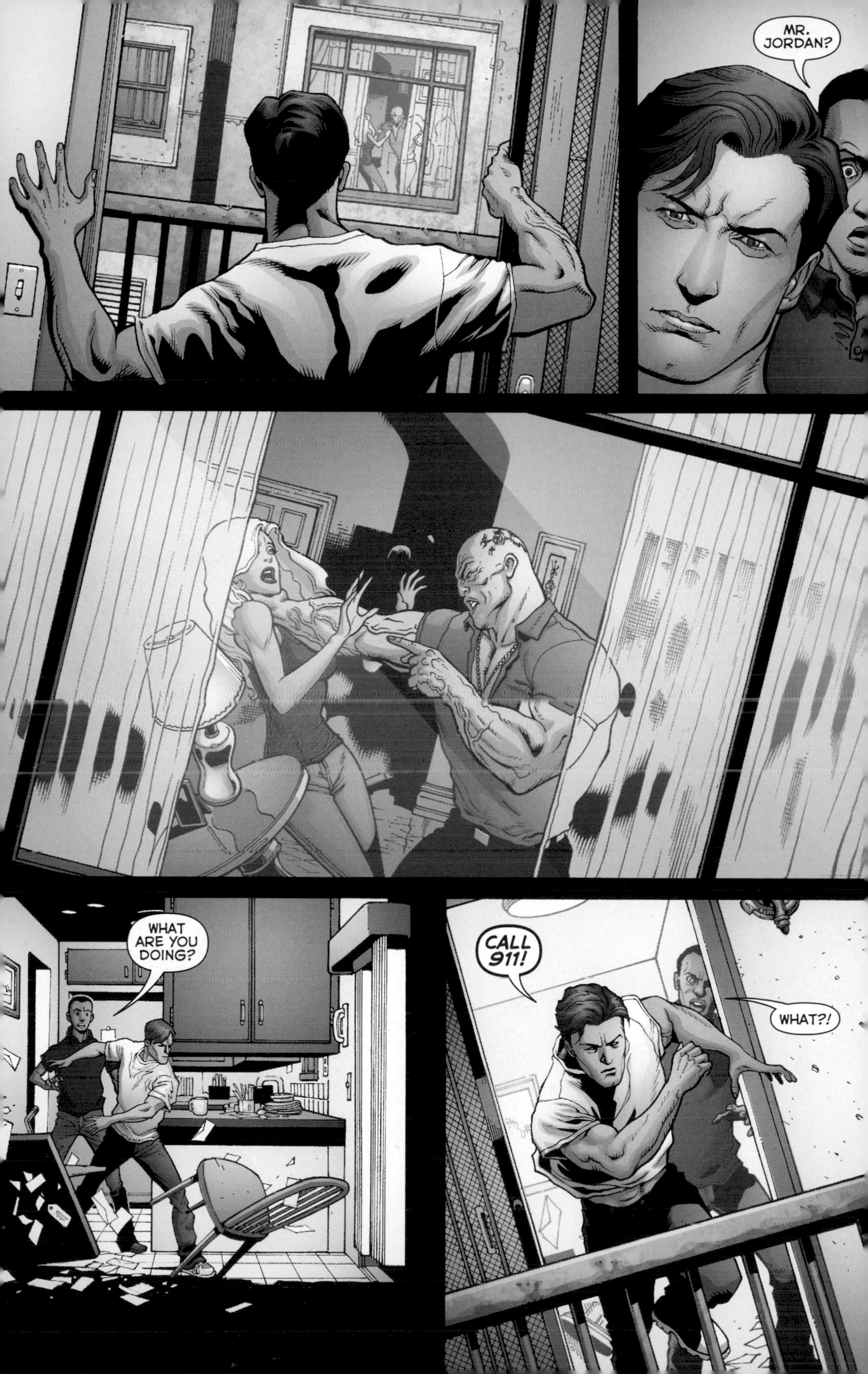
MR. JORDAN?
WHAT ARE YOU DOING?
CALL 911!
WHAT?!

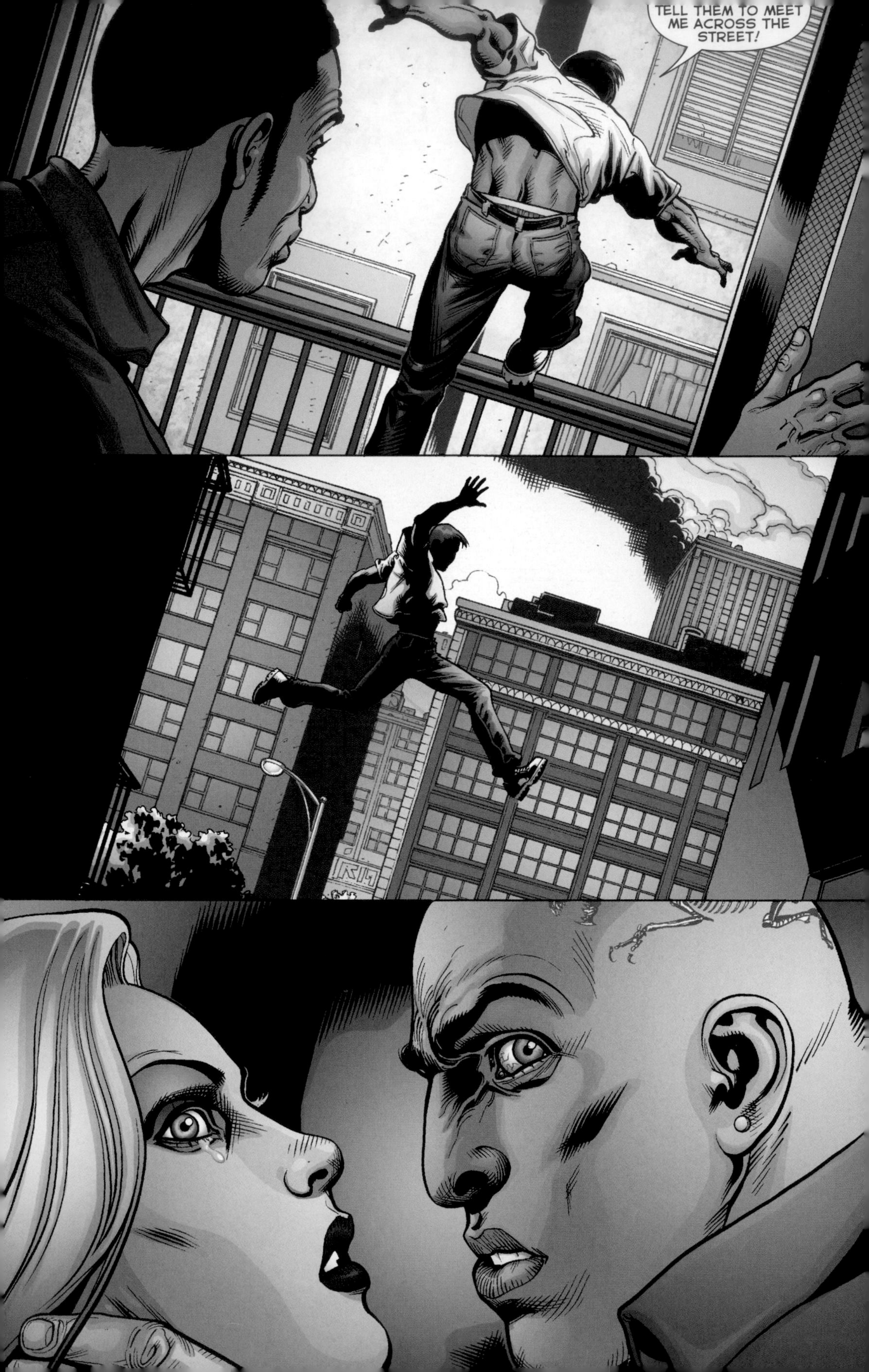
TELL THEM TO MEET ME ACROSS THE STREET!

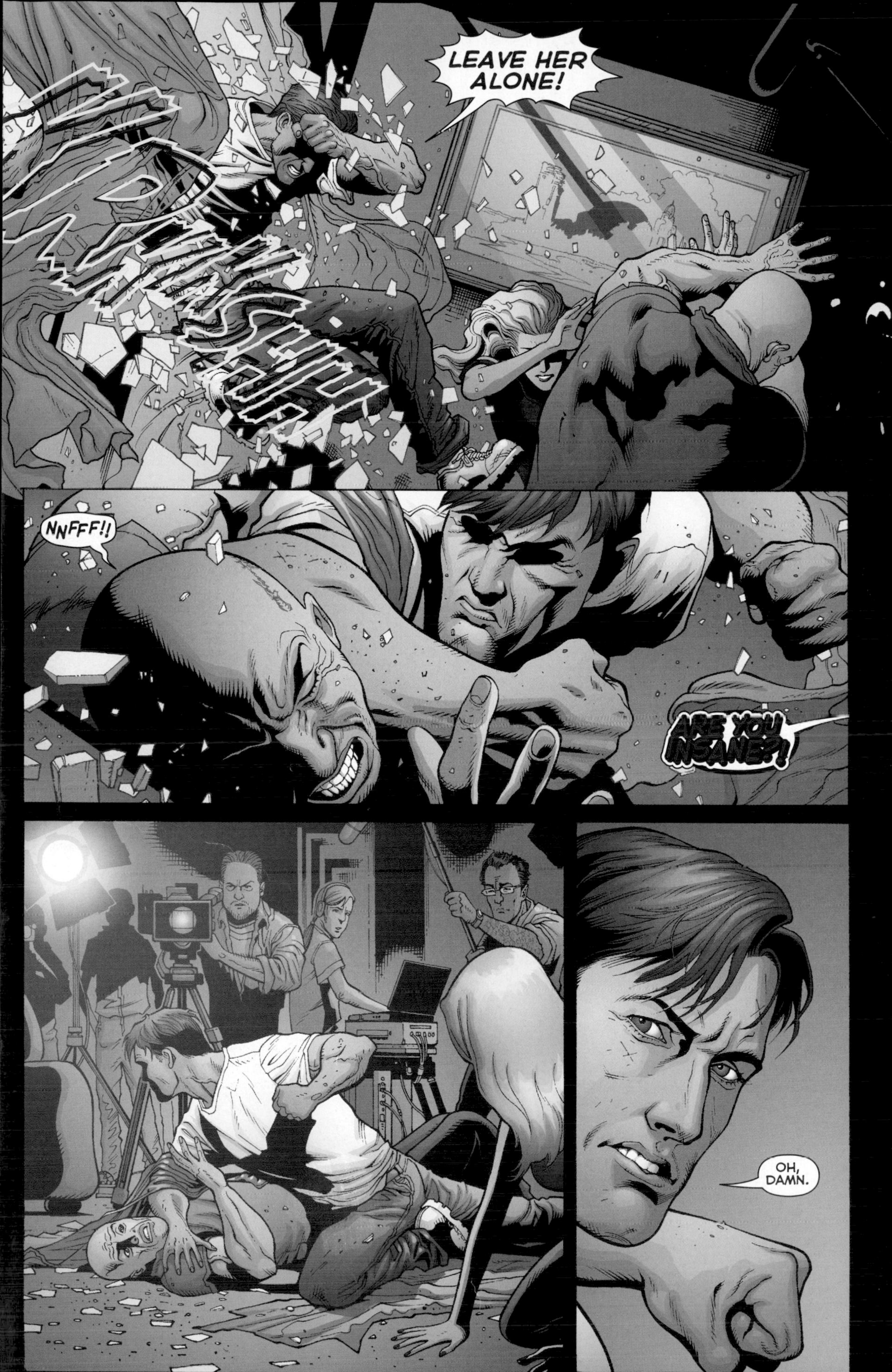
LEAVE HER ALONE!
NNFFF!!
ARE YOU INSANE?!
OH, DAMN.

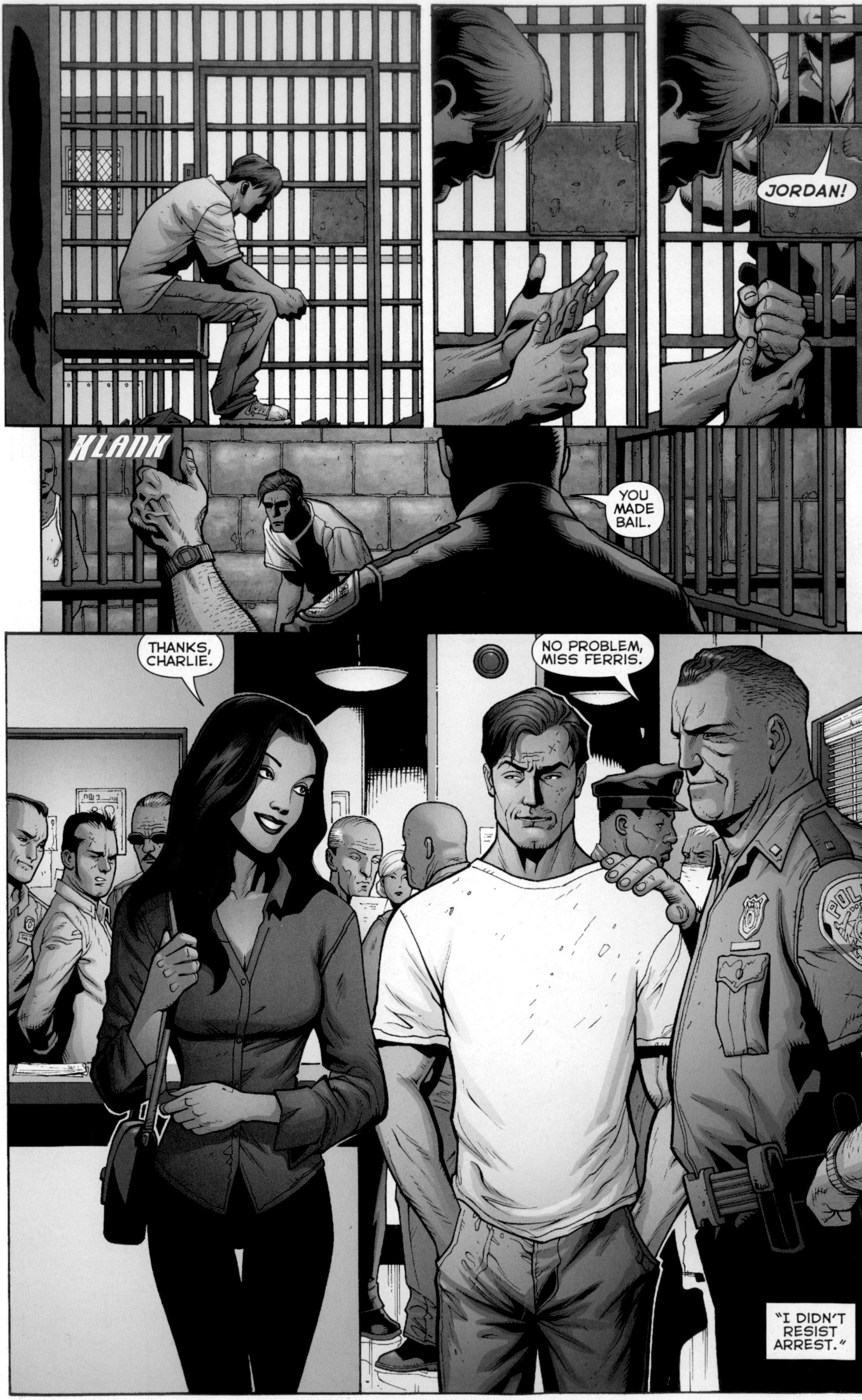
JORDAN!
KLANK
YOU MADE BAIL.
THANKS, CHARLIE.
NO PROBLEM, MISS FERRIS.
"I DIDN'T RESIST ARREST."

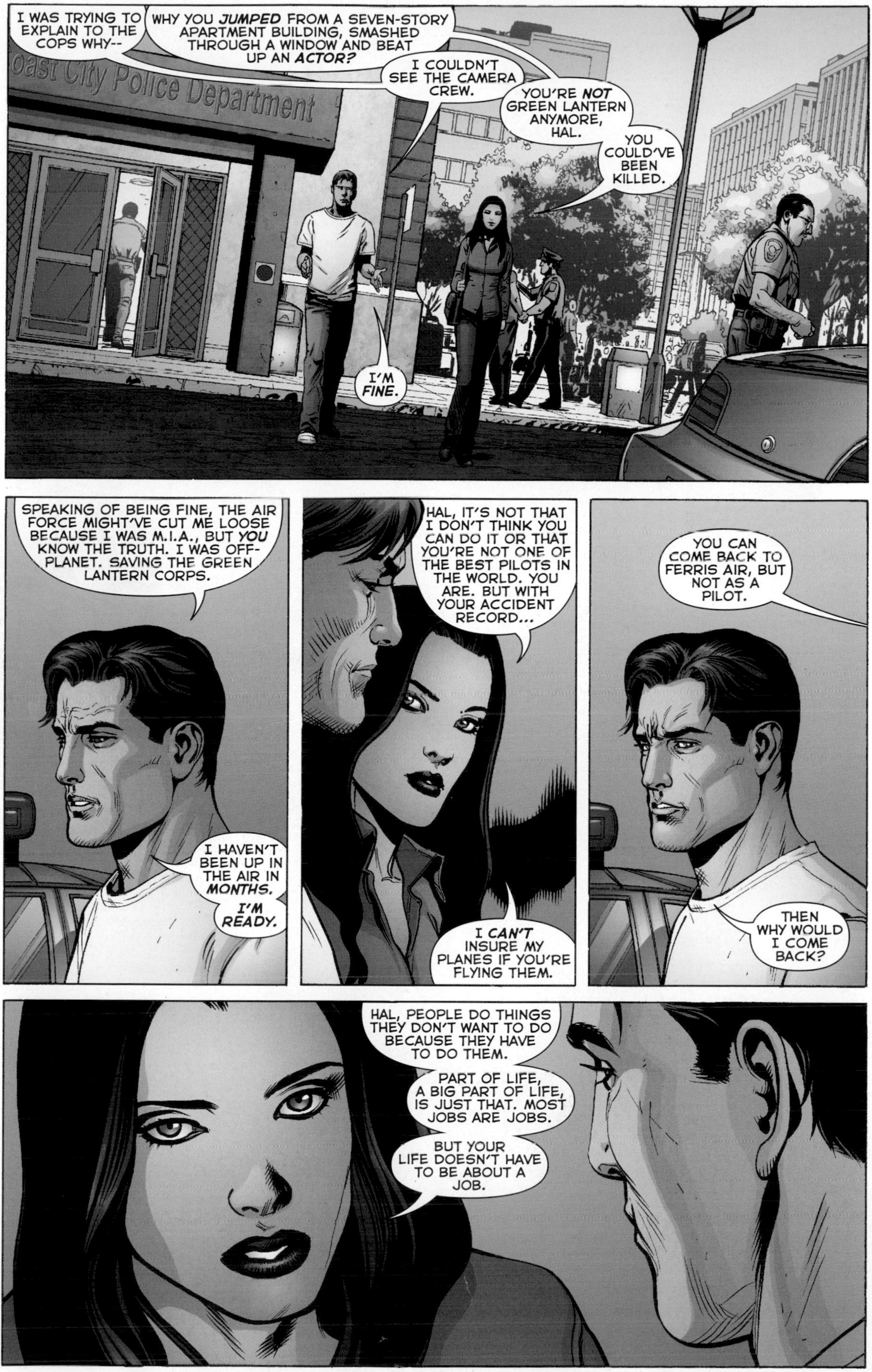
I WAS TRYING TO EXPLAIN TO THE COPS WHY--
WHY YOU JUMPED FROM A SEVEN-STORY APARTMENT BUILDING, SMASHED THROUGH A WINDOW AND BEAT UP AN ACTOR?
I COULDN'T SEE THE CAMERA CREW.
YOU'RE NOT GREEN LANTERN ANYMORE, HAL.
YOU COULD'VE BEEN KILLED.
I'M FINE.
Coast City Police Department
SPEAKING OF BEING FINE, THE AIR FORCE MIGHT'VE CUT ME LOOSE BECAUSE I WAS M.I.A., BUT YOU KNOW THE TRUTH. I WAS OFF-PLANET. SAVING THE GREEN LANTERN CORPS.
I HAVEN'T BEEN UP IN THE AIR IN MONTHS.
I'M READY.
HAL, IT'S NOT THAT I DON'T THINK YOU CAN DO IT OR THAT YOU'RE NOT ONE OF THE BEST PILOTS IN THE WORLD. YOU ARE. BUT WITH YOUR ACCIDENT RECORD...
I CAN'T INSURE MY PLANES IF YOU'RE FLYING THEM.
YOU CAN COME BACK TO FERRIS AIR, BUT NOT AS A PILOT.
THEN WHY WOULD I COME BACK?
HAL, PEOPLE DO THINGS THEY DON'T WANT TO DO BECAUSE THEY HAVE TO DO THEM.
PART OF LIFE, A BIG PART OF LIFE, IS JUST THAT. MOST JOBS ARE JOBS.
BUT YOUR LIFE DOESN'T HAVE TO BE ABOUT A JOB.

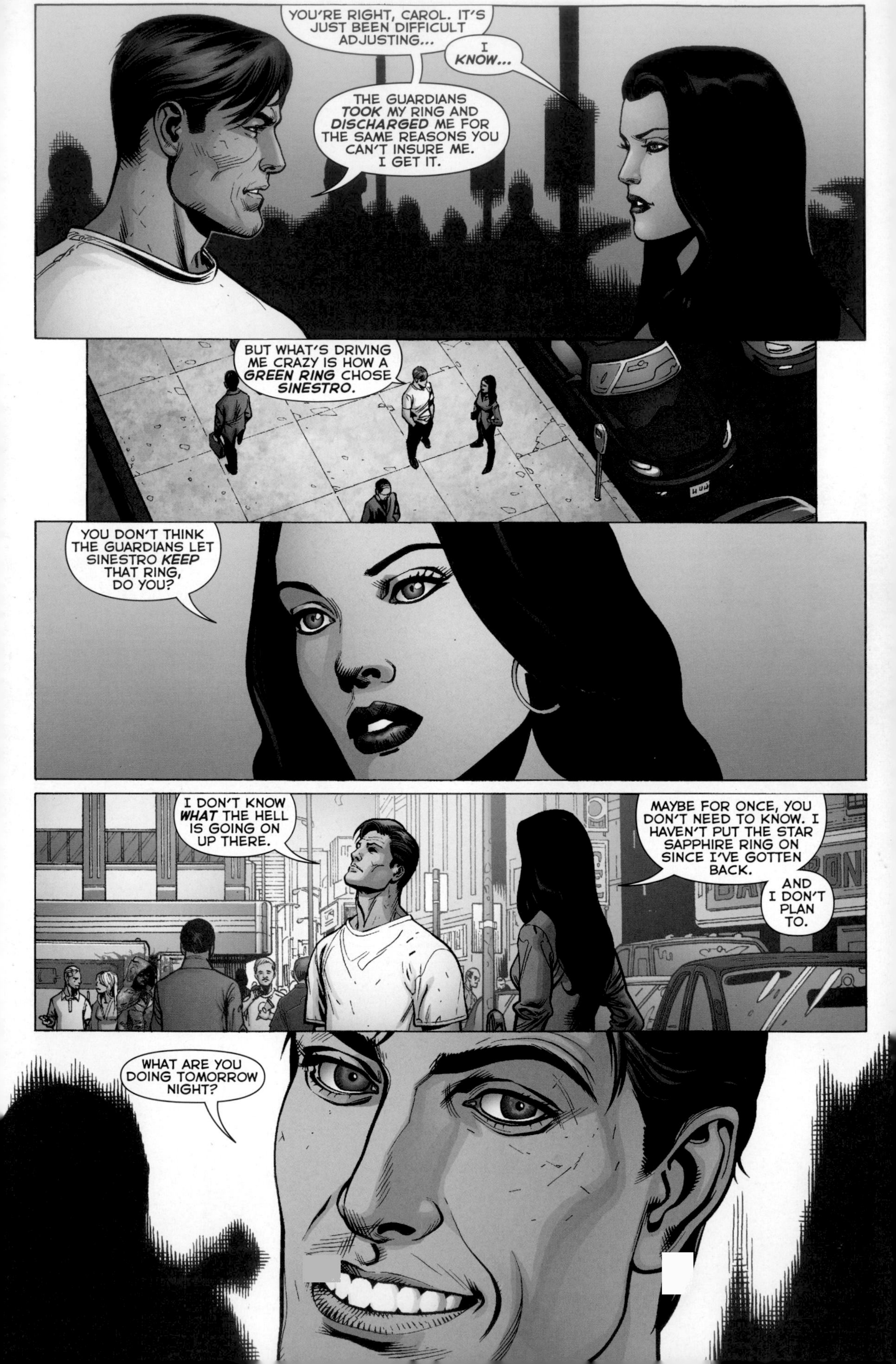
YOU'RE RIGHT, CAROL. IT'S JUST BEEN DIFFICULT ADJUSTING...
I KNOW...
THE GUARDIANS TOOK MY RING AND DISCHARGED ME FOR THE SAME REASONS YOU CAN'T INSURE ME. I GET IT.
BUT WHAT'S DRIVING ME CRAZY IS HOW A GREEN RING CHOSE SINESTRO.
YOU DON'T THINK THE GUARDIANS LET SINESTRO KEEP THAT RING, DO YOU?
I DON'T KNOW WHAT THE HELL IS GOING ON UP THERE.
MAYBE FOR ONCE, YOU DON'T NEED TO KNOW. I HAVEN'T PUT THE STAR SAPPHIRE RING ON SINCE I'VE GOTTEN BACK.
AND I DON'T PLAN TO.
WHAT ARE YOU DOING TOMORROW NIGHT?

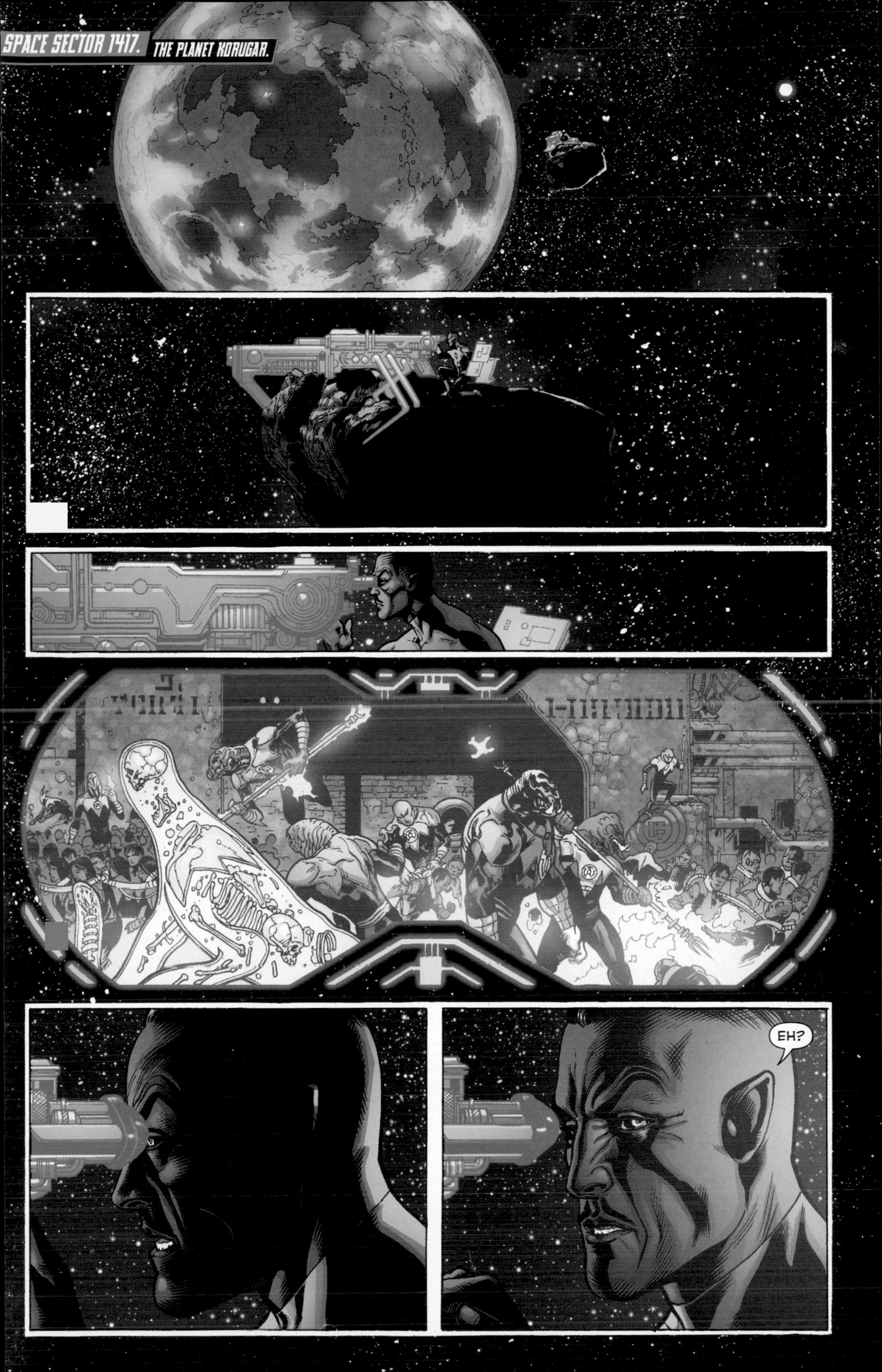
SPACE SECTOR 1417.
THE PLANET KORUGAR.
EH?

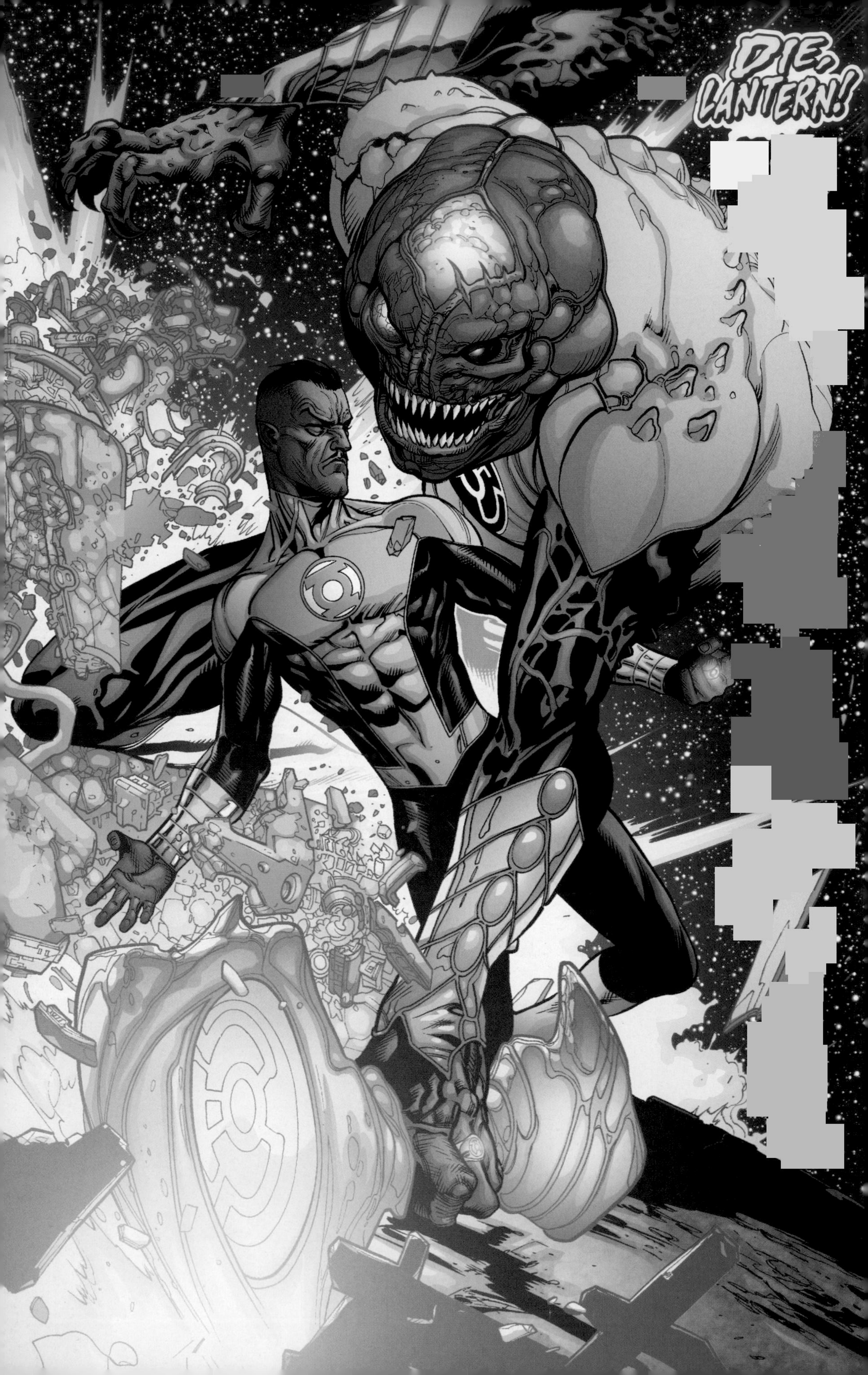
DIE, LANTERN!

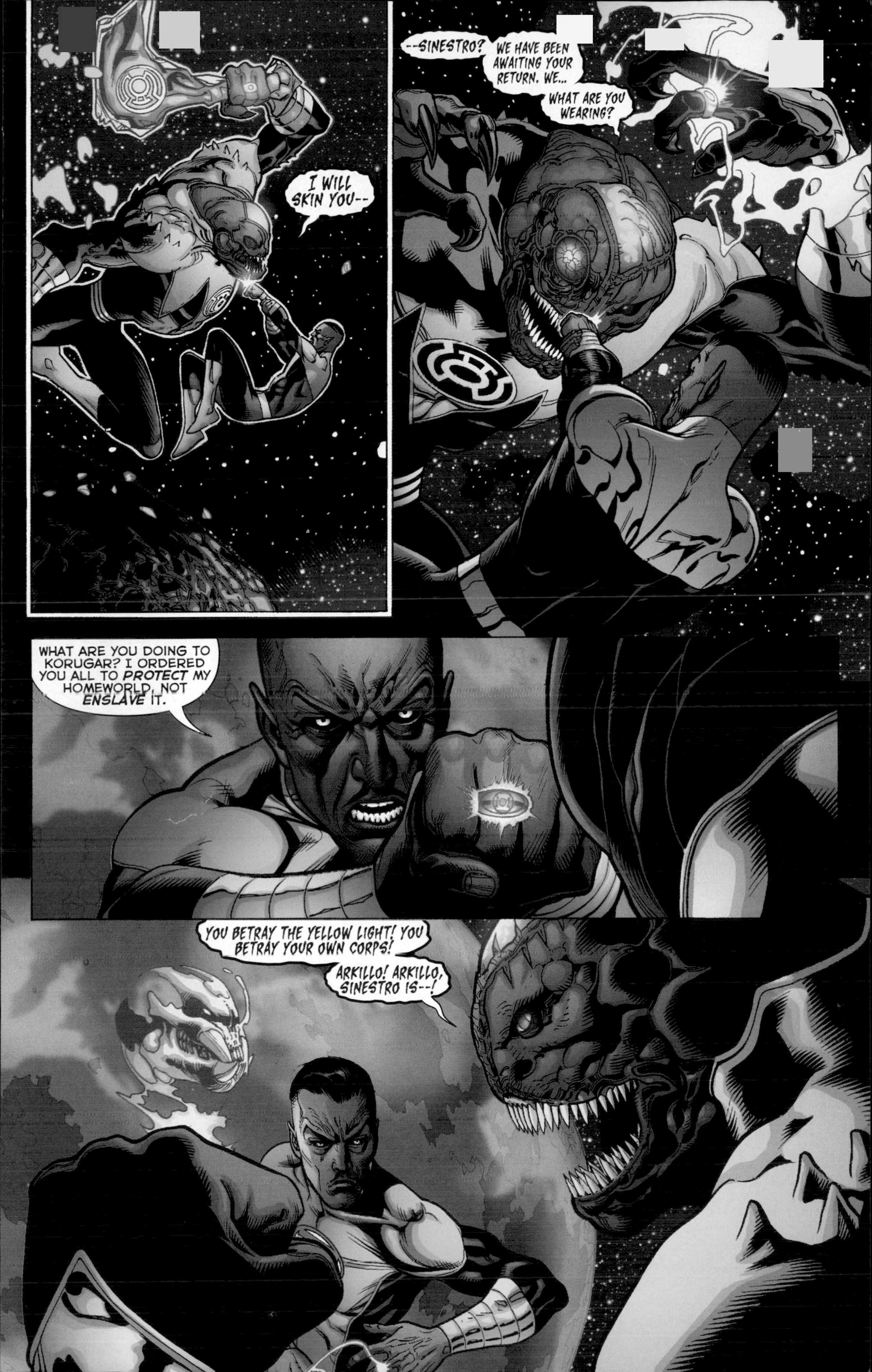
I WILL SKIN YOU--
--SINESTRO?
WE HAVE BEEN AWAITING YOUR RETURN. WE...
WHAT ARE YOU WEARING?
WHAT ARE YOU DOING TO KORUGAR? I ORDERED YOU ALL TO PROTECT MY HOMEWORLD, NOT ENSLAVE IT.
YOU BETRAY THE YELLOW LIGHT! YOU BETRAY YOUR OWN CORPS!
ARKILLO! ARKILLO, SINESTRO IS--!

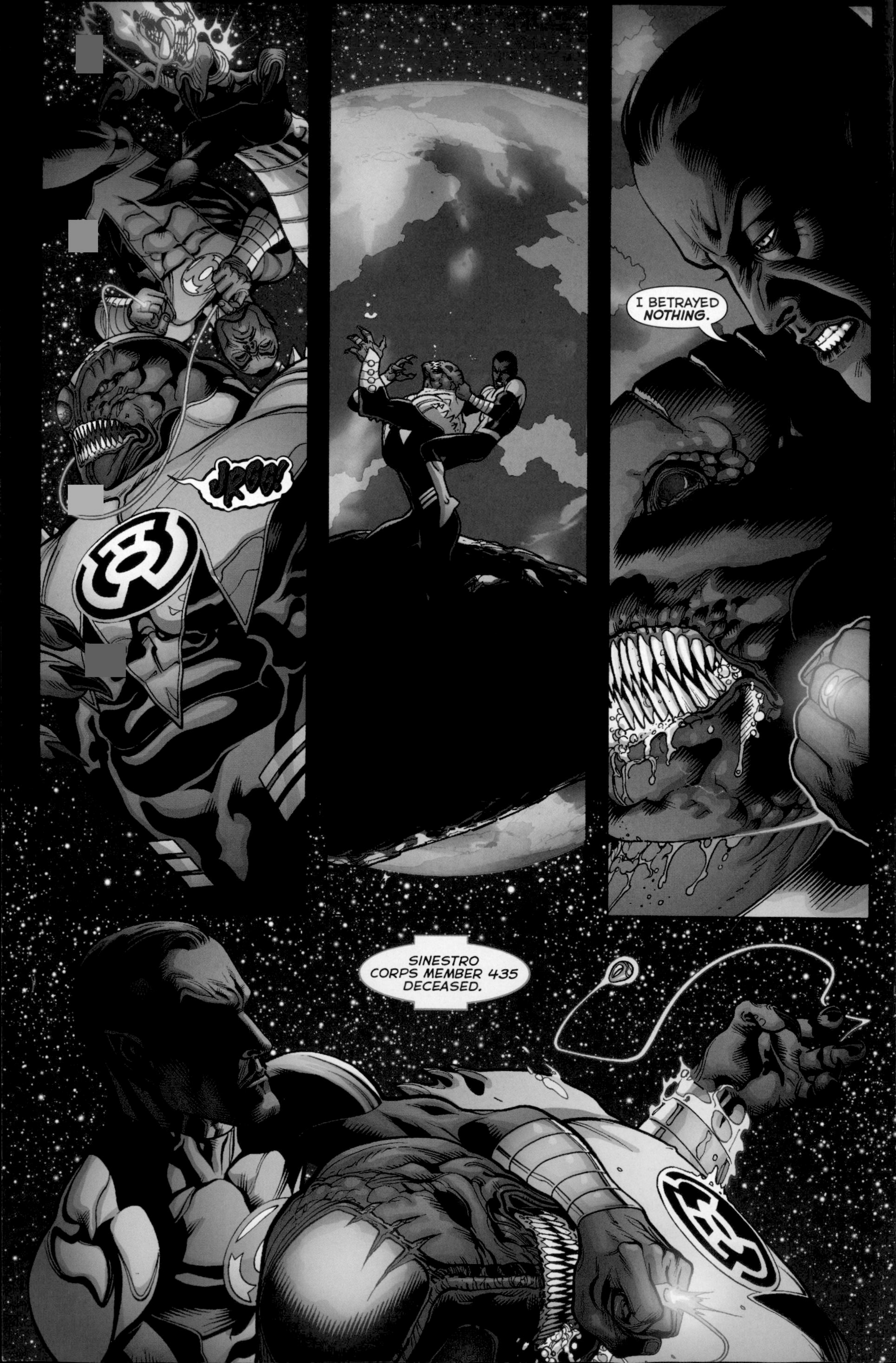
JRGG!
I BETRAYED NOTHING.
SINESTRO CORPS MEMBER 435 DECEASED.

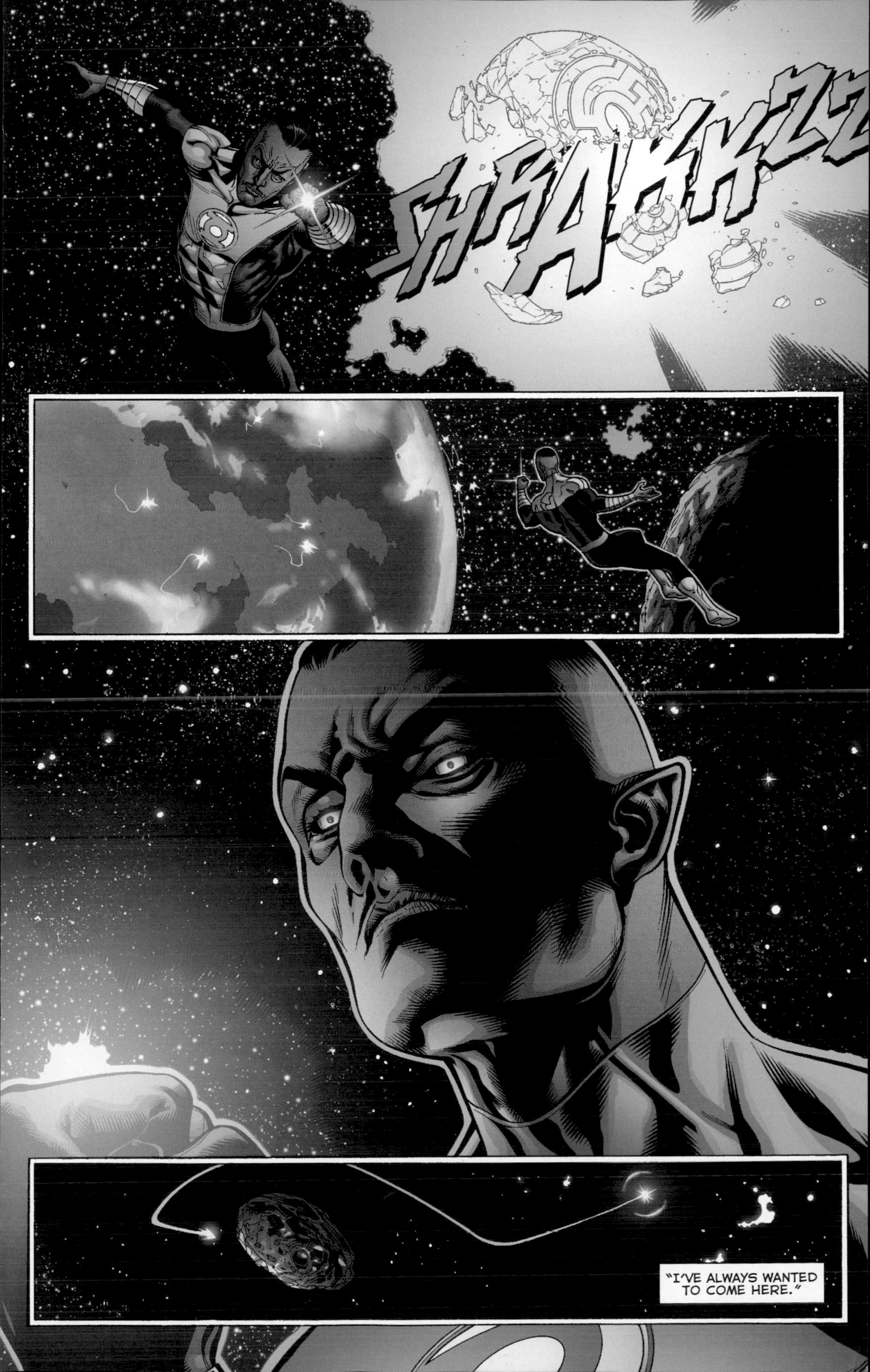
SHRAKKZZ
"I'VE ALWAYS WANTED TO COME HERE."

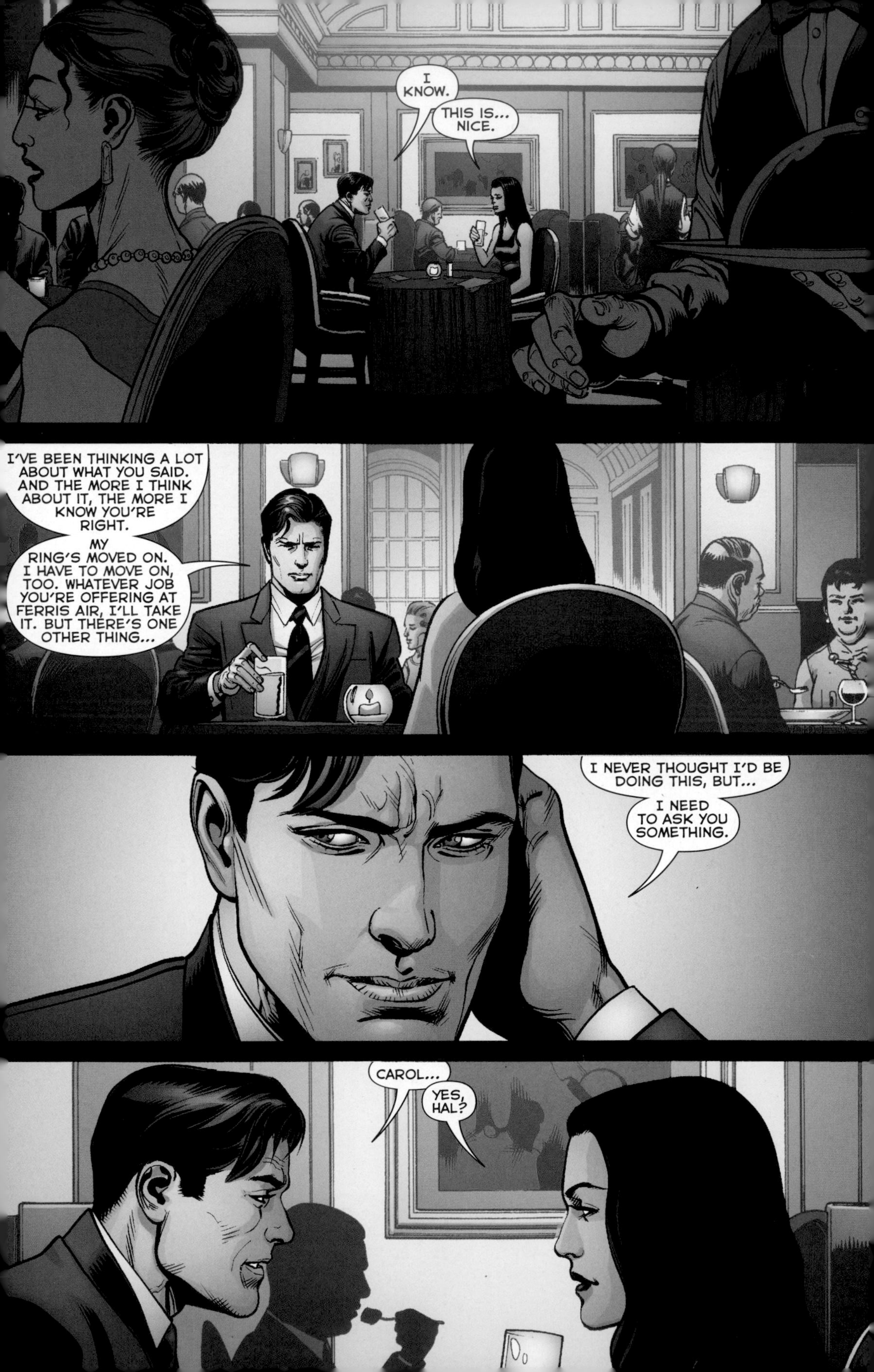
I KNOW.
THIS IS... NICE.
I'VE BEEN THINKING A LOT ABOUT WHAT YOU SAID. AND THE MORE I THINK ABOUT IT, THE MORE I KNOW YOU'RE RIGHT.
MY RING'S MOVED ON. I HAVE TO MOVE ON, TOO. WHATEVER JOB YOU'RE OFFERING AT FERRIS AIR, I'LL TAKE IT. BUT THERE'S ONE OTHER THING...
I NEVER THOUGHT I'D BE DOING THIS, BUT...
I NEED TO ASK YOU SOMETHING.
CAROL...
YES, HAL?

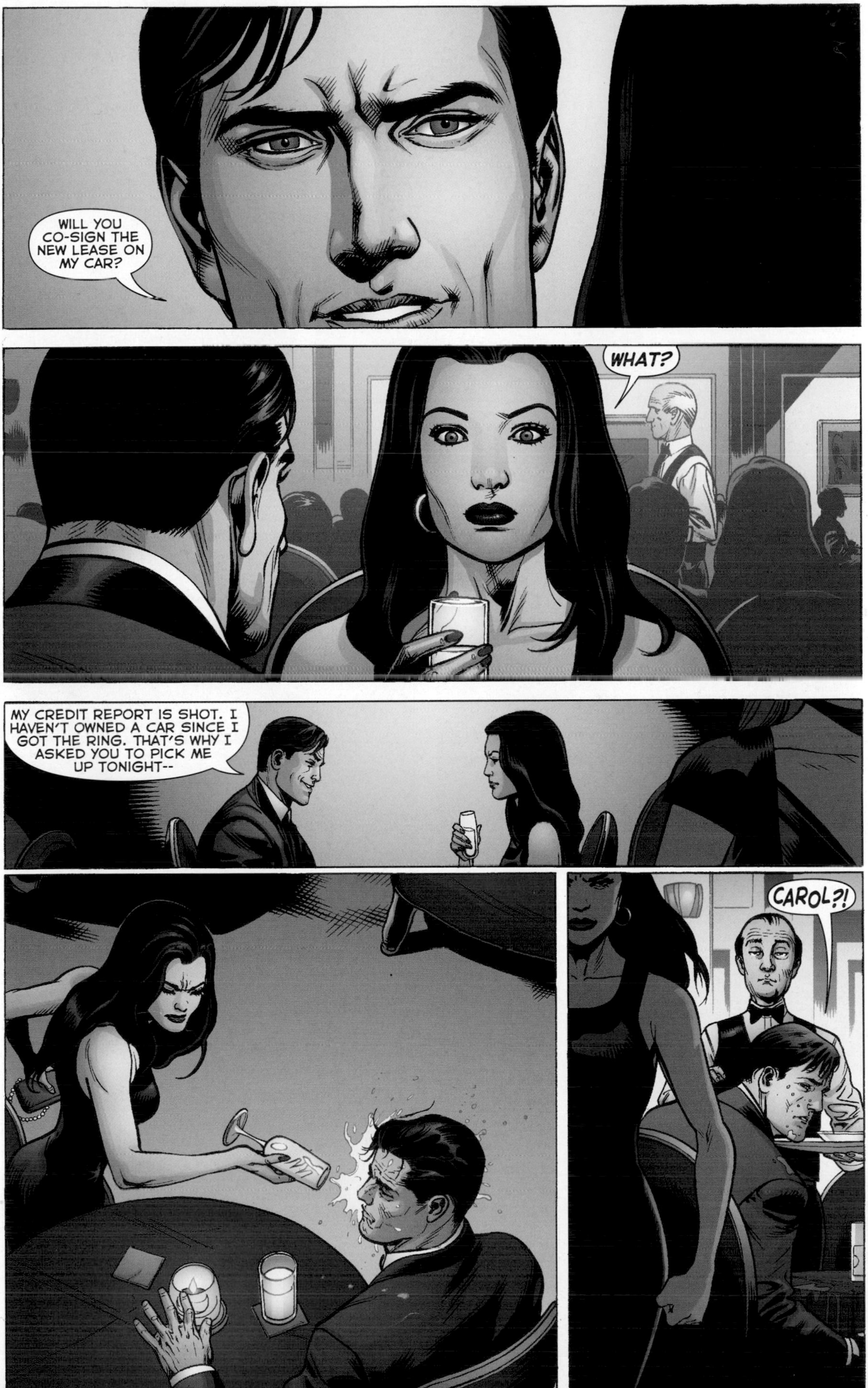
WILL YOU CO-SIGN THE NEW LEASE ON MY CAR?
WHAT?
MY CREDIT REPORT IS SHOT. I HAVEN'T OWNED A CAR SINCE I GOT THE RING. THAT'S WHY I ASKED YOU TO PICK ME UP TONIGHT--
CAROL?!

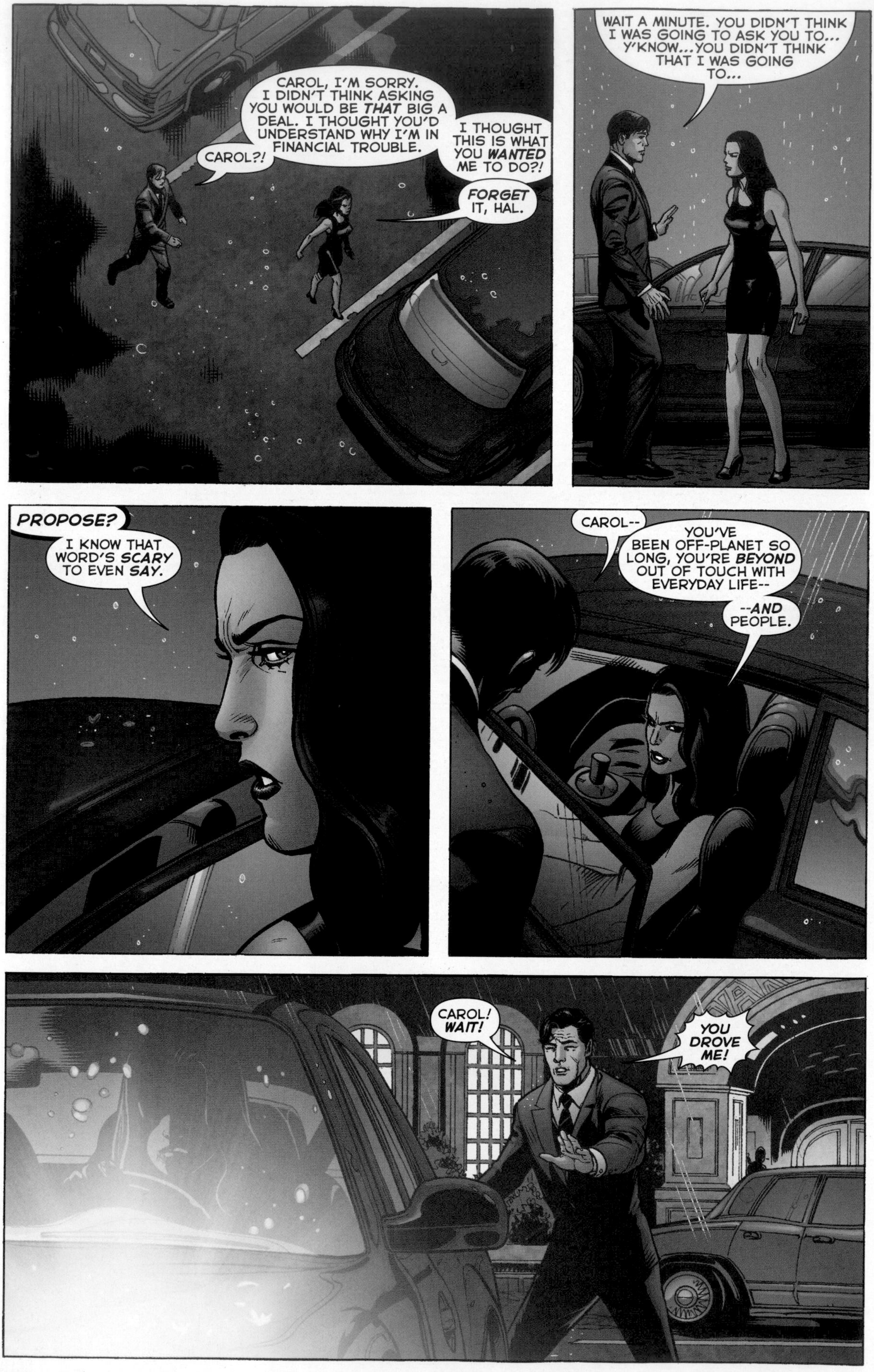
CAROL, I'M SORRY. I DIDN'T THINK ASKING YOU WOULD BE THAT BIG A DEAL. I THOUGHT YOU'D UNDERSTAND WHY I'M IN FINANCIAL TROUBLE.
CAROL?!
I THOUGHT THIS IS WHAT YOU WANTED ME TO DO?!
FORGET IT, HAL.
WAIT A MINUTE. YOU DIDN'T THINK I WAS GOING TO ASK YOU TO... Y'KNOW...YOU DIDN'T THINK THAT I WAS GOING TO...
PROPOSE?
I KNOW THAT WORD'S SCARY TO EVEN SAY.
CAROL--
YOU'VE BEEN OFF-PLANET SO LONG, YOU'RE BEYOND OUT OF TOUCH WITH EVERYDAY LIFE--
--AND PEOPLE.
CAROL! WAIT!
YOU DROVE ME!

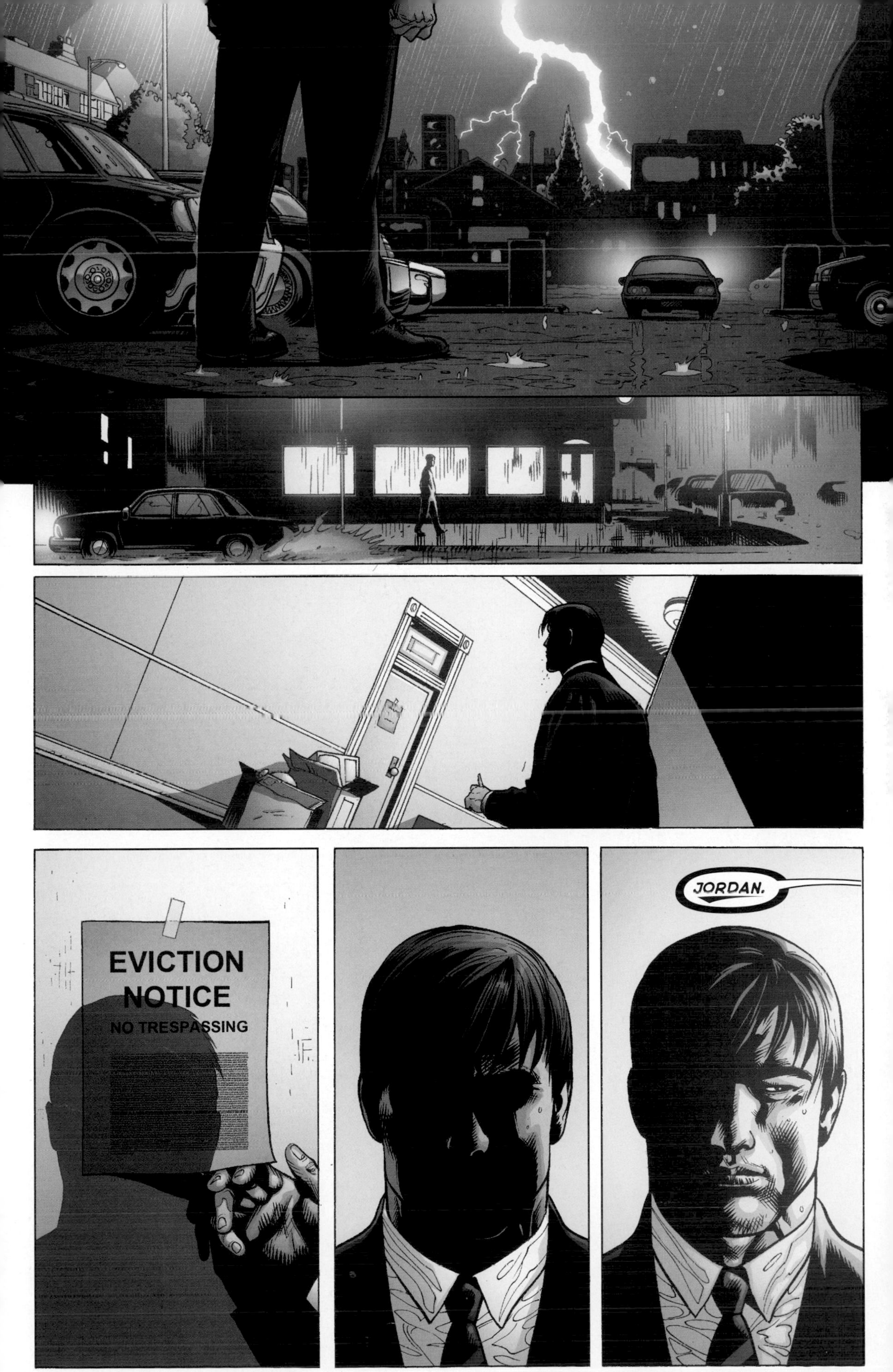
EVICTION NOTICE
NO TRESPASSING
JORDAN.

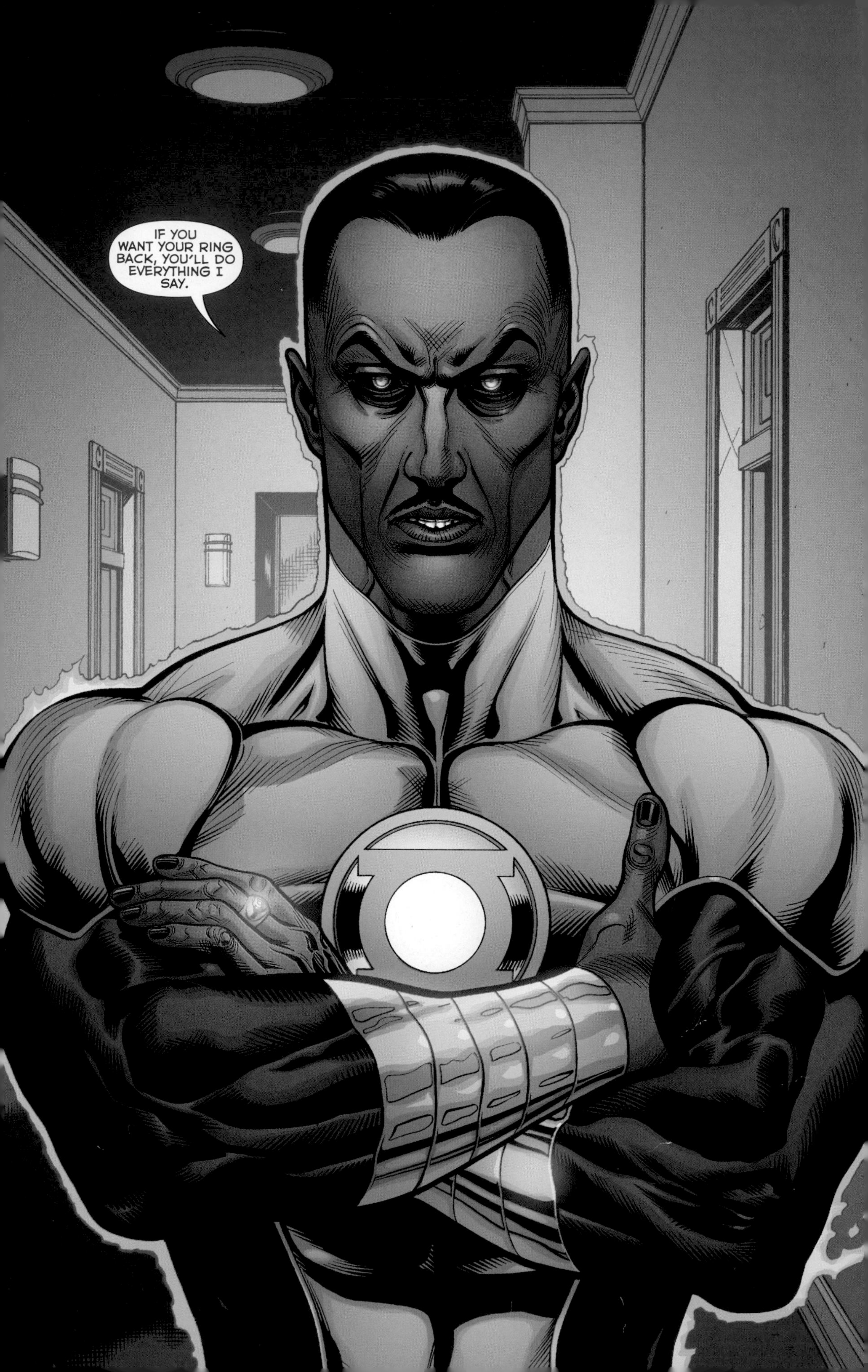
IF YOU WANT YOUR RING BACK, YOU'LL DO EVERYTHING I SAY.

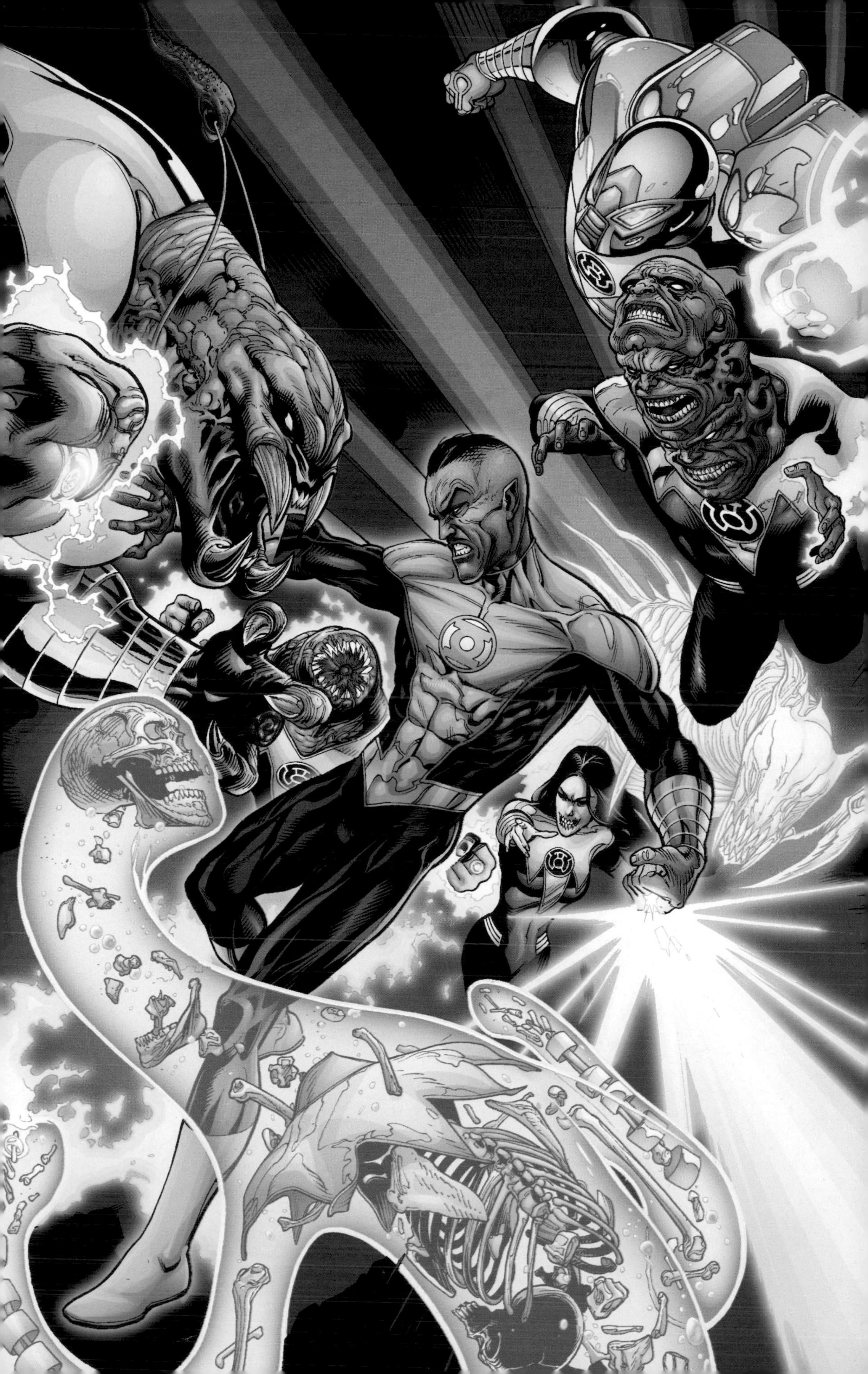

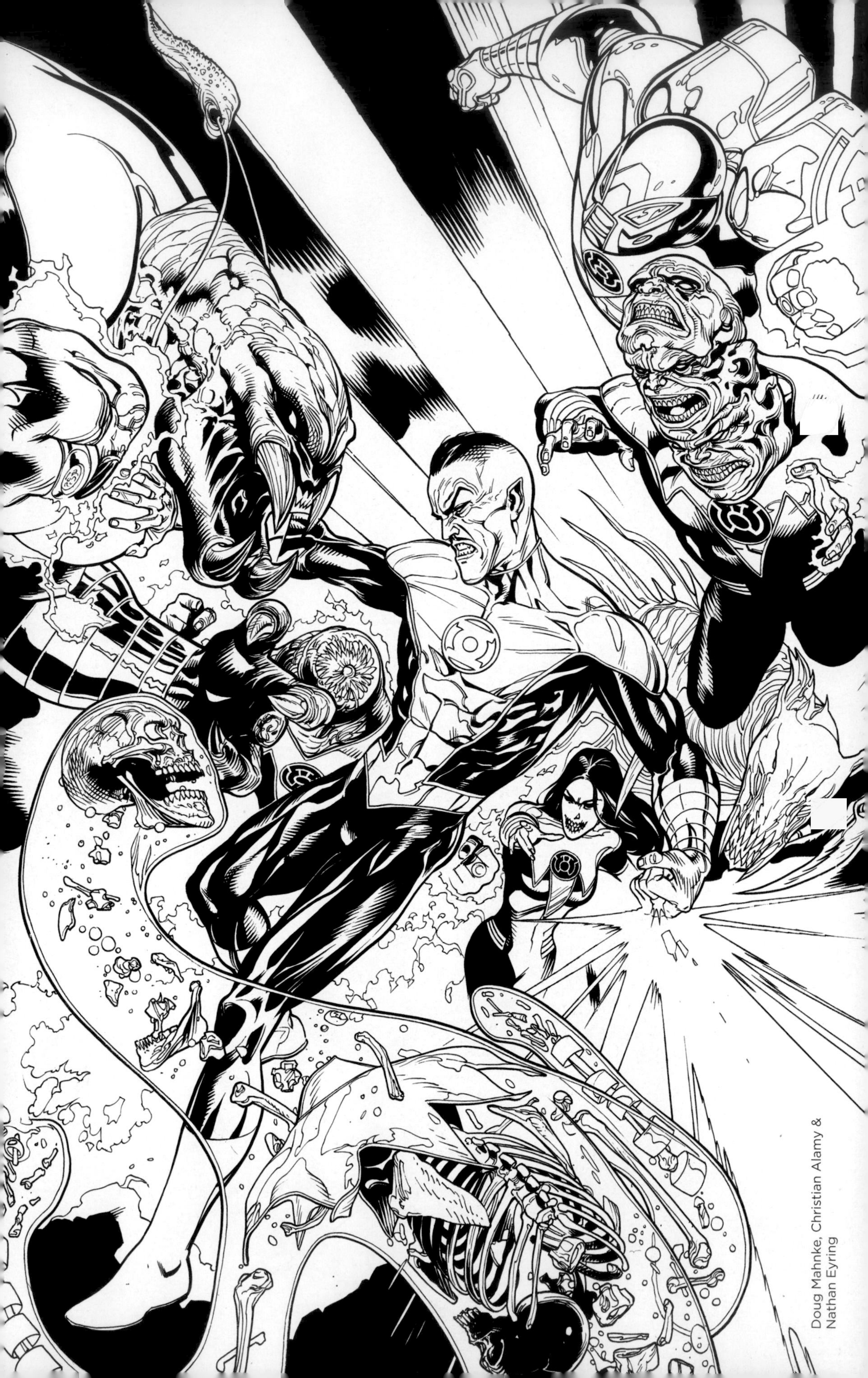

Doug Mahnke, Christian Alamy &
Nathan Eyring

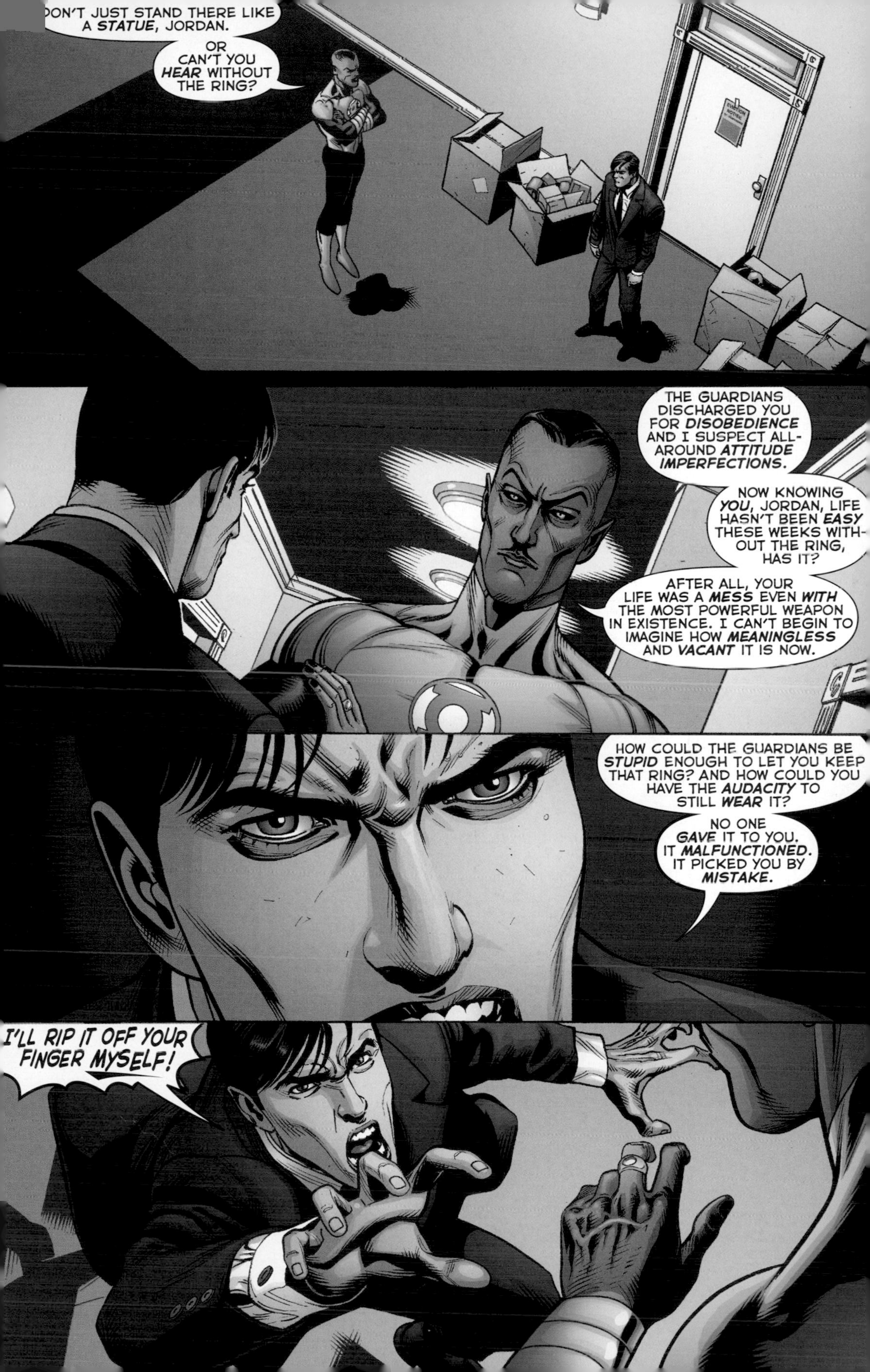
DON'T JUST STAND THERE LIKE A STATUE, JORDAN.
OR CAN'T YOU HEAR WITHOUT THE RING?
THE GUARDIANS DISCHARGED YOU FOR DISOBEDIENCE AND I SUSPECT ALL-AROUND ATTITUDE IMPERFECTIONS.
NOW KNOWING YOU, JORDAN, LIFE HASN'T BEEN EASY THESE WEEKS WITH-OUT THE RING, HAS IT?
AFTER ALL, YOUR LIFE WAS A MESS EVEN WITH THE MOST POWERFUL WEAPON IN EXISTENCE. I CAN'T BEGIN TO IMAGINE HOW MEANINGLESS AND VACANT IT IS NOW.
HOW COULD THE GUARDIANS BE STUPID ENOUGH TO LET YOU KEEP THAT RING? AND HOW COULD YOU HAVE THE AUDACITY TO STILL WEAR IT?
NO ONE GAVE IT TO YOU. IT MALFUNCTIONED. IT PICKED YOU BY MISTAKE.
I'LL RIP IT OFF YOUR FINGER MYSELF!

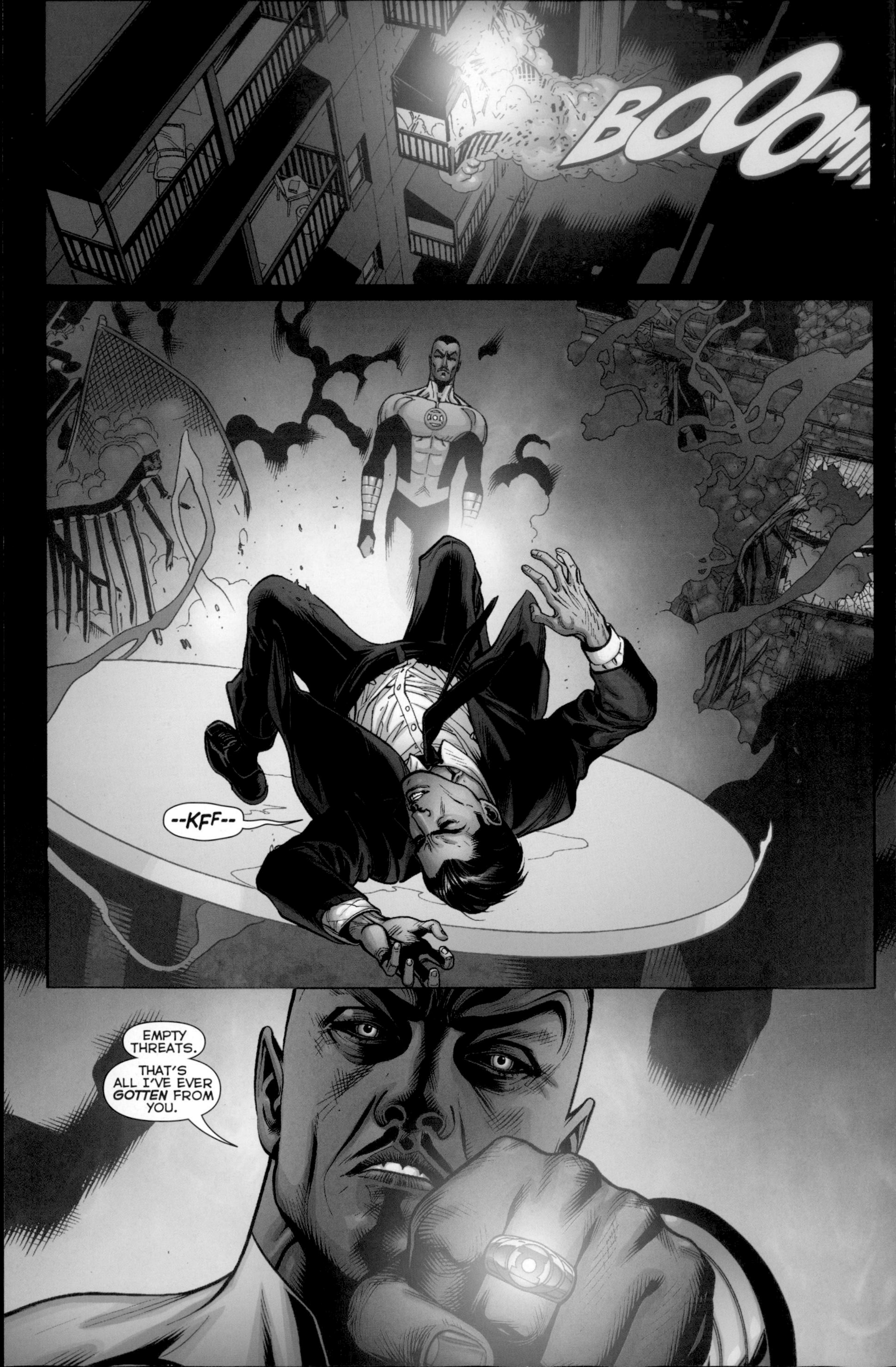
BOOOM
--KFF--
EMPTY THREATS.
THAT'S ALL I'VE EVER GOTTEN FROM YOU.

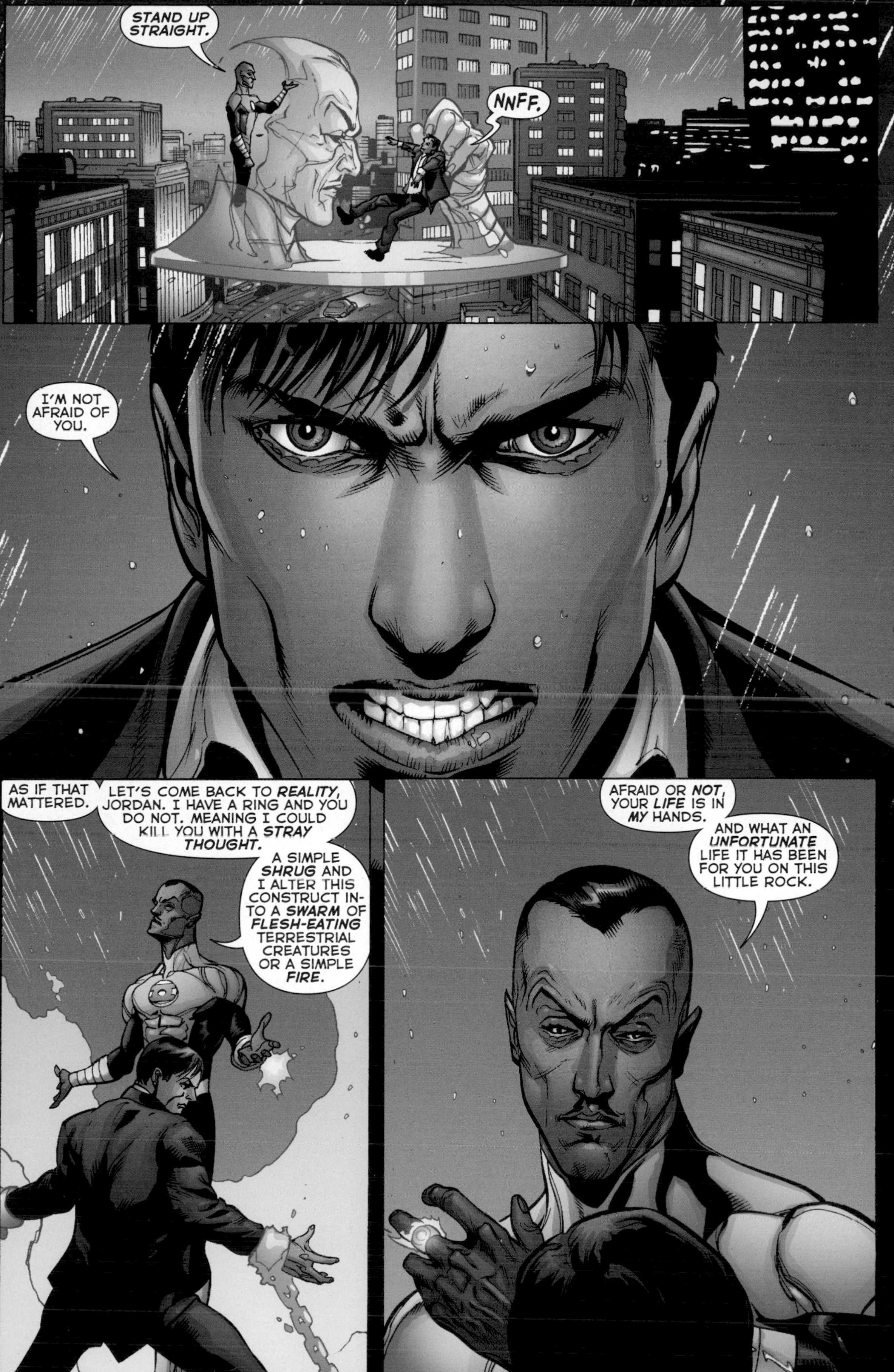
STAND UP STRAIGHT.
NNFF.
I'M NOT AFRAID OF YOU.
AS IF THAT MATTERED.
LET'S COME BACK TO *REALITY*, JORDAN. I HAVE A RING AND YOU DO NOT. MEANING I COULD KILL YOU WITH A *STRAY THOUGHT.*
A SIMPLE *SHRUG* AND I ALTER THIS CONSTRUCT INTO A *SWARM* OF *FLESH-EATING* TERRESTRIAL CREATURES OR A SIMPLE *FIRE.*
AFRAID OR *NOT*, YOUR *LIFE* IS IN *MY* HANDS.
AND WHAT AN *UNFORTUNATE* LIFE IT HAS BEEN FOR YOU ON THIS LITTLE ROCK.

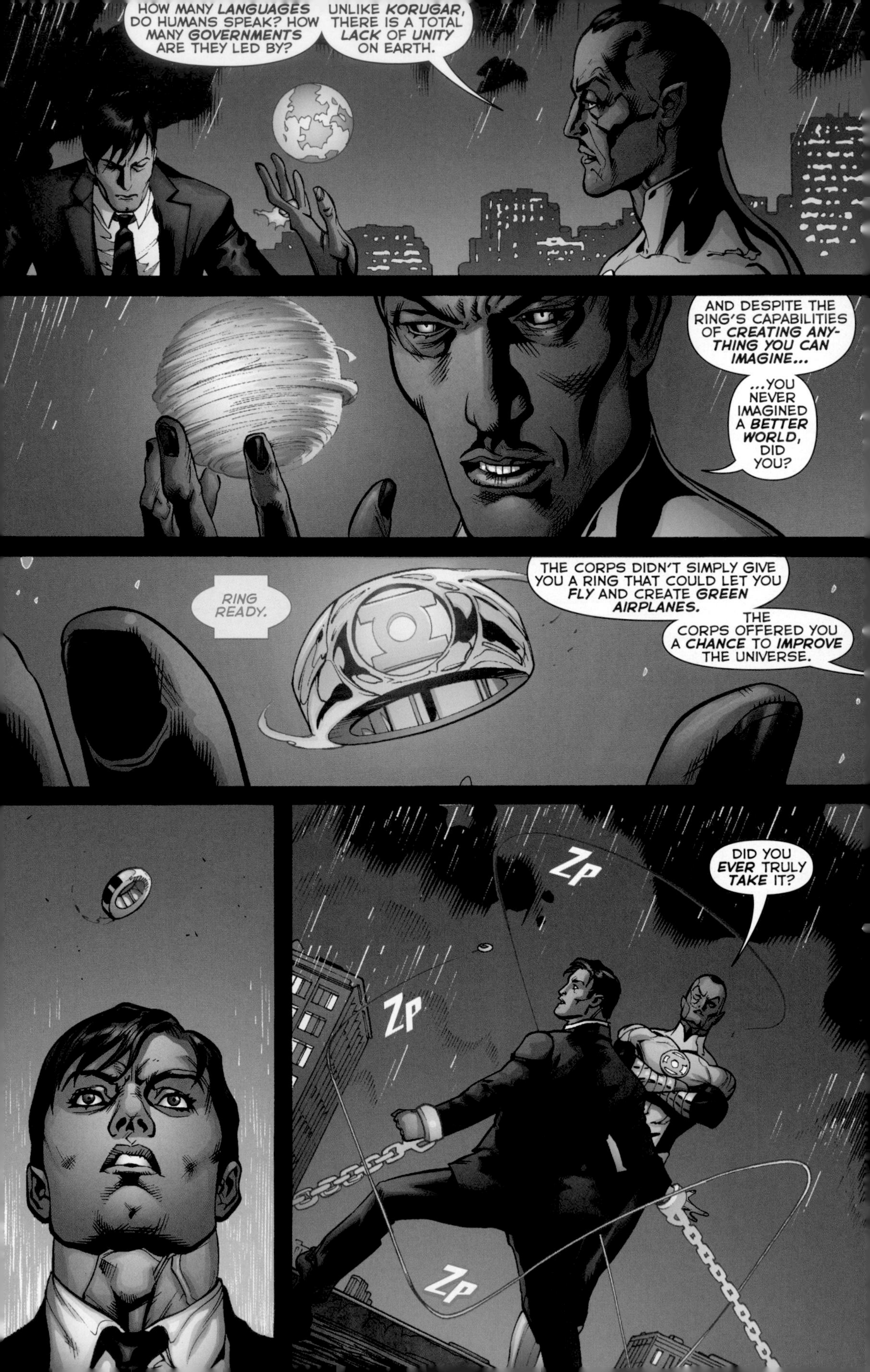
HOW MANY LANGUAGES DO HUMANS SPEAK? HOW MANY GOVERNMENTS ARE THEY LED BY?
UNLIKE KORUGAR, THERE IS A TOTAL LACK OF UNITY ON EARTH.
AND DESPITE THE RING'S CAPABILITIES OF CREATING ANYTHING YOU CAN IMAGINE...
...YOU NEVER IMAGINED A BETTER WORLD, DID YOU?
RING READY.
THE CORPS DIDN'T SIMPLY GIVE YOU A RING THAT COULD LET YOU FLY AND CREATE GREEN AIRPLANES.
THE CORPS OFFERED YOU A CHANCE TO IMPROVE THE UNIVERSE.
ZP
DID YOU EVER TRULY TAKE IT?
ZP
ZP

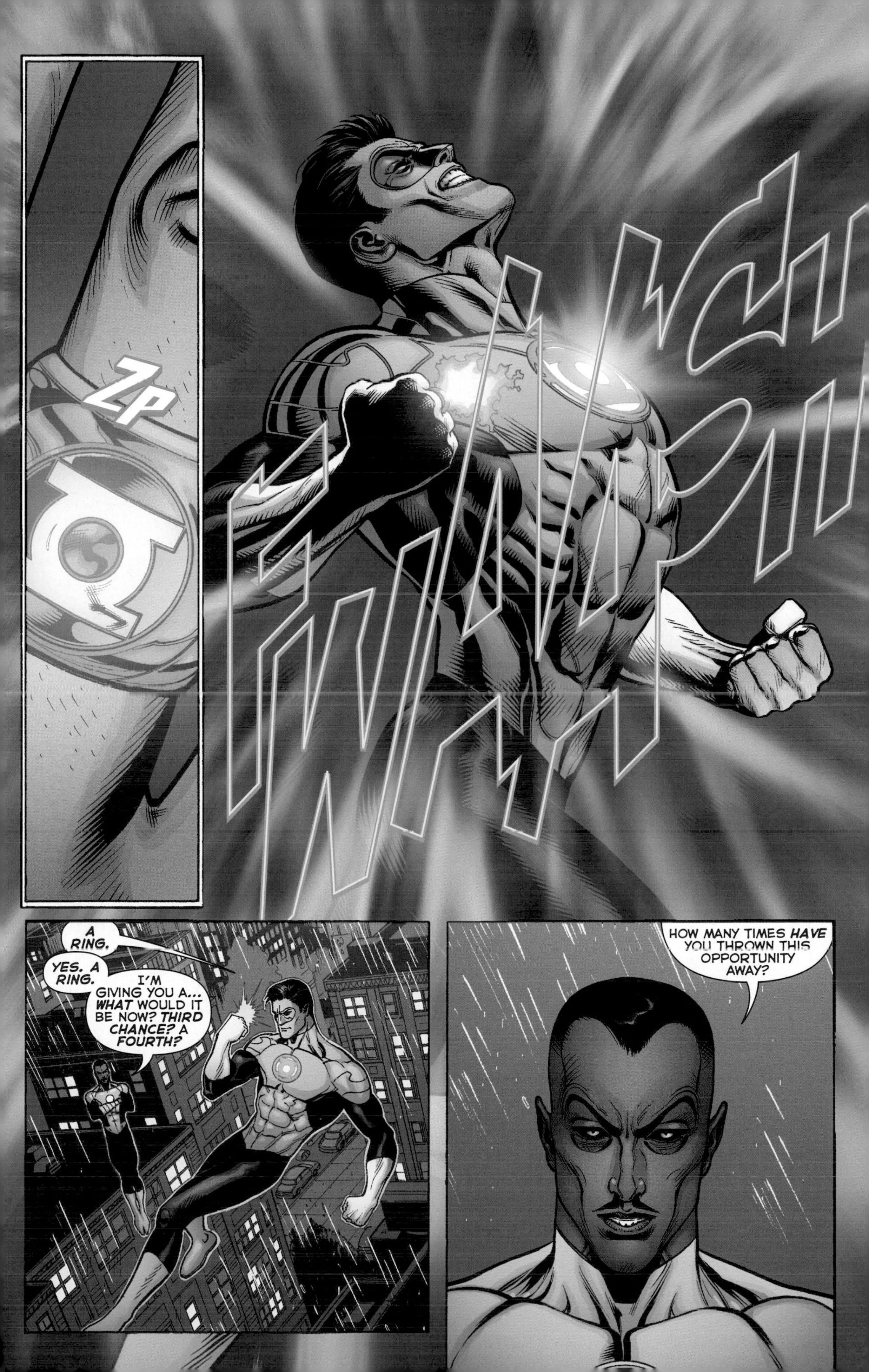
Zp
WHAAAAAAA
A RING.
YES. A RING.
I'M GIVING YOU A... WHAT WOULD IT BE NOW? THIRD CHANCE? A FOURTH?
HOW MANY TIMES HAVE YOU THROWN THIS OPPORTUNITY AWAY?

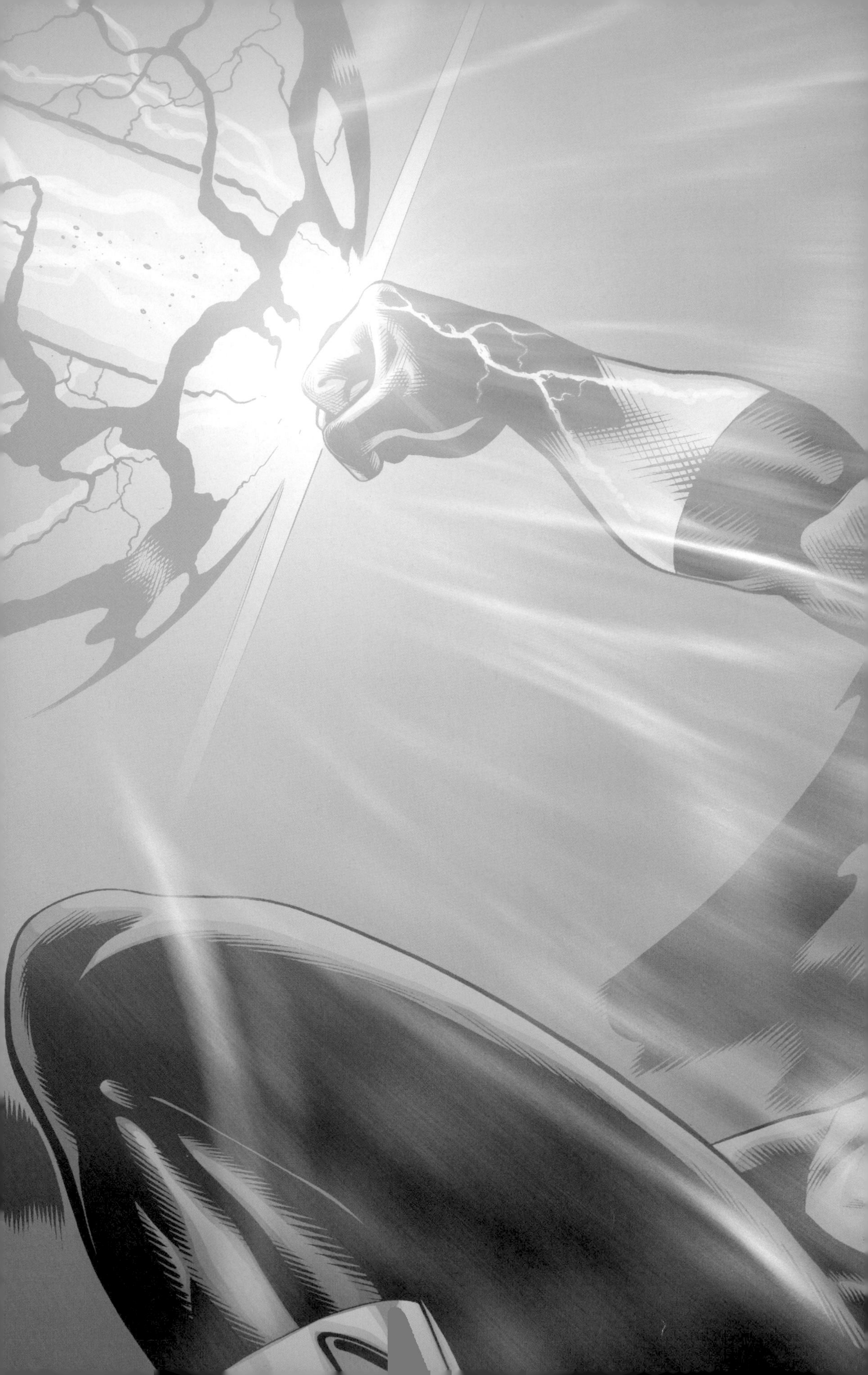

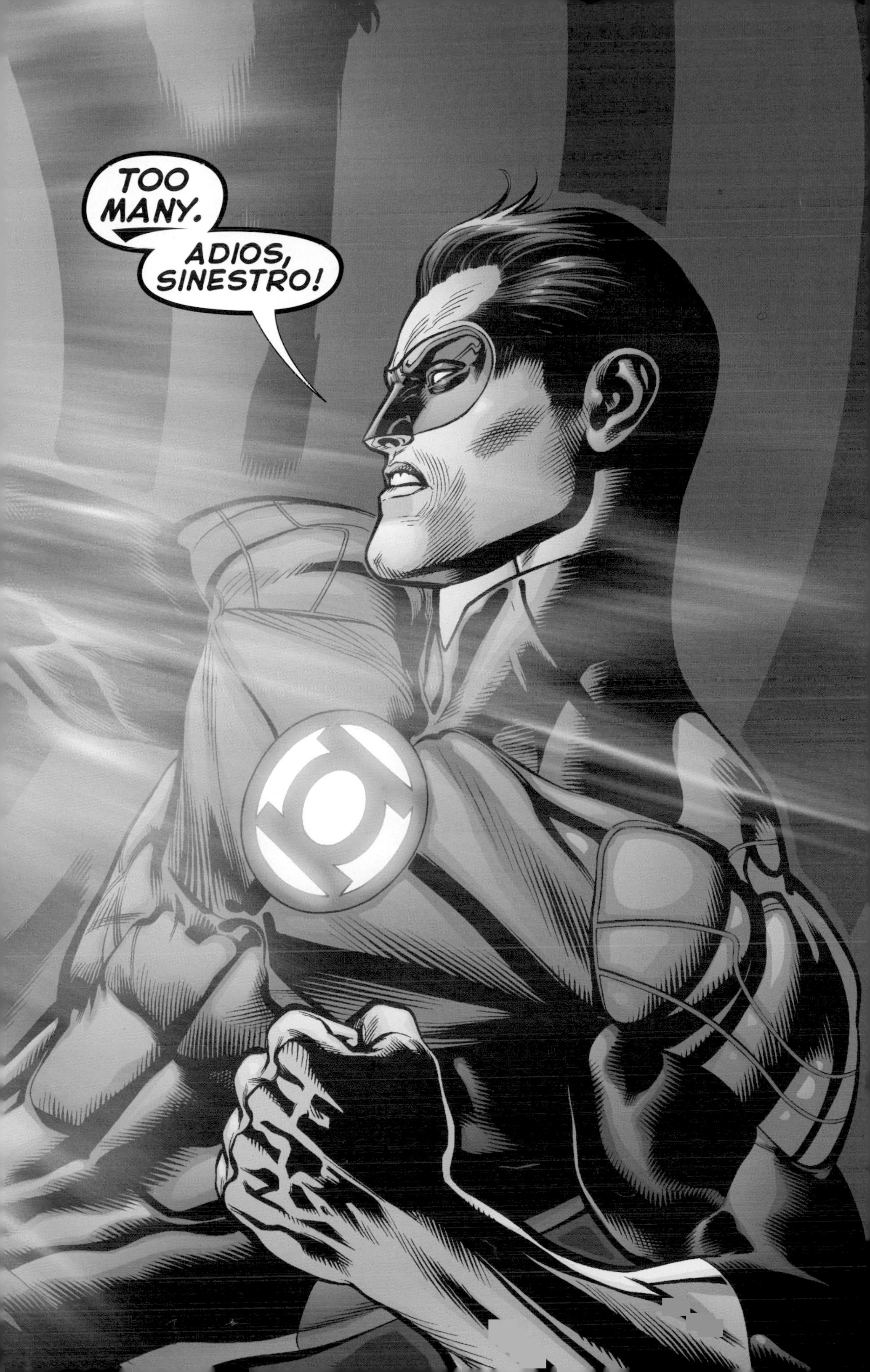
TOO MANY.
ADIOS, SINESTRO!

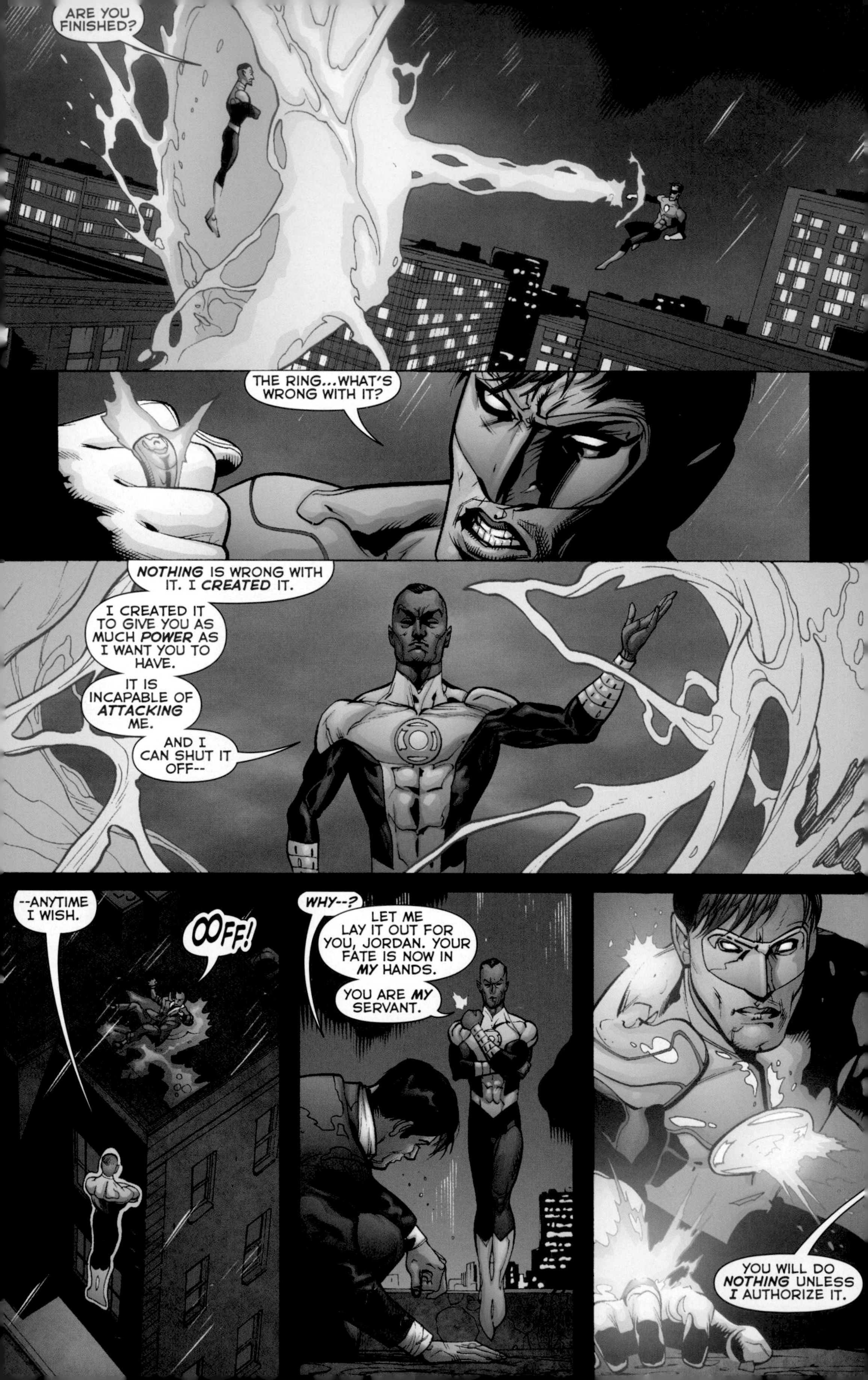
ARE YOU FINISHED?
THE RING...WHAT'S WRONG WITH IT?
NOTHING IS WRONG WITH IT. I *CREATED* IT.
I CREATED IT TO GIVE YOU AS MUCH *POWER* AS I WANT YOU TO HAVE.
IT IS INCAPABLE OF *ATTACKING* ME.
AND I CAN SHUT IT OFF--
--ANYTIME I WISH.
OOFF!
WHY--?
LET ME LAY IT OUT FOR YOU, JORDAN. YOUR FATE IS NOW IN *MY* HANDS.
YOU ARE *MY* SERVANT.
YOU WILL DO *NOTHING* UNLESS *I* AUTHORIZE IT.

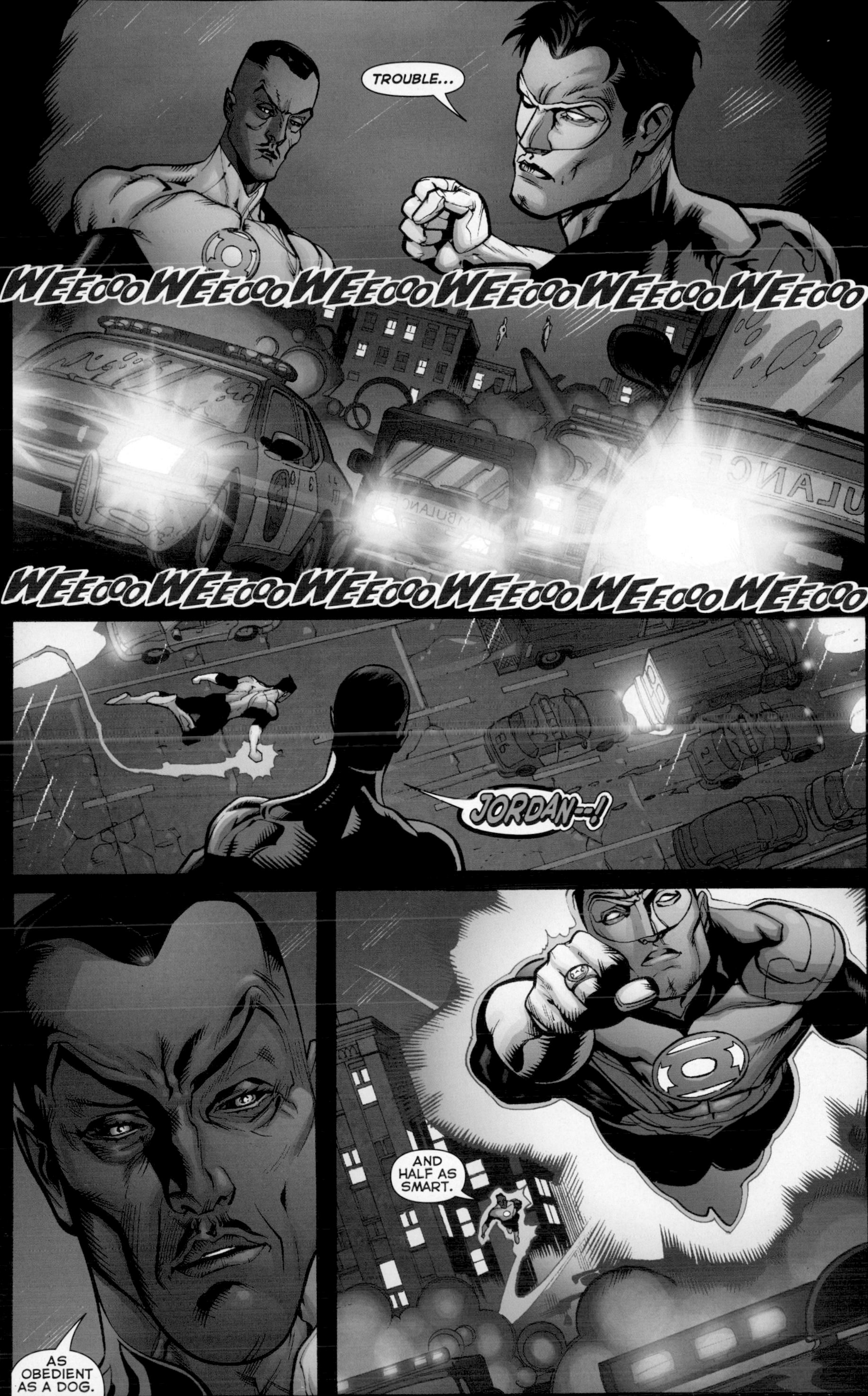
TROUBLE...
WEEOOO WEEOOO WEEOOO WEEOOO WEEOOO WEEOOO
AMBULANCE
WEEOOO WEEOOO WEEOOO WEEOOO WEEOOO WEEOOO
JORDAN--!
AS OBEDIENT AS A DOG.
AND HALF AS SMART.

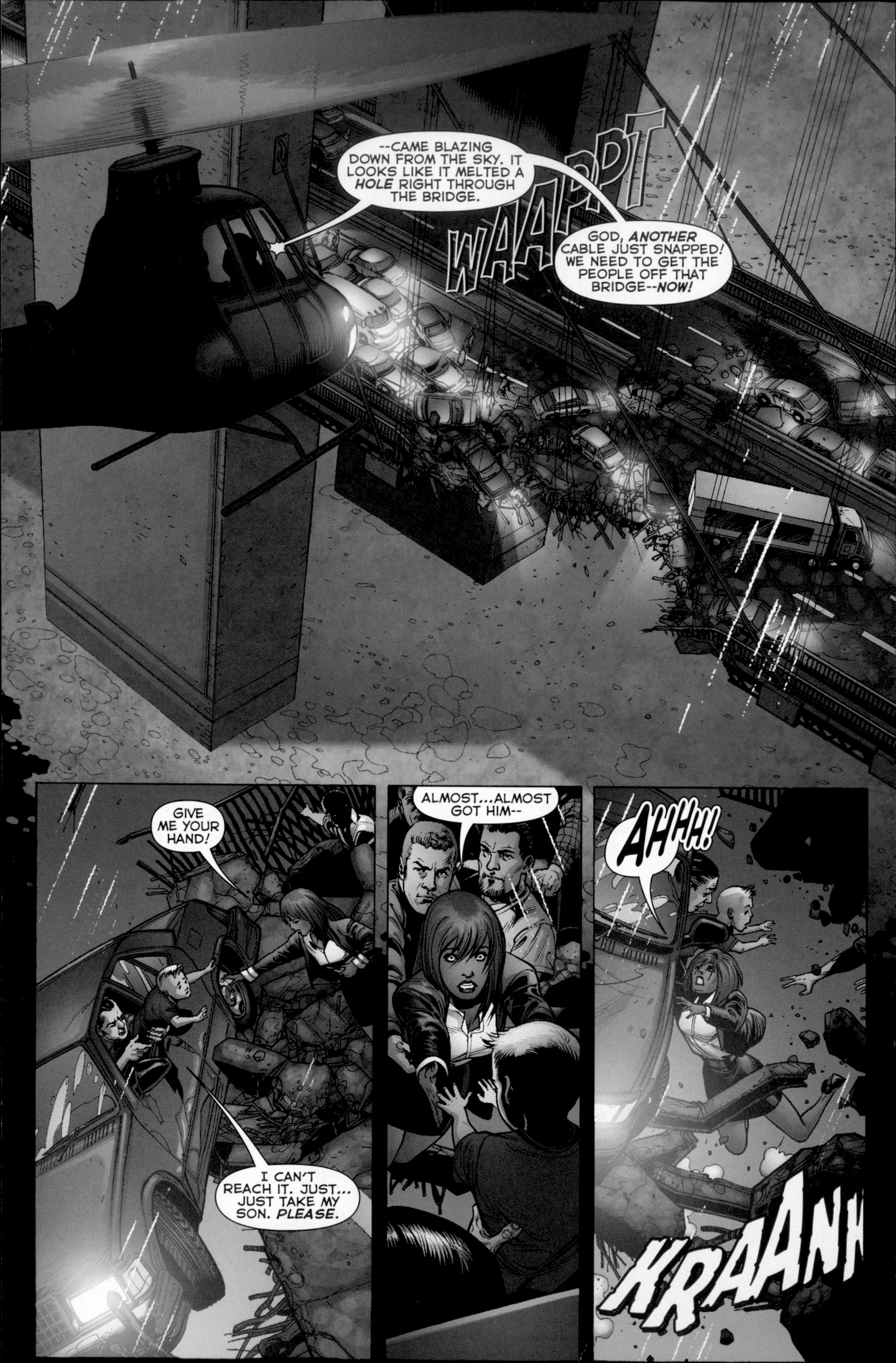
--CAME BLAZING DOWN FROM THE SKY. IT LOOKS LIKE IT MELTED A HOLE RIGHT THROUGH THE BRIDGE.
WAAPPT
GOD, ANOTHER CABLE JUST SNAPPED! WE NEED TO GET THE PEOPLE OFF THAT BRIDGE--NOW!
GIVE ME YOUR HAND!
I CAN'T REACH IT. JUST... JUST TAKE MY SON. PLEASE.
ALMOST...ALMOST GOT HIM--
AHHH!
KRAANK

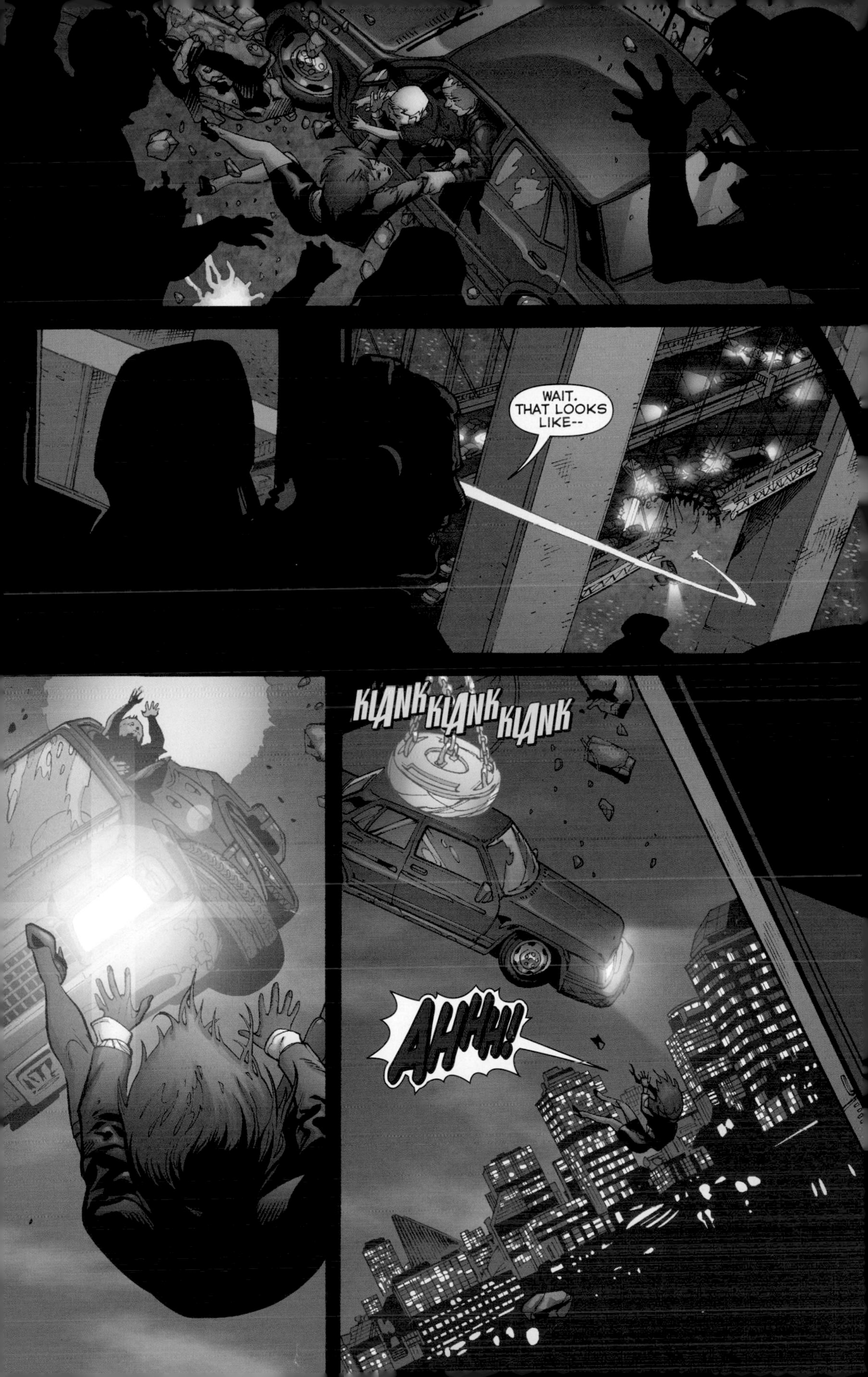
WAIT. THAT LOOKS LIKE--
KLANK KLANK KLANK
AHHH!

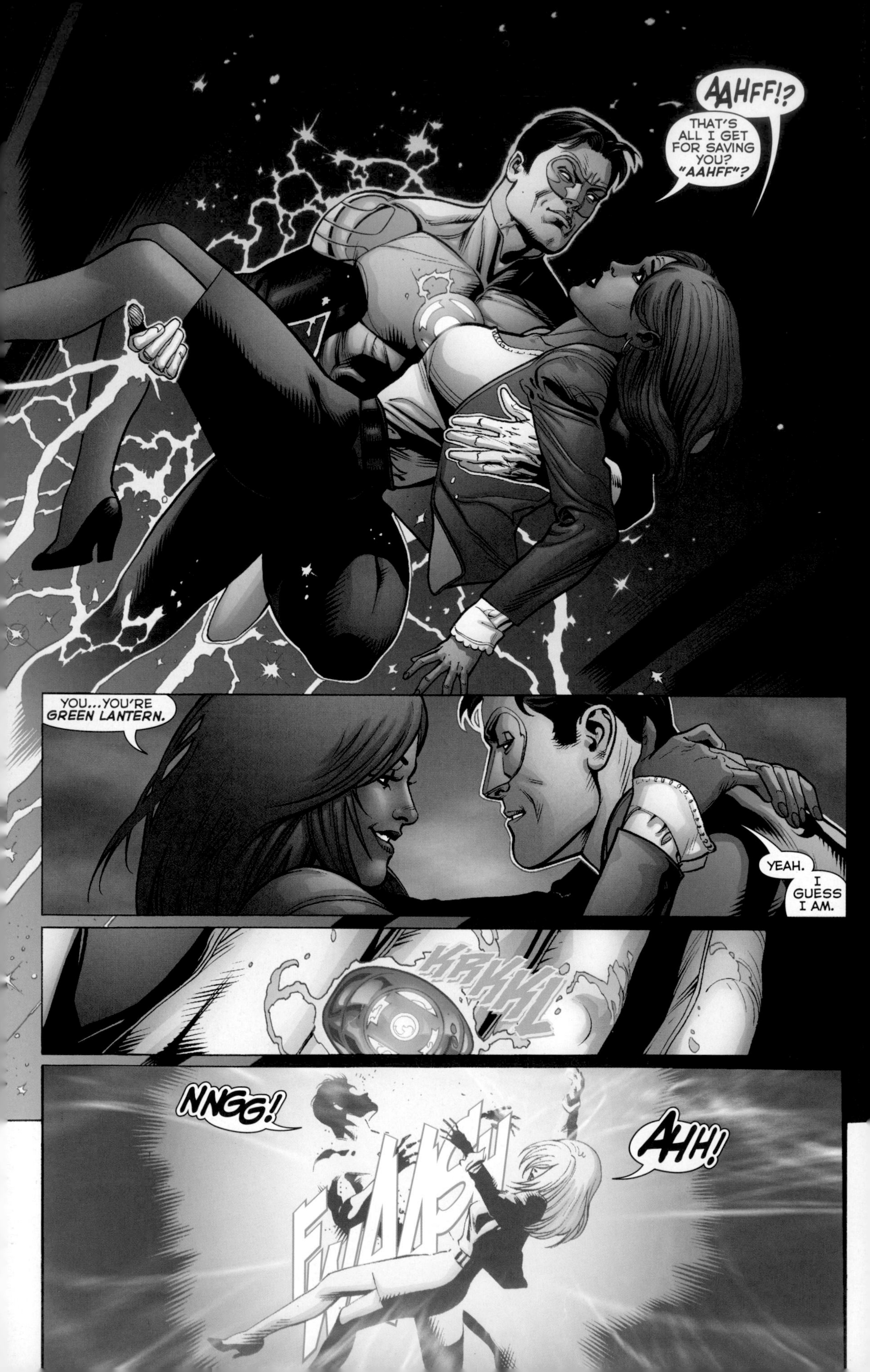
AAHFF!?
THAT'S ALL I GET FOR SAVING YOU? "AAHFF"?
YOU...YOU'RE GREEN LANTERN.
YEAH. I GUESS I AM.
KRKKL
NNGG!
AHH!
FLAASH

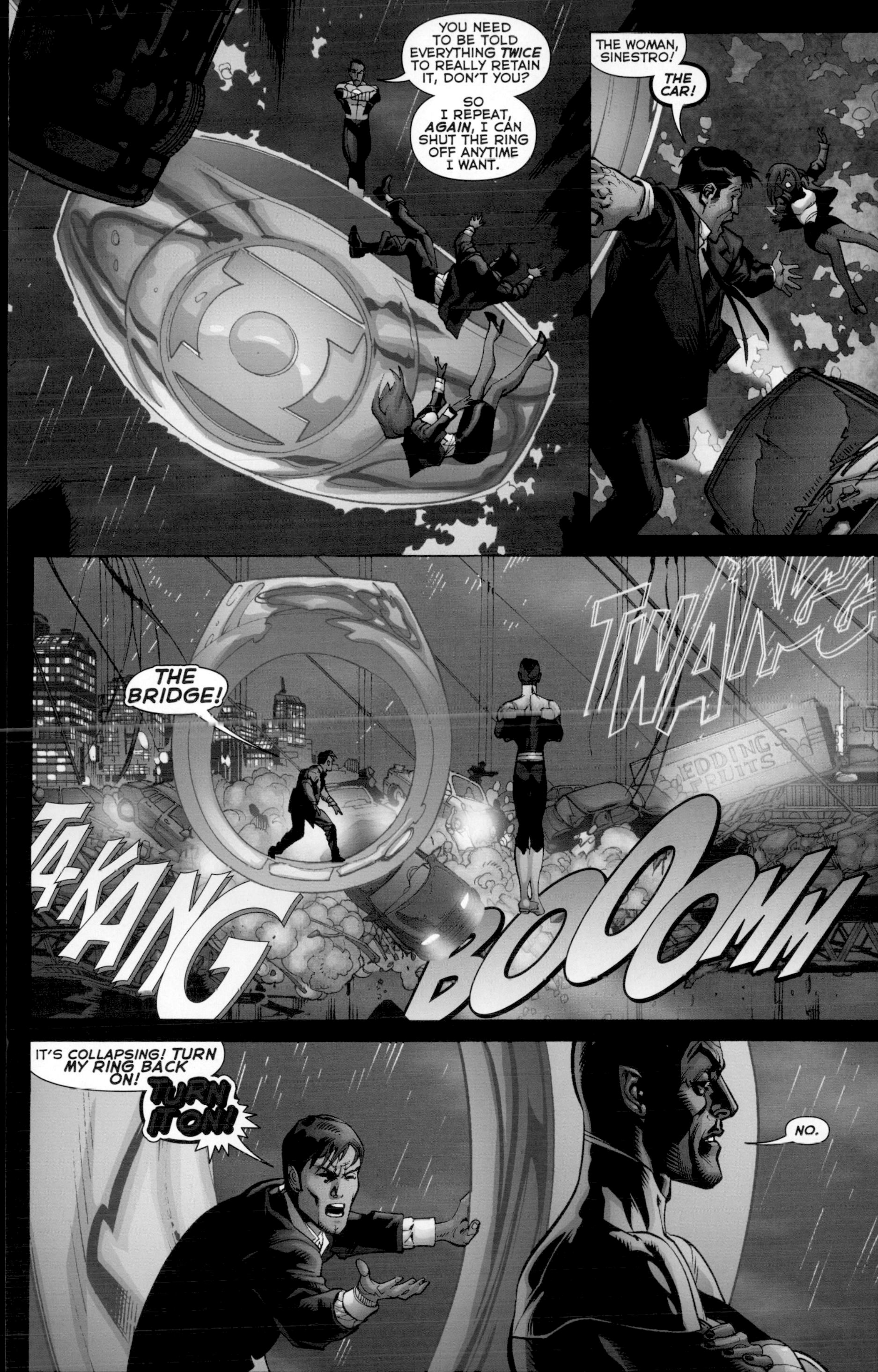

YOU NEED TO BE TOLD EVERYTHING TWICE TO REALLY RETAIN IT, DON'T YOU?
SO I REPEAT, AGAIN, I CAN SHUT THE RING OFF ANYTIME I WANT.
THE WOMAN, SINESTRO!
THE CAR!
THE BRIDGE!
TWANG
TA-KANG
BOOOOMM
EDDING FRUITS
IT'S COLLAPSING! TURN MY RING BACK ON!
TURN IT ON!
NO.

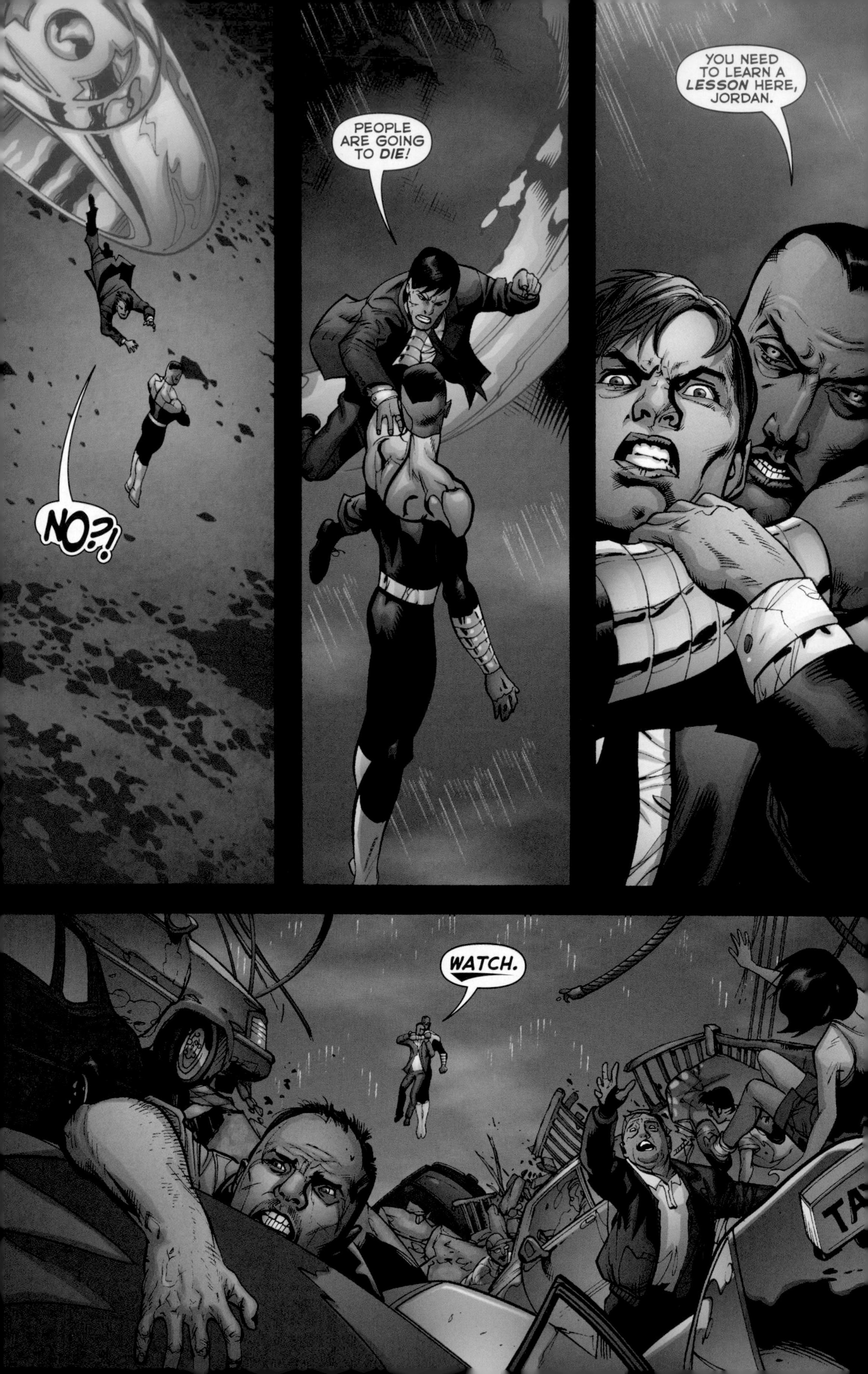
NO?!
PEOPLE ARE GOING TO DIE!
YOU NEED TO LEARN A LESSON HERE, JORDAN.
WATCH.

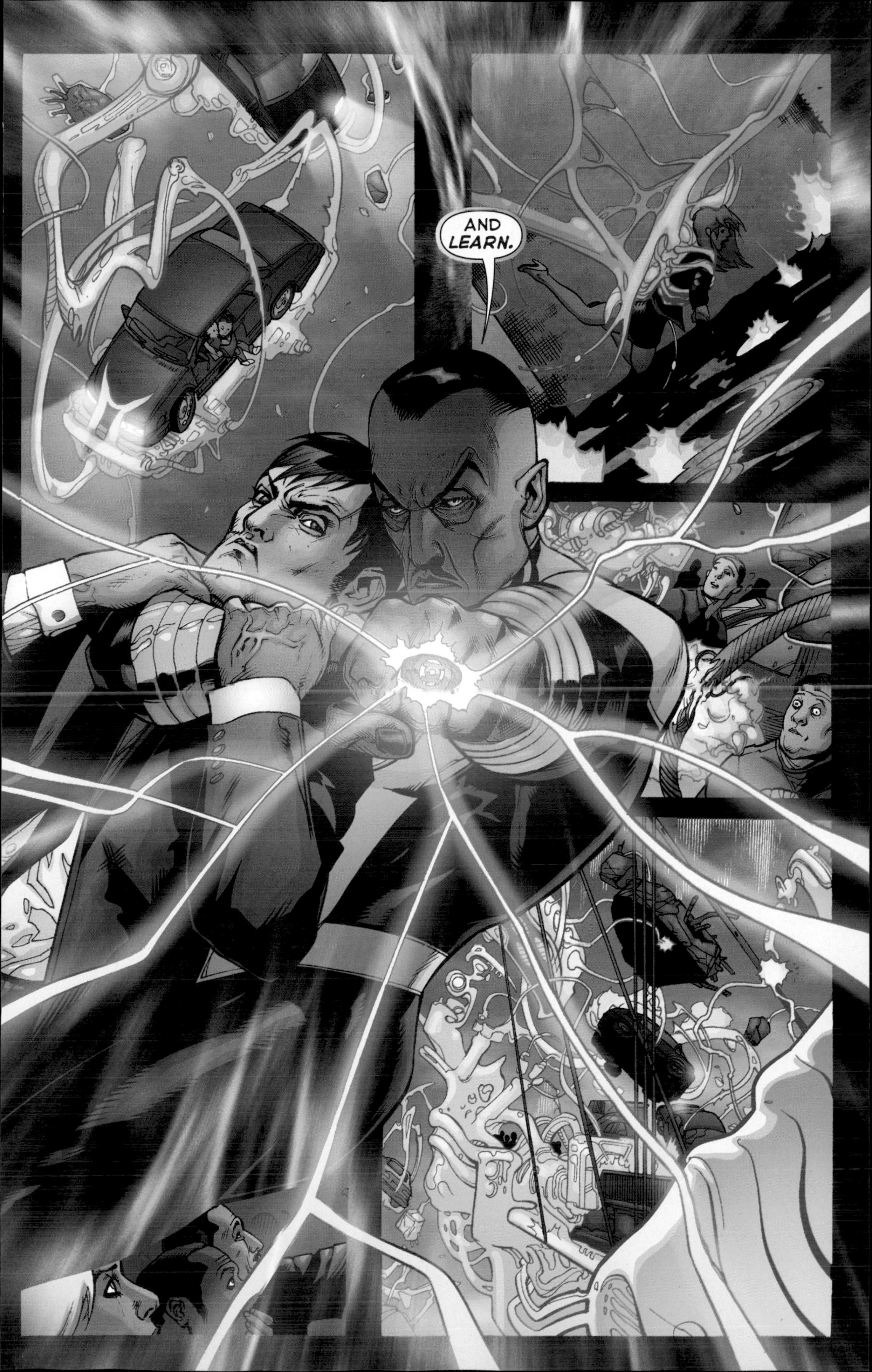
AND LEARN.

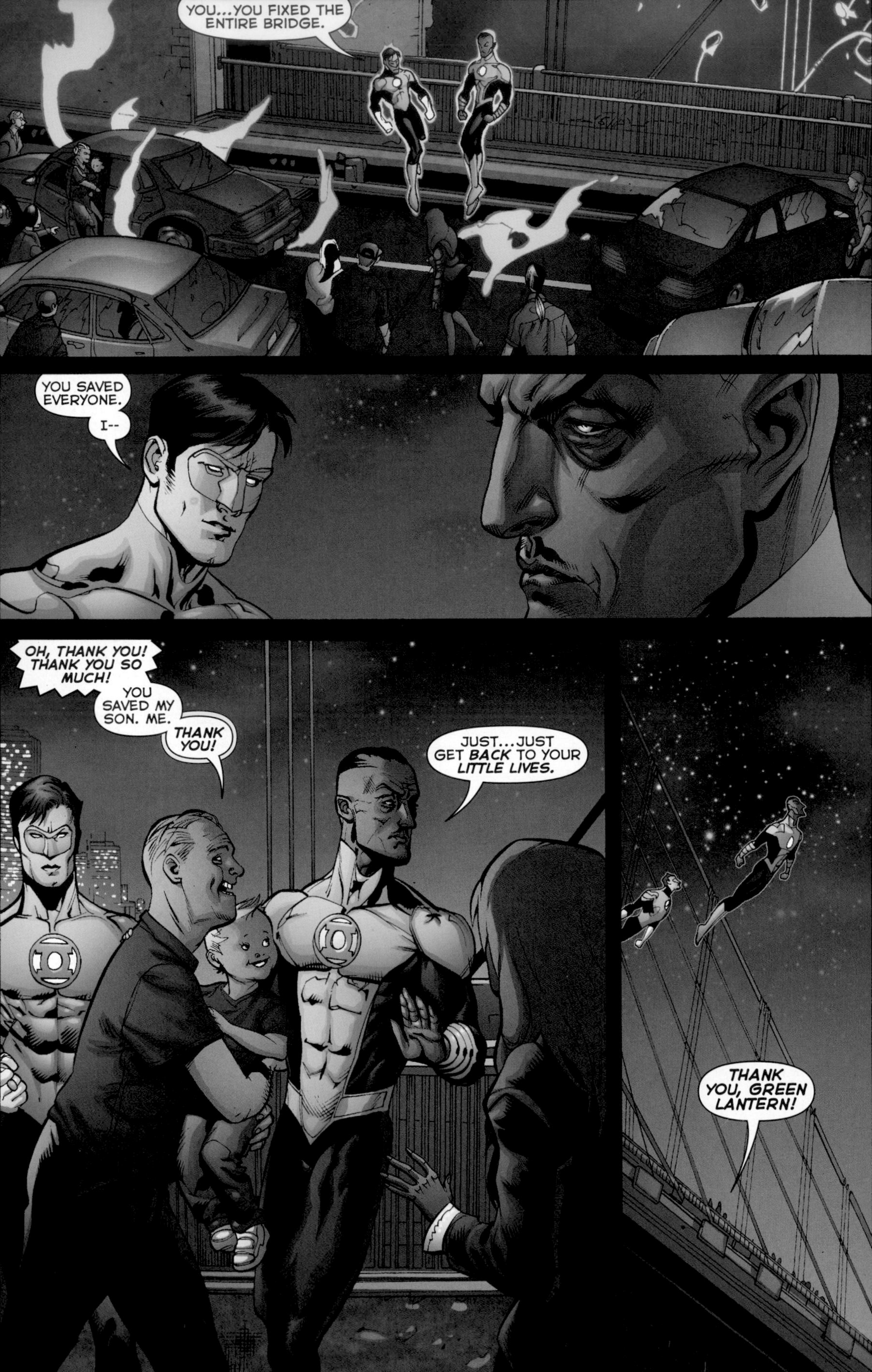
YOU...YOU FIXED THE ENTIRE BRIDGE.
YOU SAVED EVERYONE.
I--
OH, THANK YOU! THANK YOU SO MUCH!
YOU SAVED MY SON. ME.
THANK YOU!
JUST...JUST GET BACK TO YOUR LITTLE LIVES.
THANK YOU, GREEN LANTERN!

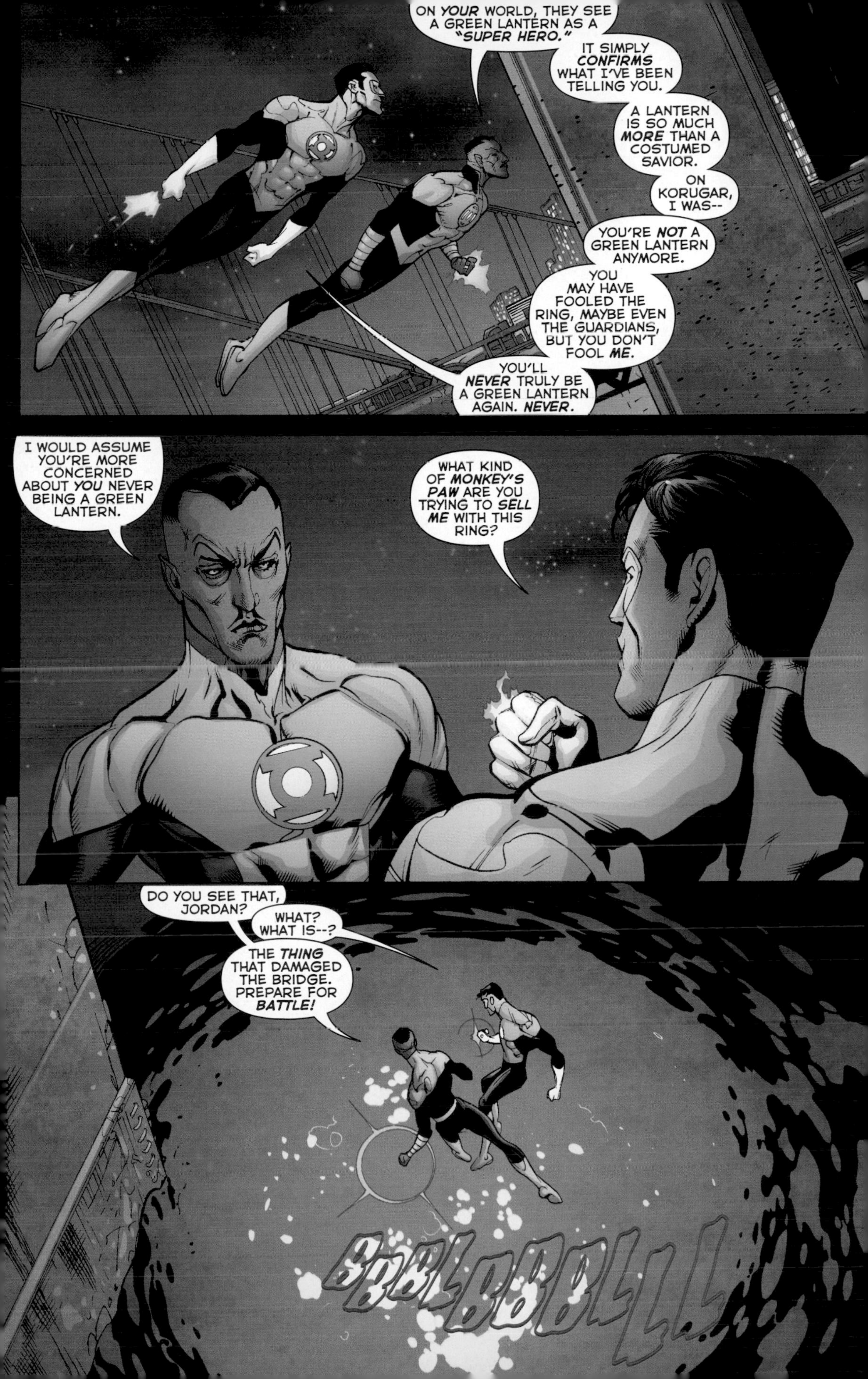
ON YOUR WORLD, THEY SEE A GREEN LANTERN AS A "SUPER HERO."
IT SIMPLY CONFIRMS WHAT I'VE BEEN TELLING YOU.
A LANTERN IS SO MUCH MORE THAN A COSTUMED SAVIOR.
ON KORUGAR, I WAS--
YOU'RE NOT A GREEN LANTERN ANYMORE.
YOU MAY HAVE FOOLED THE RING, MAYBE EVEN THE GUARDIANS, BUT YOU DON'T FOOL ME.
YOU'LL NEVER TRULY BE A GREEN LANTERN AGAIN. NEVER.
I WOULD ASSUME YOU'RE MORE CONCERNED ABOUT YOU NEVER BEING A GREEN LANTERN.
WHAT KIND OF MONKEY'S PAW ARE YOU TRYING TO SELL ME WITH THIS RING?
DO YOU SEE THAT, JORDAN?
WHAT? WHAT IS--?
THE THING THAT DAMAGED THE BRIDGE. PREPARE FOR BATTLE!
BBBLBBBLLL

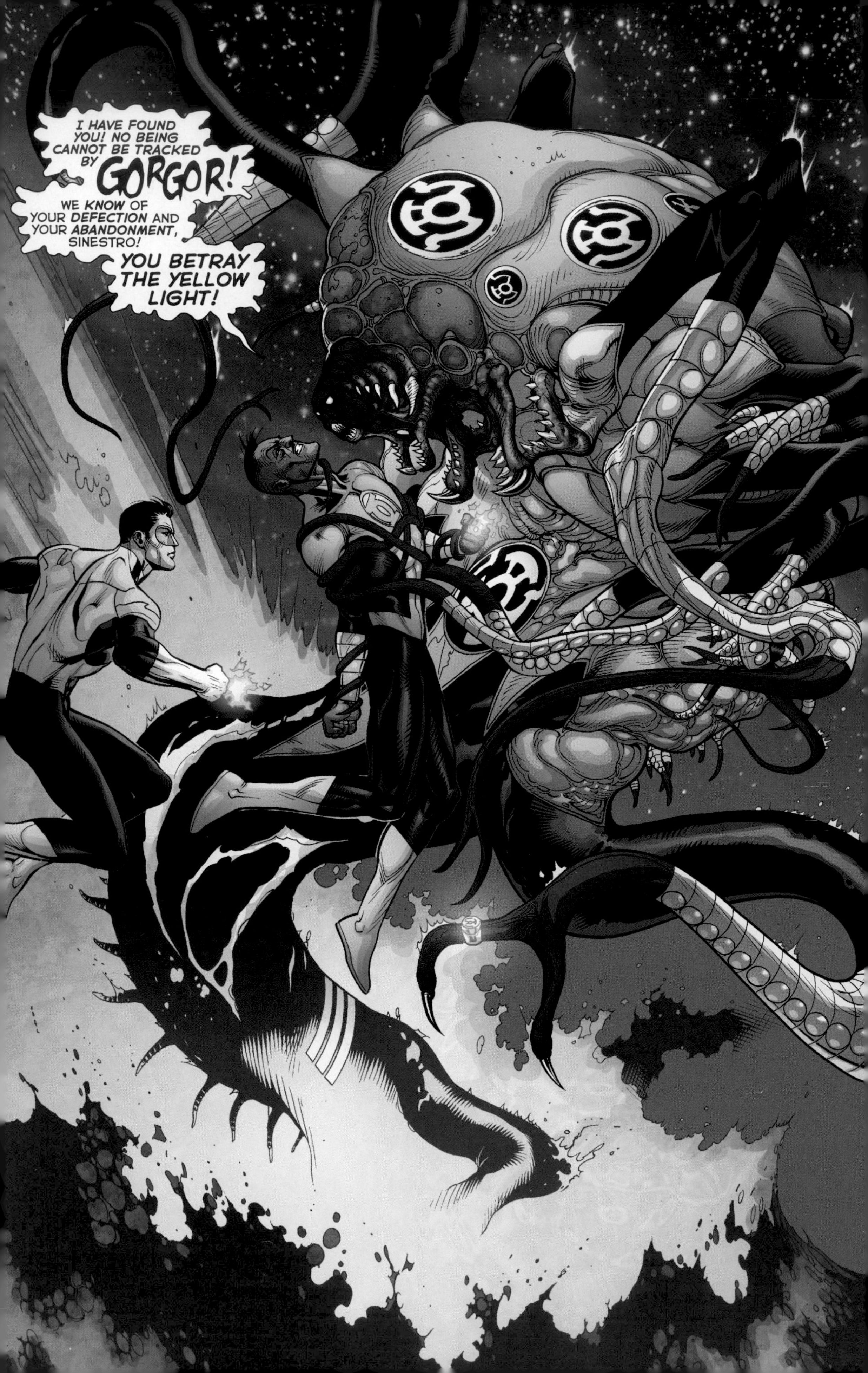
I HAVE FOUND YOU! NO BEING CANNOT BE TRACKED BY GORGOR!
WE KNOW OF YOUR DEFECTION AND YOUR ABANDONMENT, SINESTRO!
YOU BETRAY THE YELLOW LIGHT!

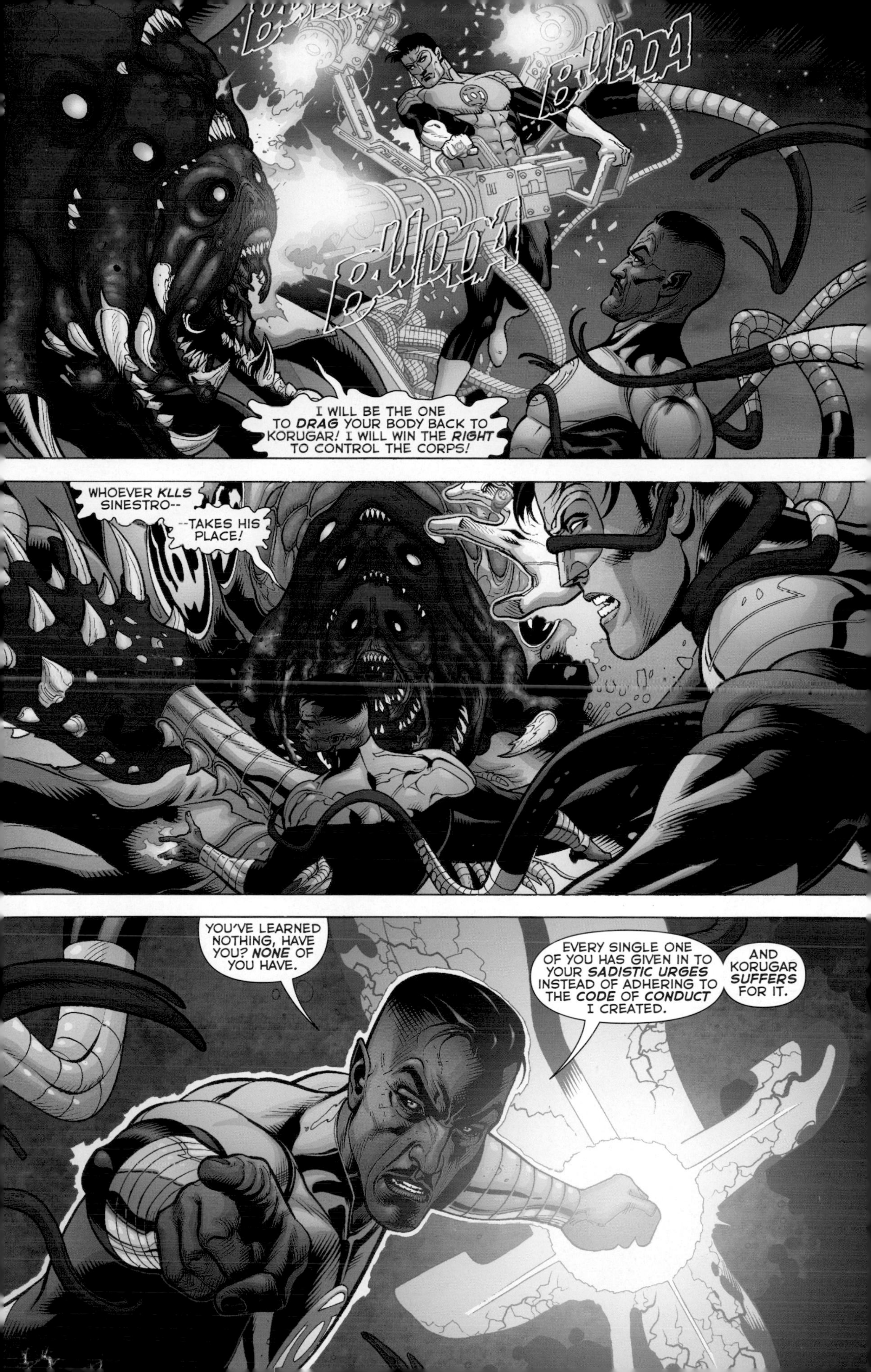
BUDDA
BUDDA
I WILL BE THE ONE TO DRAG YOUR BODY BACK TO KORUGAR! I WILL WIN THE RIGHT TO CONTROL THE CORPS!
WHOEVER KLLS SINESTRO--
--TAKES HIS PLACE!
YOU'VE LEARNED NOTHING, HAVE YOU? NONE OF YOU HAVE.
EVERY SINGLE ONE OF YOU HAS GIVEN IN TO YOUR SADISTIC URGES INSTEAD OF ADHERING TO THE CODE OF CONDUCT I CREATED.
AND KORUGAR SUFFERS FOR IT.

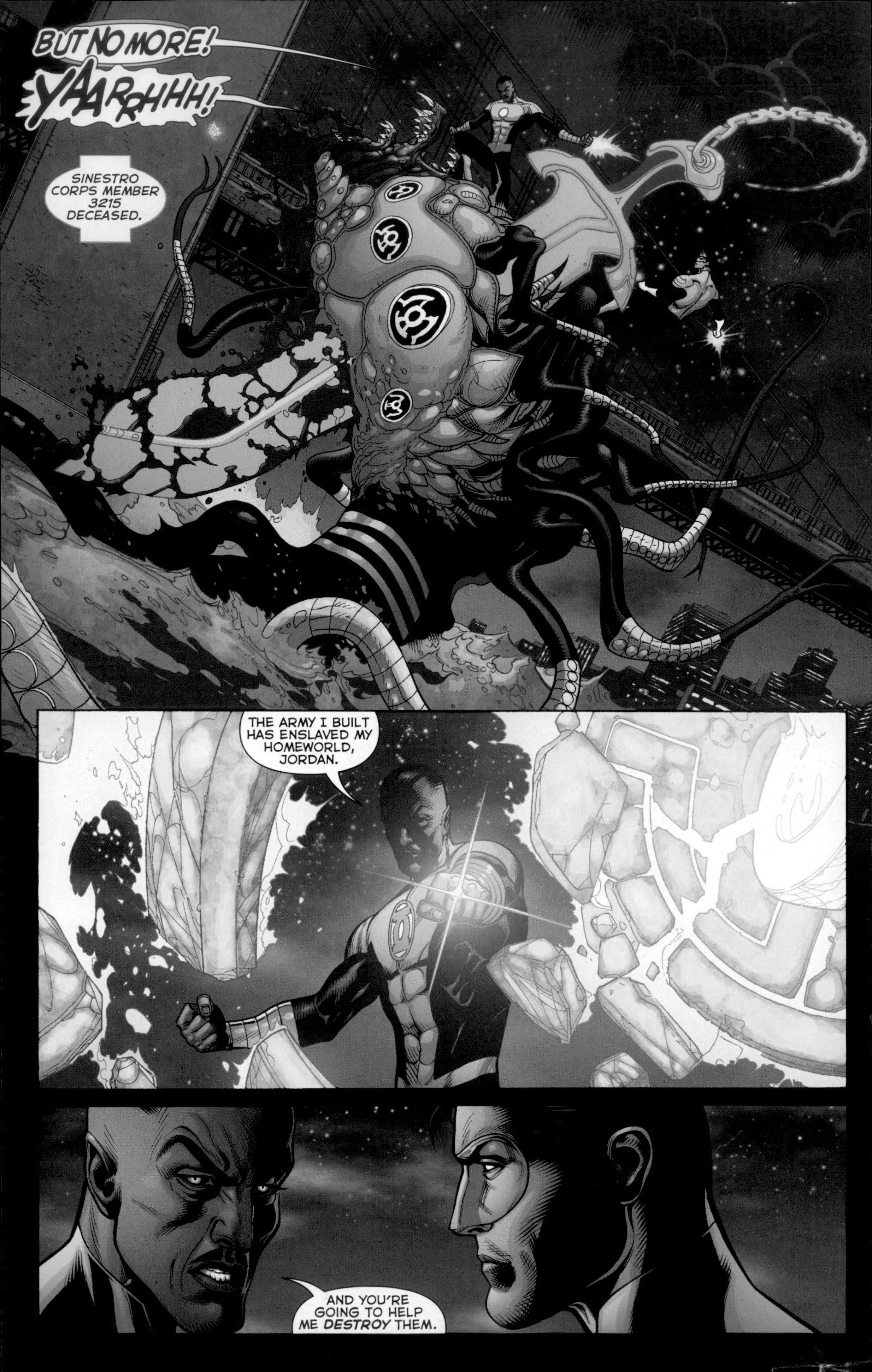
BUT NO MORE!
YAARRHHH!
SINESTRO CORPS MEMBER 3215 DECEASED.
THE ARMY I BUILT HAS ENSLAVED MY HOMEWORLD, JORDAN.
AND YOU'RE GOING TO HELP ME DESTROY THEM.

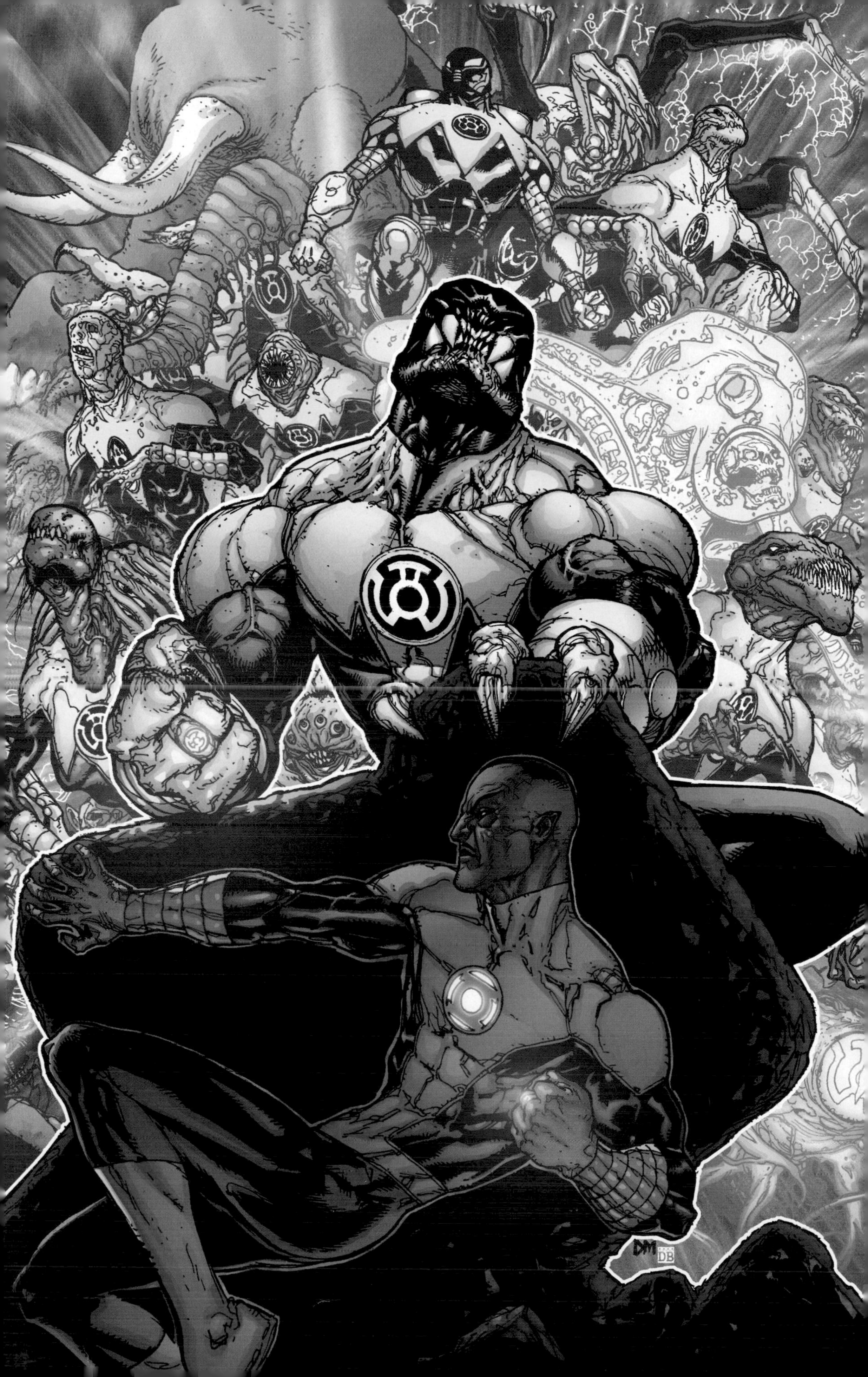

Doug Mahnke & David Baron

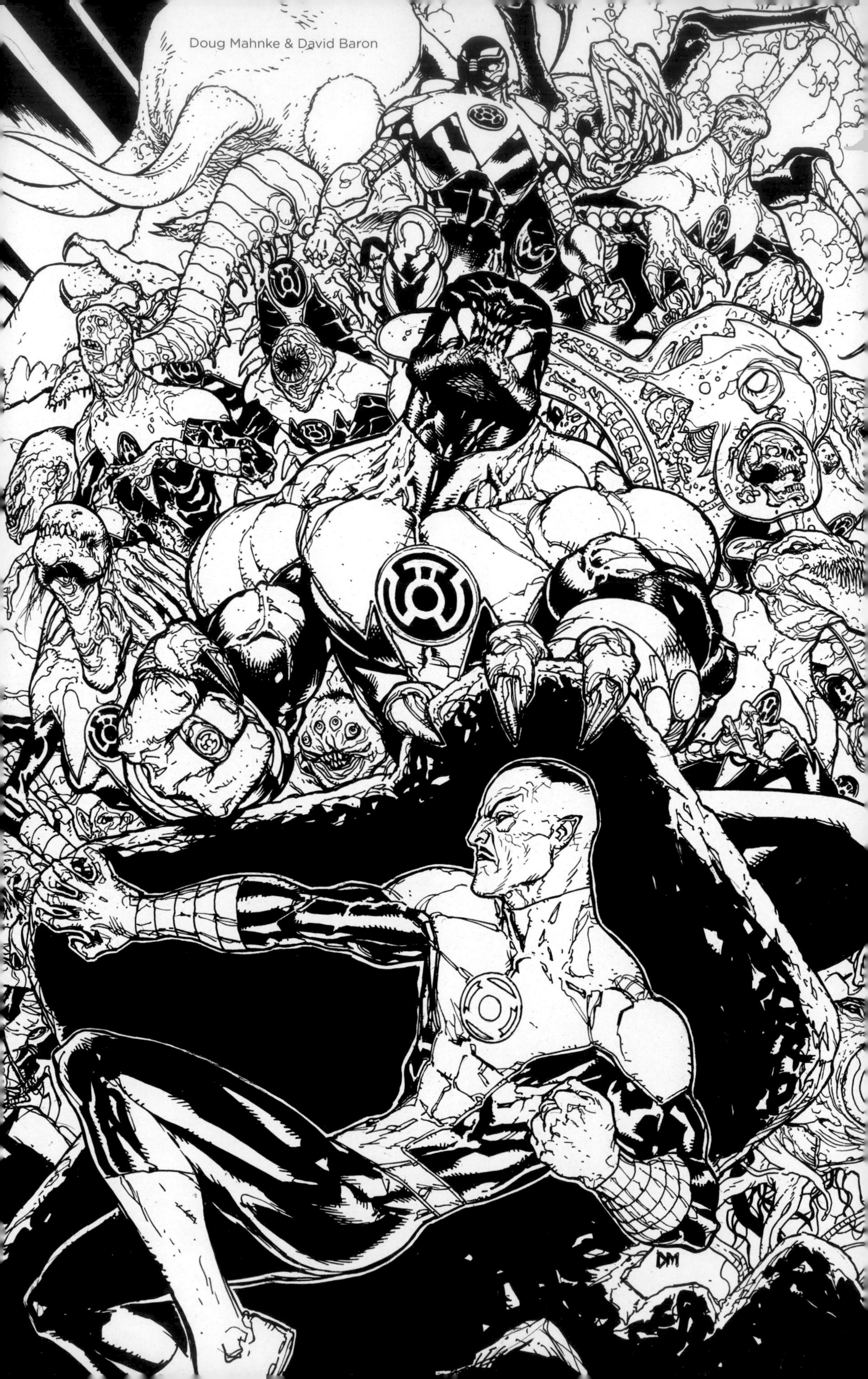

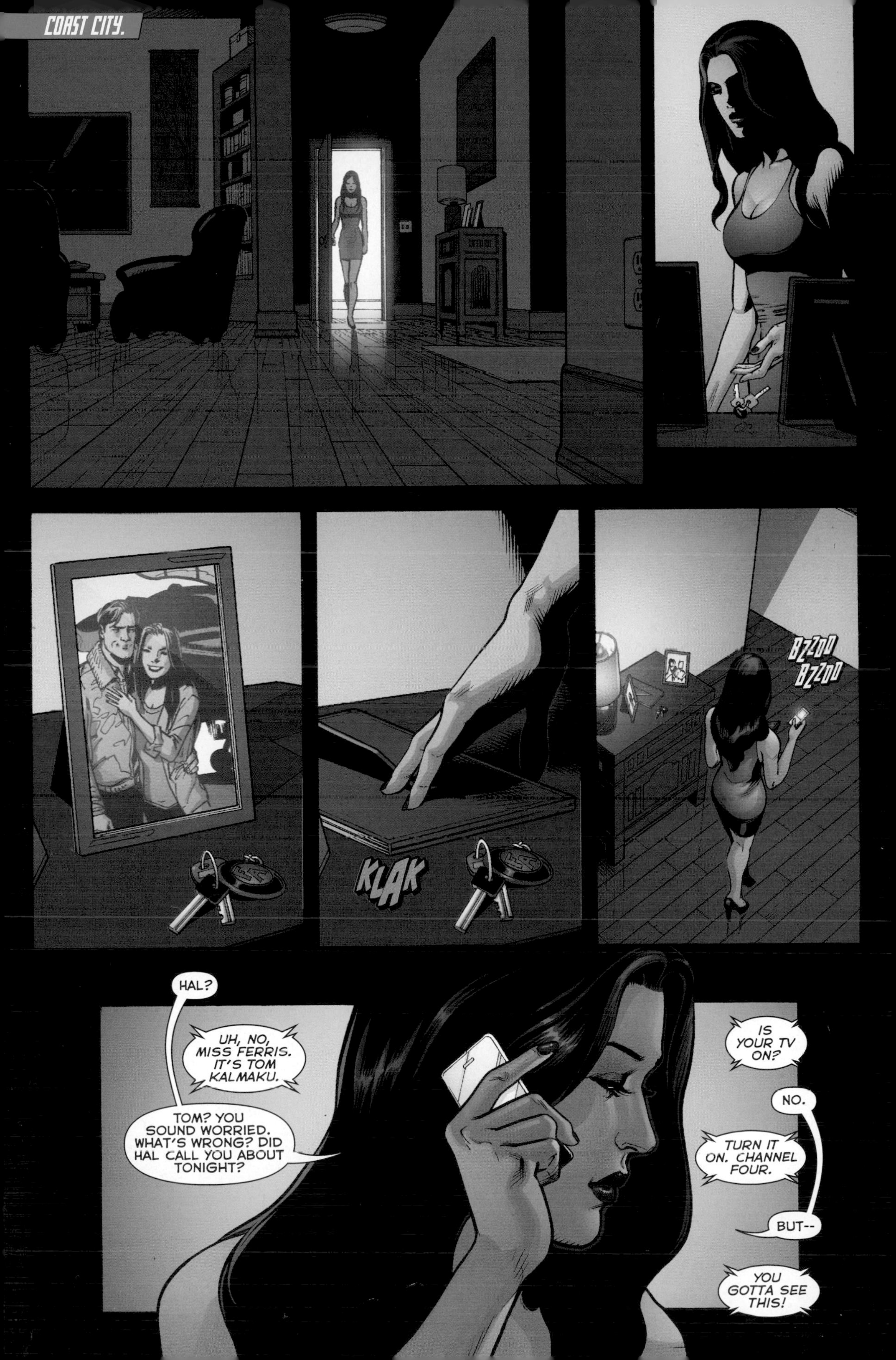
COAST CITY.
KLAK
BZZOO BZZOO
HAL?
UH, NO, MISS FERRIS. IT'S TOM KALMAKU.
TOM? YOU SOUND WORRIED. WHAT'S WRONG? DID HAL CALL YOU ABOUT TONIGHT?
IS YOUR TV ON?
NO.
TURN IT ON. CHANNEL FOUR.
BUT--
YOU GOTTA SEE THIS!

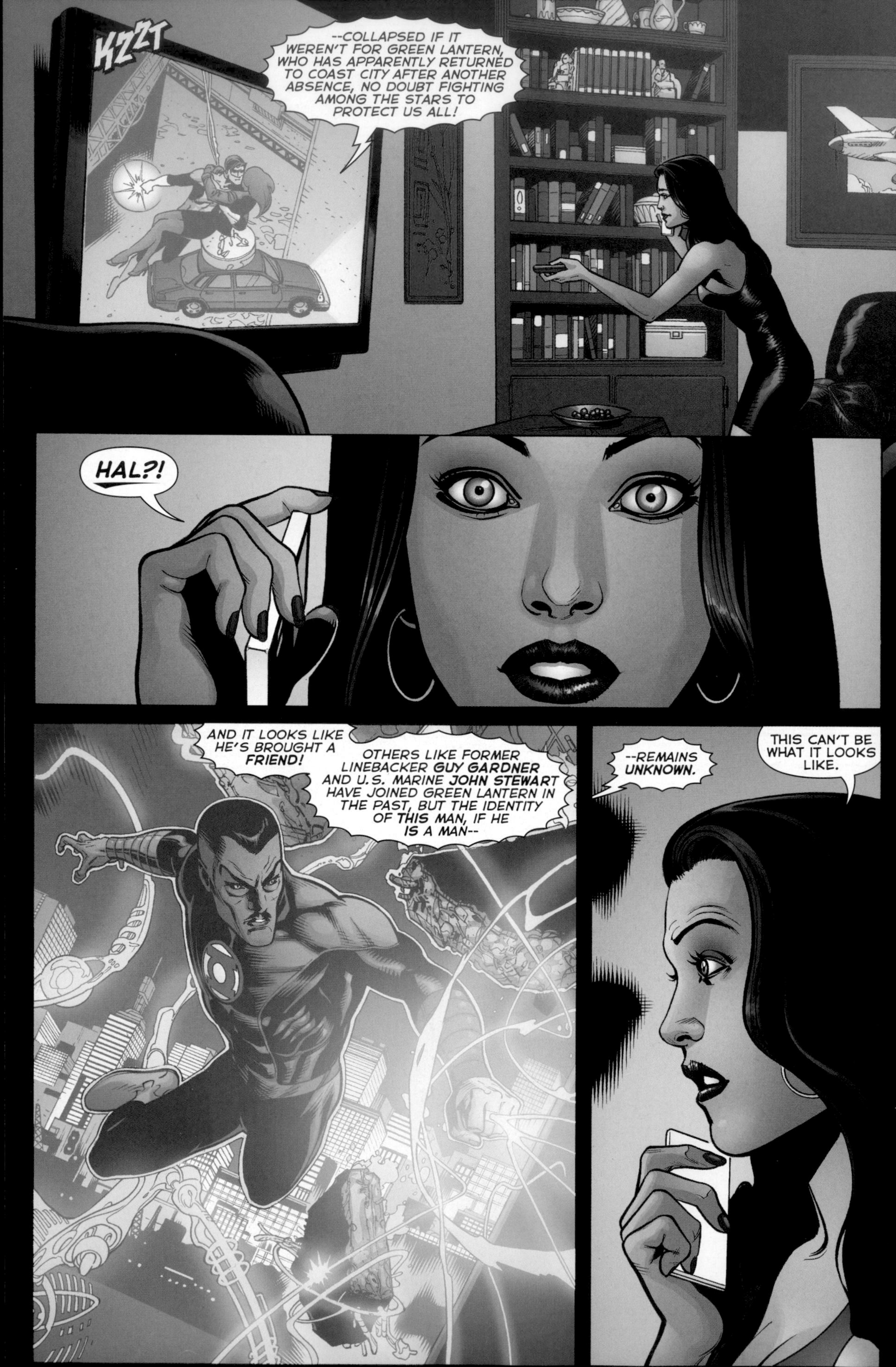
KZZT
--COLLAPSED IF IT WEREN'T FOR GREEN LANTERN, WHO HAS APPARENTLY RETURNED TO COAST CITY AFTER ANOTHER ABSENCE, NO DOUBT FIGHTING AMONG THE STARS TO PROTECT US ALL!
HAL?!
AND IT LOOKS LIKE HE'S BROUGHT A FRIEND!
OTHERS LIKE FORMER LINEBACKER GUY GARDNER AND U.S. MARINE JOHN STEWART HAVE JOINED GREEN LANTERN IN THE PAST, BUT THE IDENTITY OF THIS MAN, IF HE IS A MAN--
--REMAINS UNKNOWN.
THIS CAN'T BE WHAT IT LOOKS LIKE.

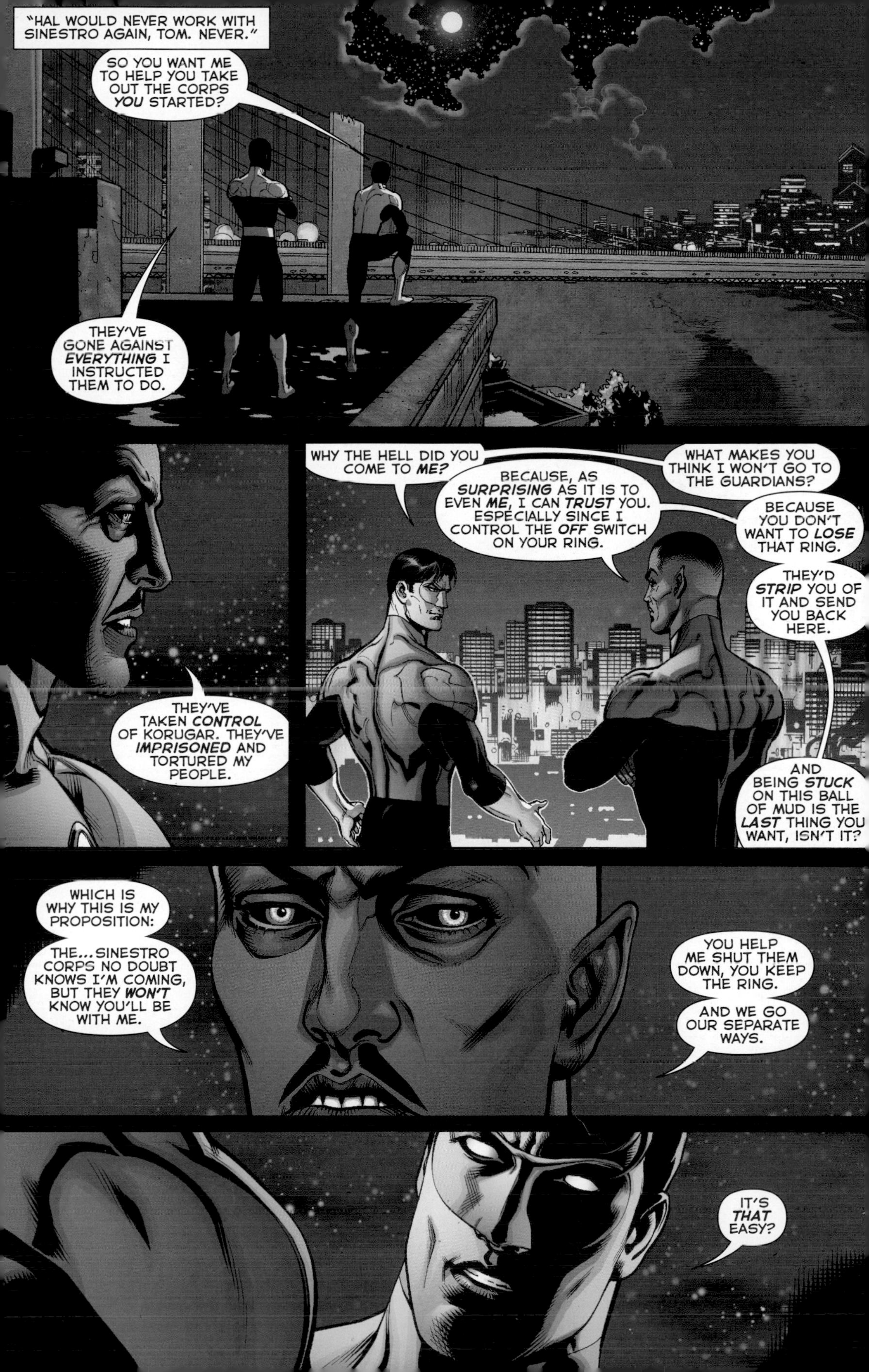
"HAL WOULD NEVER WORK WITH SINESTRO AGAIN, TOM. NEVER."
SO YOU WANT ME TO HELP YOU TAKE OUT THE CORPS YOU STARTED?
THEY'VE GONE AGAINST EVERYTHING I INSTRUCTED THEM TO DO.
THEY'VE TAKEN CONTROL OF KORUGAR. THEY'VE IMPRISONED AND TORTURED MY PEOPLE.
WHY THE HELL DID YOU COME TO ME?
BECAUSE, AS SURPRISING AS IT IS TO EVEN ME, I CAN TRUST YOU. ESPECIALLY SINCE I CONTROL THE OFF SWITCH ON YOUR RING.
WHAT MAKES YOU THINK I WON'T GO TO THE GUARDIANS?
BECAUSE YOU DON'T WANT TO LOSE THAT RING.
THEY'D STRIP YOU OF IT AND SEND YOU BACK HERE.
AND BEING STUCK ON THIS BALL OF MUD IS THE LAST THING YOU WANT, ISN'T IT?
WHICH IS WHY THIS IS MY PROPOSITION:
THE... SINESTRO CORPS NO DOUBT KNOWS I'M COMING, BUT THEY WON'T KNOW YOU'LL BE WITH ME.
YOU HELP ME SHUT THEM DOWN, YOU KEEP THE RING.
AND WE GO OUR SEPARATE WAYS.
IT'S THAT EASY?

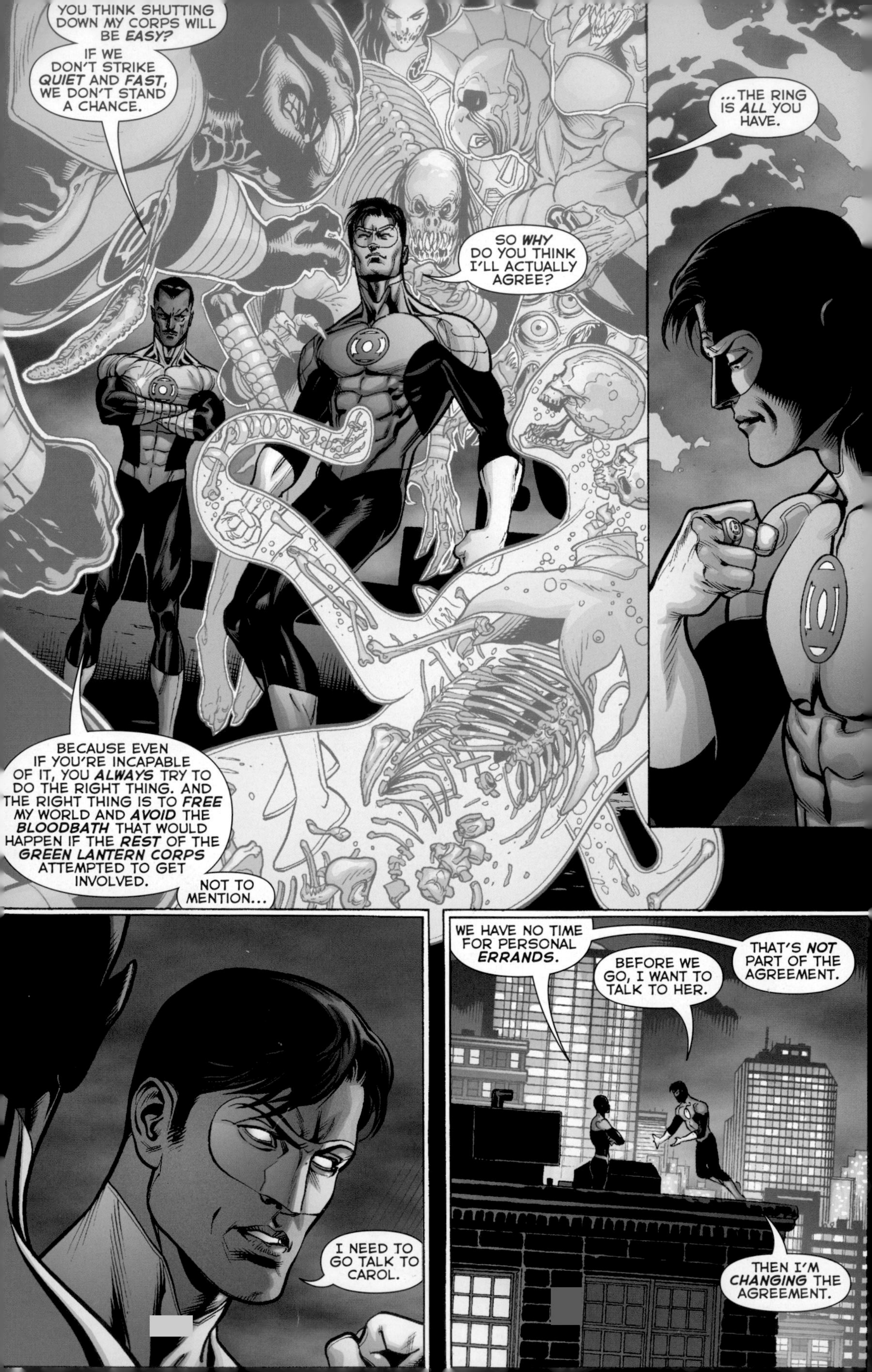
YOU THINK SHUTTING DOWN MY CORPS WILL BE *EASY?*
IF WE DON'T STRIKE *QUIET* AND *FAST*, WE DON'T STAND A CHANCE.
SO *WHY* DO YOU THINK I'LL ACTUALLY AGREE?
BECAUSE EVEN IF YOU'RE INCAPABLE OF IT, YOU *ALWAYS* TRY TO DO THE RIGHT THING. AND THE RIGHT THING IS TO *FREE* MY WORLD AND *AVOID* THE *BLOODBATH* THAT WOULD HAPPEN IF THE *REST* OF THE *GREEN LANTERN CORPS* ATTEMPTED TO GET INVOLVED.
NOT TO MENTION...
...THE RING IS *ALL* YOU HAVE.
I NEED TO GO TALK TO CAROL.
BEFORE WE GO, I WANT TO TALK TO HER.
WE HAVE NO TIME FOR PERSONAL *ERRANDS*.
THAT'S *NOT* PART OF THE AGREEMENT.
THEN I'M *CHANGING* THE AGREEMENT.

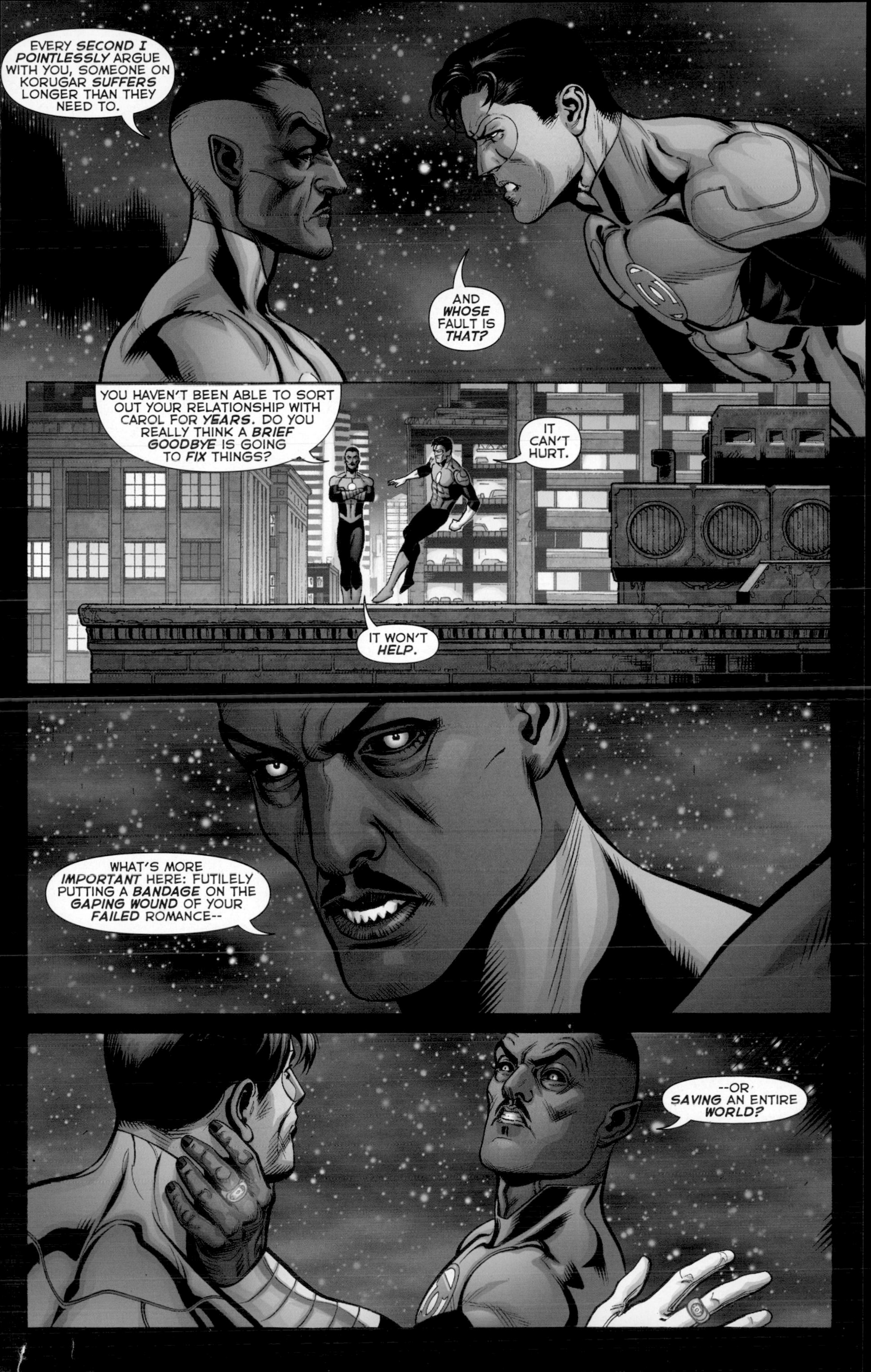
EVERY SECOND I POINTLESSLY ARGUE WITH YOU, SOMEONE ON KORUGAR SUFFERS LONGER THAN THEY NEED TO.
AND WHOSE FAULT IS THAT?
YOU HAVEN'T BEEN ABLE TO SORT OUT YOUR RELATIONSHIP WITH CAROL FOR YEARS. DO YOU REALLY THINK A BRIEF GOODBYE IS GOING TO FIX THINGS?
IT CAN'T HURT.
IT WON'T HELP.
WHAT'S MORE IMPORTANT HERE: FUTILELY PUTTING A BANDAGE ON THE GAPING WOUND OF YOUR FAILED ROMANCE--
--OR SAVING AN ENTIRE WORLD?

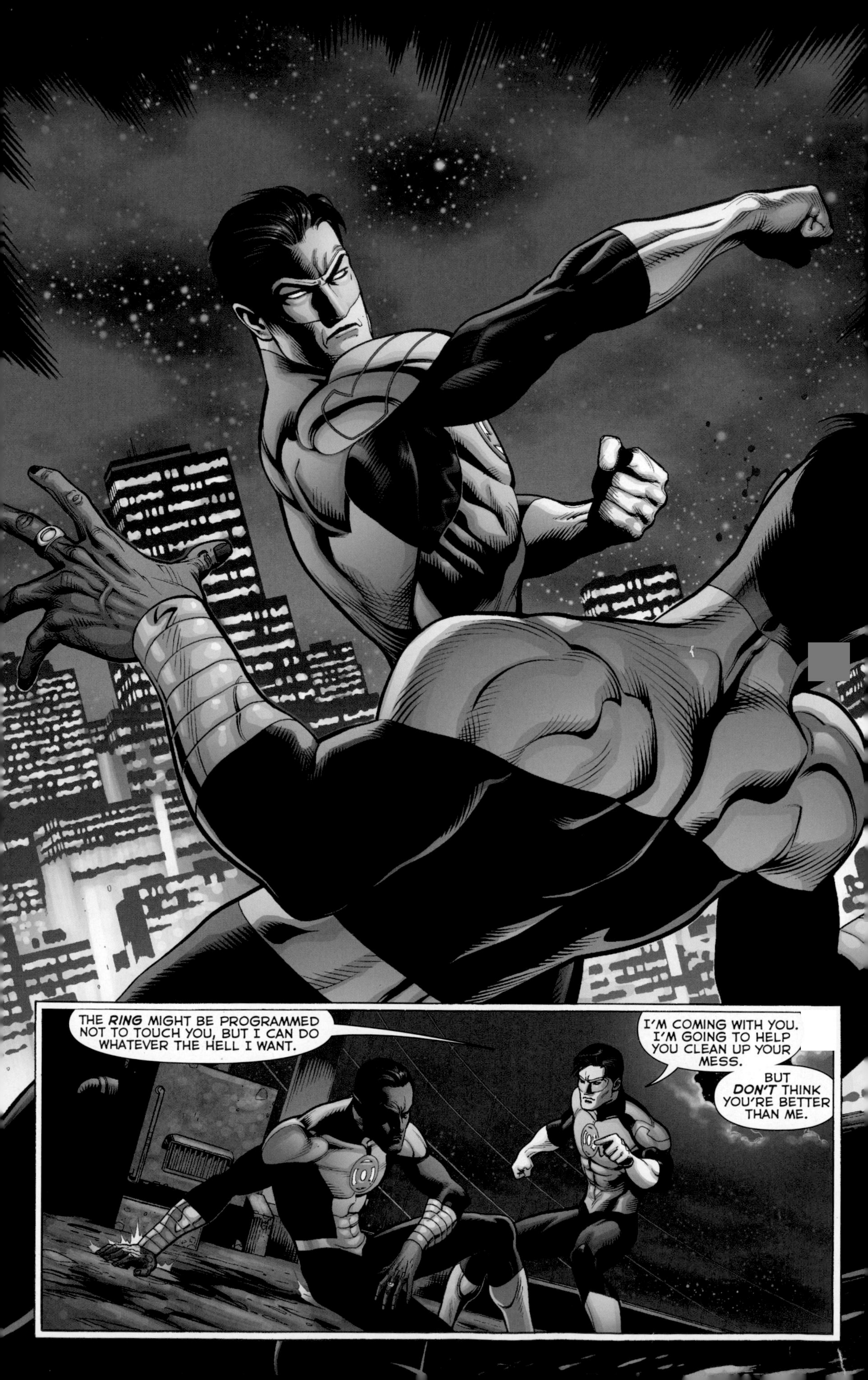
THE *RING* MIGHT BE PROGRAMMED NOT TO TOUCH YOU, BUT I CAN DO WHATEVER THE HELL I WANT.
I'M COMING WITH YOU. I'M GOING TO HELP YOU CLEAN UP YOUR MESS.
BUT *DON'T* THINK YOU'RE BETTER THAN ME.

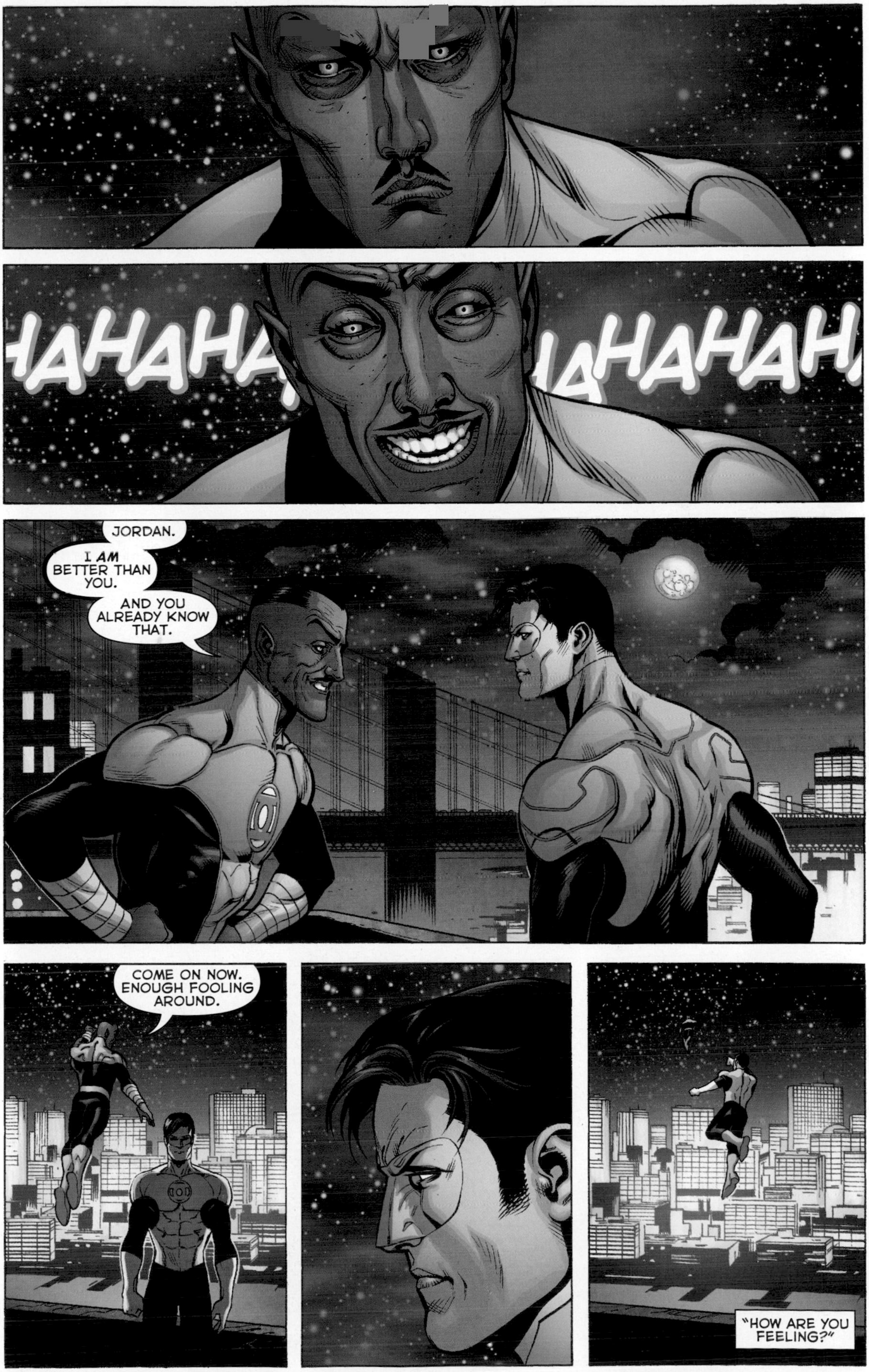
HAHAHA
HAHAHA
JORDAN.
I *AM* BETTER THAN YOU.
AND YOU ALREADY KNOW THAT.
COME ON NOW. ENOUGH FOOLING AROUND.
"HOW ARE YOU FEELING?"

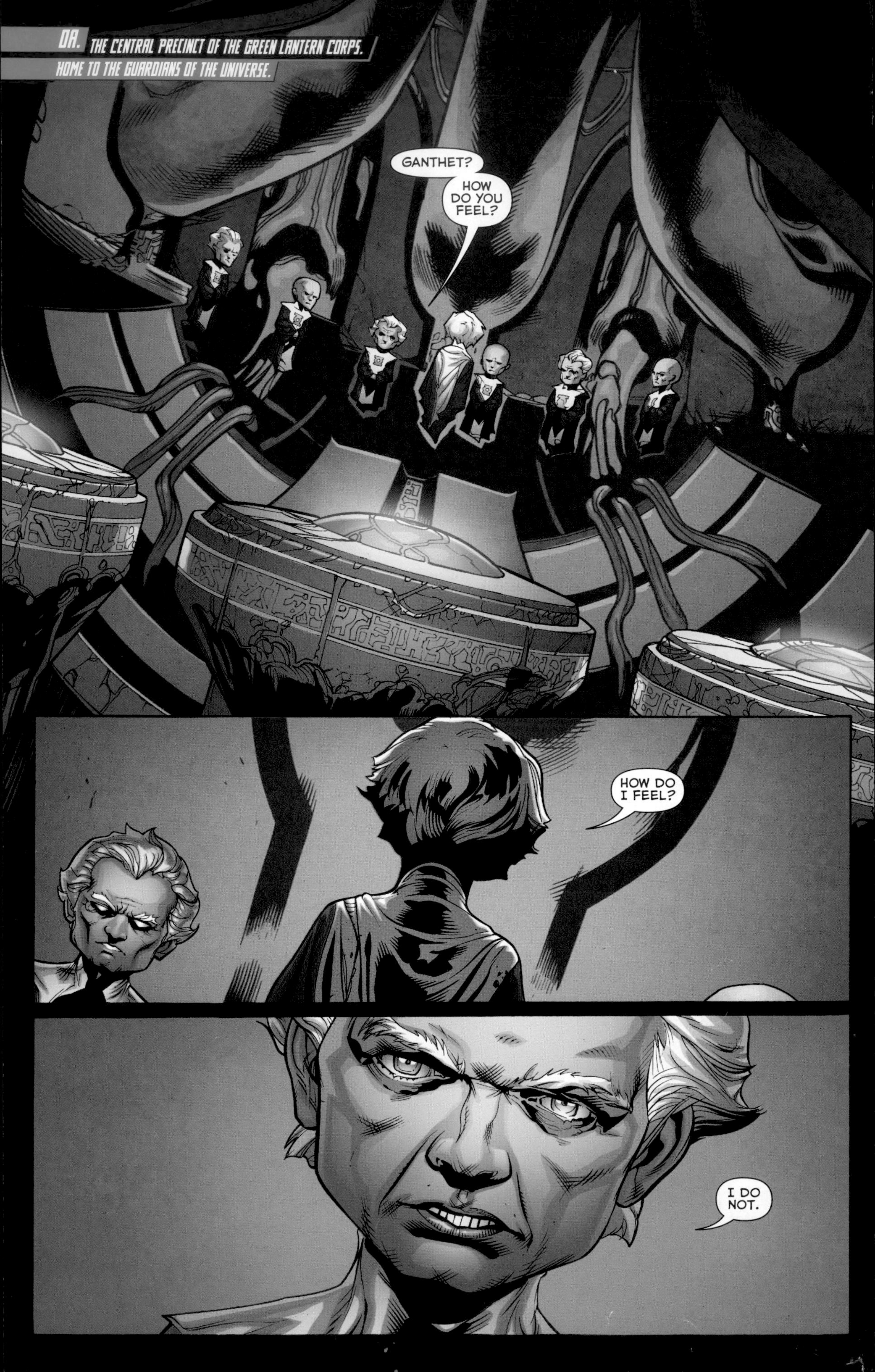

OA. THE CENTRAL PRECINCT OF THE GREEN LANTERN CORPS.
HOME TO THE GUARDIANS OF THE UNIVERSE.
GANTHET?
HOW DO YOU FEEL?
HOW DO I FEEL?
I DO NOT.

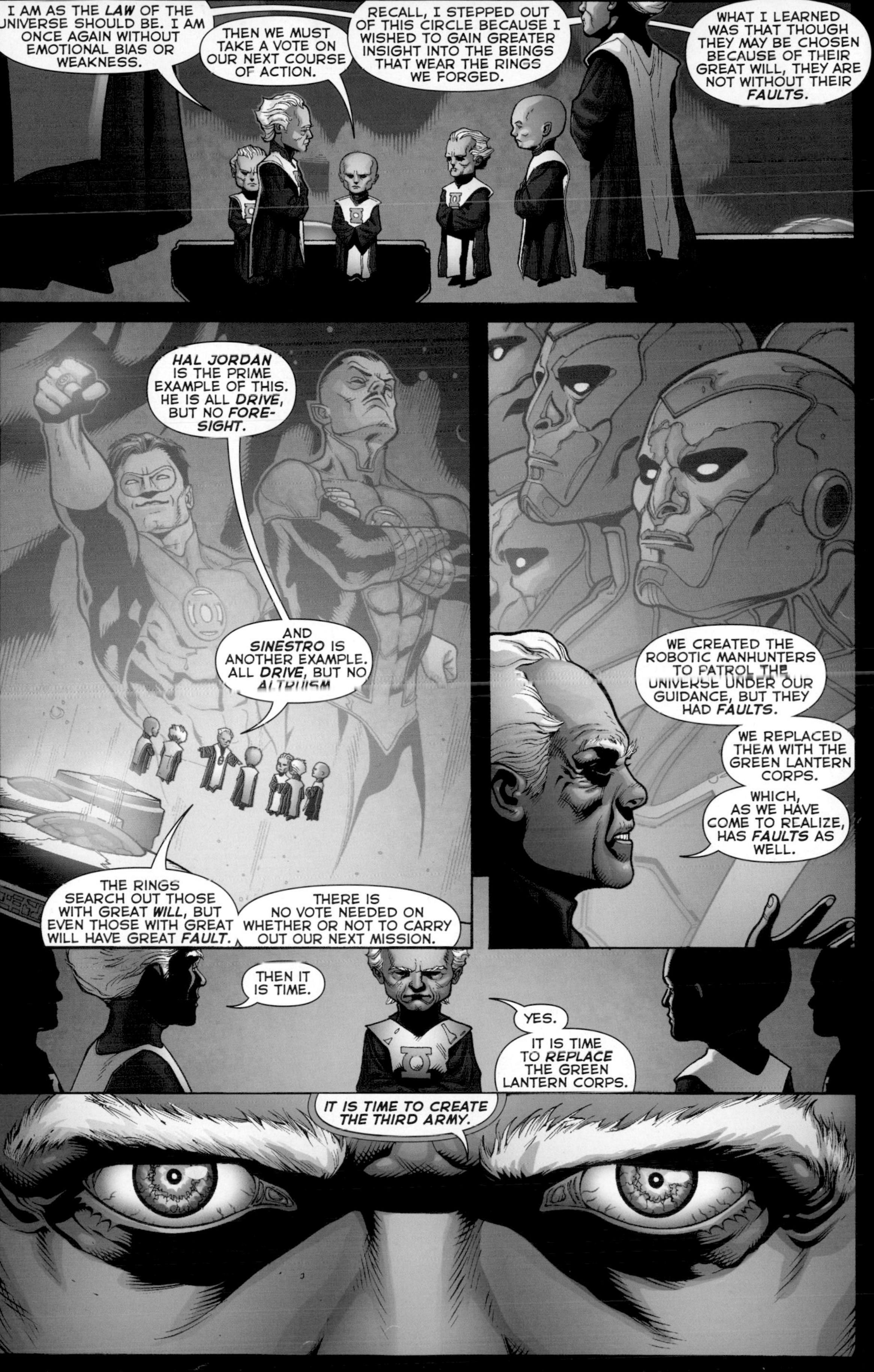
I AM AS THE LAW OF THE UNIVERSE SHOULD BE. I AM ONCE AGAIN WITHOUT EMOTIONAL BIAS OR WEAKNESS.
THEN WE MUST TAKE A VOTE ON OUR NEXT COURSE OF ACTION.
RECALL, I STEPPED OUT OF THIS CIRCLE BECAUSE I WISHED TO GAIN GREATER INSIGHT INTO THE BEINGS THAT WEAR THE RINGS WE FORGED.
WHAT I LEARNED WAS THAT THOUGH THEY MAY BE CHOSEN BECAUSE OF THEIR GREAT WILL, THEY ARE NOT WITHOUT THEIR FAULTS.
HAL JORDAN IS THE PRIME EXAMPLE OF THIS. HE IS ALL DRIVE, BUT NO FORESIGHT.
AND SINESTRO IS ANOTHER EXAMPLE. ALL DRIVE, BUT NO ALTRUISM.
THE RINGS SEARCH OUT THOSE WITH GREAT WILL, BUT EVEN THOSE WITH GREAT WILL HAVE GREAT FAULT.
THERE IS NO VOTE NEEDED ON WHETHER OR NOT TO CARRY OUT OUR NEXT MISSION.
WE CREATED THE ROBOTIC MANHUNTERS TO PATROL THE UNIVERSE UNDER OUR GUIDANCE, BUT THEY HAD FAULTS.
WE REPLACED THEM WITH THE GREEN LANTERN CORPS.
WHICH, AS WE HAVE COME TO REALIZE, HAS FAULTS AS WELL.
THEN IT IS TIME.
YES.
IT IS TIME TO REPLACE THE GREEN LANTERN CORPS.
IT IS TIME TO CREATE THE THIRD ARMY.

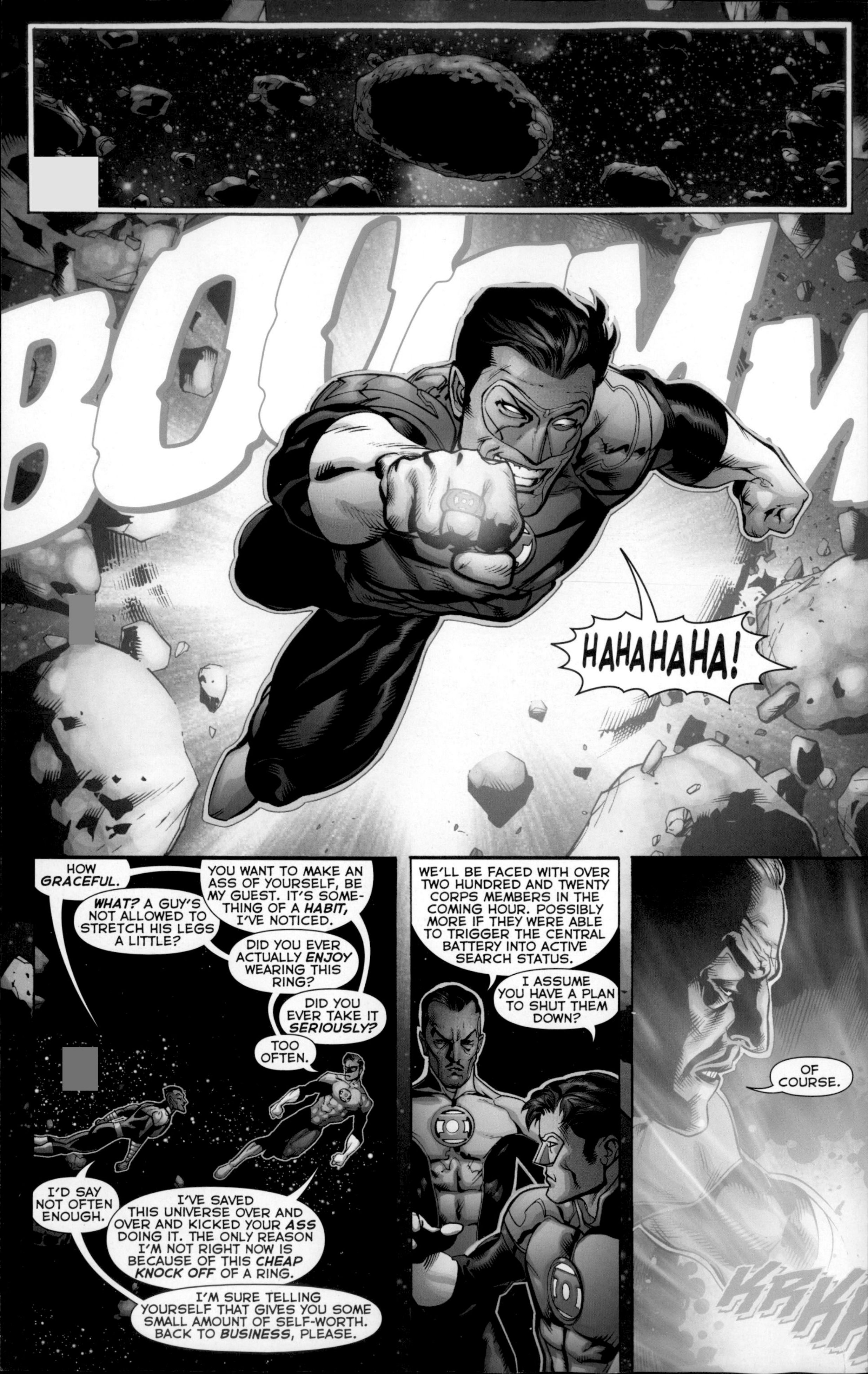
HAHAHAHA!
HOW GRACEFUL.
WHAT? A GUY'S NOT ALLOWED TO STRETCH HIS LEGS A LITTLE?
YOU WANT TO MAKE AN ASS OF YOURSELF, BE MY GUEST. IT'S SOMETHING OF A HABIT, I'VE NOTICED.
DID YOU EVER ACTUALLY ENJOY WEARING THIS RING?
DID YOU EVER TAKE IT SERIOUSLY?
TOO OFTEN.
I'D SAY NOT OFTEN ENOUGH.
I'VE SAVED THIS UNIVERSE OVER AND OVER AND KICKED YOUR ASS DOING IT. THE ONLY REASON I'M NOT RIGHT NOW IS BECAUSE OF THIS CHEAP KNOCK OFF OF A RING.
I'M SURE TELLING YOURSELF THAT GIVES YOU SOME SMALL AMOUNT OF SELF-WORTH. BACK TO BUSINESS, PLEASE.
WE'LL BE FACED WITH OVER TWO HUNDRED AND TWENTY CORPS MEMBERS IN THE COMING HOUR. POSSIBLY MORE IF THEY WERE ABLE TO TRIGGER THE CENTRAL BATTERY INTO ACTIVE SEARCH STATUS.
I ASSUME YOU HAVE A PLAN TO SHUT THEM DOWN?
OF COURSE.

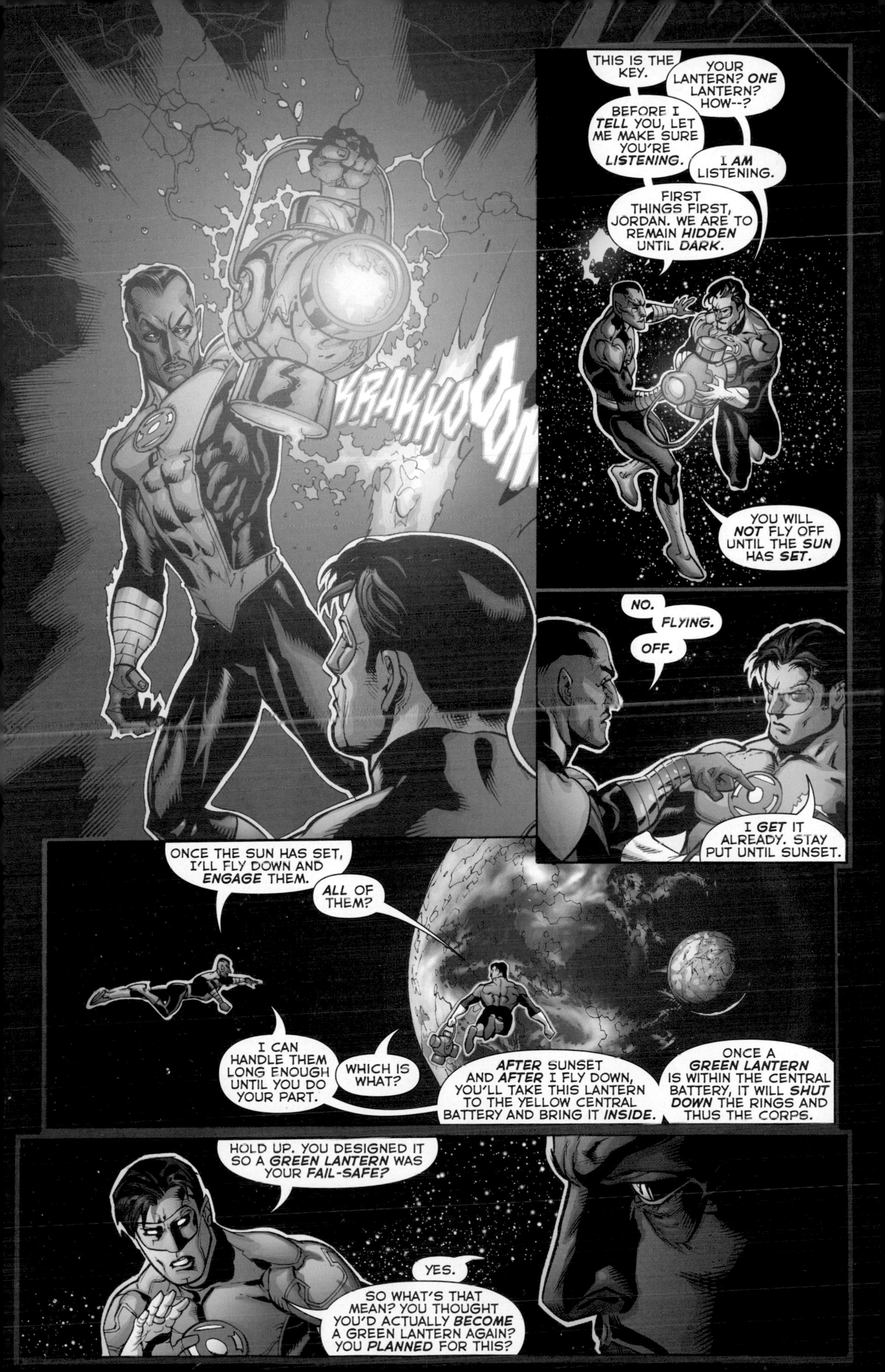
KRAKKOOOM
THIS IS THE KEY.
YOUR LANTERN? ONE LANTERN? HOW--?
BEFORE I TELL YOU, LET ME MAKE SURE YOU'RE LISTENING.
I AM LISTENING.
FIRST THINGS FIRST, JORDAN. WE ARE TO REMAIN HIDDEN UNTIL DARK.
YOU WILL NOT FLY OFF UNTIL THE SUN HAS SET.
NO.
FLYING.
OFF.
I GET IT ALREADY. STAY PUT UNTIL SUNSET.
ONCE THE SUN HAS SET, I'LL FLY DOWN AND ENGAGE THEM.
ALL OF THEM?
I CAN HANDLE THEM LONG ENOUGH UNTIL YOU DO YOUR PART.
WHICH IS WHAT?
AFTER SUNSET AND AFTER I FLY DOWN, YOU'LL TAKE THIS LANTERN TO THE YELLOW CENTRAL BATTERY AND BRING IT INSIDE.
ONCE A GREEN LANTERN IS WITHIN THE CENTRAL BATTERY, IT WILL SHUT DOWN THE RINGS AND THUS THE CORPS.
HOLD UP. YOU DESIGNED IT SO A GREEN LANTERN WAS YOUR FAIL-SAFE?
YES.
SO WHAT'S THAT MEAN? YOU THOUGHT YOU'D ACTUALLY BECOME A GREEN LANTERN AGAIN? YOU PLANNED FOR THIS?

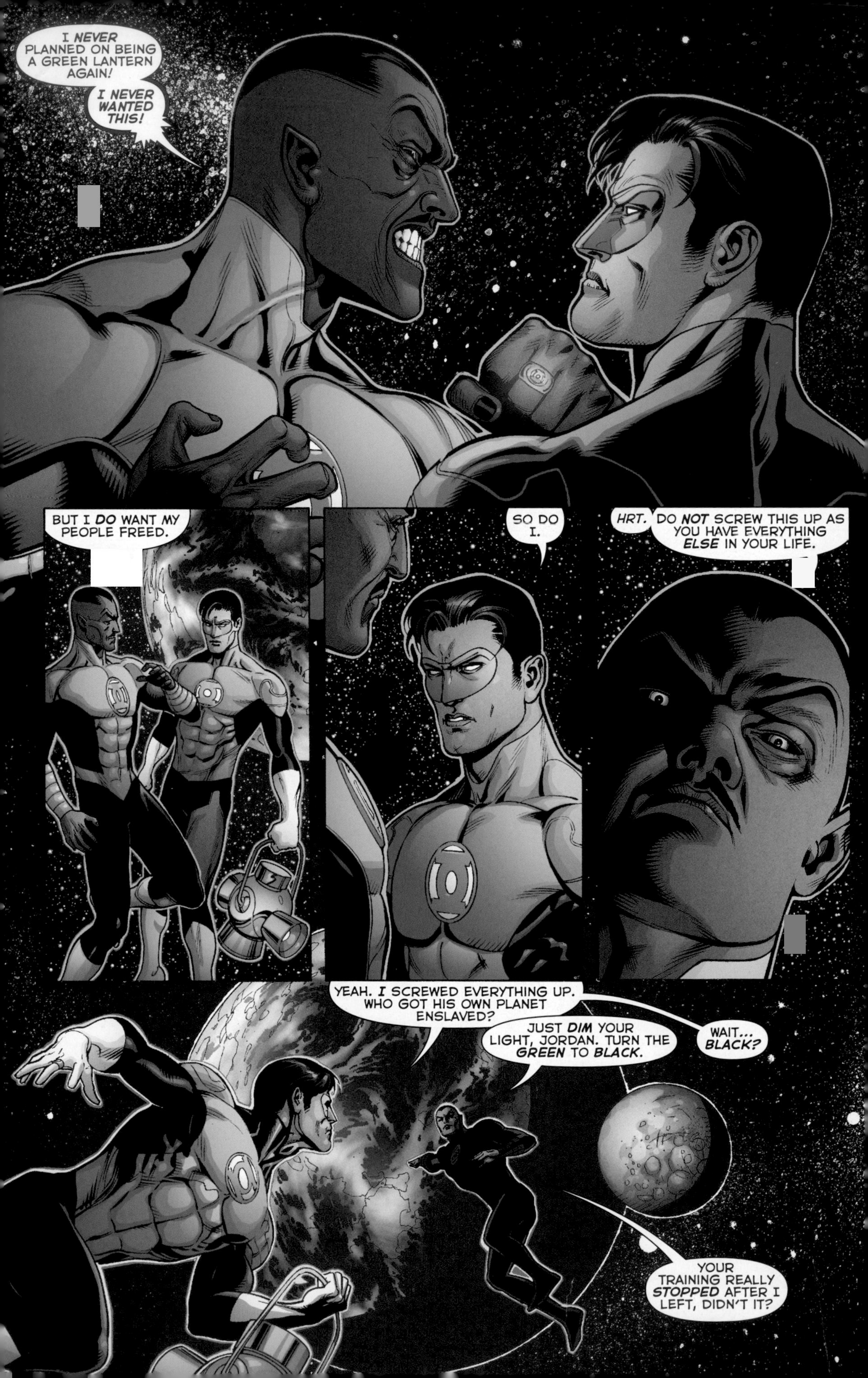
I NEVER PLANNED ON BEING A GREEN LANTERN AGAIN!
I NEVER WANTED THIS!
BUT I DO WANT MY PEOPLE FREED.
SO DO I.
HRT.
DO NOT SCREW THIS UP AS YOU HAVE EVERYTHING ELSE IN YOUR LIFE.
YEAH. I SCREWED EVERYTHING UP. WHO GOT HIS OWN PLANET ENSLAVED?
JUST DIM YOUR LIGHT, JORDAN. TURN THE GREEN TO BLACK.
WAIT... BLACK?
YOUR TRAINING REALLY STOPPED AFTER I LEFT, DIDN'T IT?

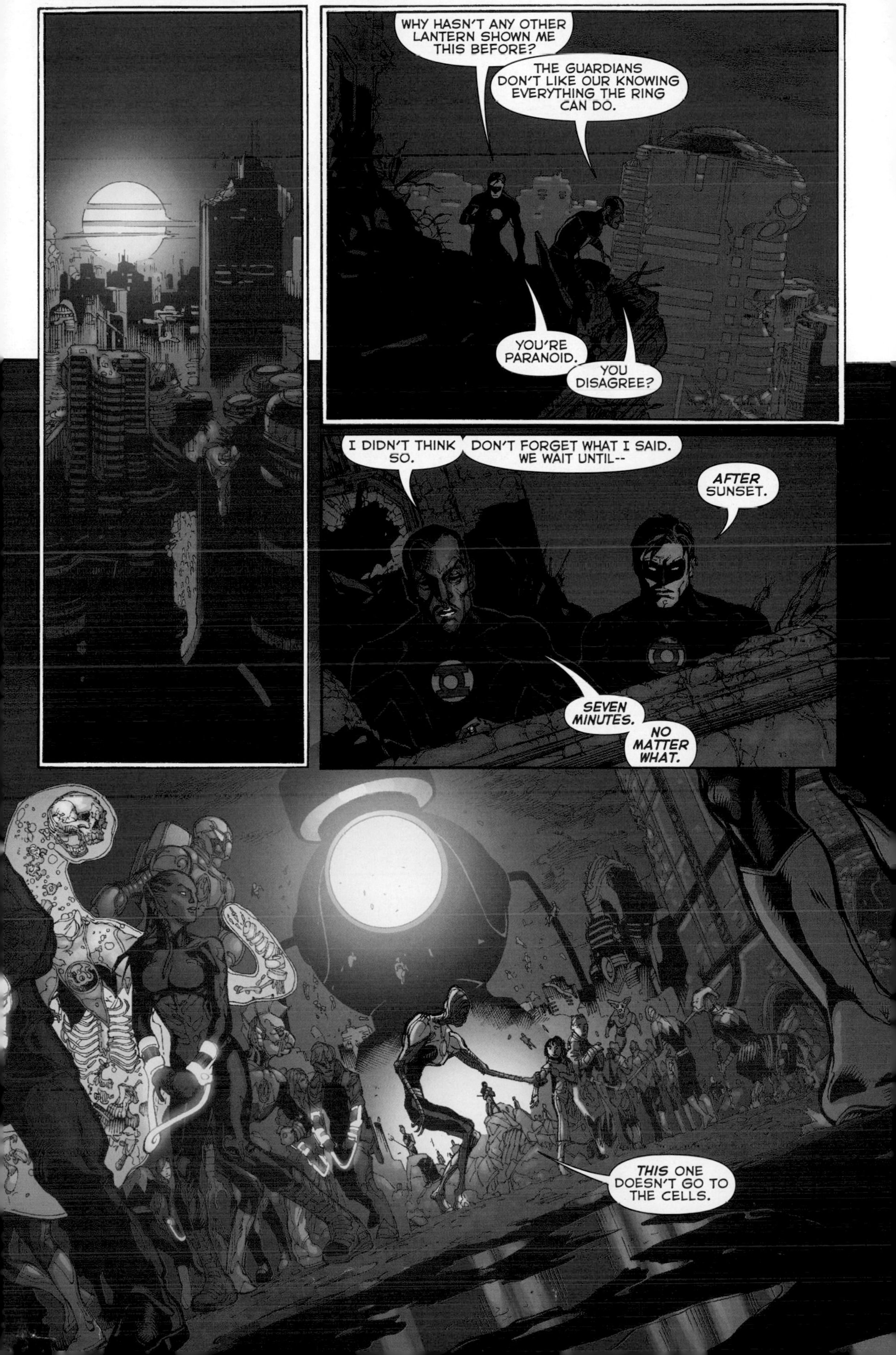

WHY HASN'T ANY OTHER LANTERN SHOWN ME THIS BEFORE?
THE GUARDIANS DON'T LIKE OUR KNOWING EVERYTHING THE RING CAN DO.
YOU'RE PARANOID.
YOU DISAGREE?
I DIDN'T THINK SO.
DON'T FORGET WHAT I SAID. WE WAIT UNTIL--
AFTER SUNSET.
SEVEN MINUTES.
NO MATTER WHAT.
THIS ONE DOESN'T GO TO THE CELLS.

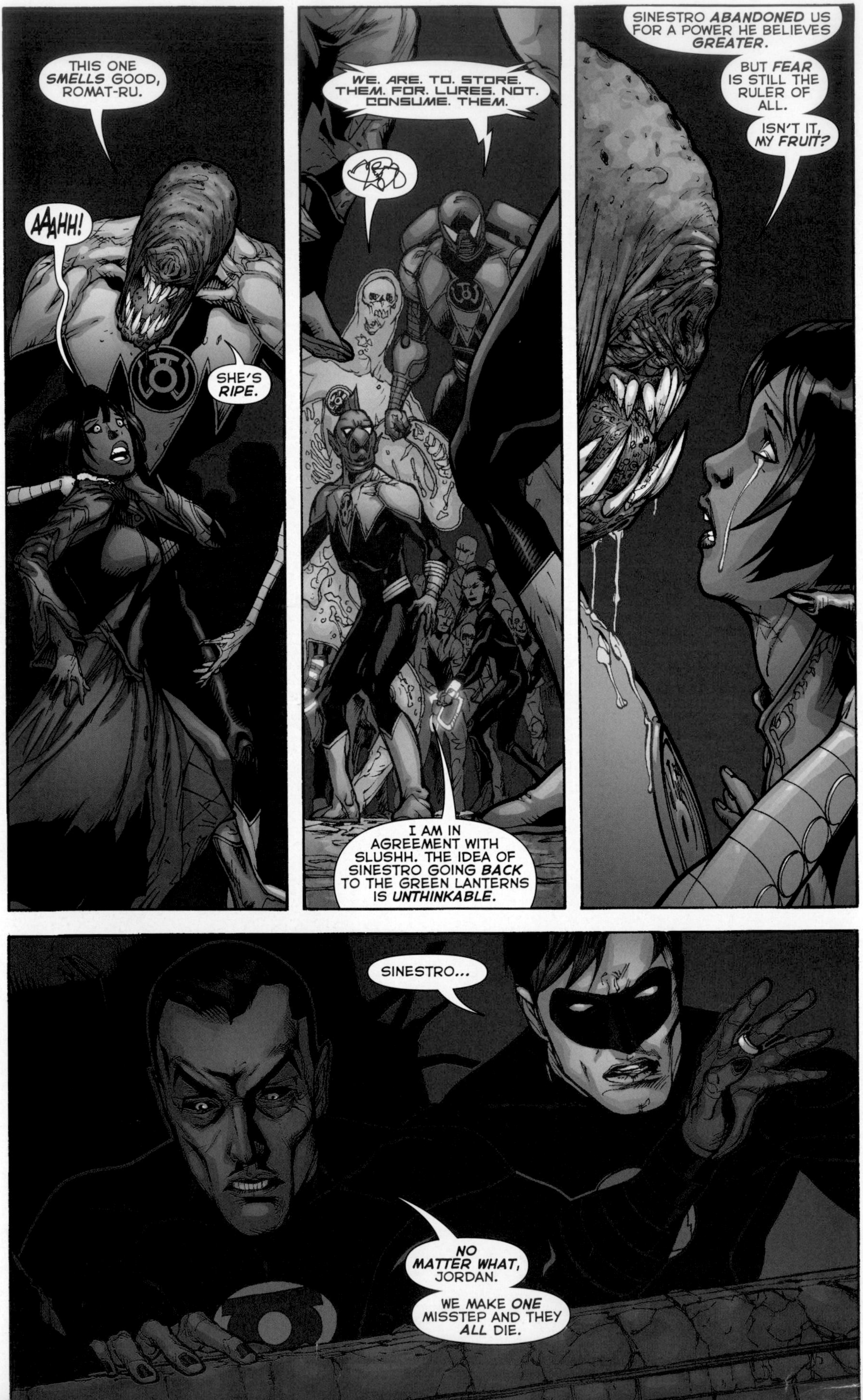

THIS ONE SMELLS GOOD, ROMAT-RU.
AAAHH!
SHE'S RIPE.
WE. ARE. TO. STORE. THEM. FOR. LURES. NOT. CONSUME. THEM.
I AM IN AGREEMENT WITH SLUSHH. THE IDEA OF SINESTRO GOING BACK TO THE GREEN LANTERNS IS UNTHINKABLE.
SINESTRO ABANDONED US FOR A POWER HE BELIEVES GREATER.
BUT FEAR IS STILL THE RULER OF ALL.
ISN'T IT, MY FRUIT?
SINESTRO...
NO MATTER WHAT, JORDAN.
WE MAKE ONE MISSTEP AND THEY ALL DIE.

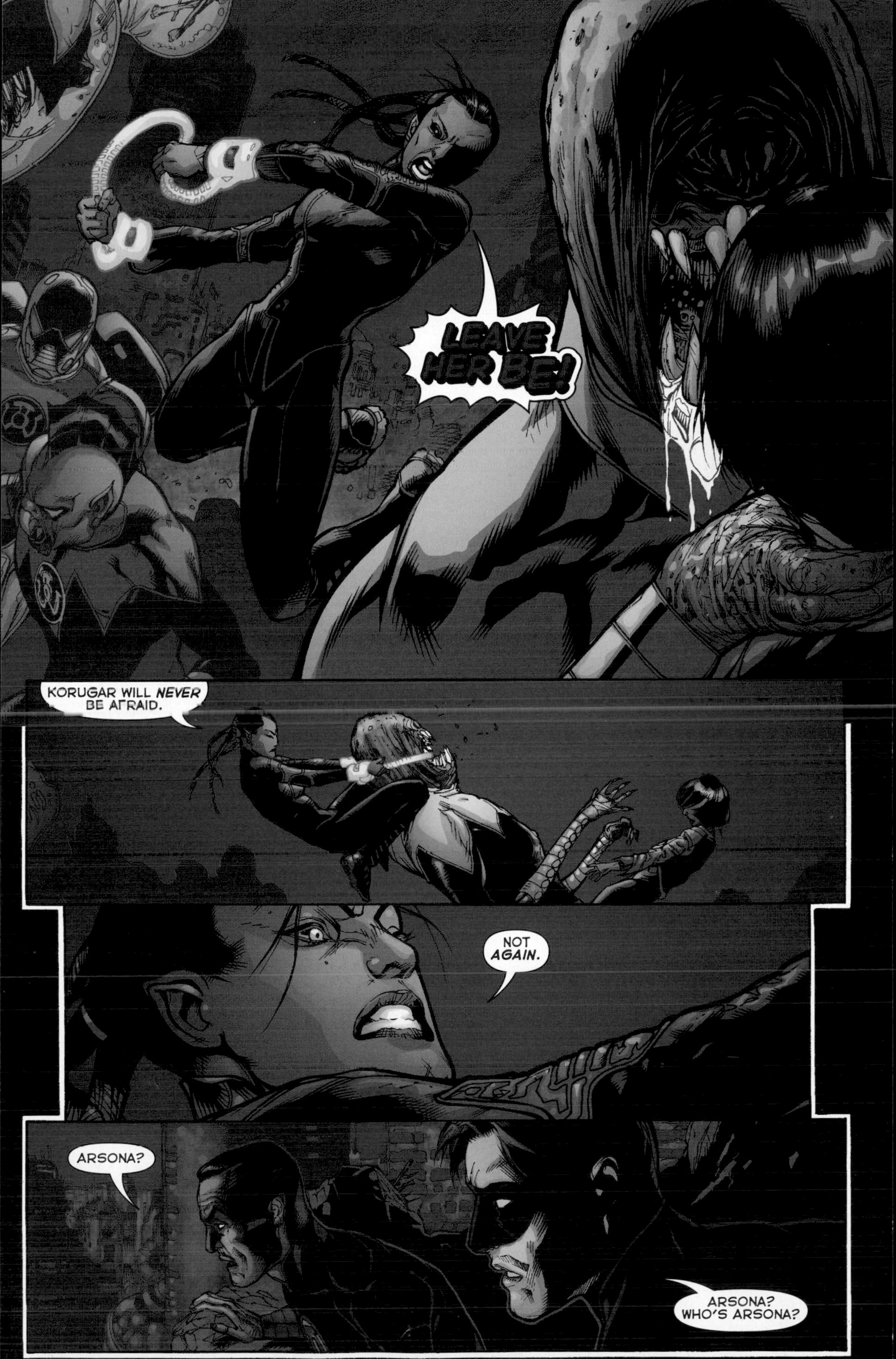
LEAVE HER BE!
KORUGAR WILL NEVER BE AFRAID.
NOT AGAIN.
ARSONA?
ARSONA? WHO'S ARSONA?

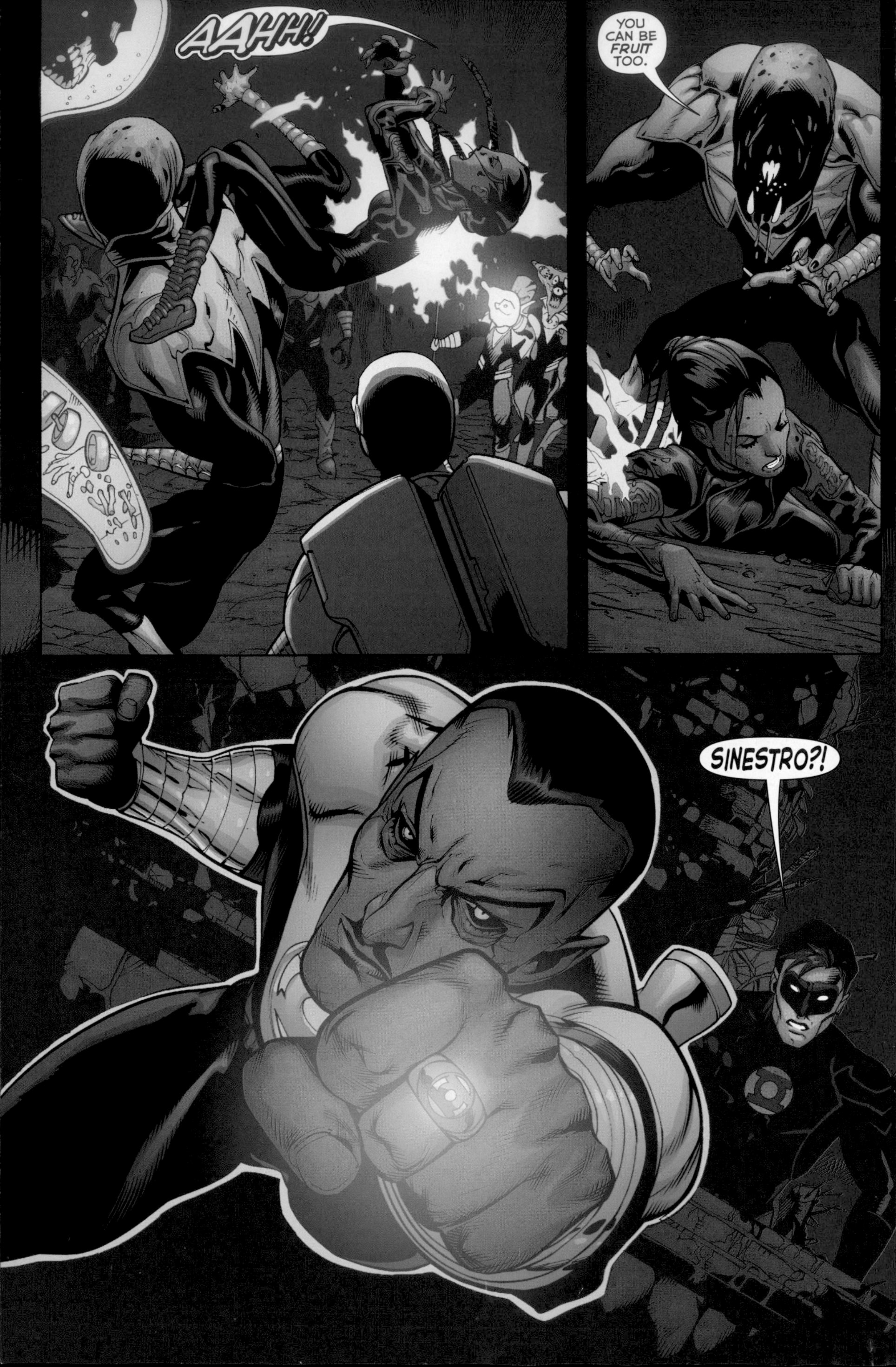
AAHH!
YOU CAN BE FRUIT TOO.
SINESTRO?!

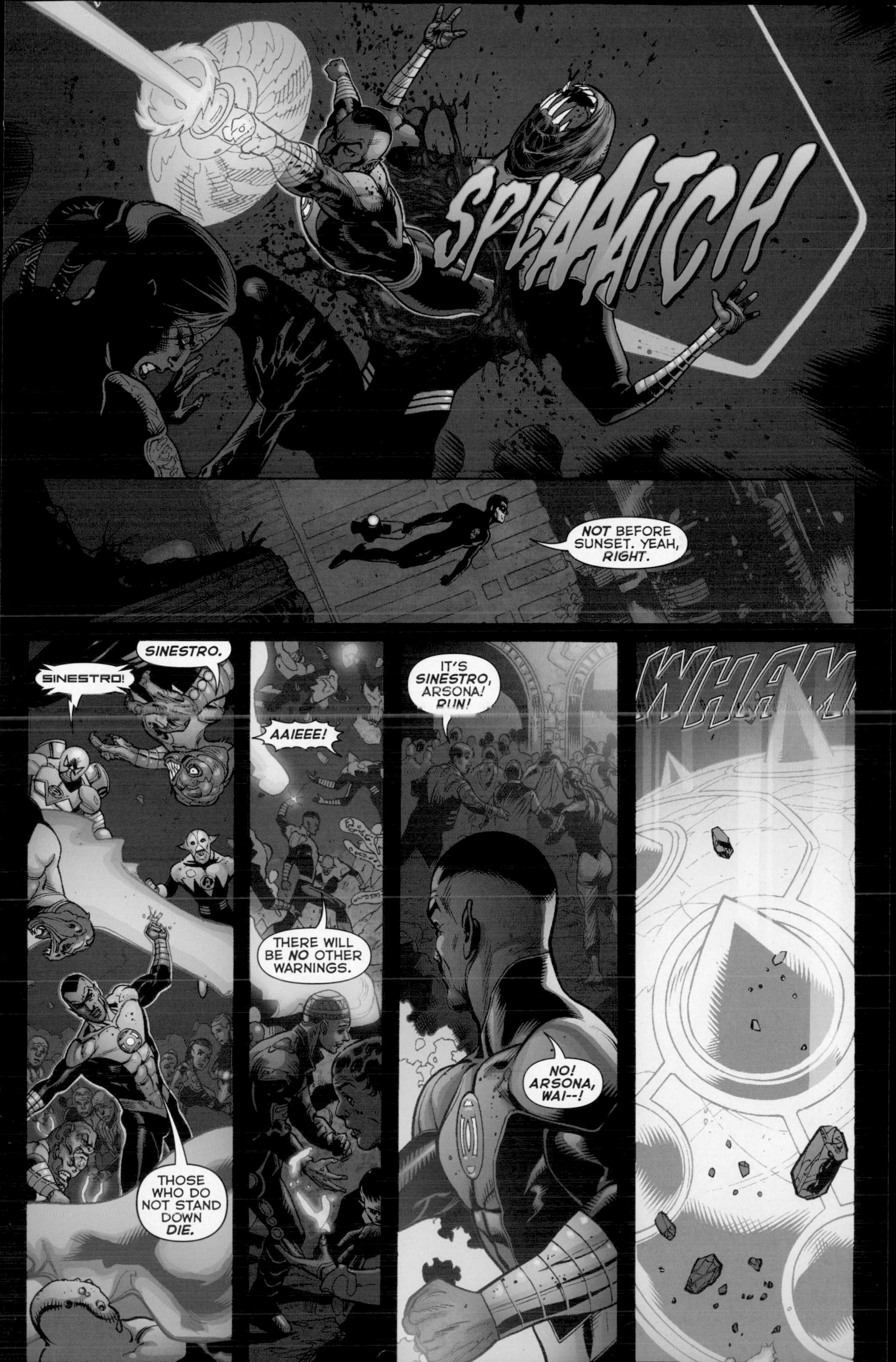

SPLAAATCH
NOT BEFORE SUNSET. YEAH, RIGHT.
SINESTRO.
SINESTRO!
THOSE WHO DO NOT STAND DOWN DIE.
AAIEEE!
THERE WILL BE NO OTHER WARNINGS.
IT'S SINESTRO, ARSONA! RUN!
NO! ARSONA, WAI--!

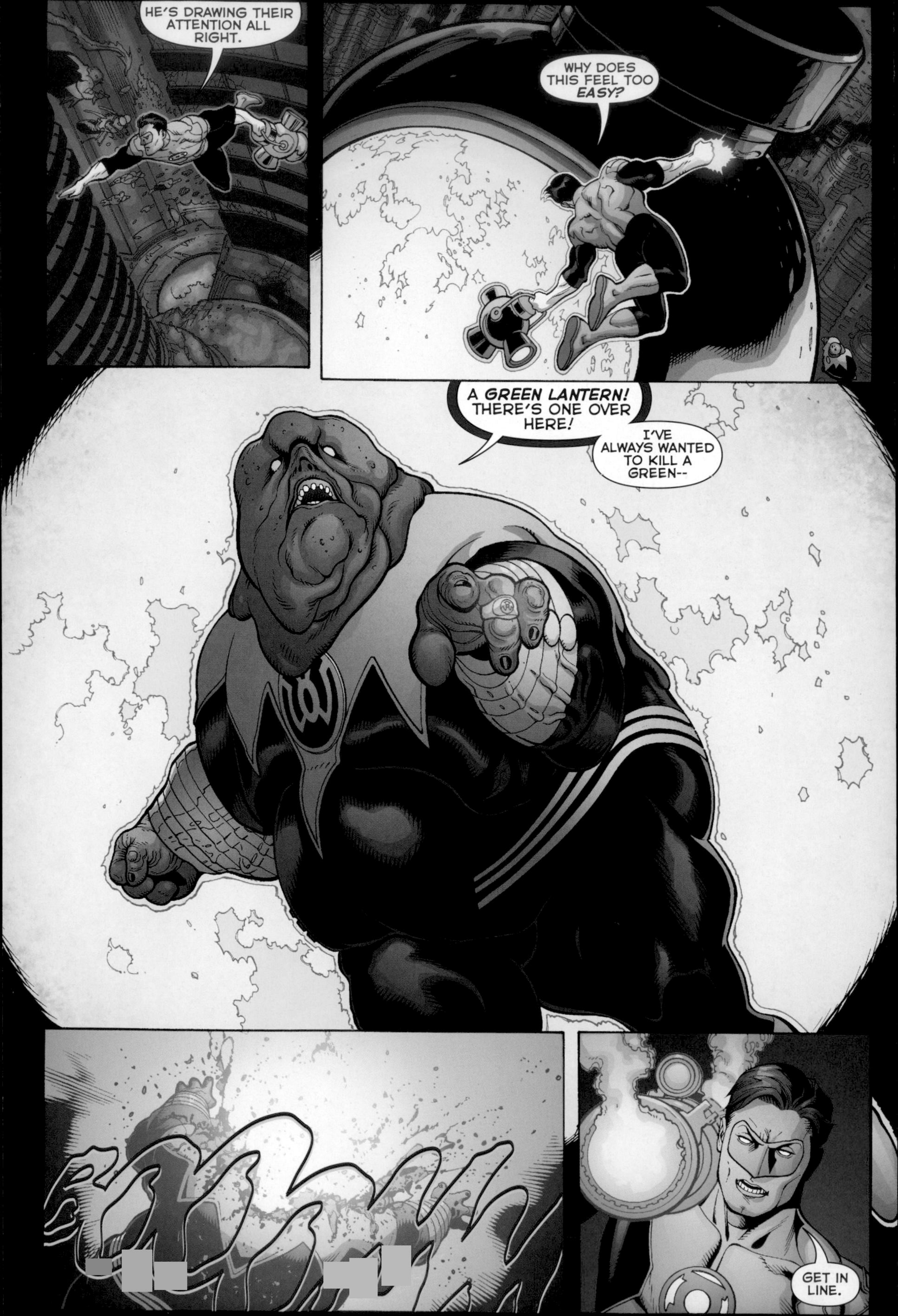
HE'S DRAWING THEIR ATTENTION ALL RIGHT.
WHY DOES THIS FEEL TOO *EASY?*
A *GREEN LANTERN!* THERE'S ONE OVER HERE!
I'VE ALWAYS WANTED TO KILL A GREEN--
GET IN LINE.

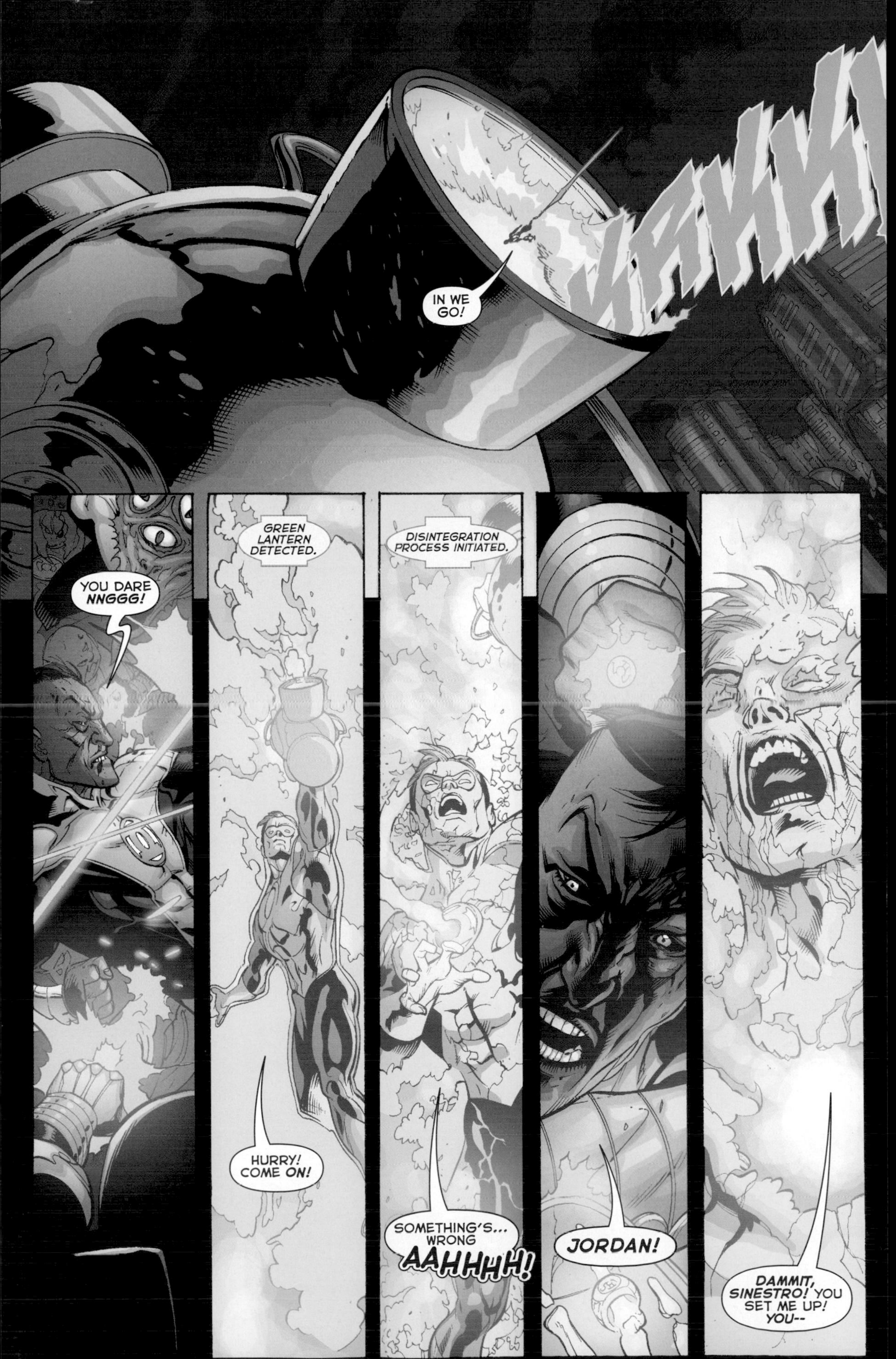
IN WE GO!
YOU DARE NNGGG!
GREEN LANTERN DETECTED.
HURRY! COME ON!
DISINTEGRATION PROCESS INITIATED.
SOMETHING'S... WRONG
AAHHHHH!
JORDAN!
DAMMIT, SINESTRO! YOU SET ME UP! YOU--

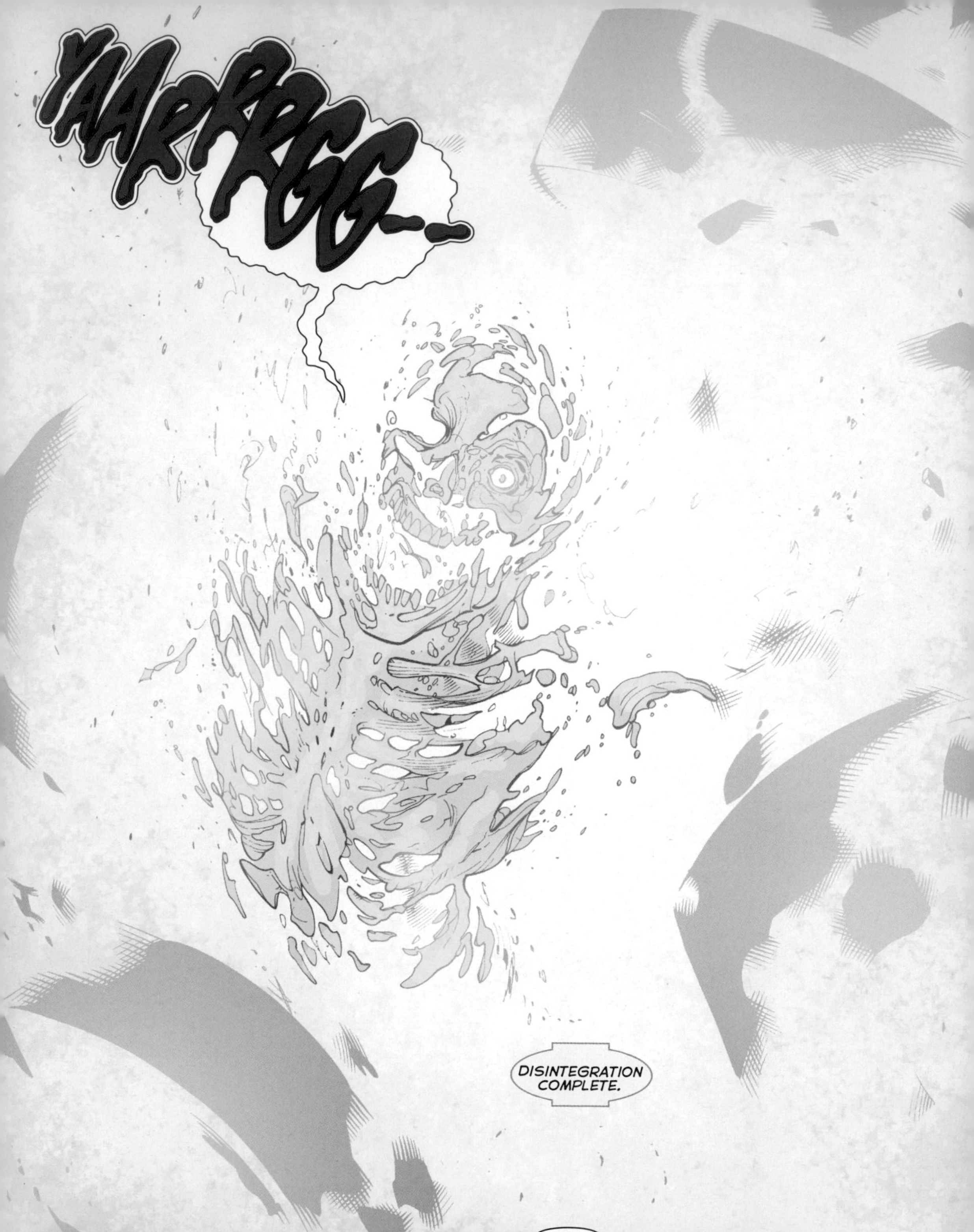
YAARRGG--
DISINTEGRATION COMPLETE.
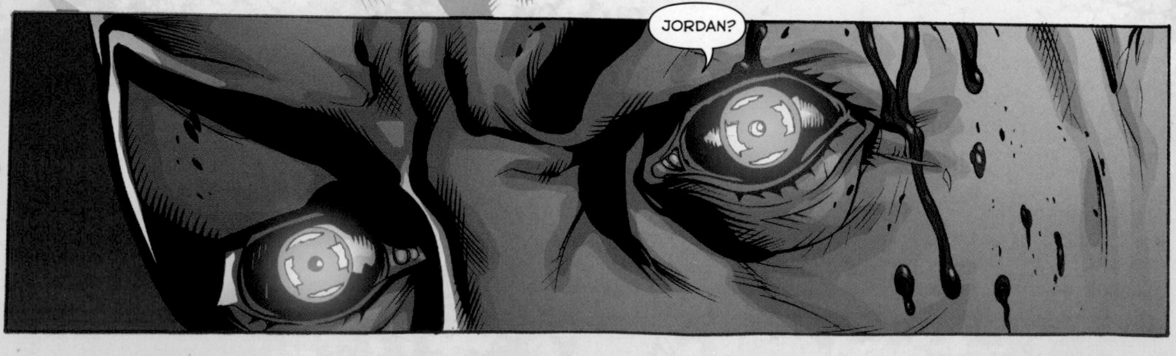
JORDAN?

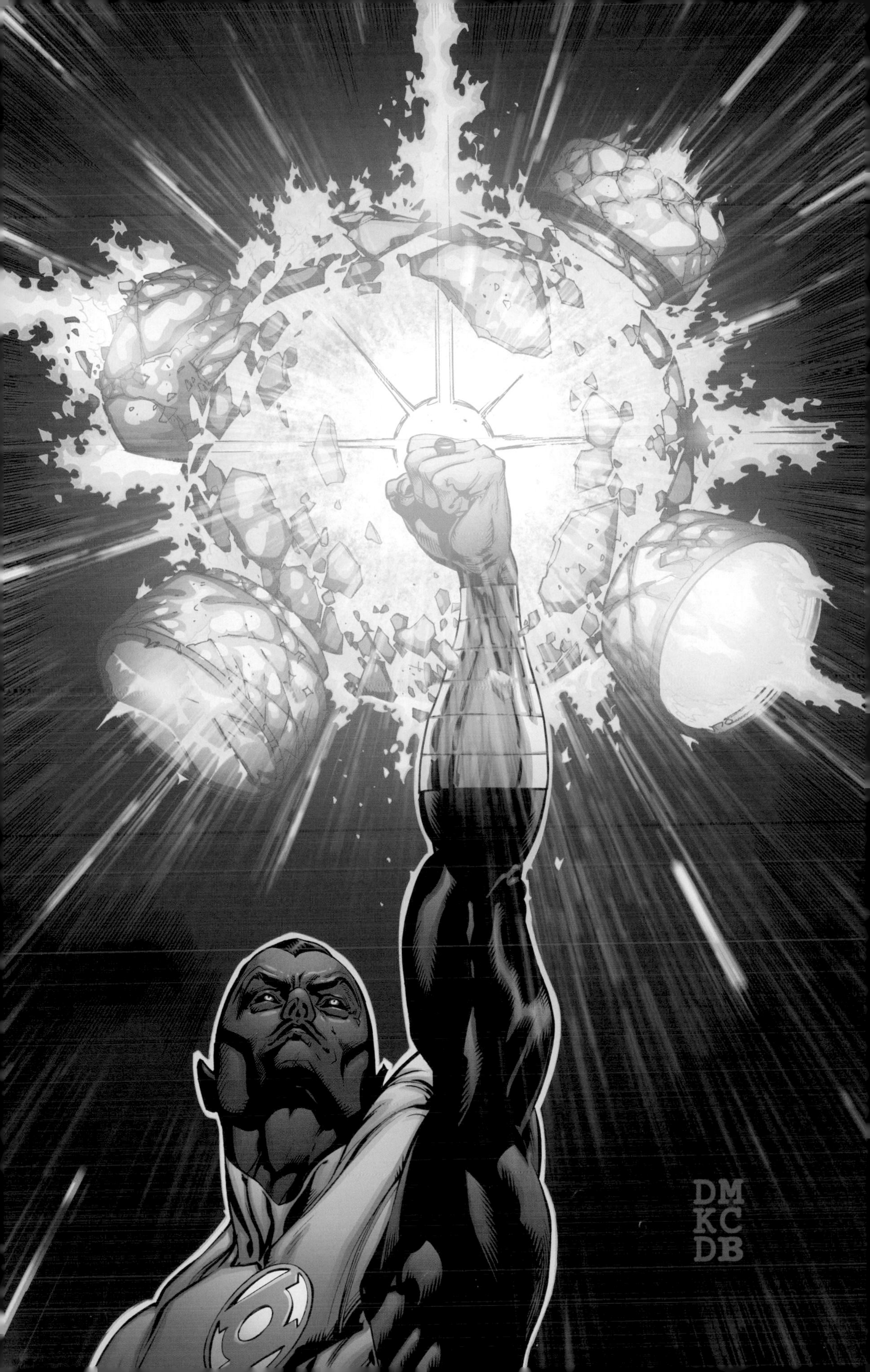
DM
KC
DB

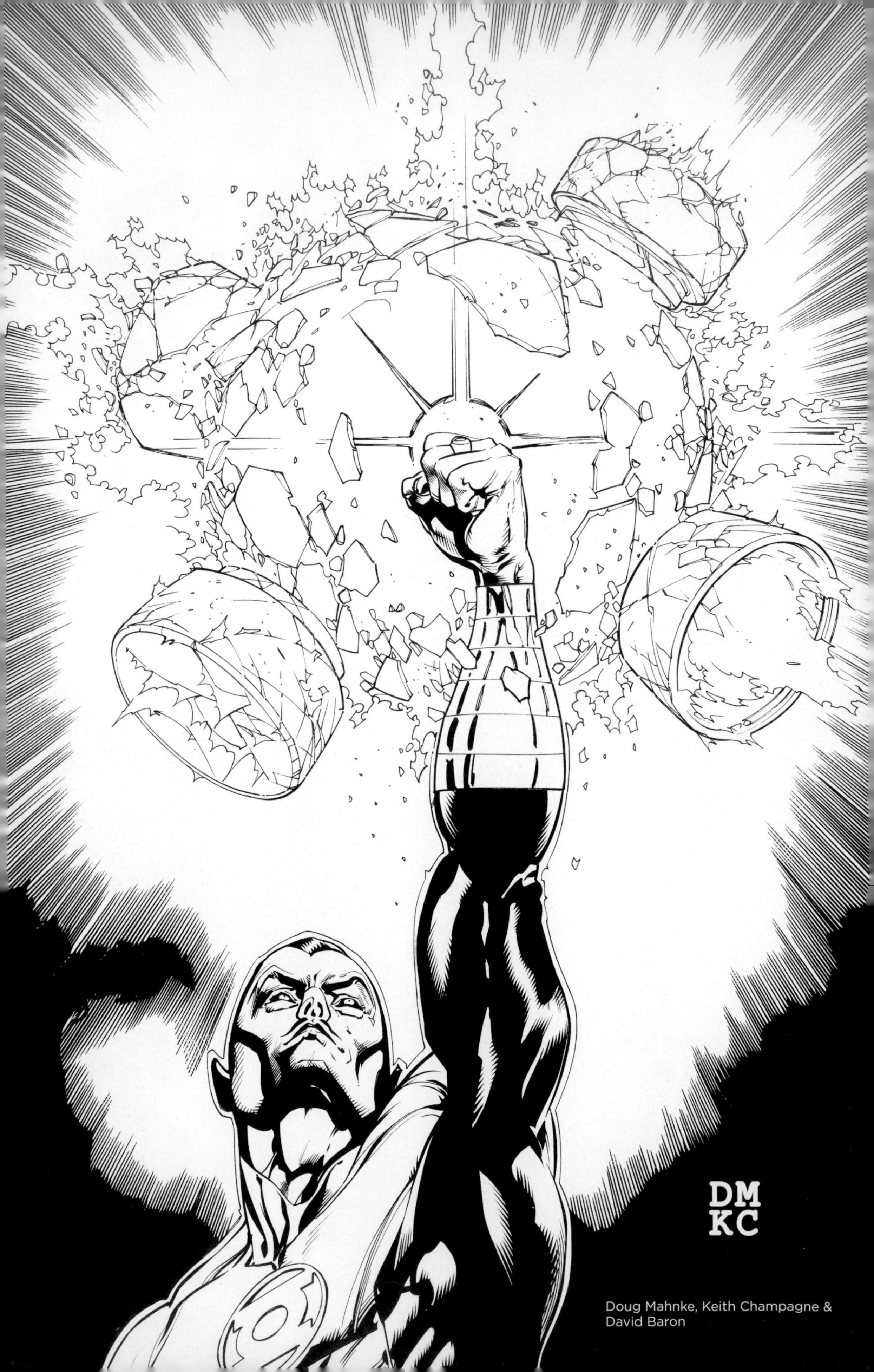
DM
KC

Doug Mahnke, Keith Champagne &
David Baron

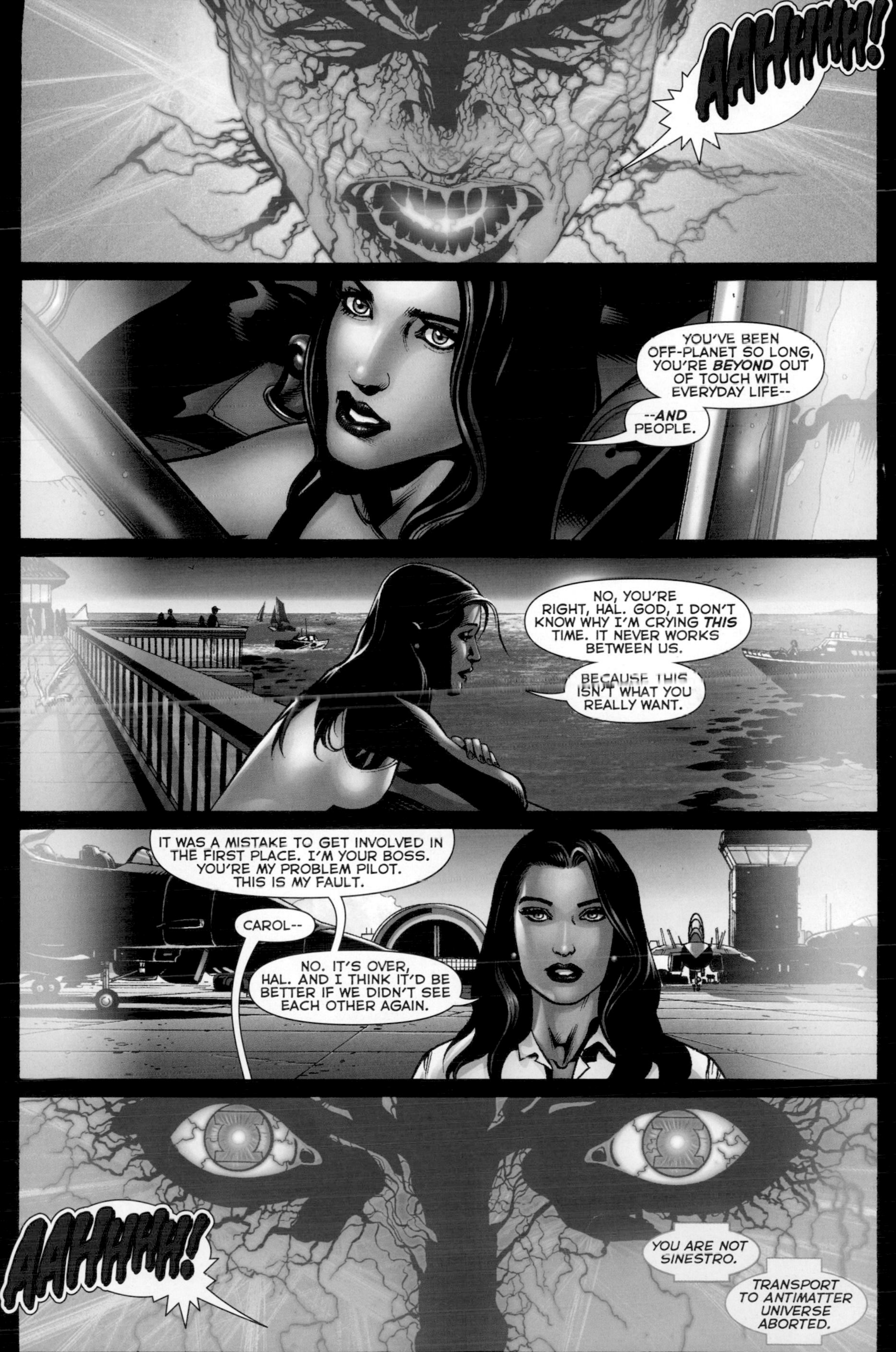
AAHHHHH!
YOU'VE BEEN OFF-PLANET SO LONG, YOU'RE *BEYOND* OUT OF TOUCH WITH EVERYDAY LIFE--
--*AND* PEOPLE.
NO, YOU'RE RIGHT, HAL. GOD, I DON'T KNOW WHY I'M CRYING *THIS* TIME. IT NEVER WORKS BETWEEN US.
BECAUSE THIS ISN'T WHAT YOU REALLY WANT.
IT WAS A MISTAKE TO GET INVOLVED IN THE FIRST PLACE. I'M YOUR BOSS. YOU'RE MY PROBLEM PILOT. THIS IS MY FAULT.
CAROL--
NO. IT'S OVER, HAL. AND I THINK IT'D BE BETTER IF WE DIDN'T SEE EACH OTHER AGAIN.
AAHHHHH!
YOU ARE NOT SINESTRO.
TRANSPORT TO ANTIMATTER UNIVERSE ABORTED.

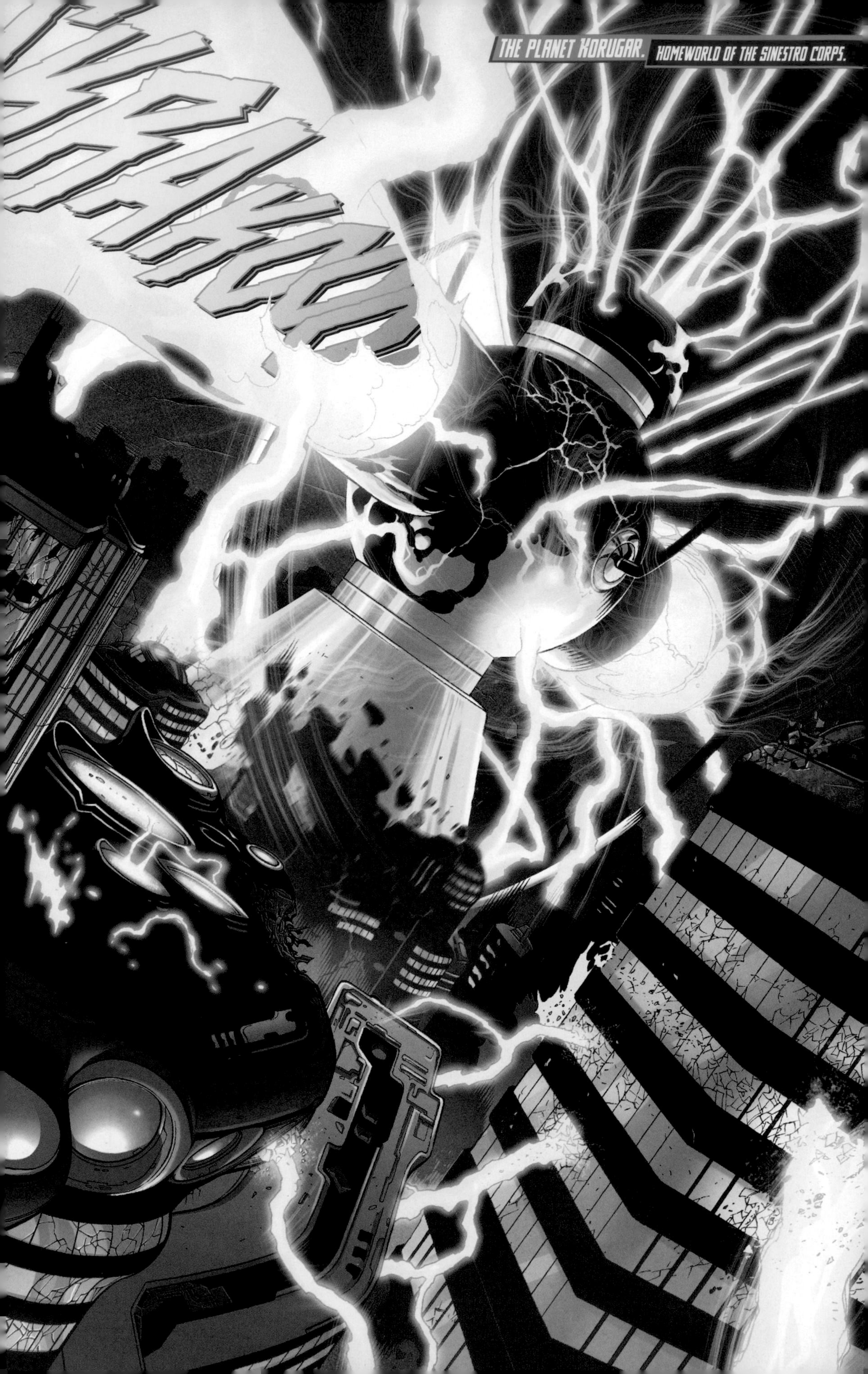
THE PLANET KORUGAR.
HOMEWORLD OF THE SINESTRO CORPS.

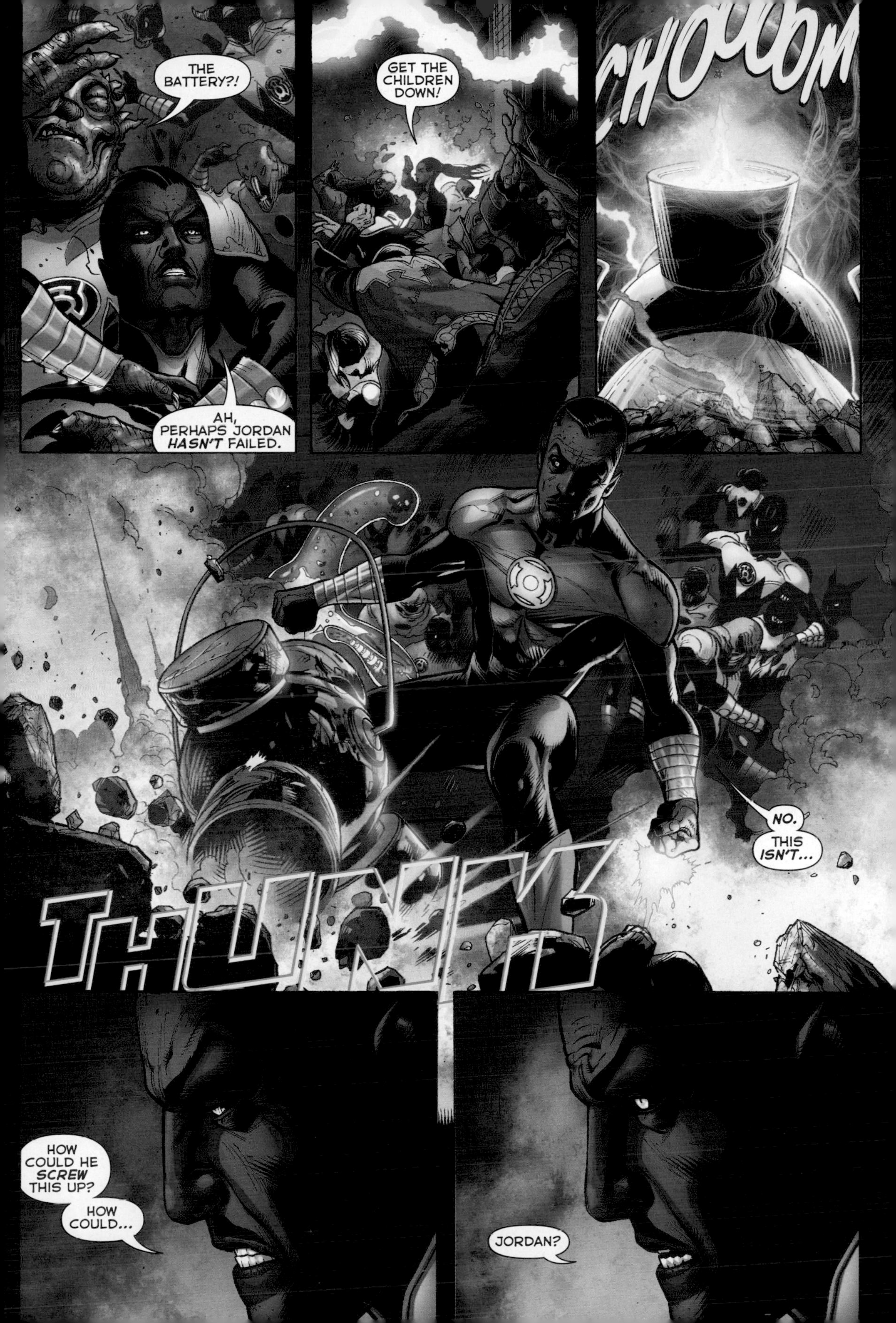
THE BATTERY?!
AH, PERHAPS JORDAN HASN'T FAILED.
GET THE CHILDREN DOWN!
NO. THIS ISN'T...
THUNK
HOW COULD HE SCREW THIS UP?
HOW COULD...
JORDAN?

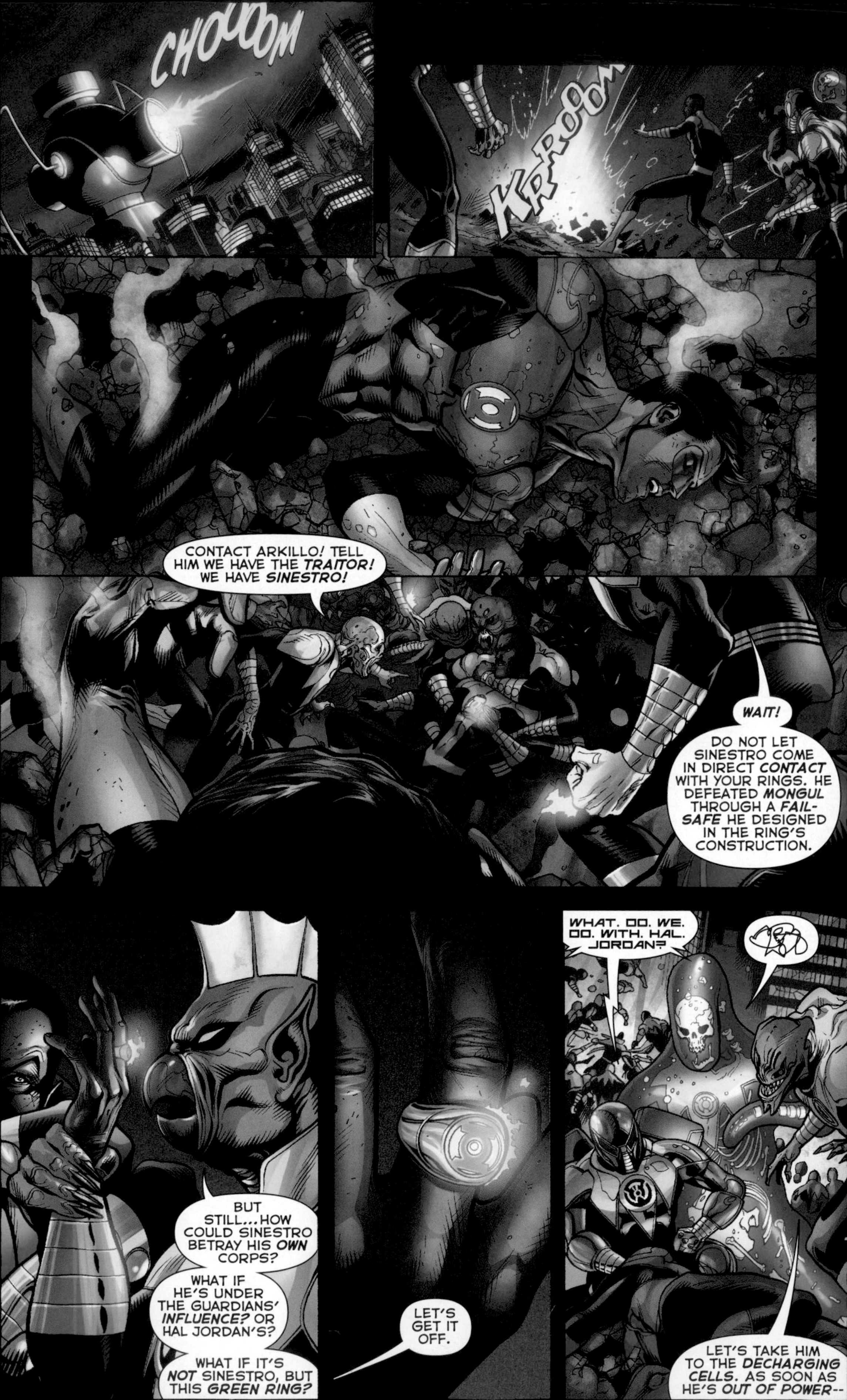

CHOOOOM
KRROOOM
CONTACT ARKILLO! TELL HIM WE HAVE THE *TRAITOR!* WE HAVE *SINESTRO!*
WAIT!
DO NOT LET SINESTRO COME IN DIRECT *CONTACT* WITH YOUR RINGS. HE DEFEATED *MONGUL* THROUGH A *FAIL-SAFE* HE DESIGNED IN THE RING'S CONSTRUCTION.
BUT STILL...HOW COULD SINESTRO BETRAY HIS *OWN* CORPS?
WHAT IF HE'S UNDER THE GUARDIANS' *INFLUENCE?* OR HAL JORDAN'S?
WHAT IF IT'S *NOT* SINESTRO, BUT THIS *GREEN RING?*
LET'S GET IT OFF.
WHAT. DO. WE. DO. WITH. HAL. JORDAN?
LET'S TAKE HIM TO THE *DECHARGING CELLS.* AS SOON AS HE'S *OUT OF POWER--*

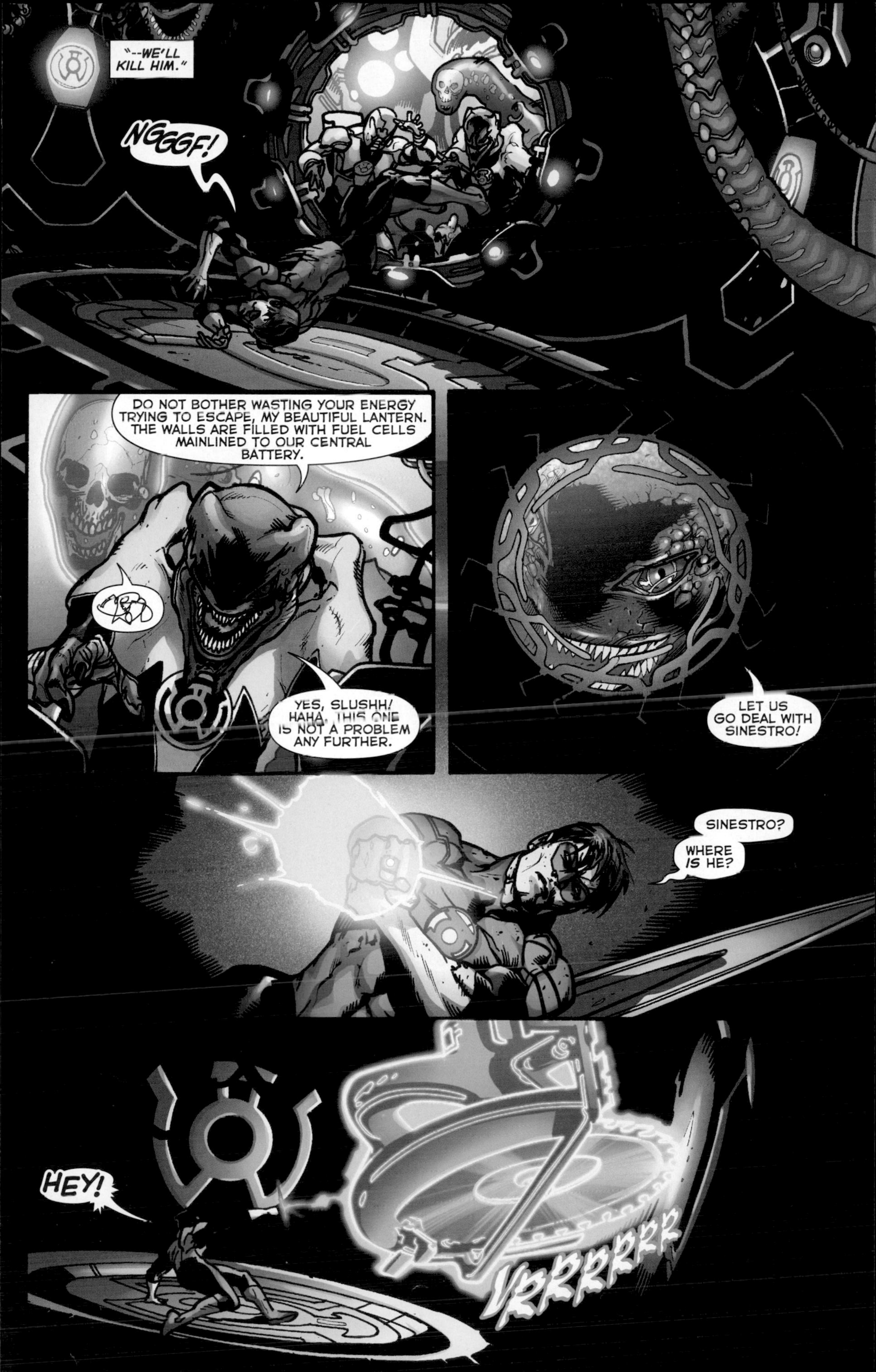
"--WE'LL KILL HIM."
NGGGF!
DO NOT BOTHER WASTING YOUR ENERGY TRYING TO ESCAPE, MY BEAUTIFUL LANTERN. THE WALLS ARE FILLED WITH FUEL CELLS MAINLINED TO OUR CENTRAL BATTERY.
YES, SLUSHH! HAHA. THIS ONE IS NOT A PROBLEM ANY FURTHER.
LET US GO DEAL WITH SINESTRO!
SINESTRO?
WHERE IS HE?
HEY!
VRRRRRR

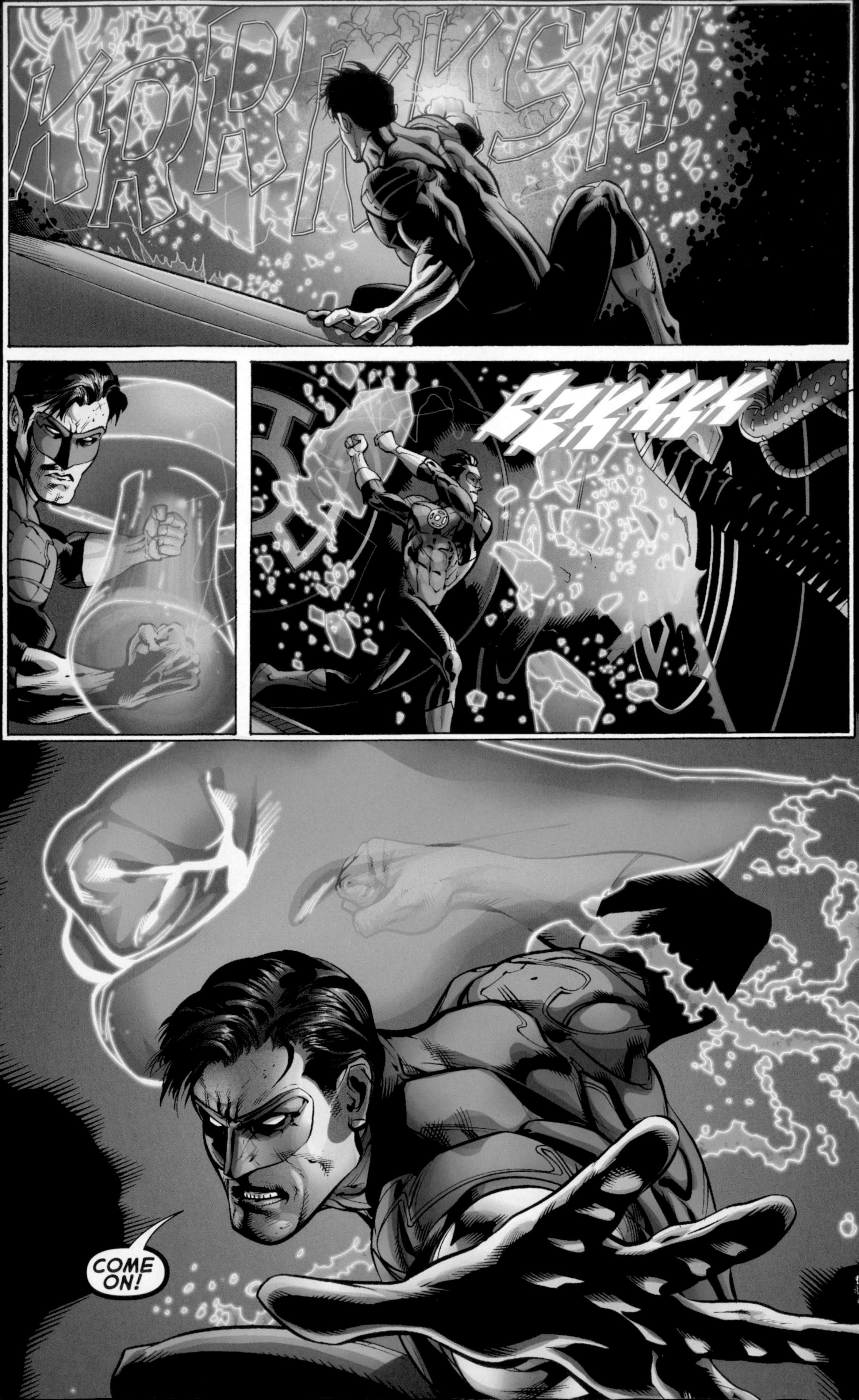
KRRAKKSH
COME ON!

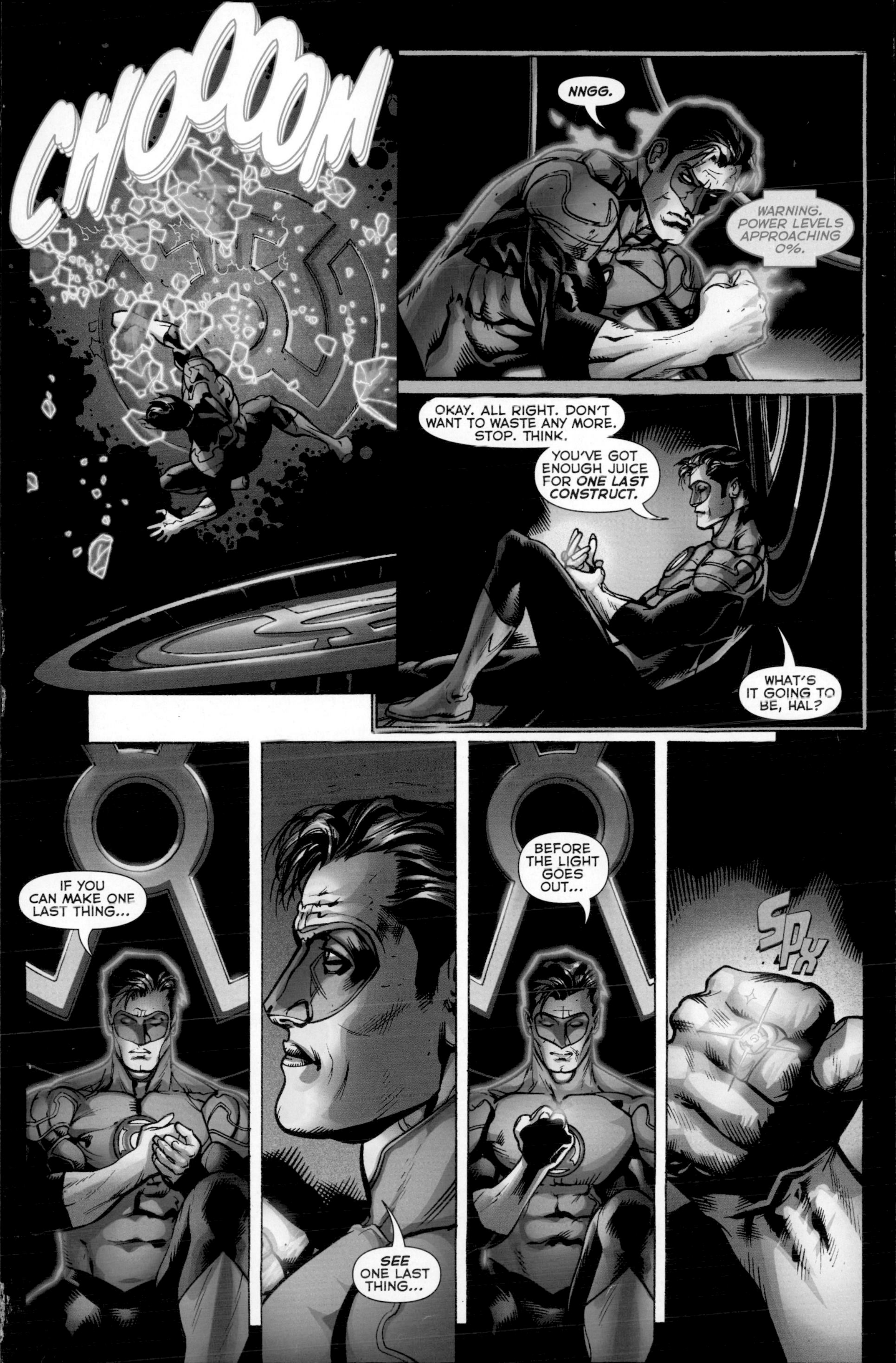
CHOOOOM
NNGG.
WARNING. POWER LEVELS APPROACHING 0%.
OKAY. ALL RIGHT. DON'T WANT TO WASTE ANY MORE. STOP. THINK.
YOU'VE GOT ENOUGH JUICE FOR ONE LAST CONSTRUCT.
WHAT'S IT GOING TO BE, HAL?
IF YOU CAN MAKE ONE LAST THING...
SEE ONE LAST THING...
BEFORE THE LIGHT GOES OUT...
SPX

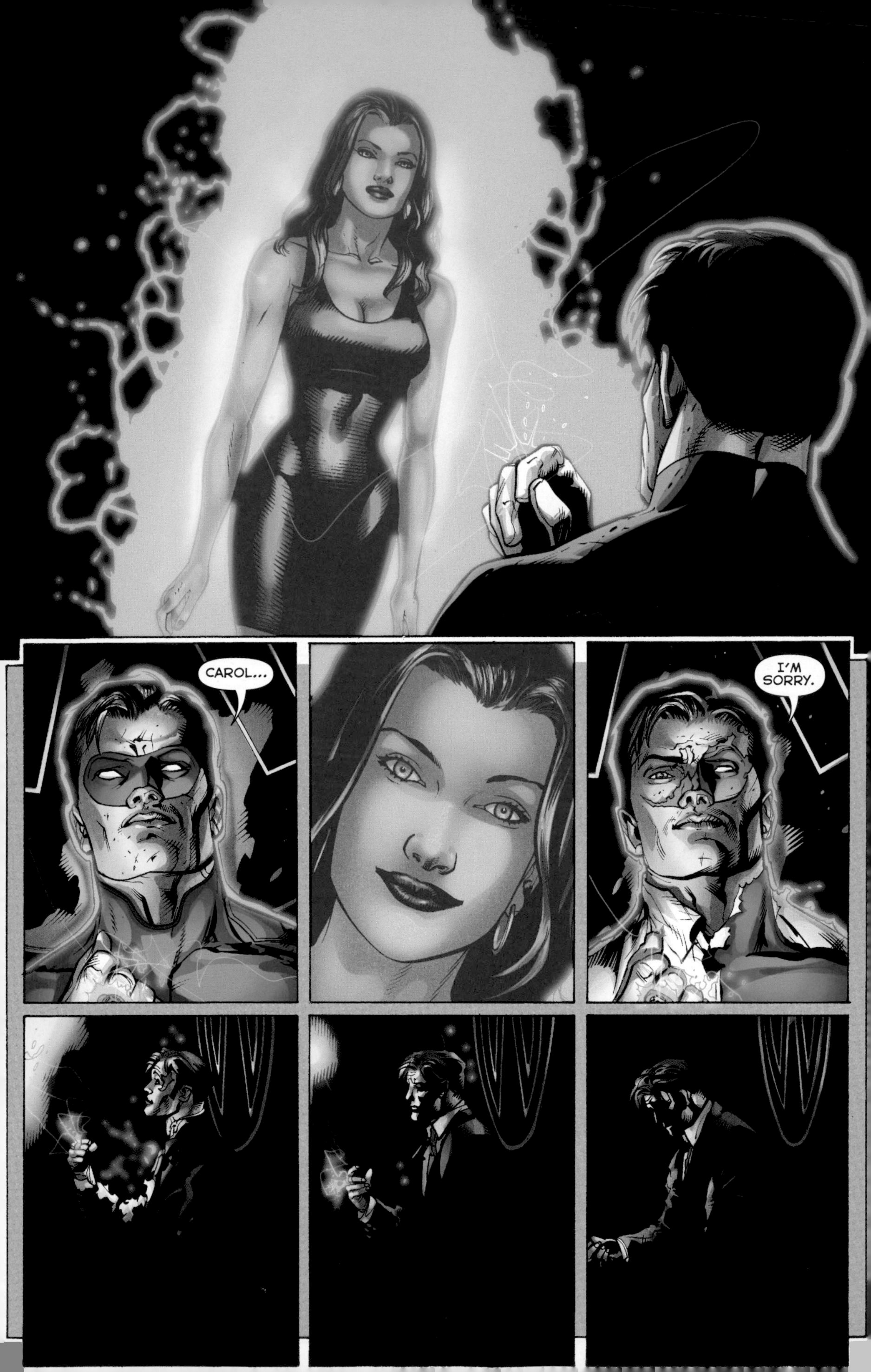
CAROL...
I'M SORRY.

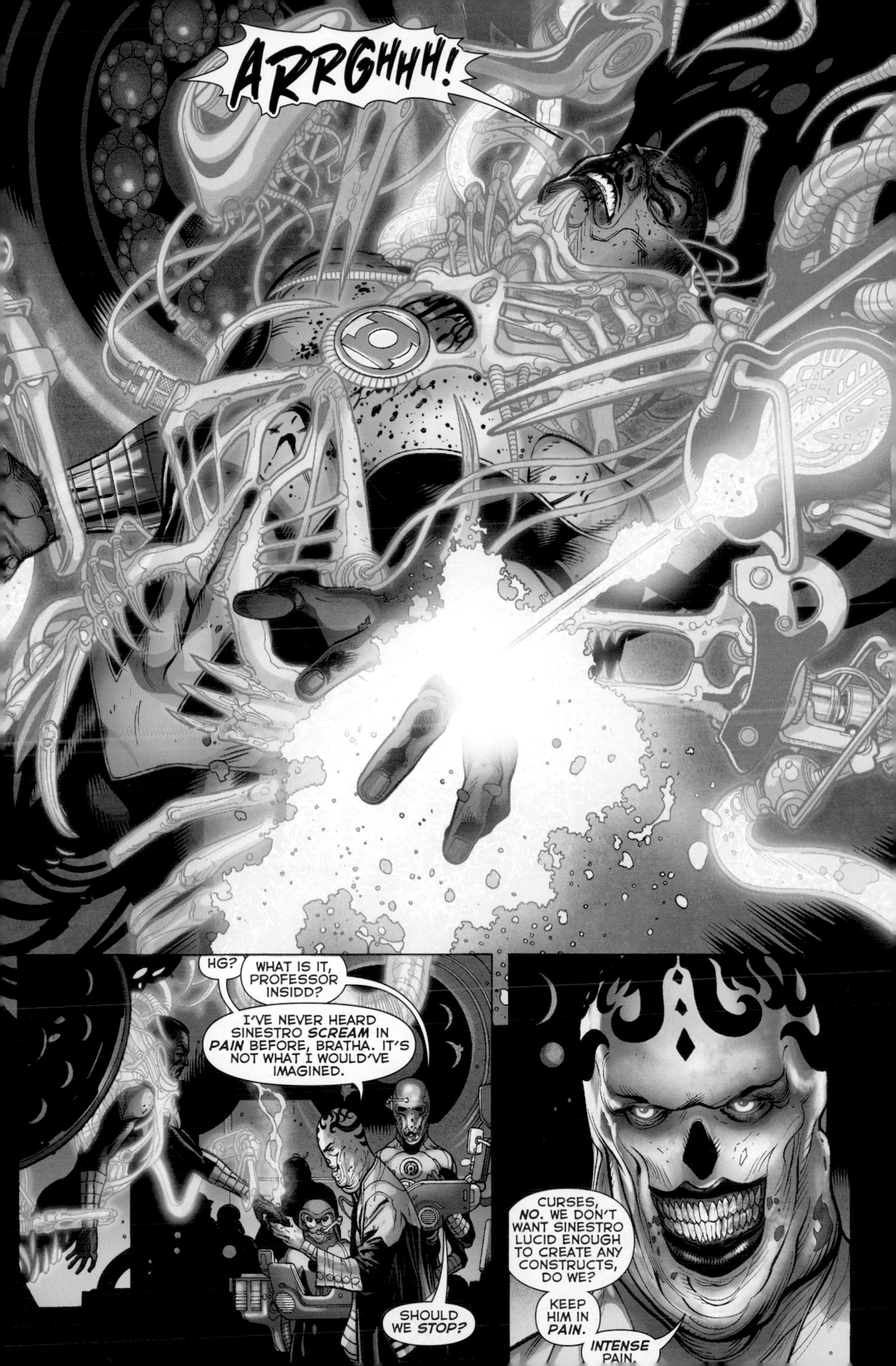

ARRGHHH!
HG?
WHAT IS IT, PROFESSOR INSIDD?
I'VE NEVER HEARD SINESTRO *SCREAM* IN *PAIN* BEFORE, BRATHA. IT'S NOT WHAT I WOULD'VE IMAGINED.
SHOULD WE *STOP?*
CURSES, *NO.* WE DON'T WANT SINESTRO LUCID ENOUGH TO CREATE ANY CONSTRUCTS, DO WE?
KEEP HIM IN *PAIN.*
INTENSE PAIN.

ARRGHHH!

THE RING SHOULD'VE **SHATTERED** BY NOW. IT'S INCREDIBLY **RESILIENT.**

NO. **I** AM. PROFESSOR INSIDD, YOU HAVE A CHOICE: RELEASE ME OR DIE.

I SUPPOSE A BEAM WILL COME OUT OF THERE AND MAKE MY BRAIN **EXPLODE,** HM? NOT WHEN YOUR PAIN LEVELS ARE AT SIXTEEN HEGATOX!

SEVENTEEN, PROFESSOR INSIDD!

SO THEY ARE!

THREATENING THOSE YOU **HANDPICKED** FOR YOUR ARMY?

THE GREEN POWER HAS TRULY **INFECTED** YOUR BRAIN, HASN'T IT? NOT TO WORRY.

I WILL **FREE** YOU FROM THE EMERALD POISON.

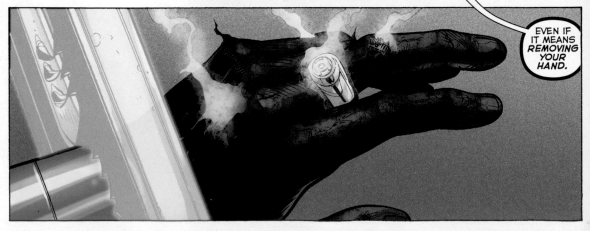

EVEN IF IT MEANS **REMOVING YOUR HAND.**

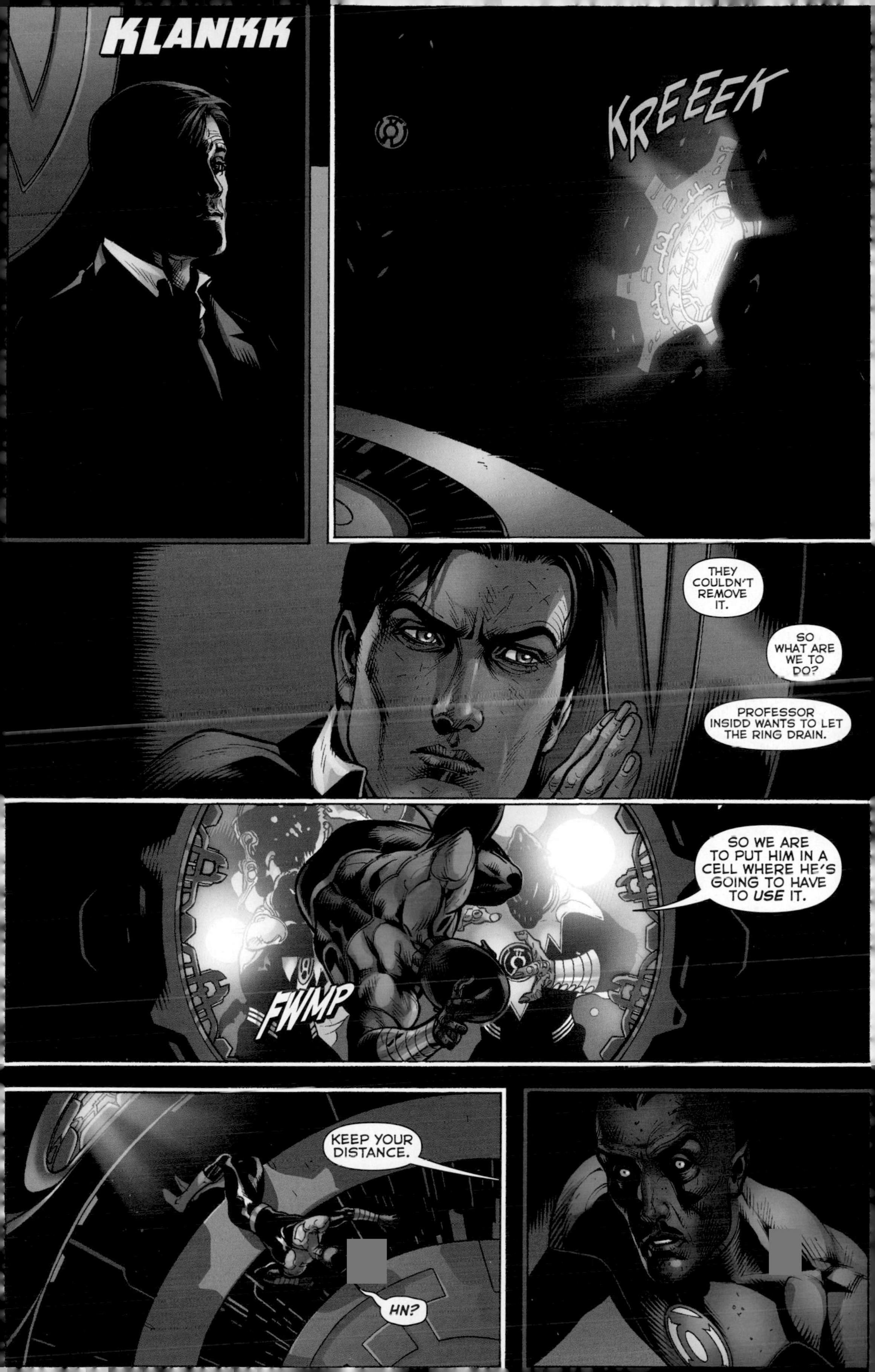
KLANKK
KREEEK
THEY COULDN'T REMOVE IT.
SO WHAT ARE WE TO DO?
PROFESSOR INSIDD WANTS TO LET THE RING DRAIN.
SO WE ARE TO PUT HIM IN A CELL WHERE HE'S GOING TO HAVE TO USE IT.
FWMP
KEEP YOUR DISTANCE.
HN?

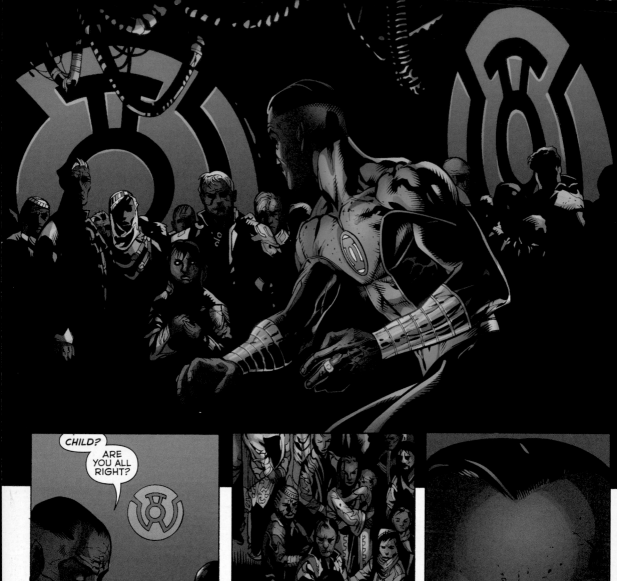

CHILD? ARE YOU ALL RIGHT?

WHAT?

WHAT ARE YOU AFRAID OF?

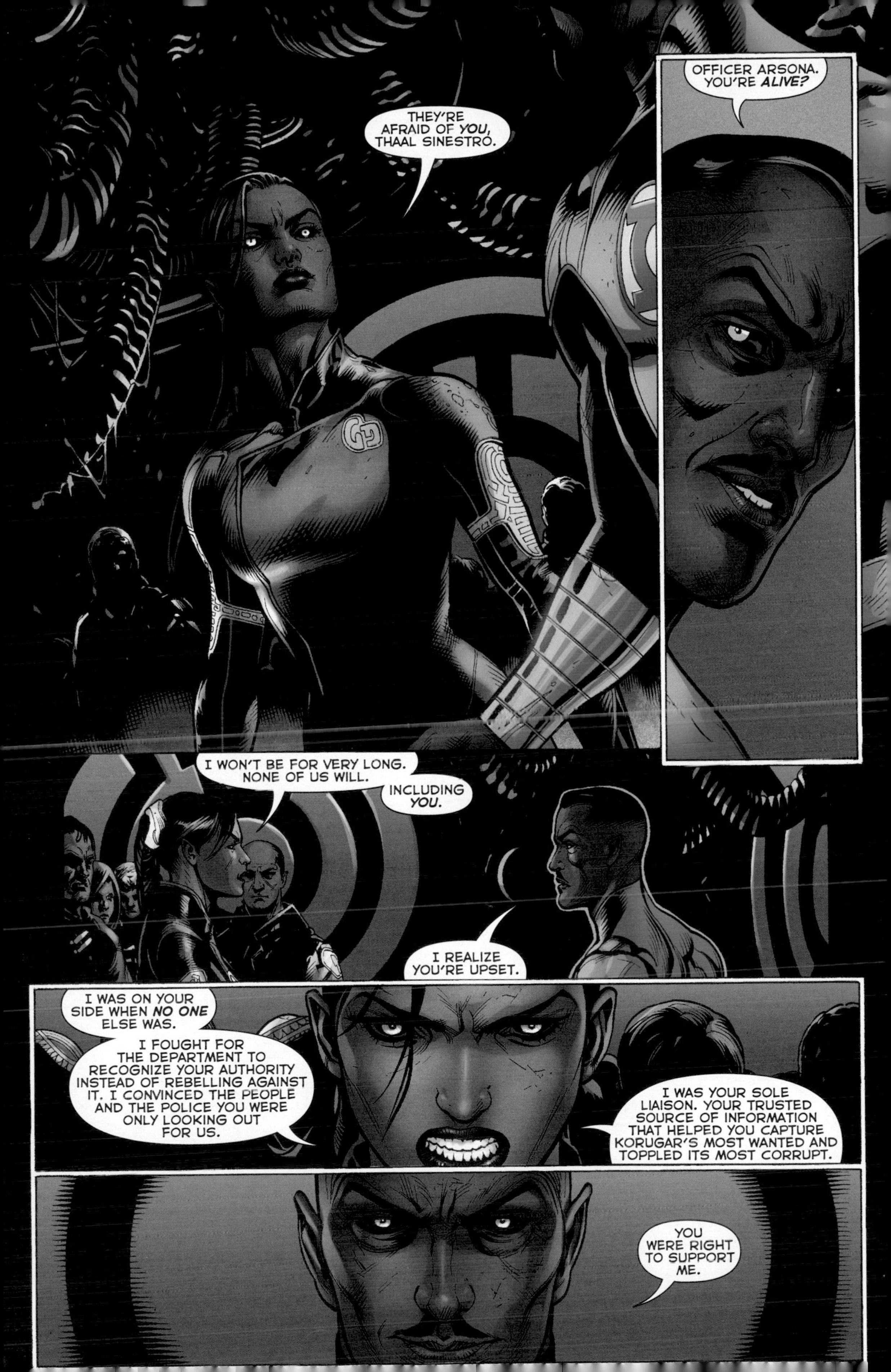
THEY'RE AFRAID OF YOU, THAAL SINESTRO.
OFFICER ARSONA. YOU'RE ALIVE?
I WON'T BE FOR VERY LONG. NONE OF US WILL.
INCLUDING YOU.
I REALIZE YOU'RE UPSET.
I WAS ON YOUR SIDE WHEN NO ONE ELSE WAS.
I FOUGHT FOR THE DEPARTMENT TO RECOGNIZE YOUR AUTHORITY INSTEAD OF REBELLING AGAINST IT. I CONVINCED THE PEOPLE AND THE POLICE YOU WERE ONLY LOOKING OUT FOR US.
I WAS YOUR SOLE LIAISON. YOUR TRUSTED SOURCE OF INFORMATION THAT HELPED YOU CAPTURE KORUGAR'S MOST WANTED AND TOPPLED ITS MOST CORRUPT.
YOU WERE RIGHT TO SUPPORT ME.

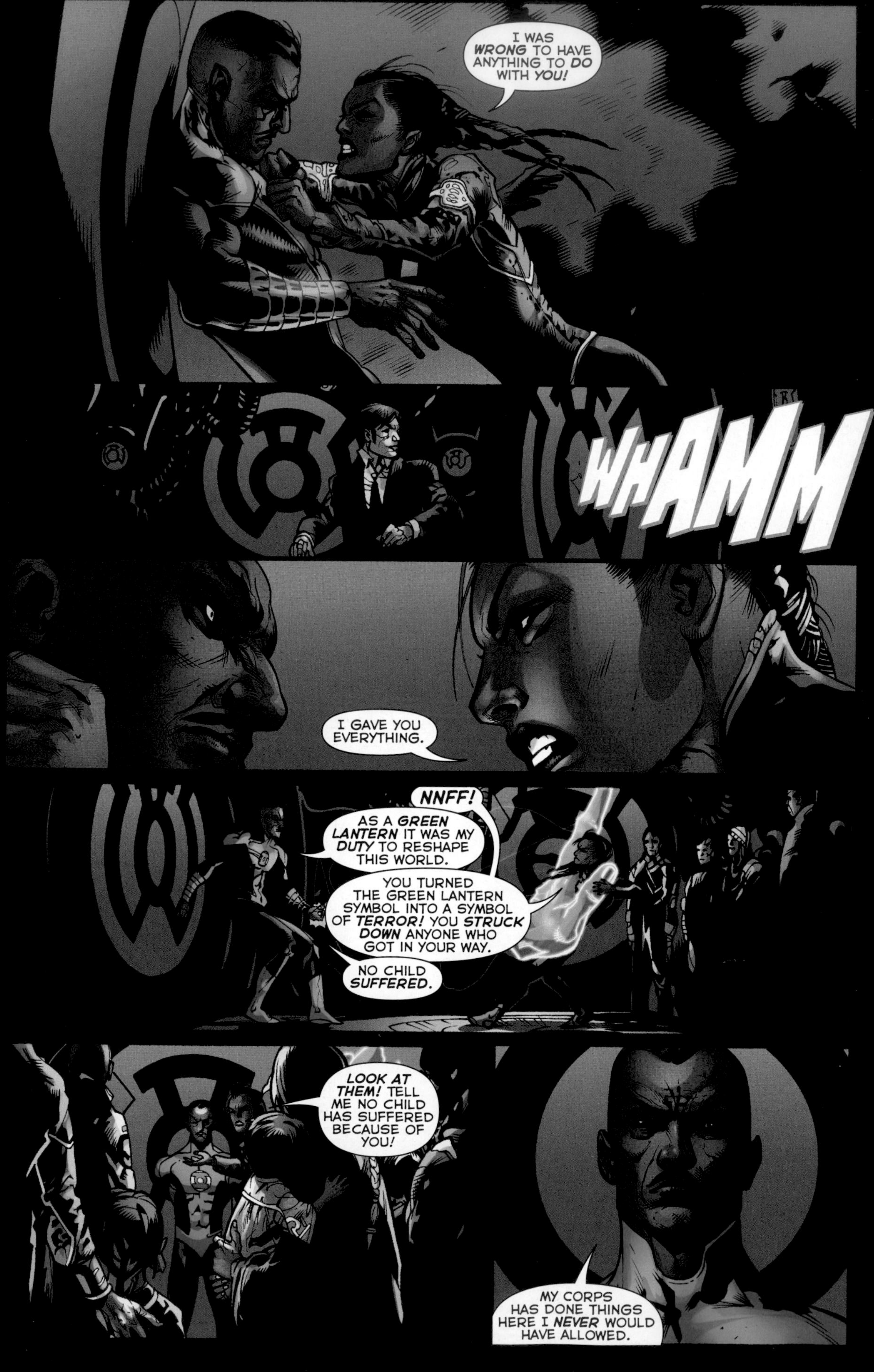
I WAS WRONG TO HAVE ANYTHING TO DO WITH YOU!
WHAMM
I GAVE YOU EVERYTHING.
NNFF!
AS A GREEN LANTERN IT WAS MY DUTY TO RESHAPE THIS WORLD.
YOU TURNED THE GREEN LANTERN SYMBOL INTO A SYMBOL OF TERROR! YOU STRUCK DOWN ANYONE WHO GOT IN YOUR WAY.
NO CHILD SUFFERED.
LOOK AT THEM! TELL ME NO CHILD HAS SUFFERED BECAUSE OF YOU!
MY CORPS HAS DONE THINGS HERE I NEVER WOULD HAVE ALLOWED.

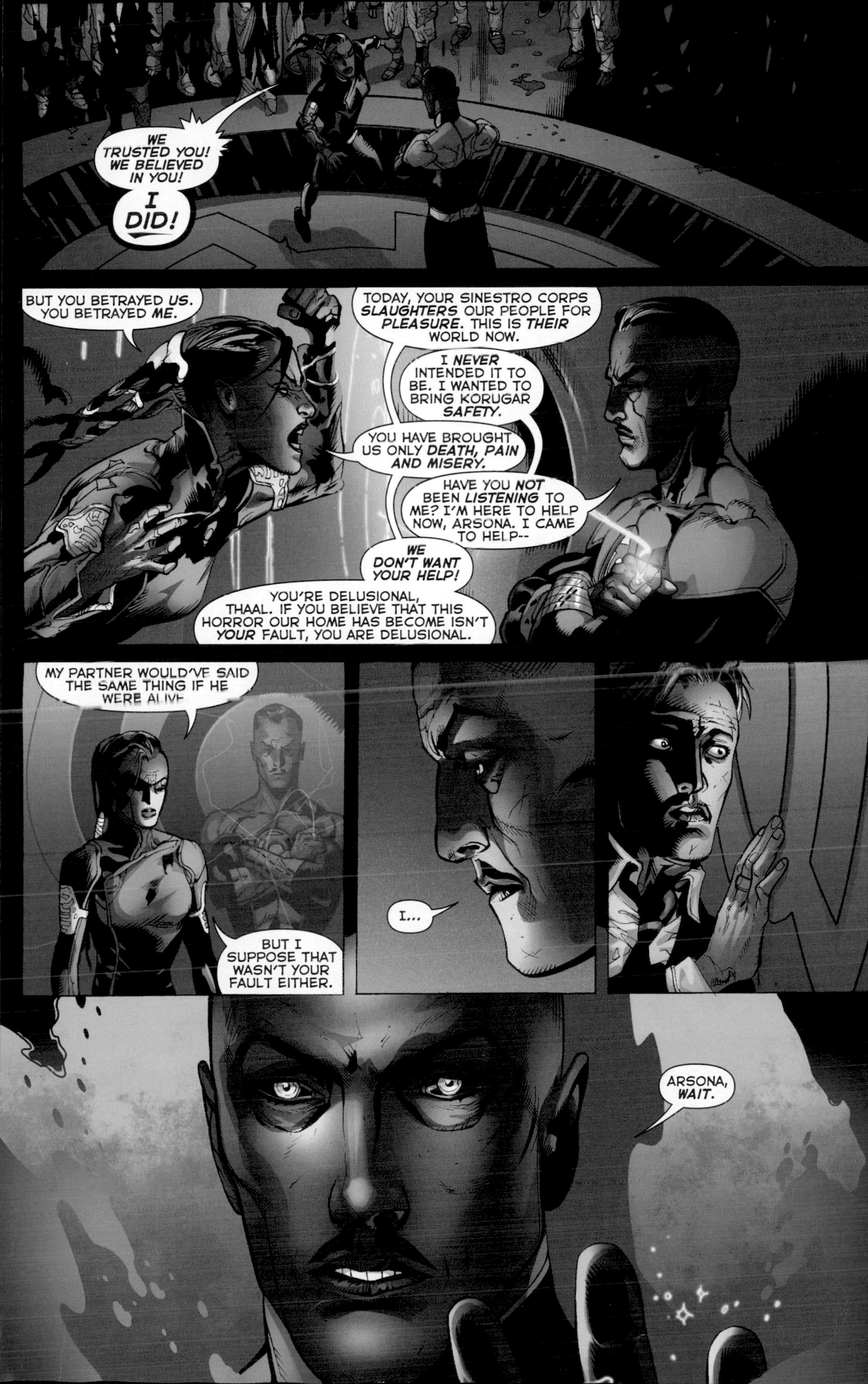
WE TRUSTED YOU! WE BELIEVED IN YOU!
I DID!
BUT YOU BETRAYED US. YOU BETRAYED ME.
TODAY, YOUR SINESTRO CORPS SLAUGHTERS OUR PEOPLE FOR PLEASURE. THIS IS THEIR WORLD NOW.
I NEVER INTENDED IT TO BE. I WANTED TO BRING KORUGAR SAFETY.
YOU HAVE BROUGHT US ONLY DEATH, PAIN AND MISERY.
HAVE YOU NOT BEEN LISTENING TO ME? I'M HERE TO HELP NOW, ARSONA. I CAME TO HELP--
WE DON'T WANT YOUR HELP!
YOU'RE DELUSIONAL, THAAL. IF YOU BELIEVE THAT THIS HORROR OUR HOME HAS BECOME ISN'T YOUR FAULT, YOU ARE DELUSIONAL.
MY PARTNER WOULD'VE SAID THE SAME THING IF HE WERE ALIVE
BUT I SUPPOSE THAT WASN'T YOUR FAULT EITHER.
I...
ARSONA, WAIT.

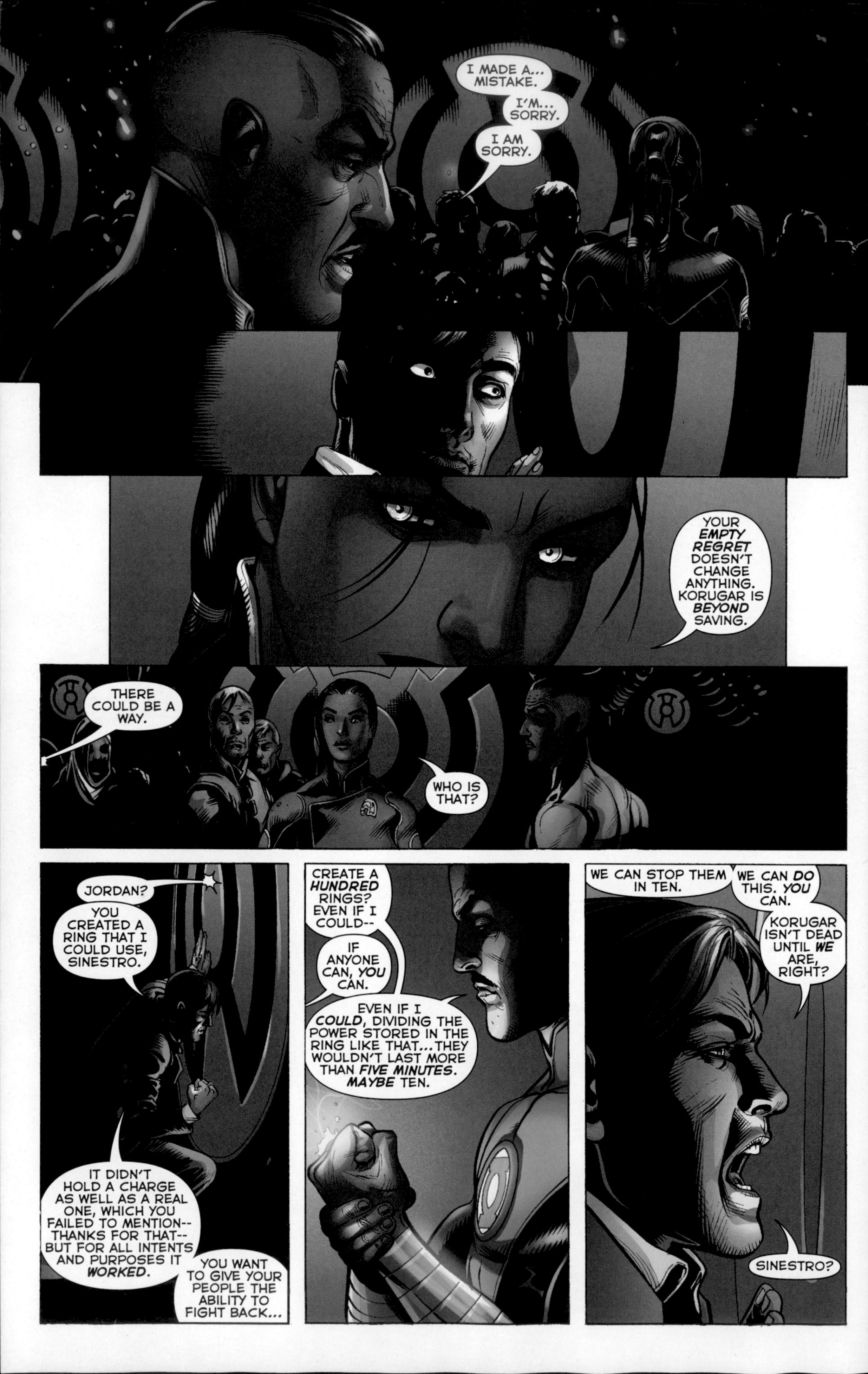
I MADE A... MISTAKE.
I'M... SORRY.
I AM SORRY.
YOUR *EMPTY REGRET* DOESN'T CHANGE ANYTHING. KORUGAR IS *BEYOND* SAVING.
THERE COULD BE A WAY.
WHO IS THAT?
JORDAN?
YOU CREATED A RING THAT I COULD USE, SINESTRO.
IT DIDN'T HOLD A CHARGE AS WELL AS A REAL ONE, WHICH YOU FAILED TO MENTION--THANKS FOR THAT--BUT FOR ALL INTENTS AND PURPOSES IT *WORKED*.
YOU WANT TO GIVE YOUR PEOPLE THE ABILITY TO FIGHT BACK...
CREATE A *HUNDRED* RINGS? EVEN IF I COULD--
IF ANYONE CAN, *YOU* CAN.
EVEN IF I *COULD*, DIVIDING THE POWER STORED IN THE RING LIKE THAT...THEY WOULDN'T LAST MORE THAN *FIVE MINUTES*. *MAYBE* TEN.
WE CAN STOP THEM IN TEN.
WE CAN *DO* THIS. *YOU* CAN.
KORUGAR ISN'T DEAD UNTIL *WE* ARE, RIGHT?
SINESTRO?

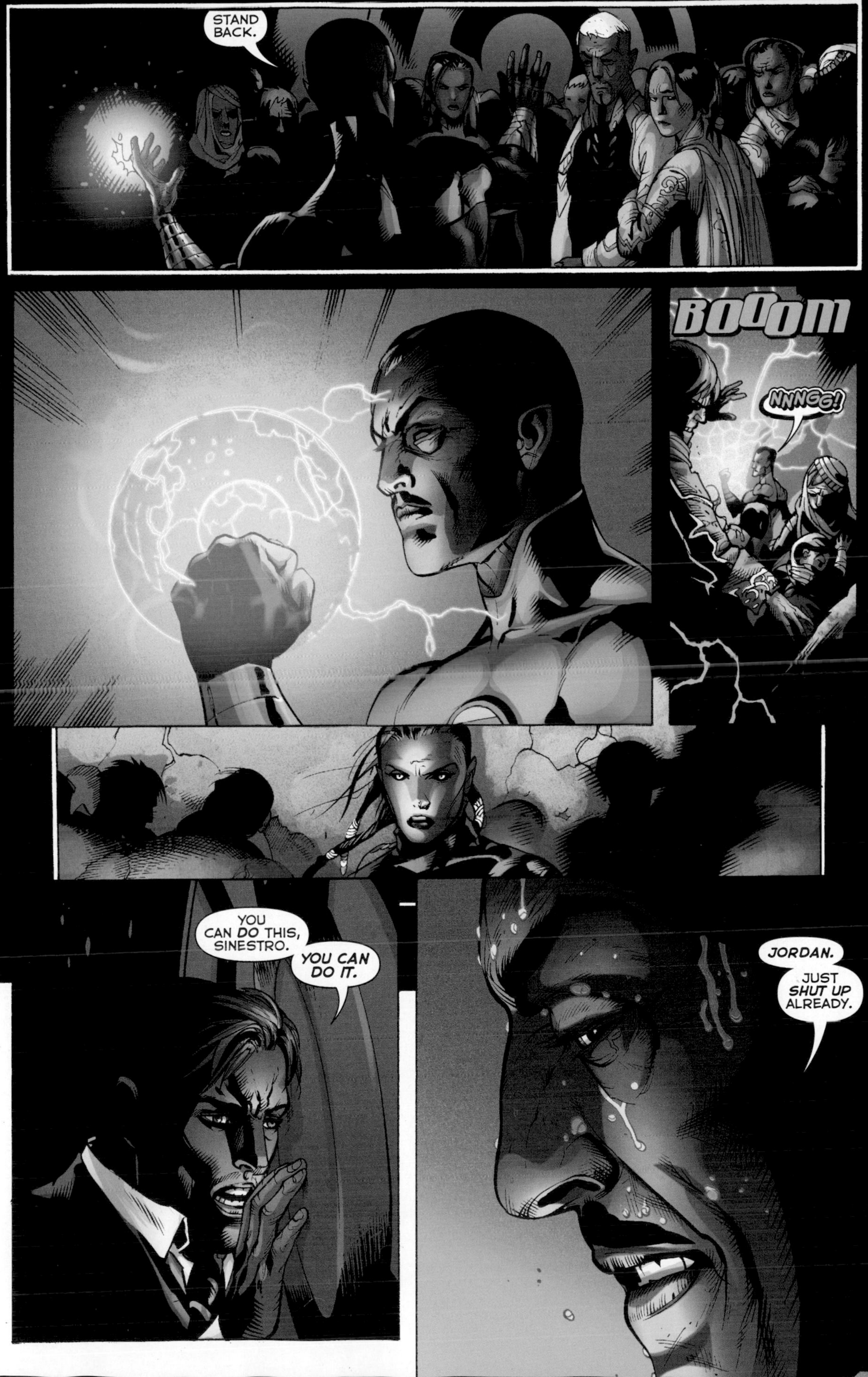
STAND BACK.
BOOOOM
NNNGG!
YOU CAN DO THIS, SINESTRO.
YOU CAN DO IT.
JORDAN.
JUST SHUT UP ALREADY.

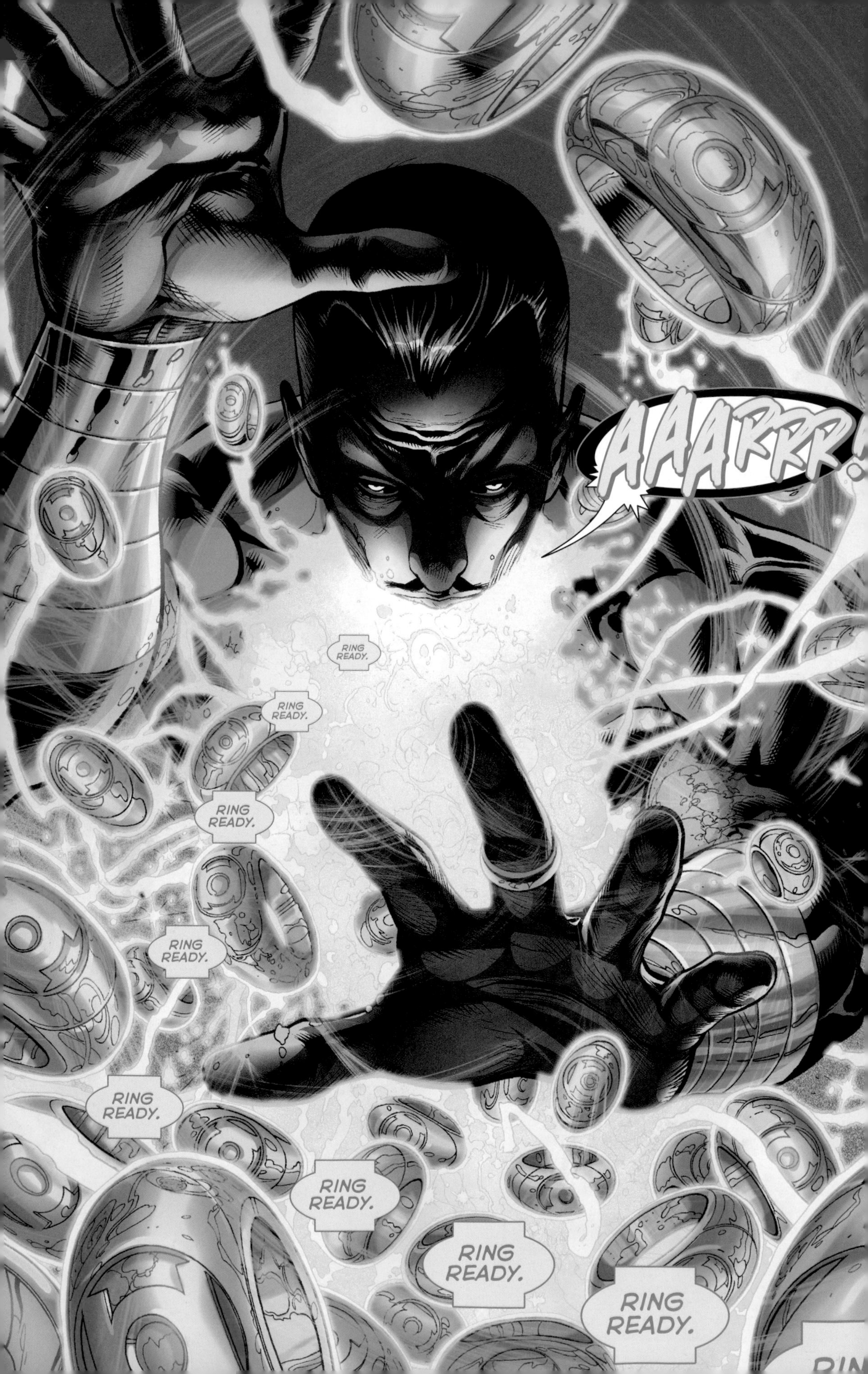
AAARRR!
RING READY.
RING READY.
RING READY.
RING READY.
RING READY.
RING READY.
RING READY.
RING READY.

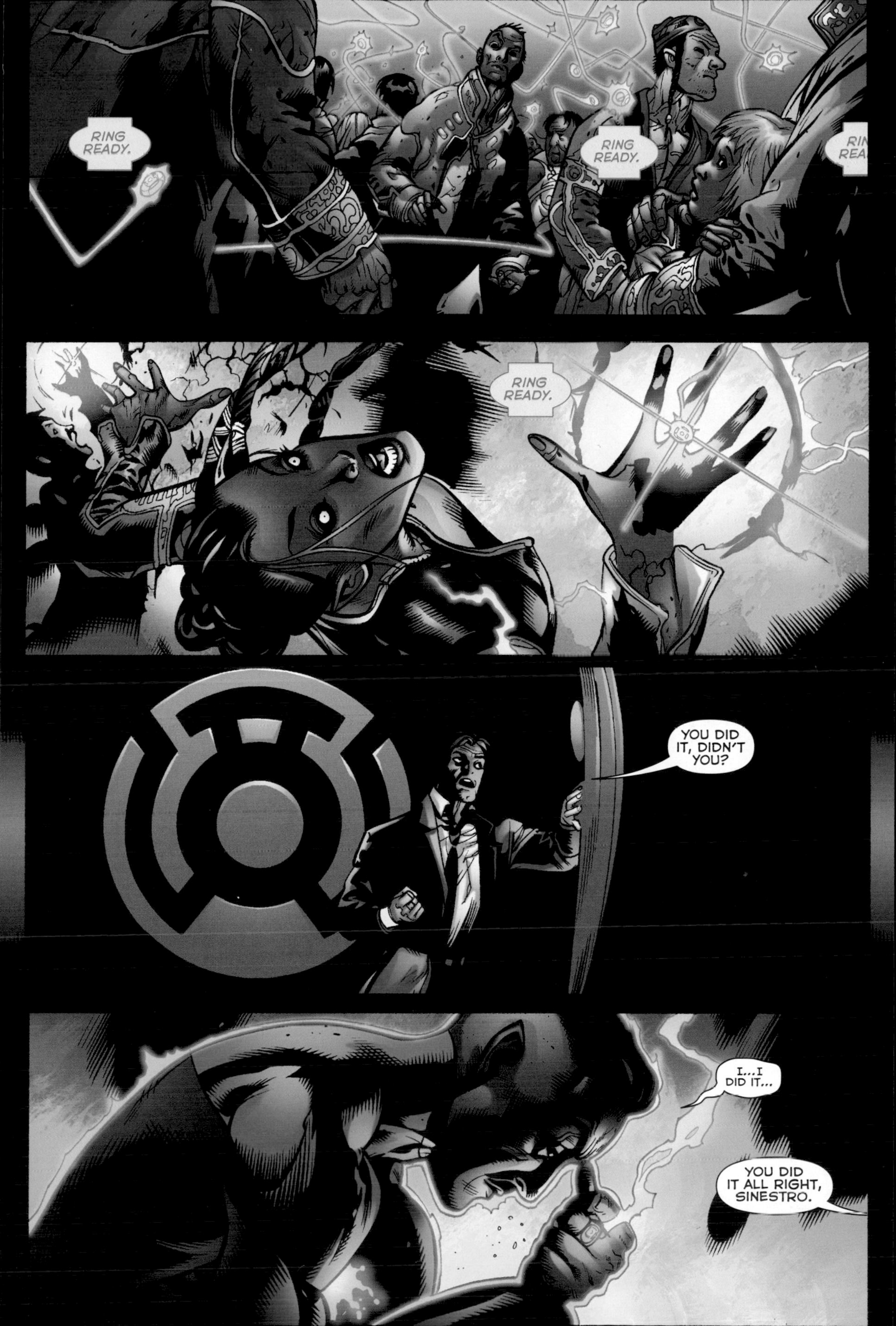

RING READY.
RING READY.
RING READY.
YOU DID IT, DIDN'T YOU?
I...I DID IT...
YOU DID IT ALL RIGHT, SINESTRO.

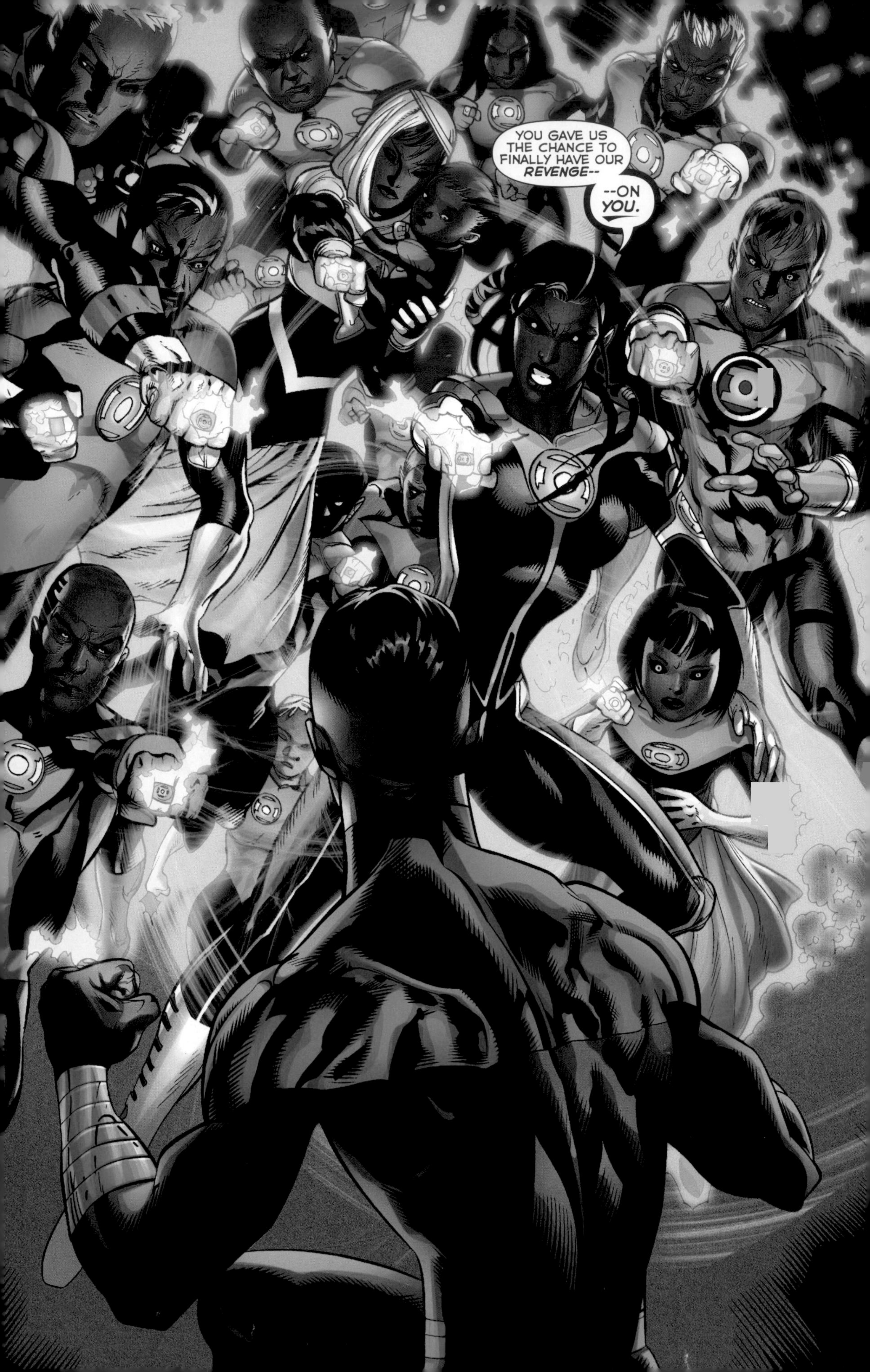
YOU GAVE US THE CHANCE TO FINALLY HAVE OUR REVENGE--
--ON YOU.

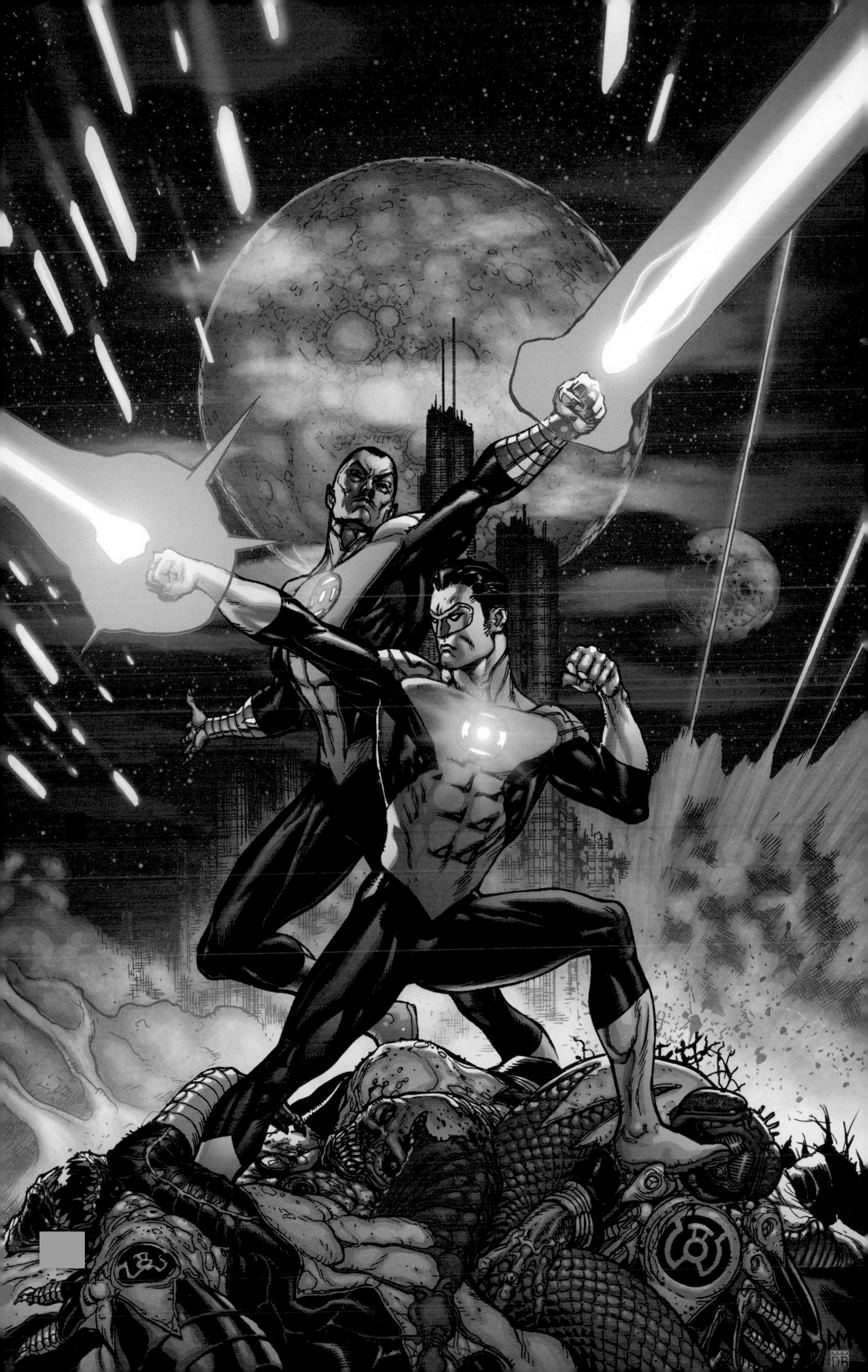

Doug Mahnke & David Baron

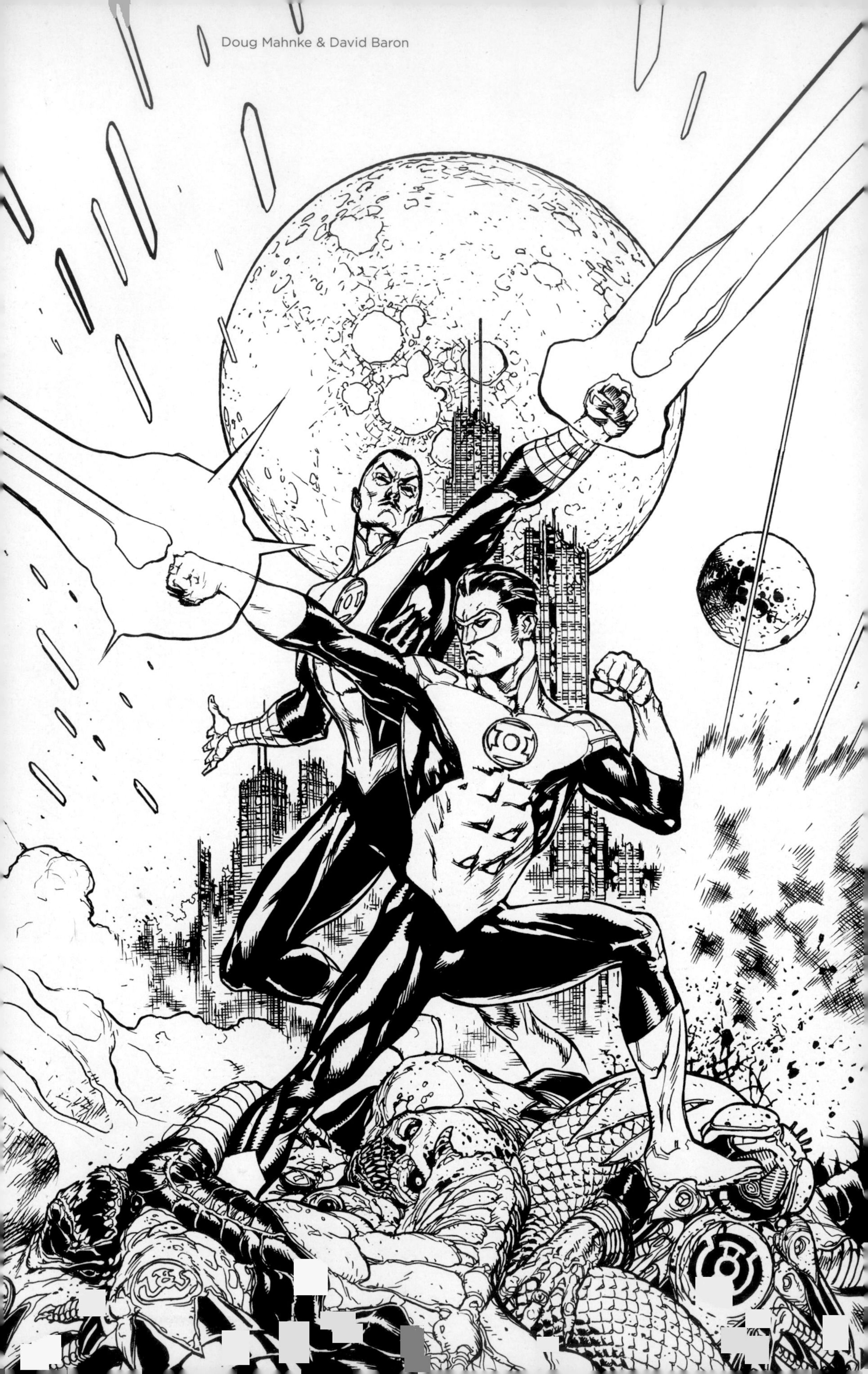

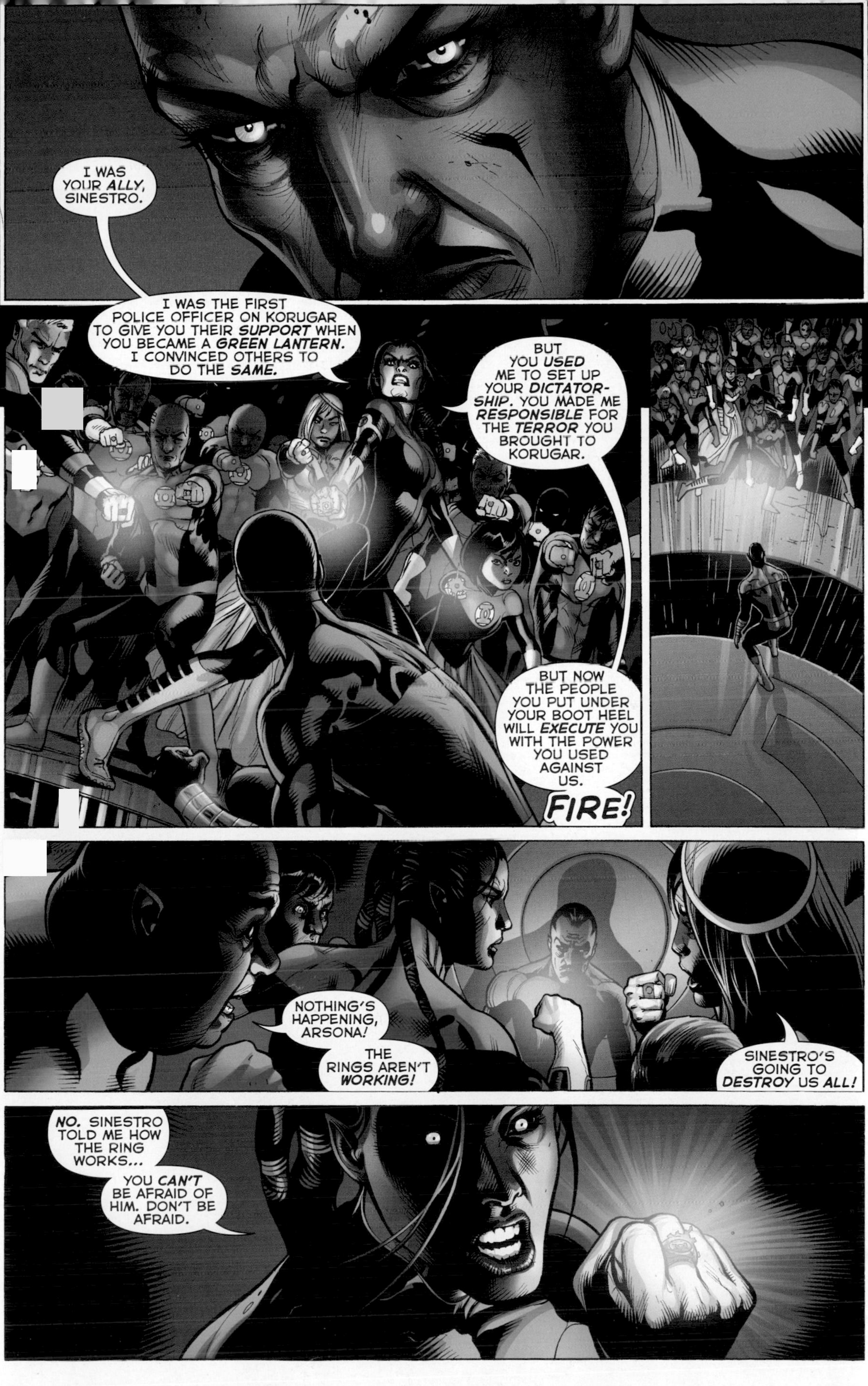
I WAS YOUR ALLY, SINESTRO.
I WAS THE FIRST POLICE OFFICER ON KORUGAR TO GIVE YOU THEIR SUPPORT WHEN YOU BECAME A GREEN LANTERN. I CONVINCED OTHERS TO DO THE SAME.
BUT YOU USED ME TO SET UP YOUR DICTATOR-SHIP. YOU MADE ME RESPONSIBLE FOR THE TERROR YOU BROUGHT TO KORUGAR.
BUT NOW THE PEOPLE YOU PUT UNDER YOUR BOOT HEEL WILL EXECUTE YOU WITH THE POWER YOU USED AGAINST US.
FIRE!
NOTHING'S HAPPENING, ARSONA!
THE RINGS AREN'T WORKING!
SINESTRO'S GOING TO DESTROY US ALL!
NO. SINESTRO TOLD ME HOW THE RING WORKS...
YOU CAN'T BE AFRAID OF HIM. DON'T BE AFRAID.

OVERCOME YOUR FEAR AND YOU CAN *USE* THE RINGS.

YOU CAN HAVE *VENGEANCE!*

I CAN.

HEY, GUYS?!

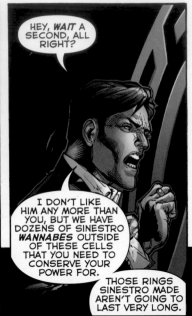

HEY, *WAIT* A SECOND, ALL RIGHT?

I DON'T LIKE HIM ANY MORE THAN YOU, BUT WE HAVE DOZENS OF SINESTRO *WANNABES* OUTSIDE OF THESE CELLS THAT YOU NEED TO CONSERVE YOUR POWER FOR.

THOSE RINGS SINESTRO MADE AREN'T GOING TO LAST VERY LONG.

HELLO?!

I WAS *NOTHING* TO YOU, WAS I?

LESS THAN *NOTHING.*

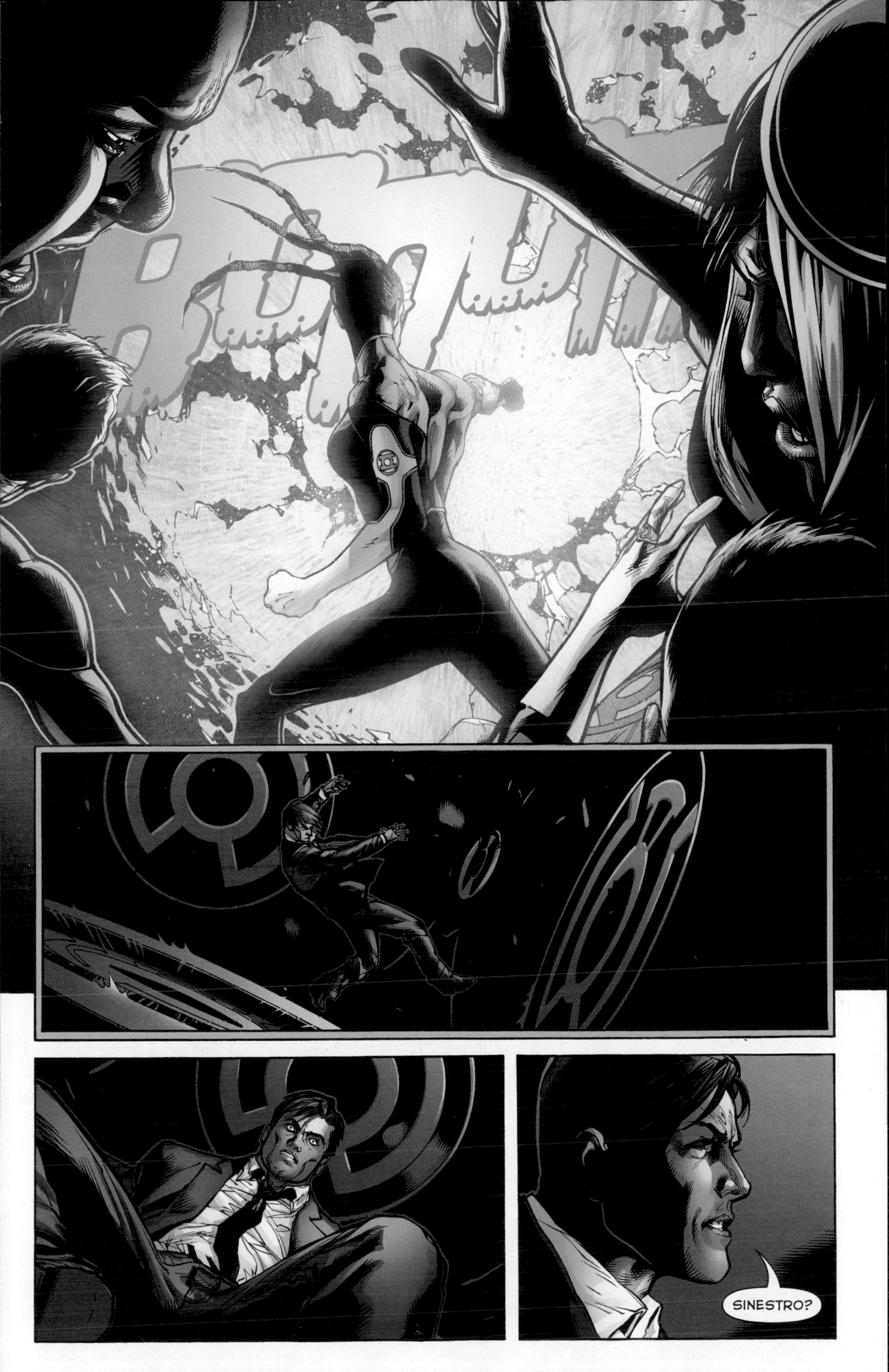
SINESTRO?

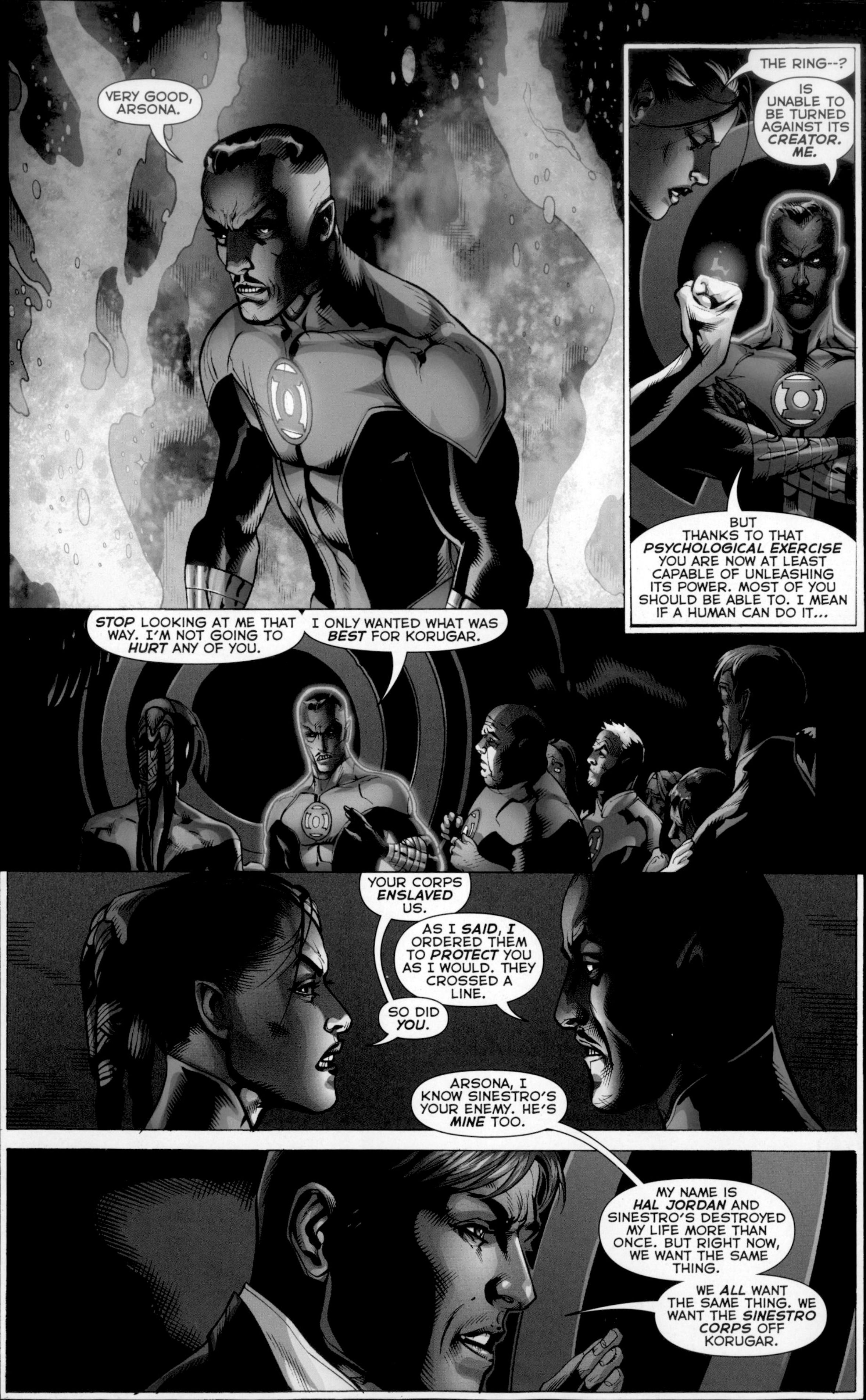

VERY GOOD, ARSONA.
THE RING--?
IS UNABLE TO BE TURNED AGAINST ITS *CREATOR. ME.*
BUT THANKS TO THAT *PSYCHOLOGICAL EXERCISE* YOU ARE NOW AT LEAST CAPABLE OF UNLEASHING ITS POWER. MOST OF YOU SHOULD BE ABLE TO. I MEAN IF A HUMAN CAN DO IT...
STOP LOOKING AT ME THAT WAY. I'M NOT GOING TO *HURT* ANY OF YOU.
I ONLY WANTED WHAT WAS *BEST* FOR KORUGAR.
YOUR CORPS *ENSLAVED* US.
AS I *SAID, I* ORDERED THEM TO *PROTECT* YOU AS I WOULD. THEY CROSSED A LINE.
SO DID *YOU.*
ARSONA, I KNOW SINESTRO'S YOUR ENEMY. HE'S *MINE* TOO.
MY NAME IS *HAL JORDAN* AND SINESTRO'S DESTROYED MY LIFE MORE THAN ONCE. BUT RIGHT NOW, WE WANT THE SAME THING.
WE *ALL* WANT THE SAME THING. WE WANT THE *SINESTRO CORPS* OFF KORUGAR.

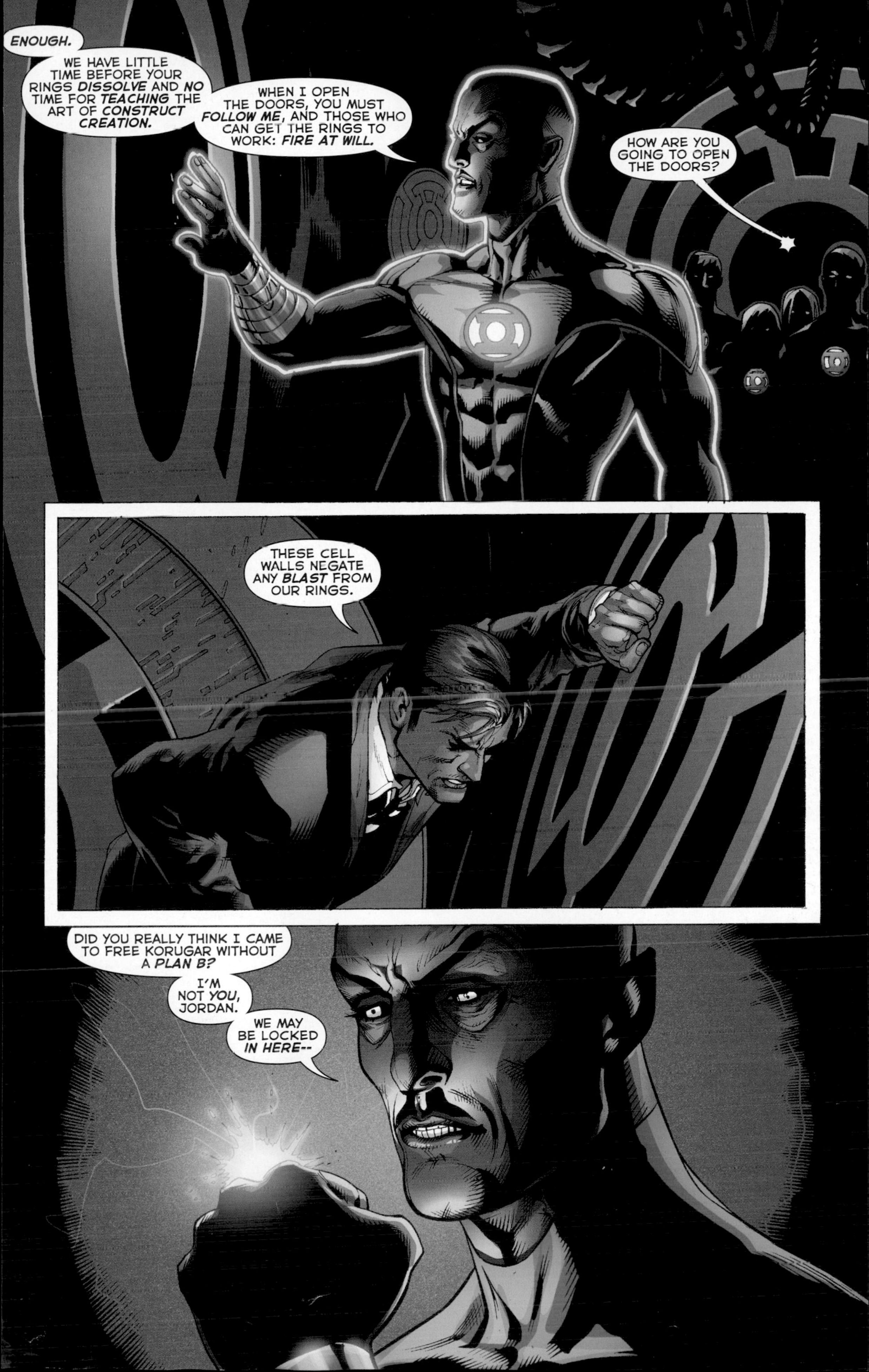
ENOUGH.
WE HAVE LITTLE TIME BEFORE YOUR RINGS DISSOLVE AND NO TIME FOR TEACHING THE ART OF CONSTRUCT CREATION.
WHEN I OPEN THE DOORS, YOU MUST FOLLOW ME, AND THOSE WHO CAN GET THE RINGS TO WORK: FIRE AT WILL.
HOW ARE YOU GOING TO OPEN THE DOORS?
THESE CELL WALLS NEGATE ANY BLAST FROM OUR RINGS.
DID YOU REALLY THINK I CAME TO FREE KORUGAR WITHOUT A PLAN B?
I'M NOT YOU, JORDAN.
WE MAY BE LOCKED IN HERE--

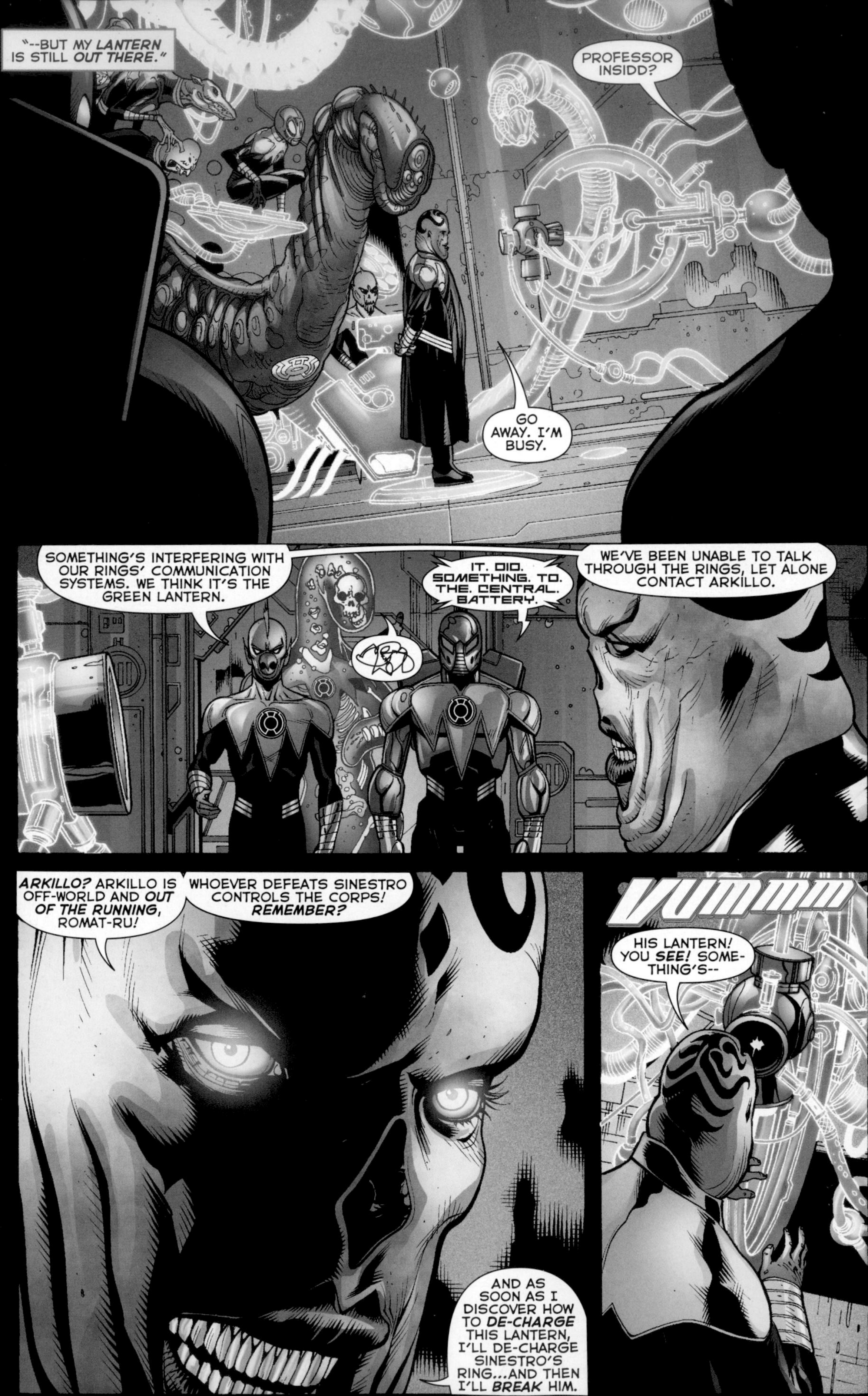
"--BUT MY LANTERN IS STILL OUT THERE."
PROFESSOR INSIDD?
GO AWAY. I'M BUSY.
SOMETHING'S INTERFERING WITH OUR RINGS' COMMUNICATION SYSTEMS. WE THINK IT'S THE GREEN LANTERN.
IT. DID. SOMETHING. TO. THE. CENTRAL. BATTERY.
WE'VE BEEN UNABLE TO TALK THROUGH THE RINGS, LET ALONE CONTACT ARKILLO.
ARKILLO? ARKILLO IS OFF-WORLD AND OUT OF THE RUNNING, ROMAT-RU!
WHOEVER DEFEATS SINESTRO CONTROLS THE CORPS! REMEMBER?
AND AS SOON AS I DISCOVER HOW TO DE-CHARGE THIS LANTERN, I'LL DE-CHARGE SINESTRO'S RING...AND THEN I'LL BREAK HIM.
VUMMM
HIS LANTERN! YOU SEE! SOMETHING'S--

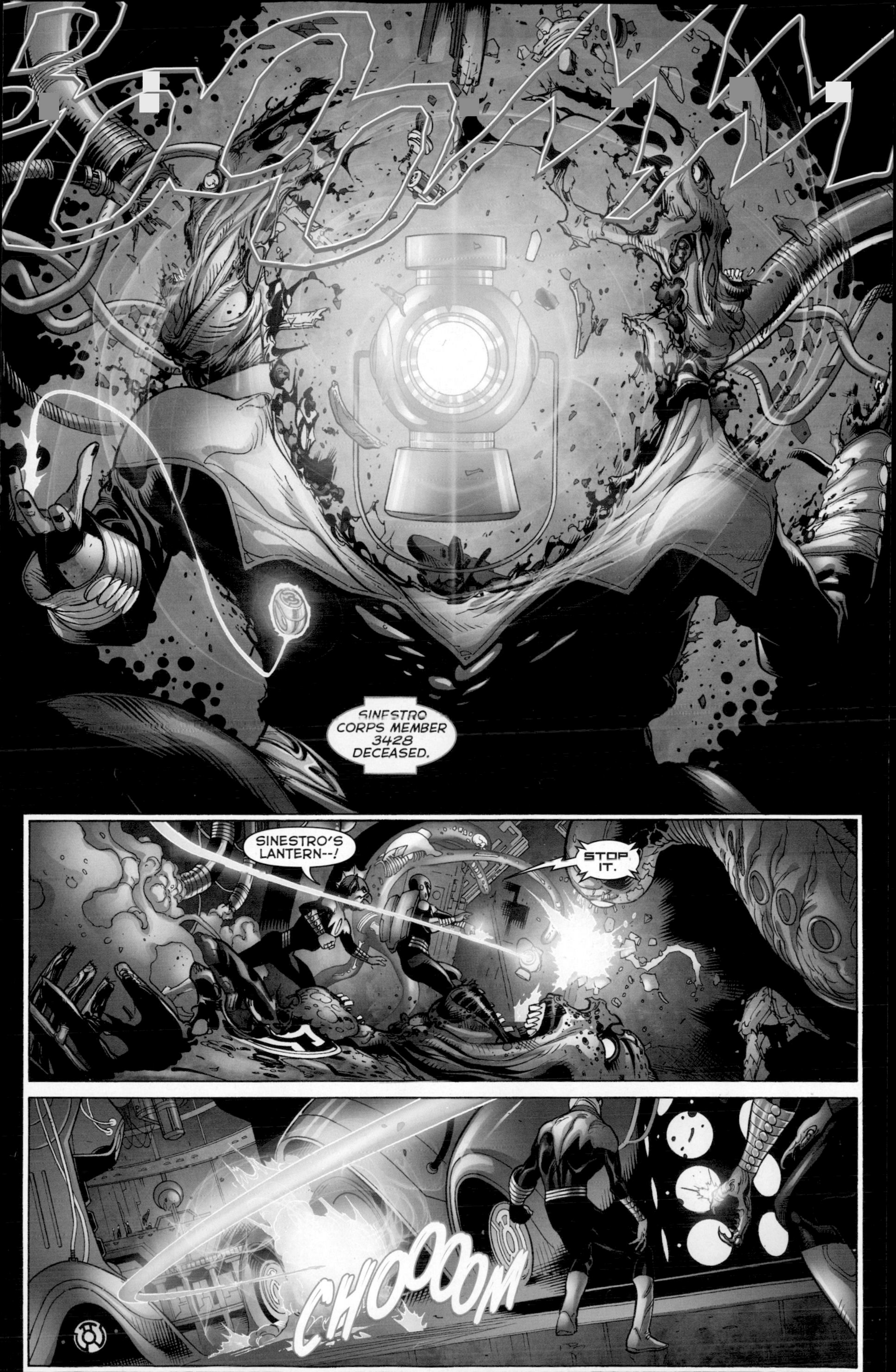
SINESTRO CORPS MEMBER 3428 DECEASED.
SINESTRO'S LANTERN--!
STOP IT.
CHOOOOM

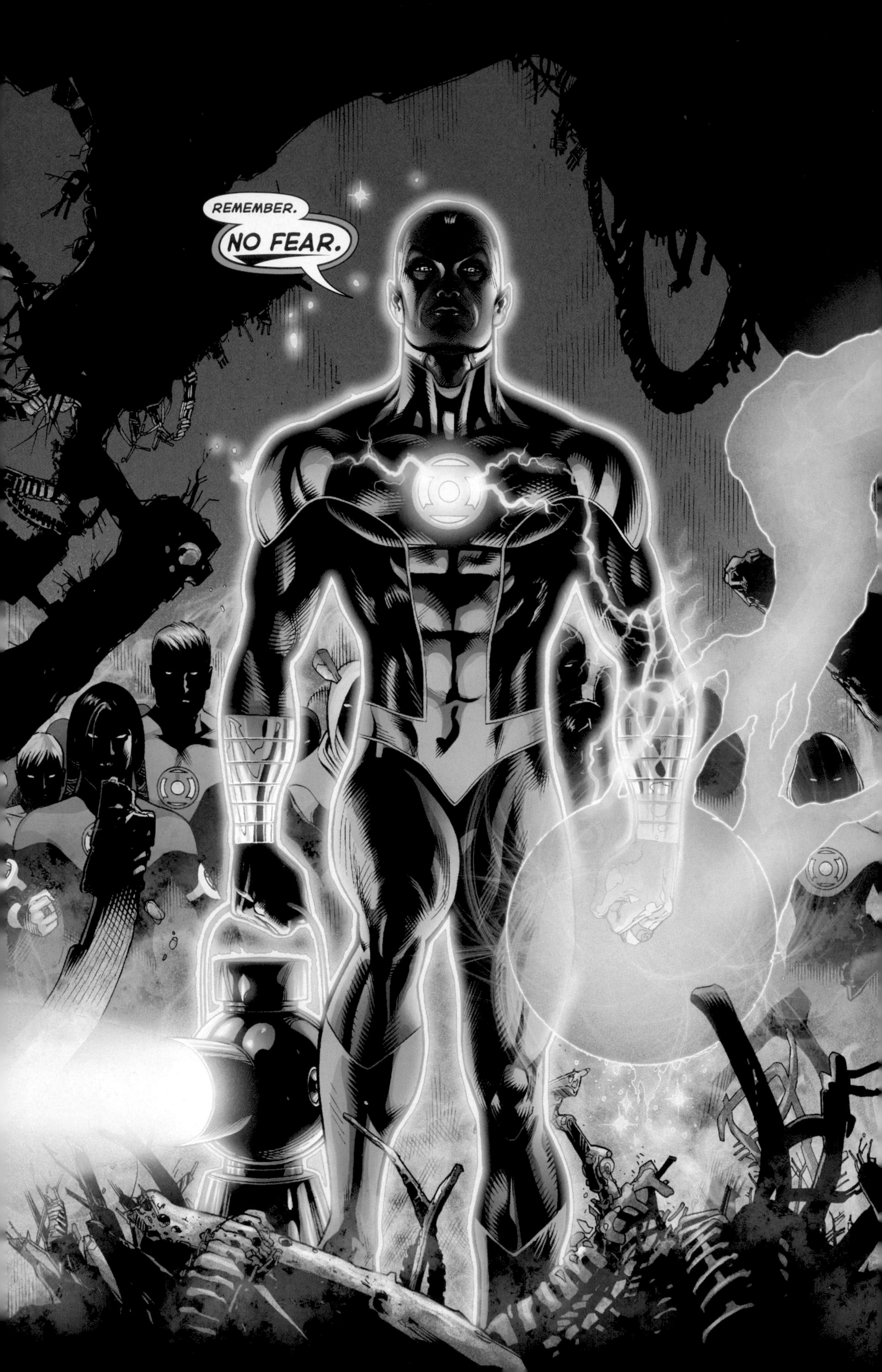
REMEMBER.
NO FEAR.

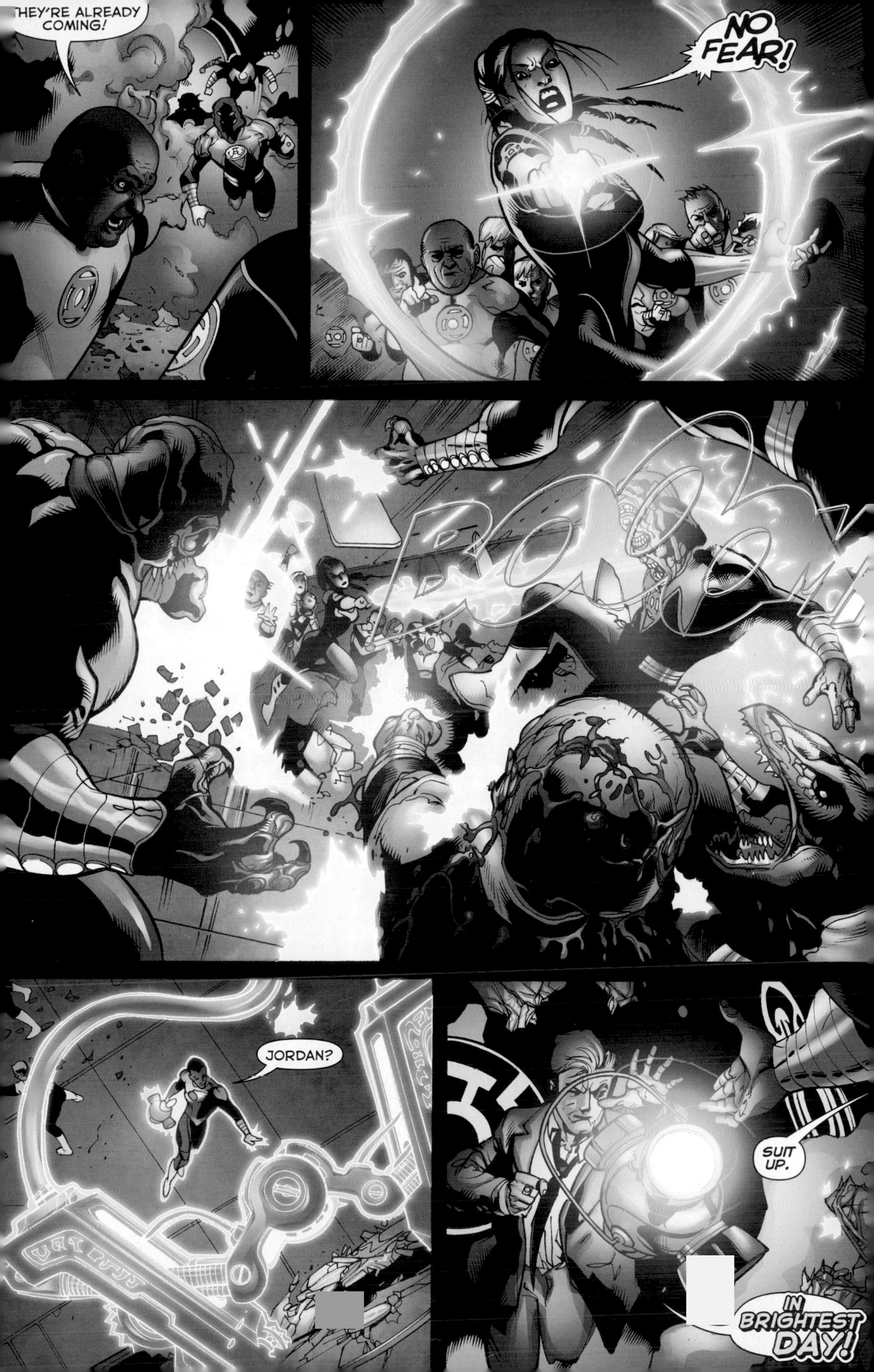
THEY'RE ALREADY COMING!
NO FEAR!
JORDAN?
SUIT UP.
IN BRIGHTEST DAY!

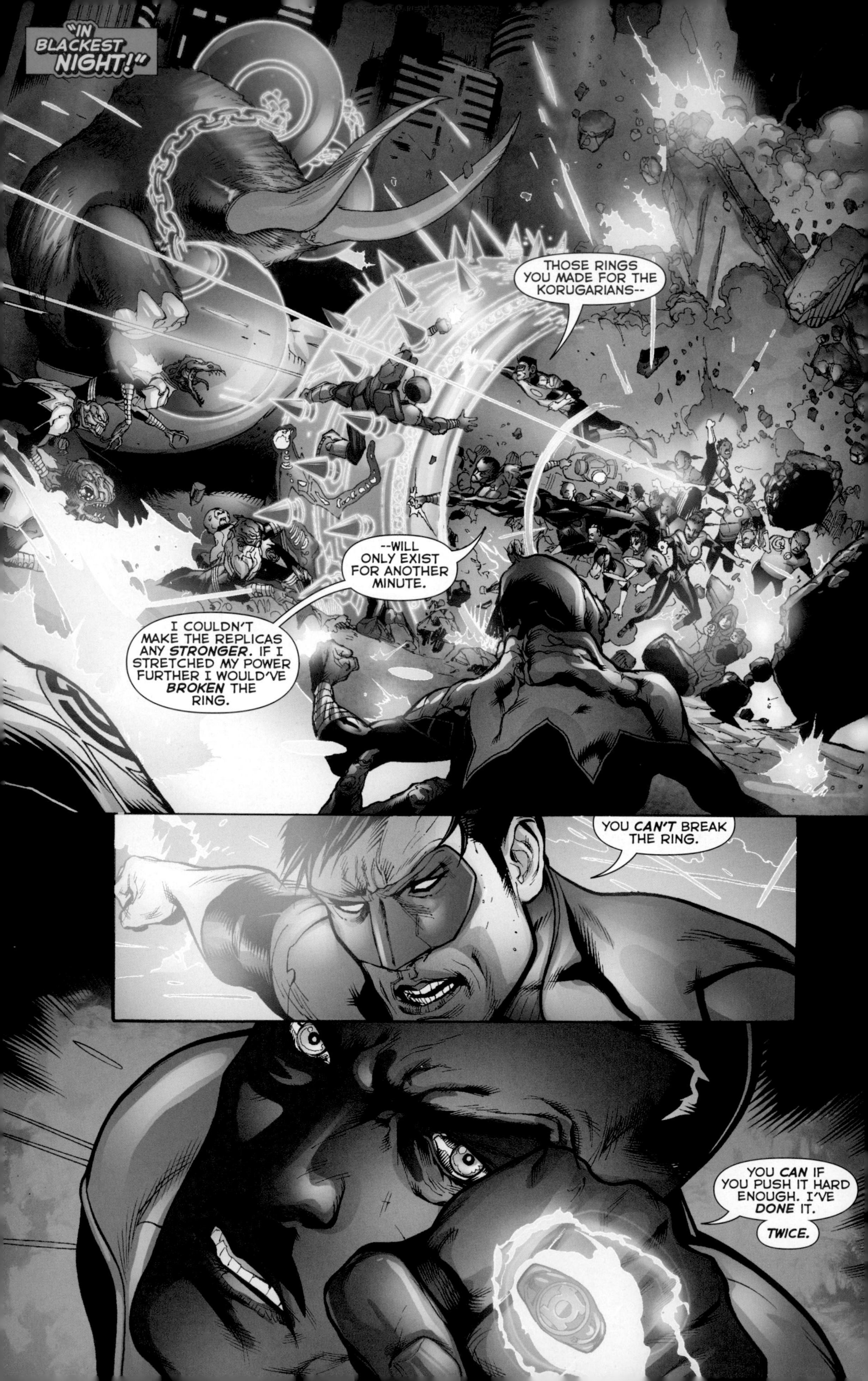
"IN BLACKEST NIGHT!"
THOSE RINGS YOU MADE FOR THE KORUGARIANS--
--WILL ONLY EXIST FOR ANOTHER MINUTE.
I COULDN'T MAKE THE REPLICAS ANY STRONGER. IF I STRETCHED MY POWER FURTHER I WOULD'VE BROKEN THE RING.
YOU CAN'T BREAK THE RING.
YOU CAN IF YOU PUSH IT HARD ENOUGH. I'VE DONE IT.
TWICE.

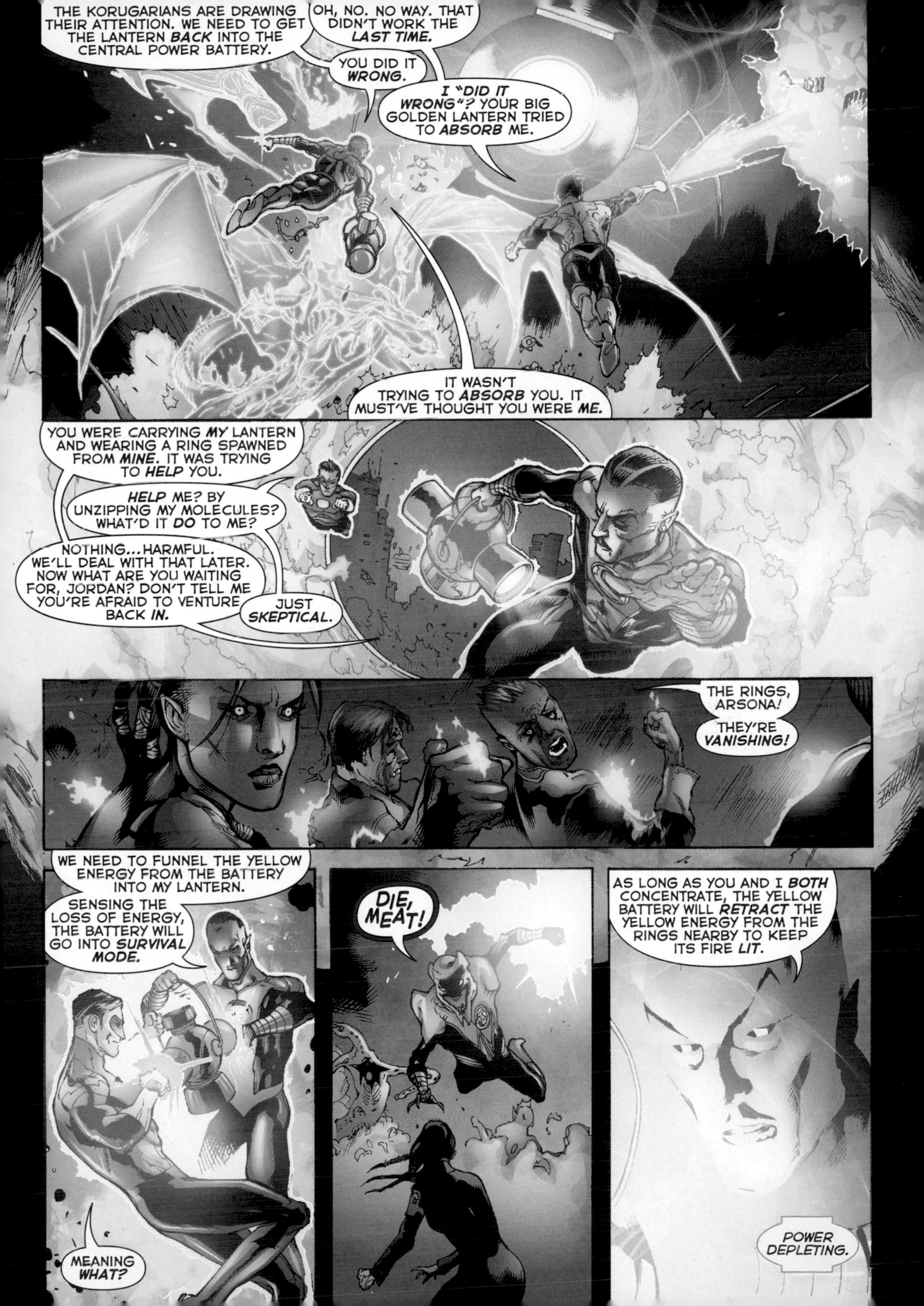

THE KORUGARIANS ARE DRAWING THEIR ATTENTION. WE NEED TO GET THE LANTERN BACK INTO THE CENTRAL POWER BATTERY.
OH, NO. NO WAY. THAT DIDN'T WORK THE LAST TIME.
YOU DID IT WRONG.
I "DID IT WRONG"? YOUR BIG GOLDEN LANTERN TRIED TO ABSORB ME.
IT WASN'T TRYING TO ABSORB YOU. IT MUST'VE THOUGHT YOU WERE ME.
YOU WERE CARRYING MY LANTERN AND WEARING A RING SPAWNED FROM MINE. IT WAS TRYING TO HELP YOU.
HELP ME? BY UNZIPPING MY MOLECULES? WHAT'D IT DO TO ME?
NOTHING... HARMFUL. WE'LL DEAL WITH THAT LATER. NOW WHAT ARE YOU WAITING FOR, JORDAN? DON'T TELL ME YOU'RE AFRAID TO VENTURE BACK IN.
JUST SKEPTICAL.
THE RINGS, ARSONA!
THEY'RE VANISHING!
WE NEED TO FUNNEL THE YELLOW ENERGY FROM THE BATTERY INTO MY LANTERN.
SENSING THE LOSS OF ENERGY, THE BATTERY WILL GO INTO SURVIVAL MODE.
MEANING WHAT?
DIE, MEAT!
AS LONG AS YOU AND I BOTH CONCENTRATE, THE YELLOW BATTERY WILL RETRACT THE YELLOW ENERGY FROM THE RINGS NEARBY TO KEEP ITS FIRE LIT.
POWER DEPLETING.

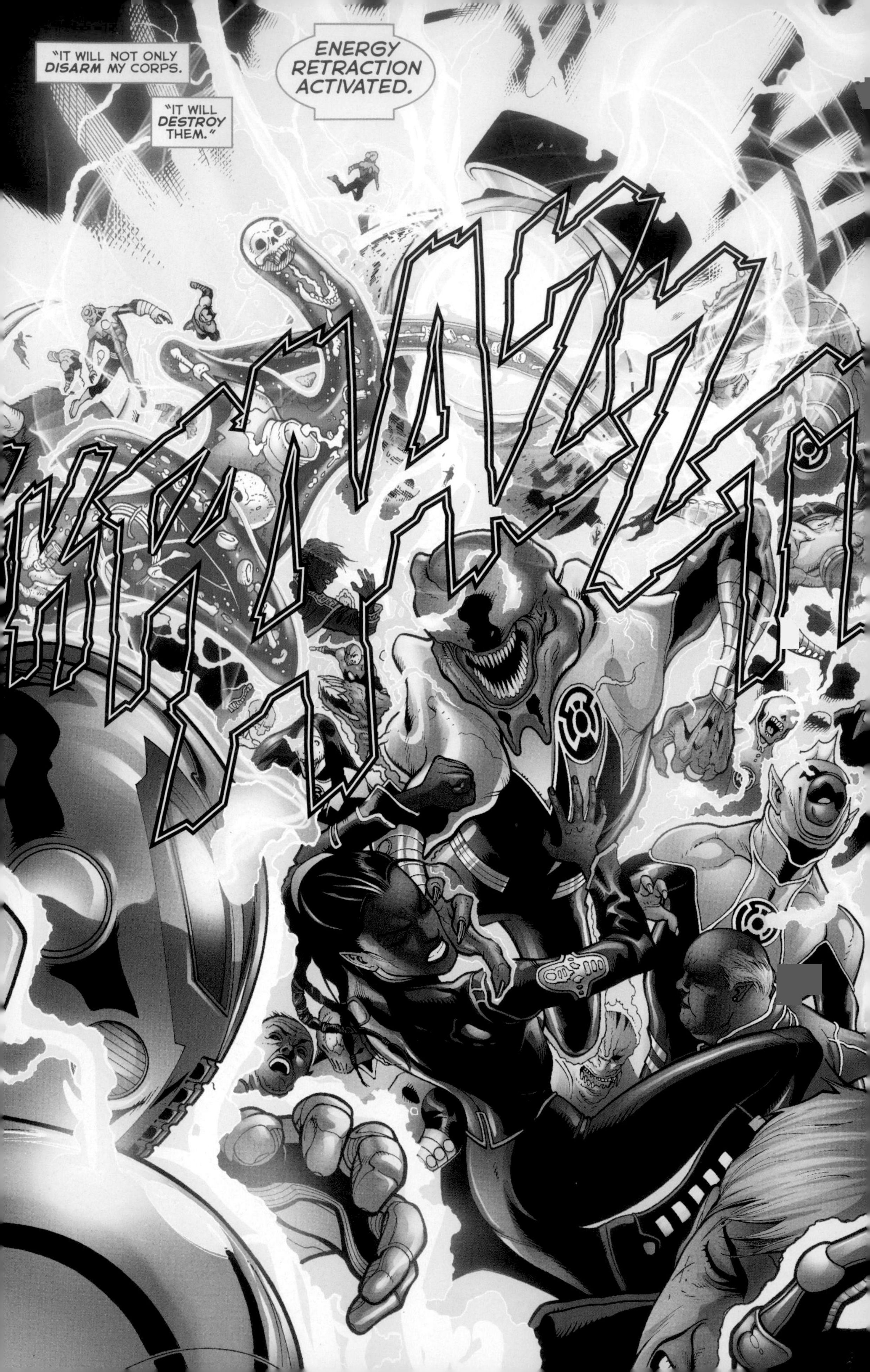
"IT WILL NOT ONLY DISARM MY CORPS.
ENERGY RETRACTION ACTIVATED.
"IT WILL DESTROY THEM."

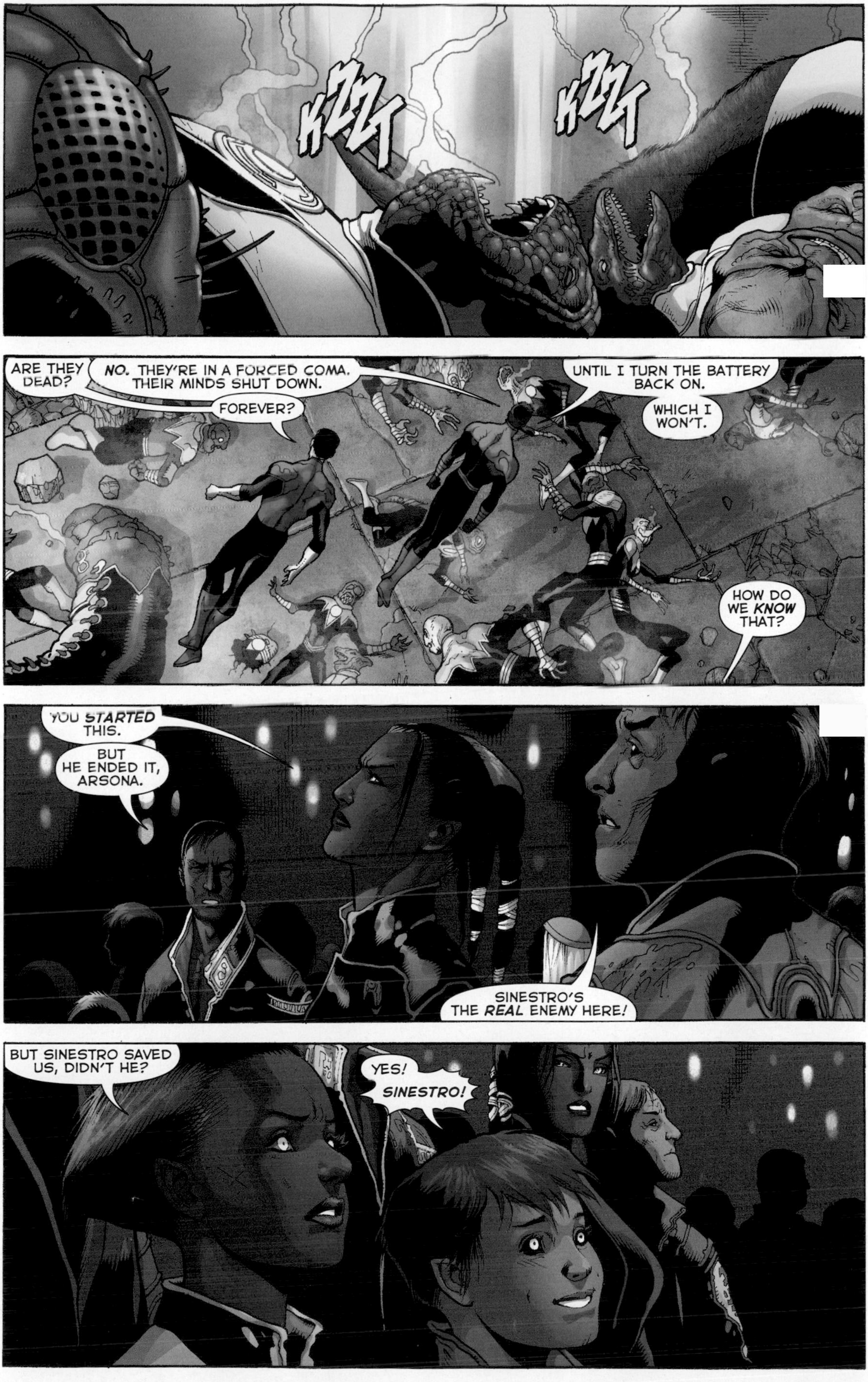
KZZZT
KZZZT
ARE THEY DEAD?
NO. THEY'RE IN A FORCED COMA. THEIR MINDS SHUT DOWN.
FOREVER?
UNTIL I TURN THE BATTERY BACK ON.
WHICH I WON'T.
HOW DO WE KNOW THAT?
YOU STARTED THIS.
BUT HE ENDED IT, ARSONA.
SINESTRO'S THE REAL ENEMY HERE!
BUT SINESTRO SAVED US, DIDN'T HE?
YES! SINESTRO!

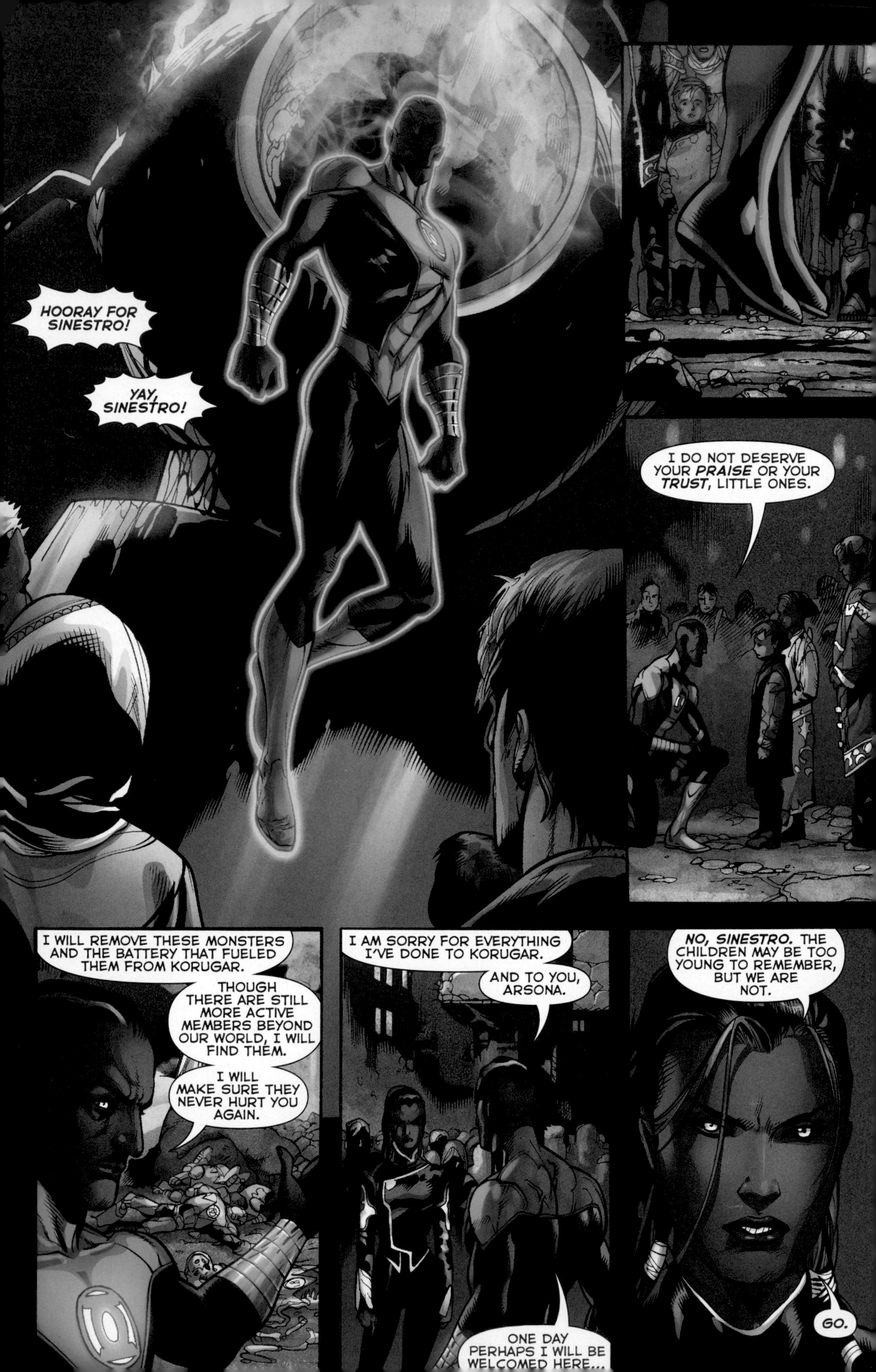
HOORAY FOR SINESTRO!
YAY, SINESTRO!
I DO NOT DESERVE YOUR *PRAISE* OR YOUR *TRUST*, LITTLE ONES.
I WILL REMOVE THESE MONSTERS AND THE BATTERY THAT FUELED THEM FROM KORUGAR.
THOUGH THERE ARE STILL MORE ACTIVE MEMBERS BEYOND OUR WORLD, I WILL FIND THEM.
I WILL MAKE SURE THEY NEVER HURT YOU AGAIN.
I AM SORRY FOR EVERYTHING I'VE DONE TO KORUGAR.
AND TO YOU, ARSONA.
ONE DAY PERHAPS I WILL BE WELCOMED HERE...
NO, SINESTRO. THE CHILDREN MAY BE TOO YOUNG TO REMEMBER, BUT WE ARE NOT.
GO.

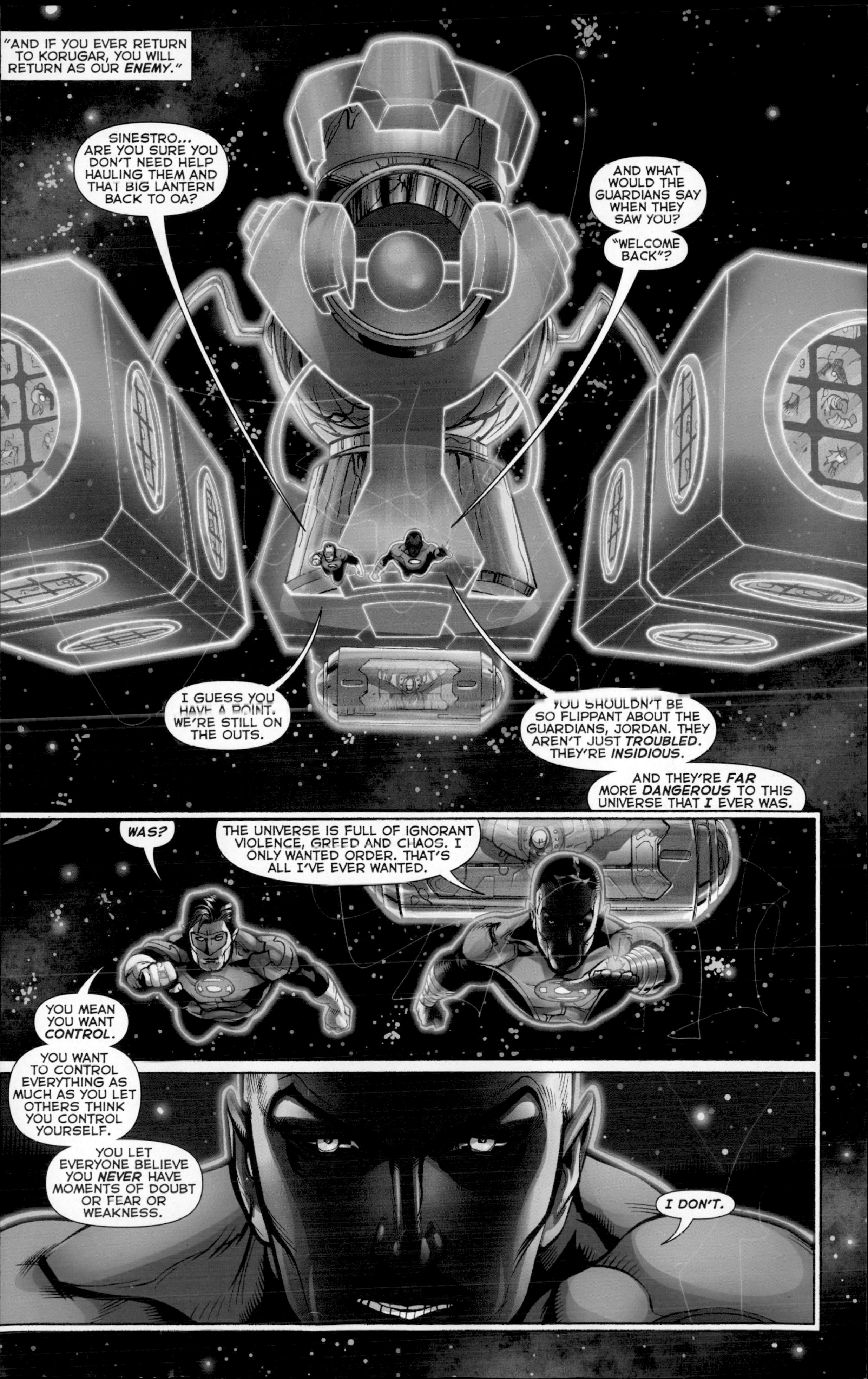
"AND IF YOU EVER RETURN TO KORUGAR, YOU WILL RETURN AS OUR *ENEMY*."
SINESTRO... ARE YOU SURE YOU DON'T NEED HELP HAULING THEM AND THAT BIG LANTERN BACK TO OA?
AND WHAT WOULD THE GUARDIANS SAY WHEN THEY SAW YOU?
"WELCOME BACK"?
I GUESS YOU HAVE A POINT. WE'RE STILL ON THE OUTS.
YOU SHOULDN'T BE SO FLIPPANT ABOUT THE GUARDIANS, JORDAN. THEY AREN'T JUST *TROUBLED*. THEY'RE *INSIDIOUS*.
AND THEY'RE *FAR* MORE *DANGEROUS* TO THIS UNIVERSE THAT *I* EVER WAS.
WAS?
THE UNIVERSE IS FULL OF IGNORANT VIOLENCE, GREED AND CHAOS. I ONLY WANTED ORDER. THAT'S ALL I'VE EVER WANTED.
YOU MEAN YOU WANT *CONTROL*.
YOU WANT TO CONTROL EVERYTHING AS MUCH AS YOU LET OTHERS THINK YOU CONTROL YOURSELF.
YOU LET EVERYONE BELIEVE YOU *NEVER* HAVE MOMENTS OF DOUBT OR FEAR OR WEAKNESS.
I DON'T.

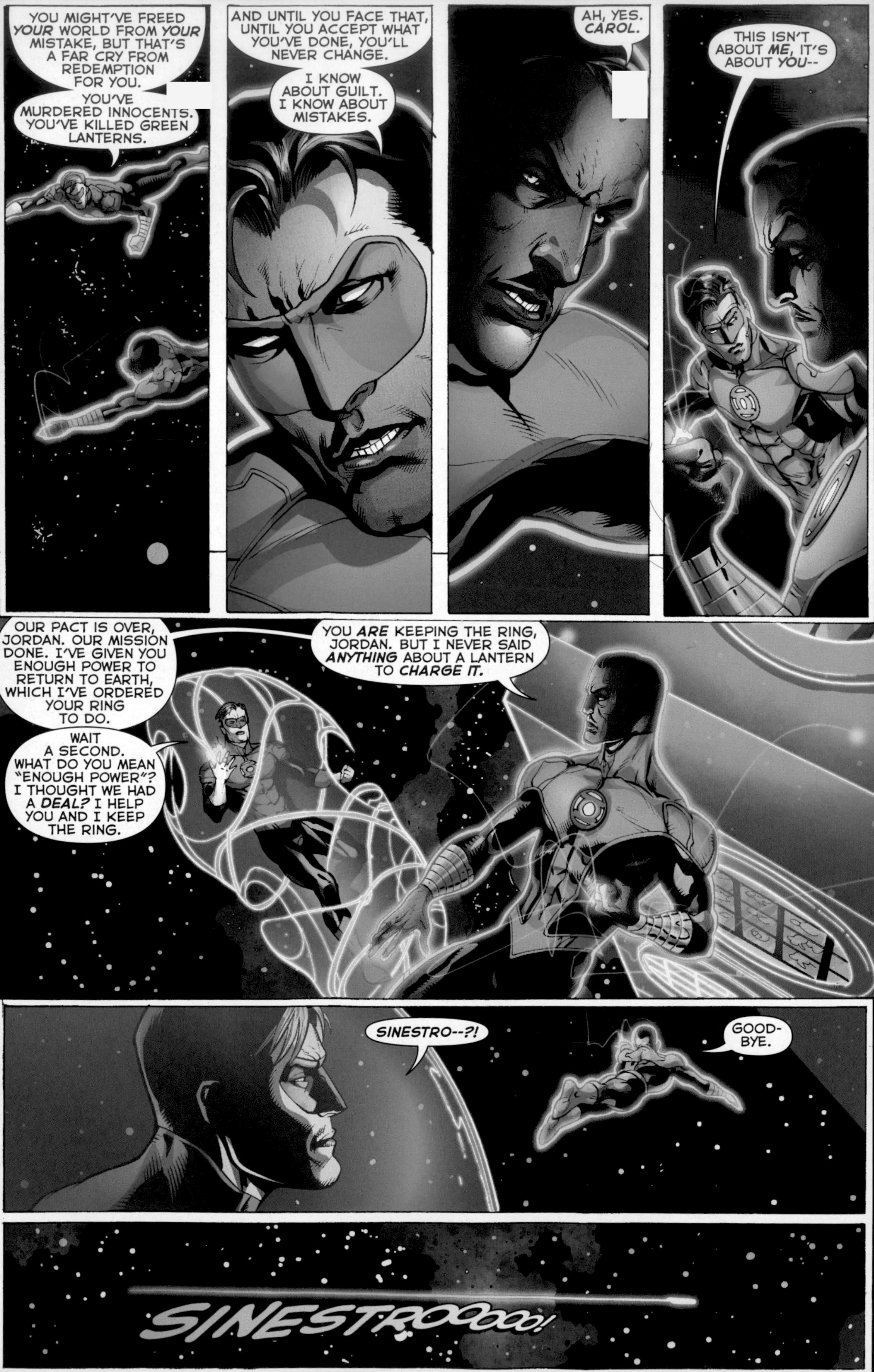

YOU MIGHT'VE FREED *YOUR* WORLD FROM *YOUR* MISTAKE, BUT THAT'S A FAR CRY FROM REDEMPTION FOR YOU.
YOU'VE MURDERED INNOCENTS. YOU'VE KILLED GREEN LANTERNS.
AND UNTIL YOU FACE THAT, UNTIL YOU ACCEPT WHAT YOU'VE DONE, YOU'LL NEVER CHANGE.
I KNOW ABOUT GUILT. I KNOW ABOUT MISTAKES.
AH, YES. *CAROL.*
THIS ISN'T ABOUT *ME*, IT'S ABOUT *YOU*--
OUR PACT IS OVER, JORDAN. OUR MISSION DONE. I'VE GIVEN YOU ENOUGH POWER TO RETURN TO EARTH, WHICH I'VE ORDERED YOUR RING TO DO.
WAIT A SECOND. WHAT DO YOU MEAN "ENOUGH POWER"? I THOUGHT WE HAD A *DEAL?* I HELP YOU AND I KEEP THE RING.
YOU *ARE* KEEPING THE RING, JORDAN. BUT I NEVER SAID *ANYTHING* ABOUT A LANTERN TO *CHARGE IT.*
SINESTRO--?!
GOOD-BYE.
SINESTROOooo!

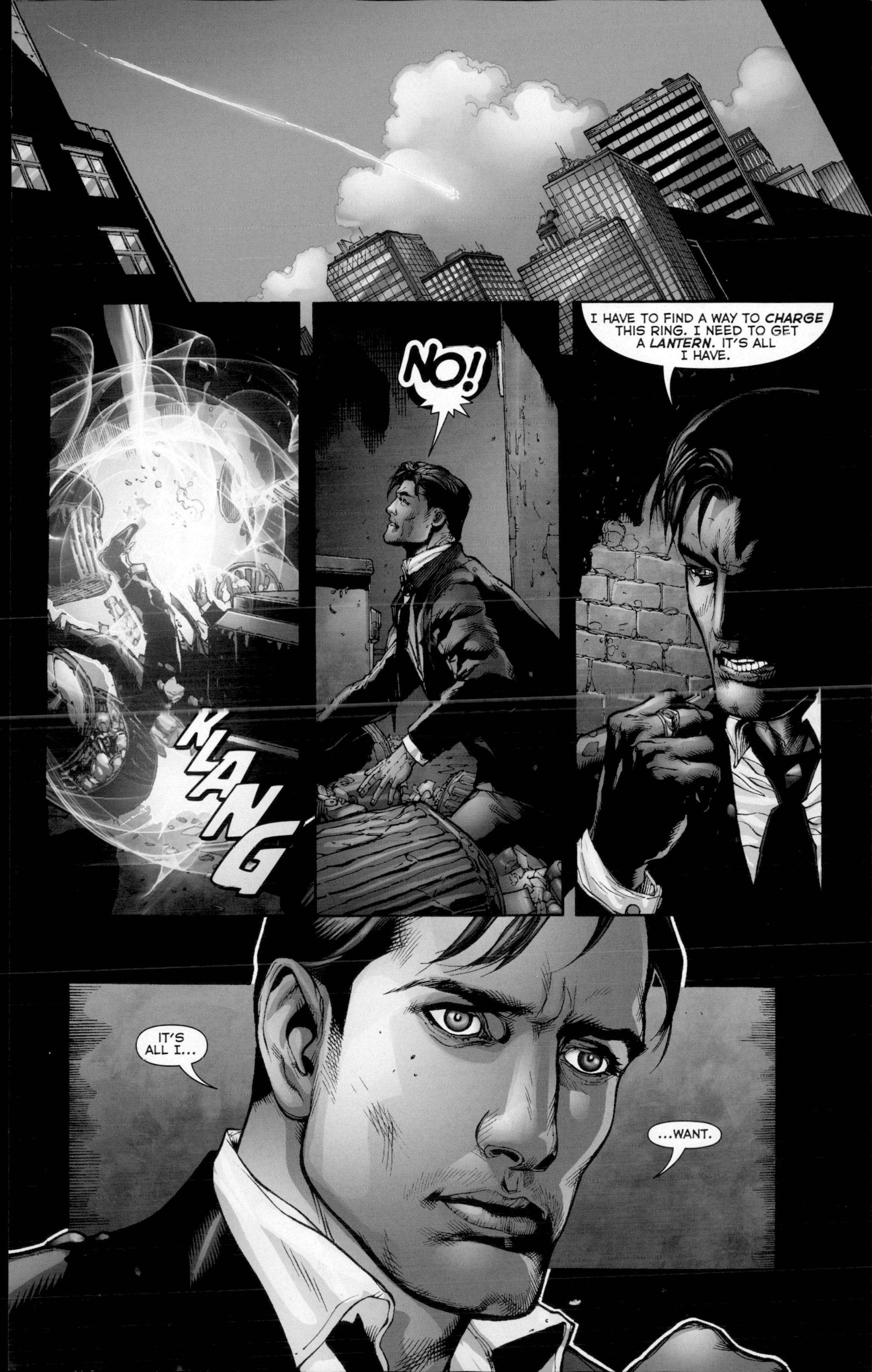
KLANG
NO!
I HAVE TO FIND A WAY TO CHARGE THIS RING. I NEED TO GET A LANTERN. IT'S ALL I HAVE.
IT'S ALL I...
...WANT.

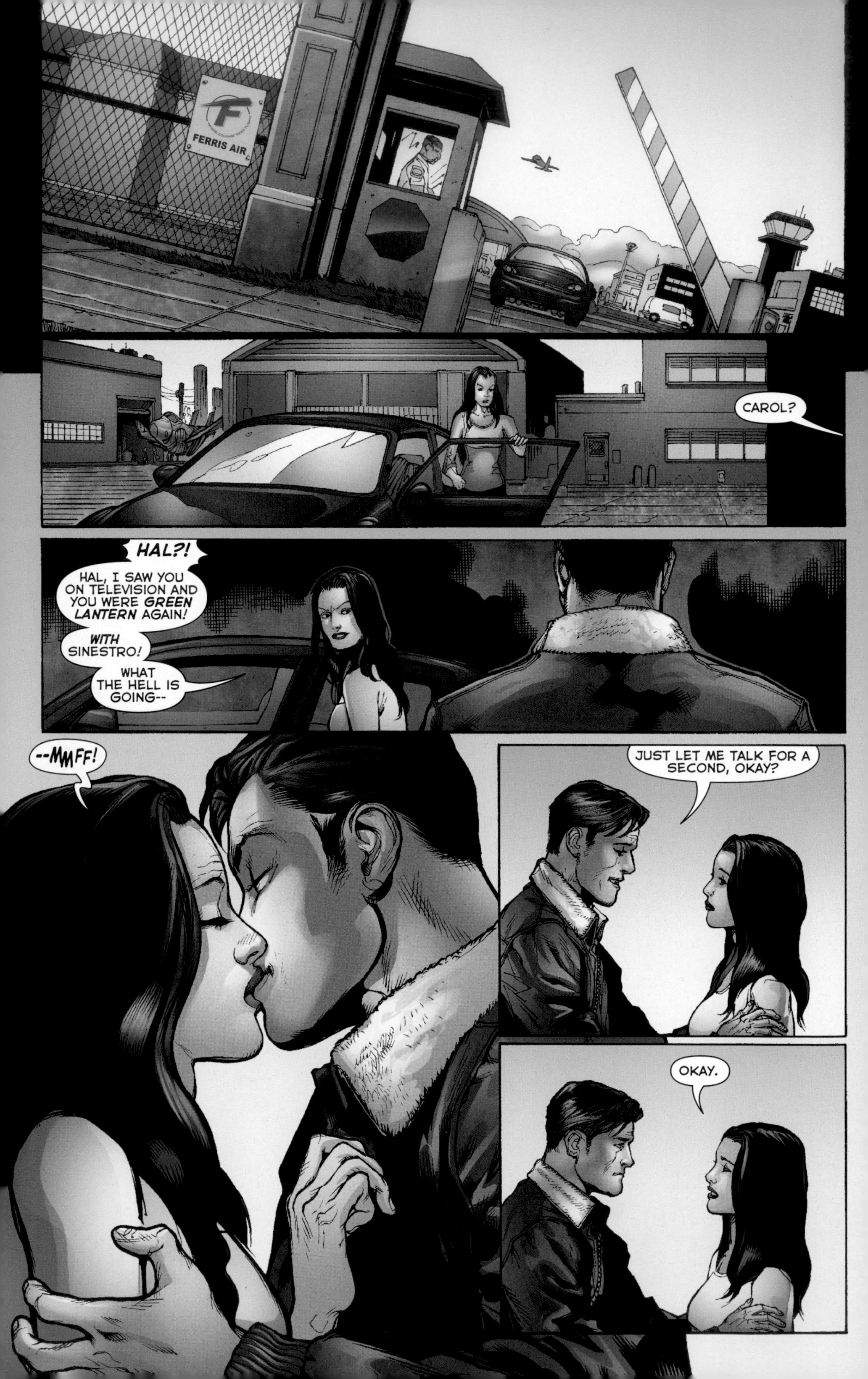
FERRIS AIR
CAROL?
HAL?!
HAL, I SAW YOU ON TELEVISION AND YOU WERE GREEN LANTERN AGAIN!
WITH SINESTRO!
WHAT THE HELL IS GOING--
--MMFF!
JUST LET ME TALK FOR A SECOND, OKAY?
OKAY.

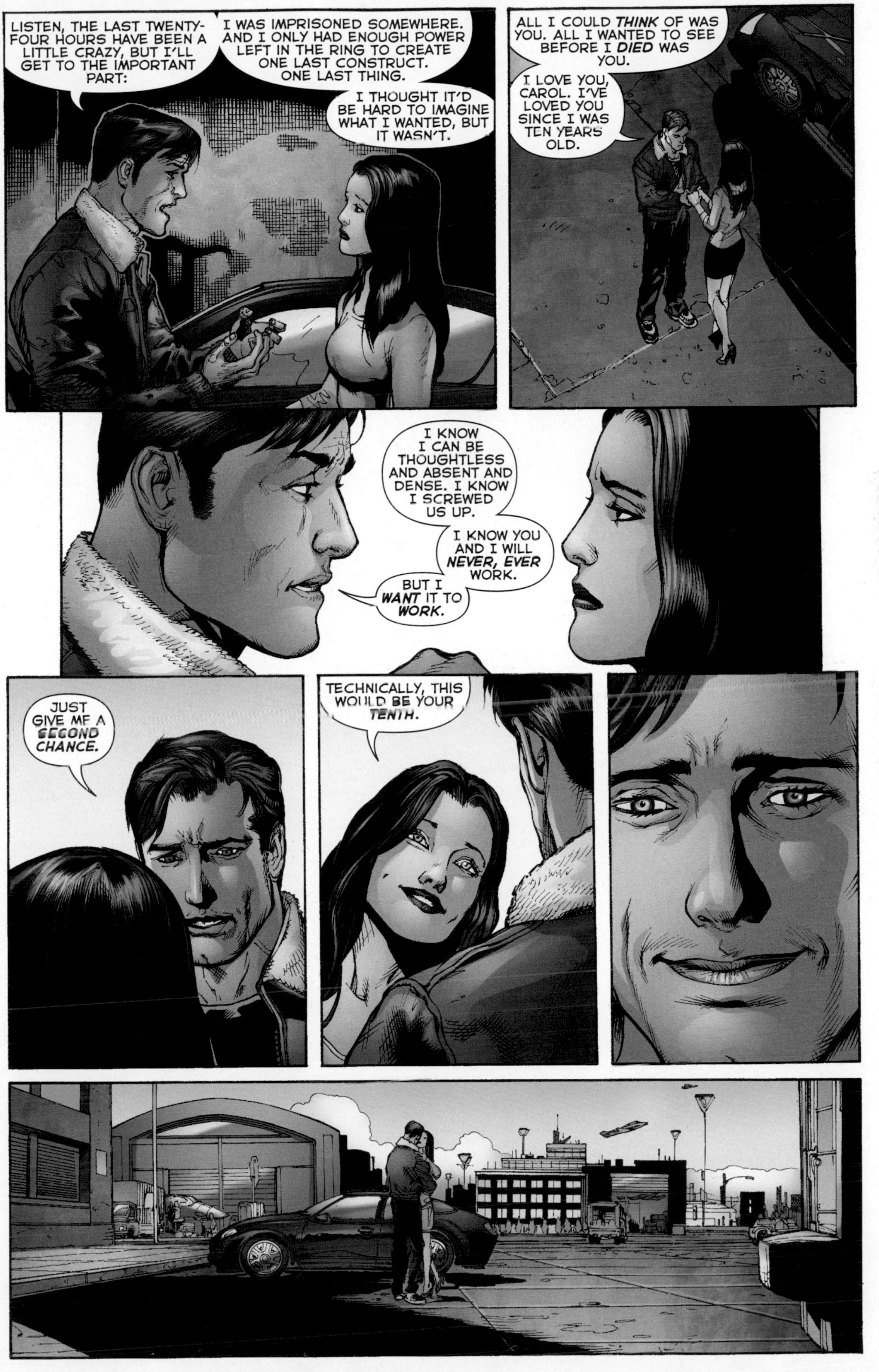
LISTEN, THE LAST TWENTY-FOUR HOURS HAVE BEEN A LITTLE CRAZY, BUT I'LL GET TO THE IMPORTANT PART:
I WAS IMPRISONED SOMEWHERE. AND I ONLY HAD ENOUGH POWER LEFT IN THE RING TO CREATE ONE LAST CONSTRUCT. ONE LAST THING.
I THOUGHT IT'D BE HARD TO IMAGINE WHAT I WANTED, BUT IT WASN'T.
ALL I COULD THINK OF WAS YOU. ALL I WANTED TO SEE BEFORE I DIED WAS YOU.
I LOVE YOU, CAROL. I'VE LOVED YOU SINCE I WAS TEN YEARS OLD.
I KNOW I CAN BE THOUGHTLESS AND ABSENT AND DENSE. I KNOW I SCREWED US UP.
I KNOW YOU AND I WILL NEVER, EVER WORK.
BUT I WANT IT TO WORK.
JUST GIVE ME A SECOND CHANCE.
TECHNICALLY, THIS WOULD BE YOUR TENTH.

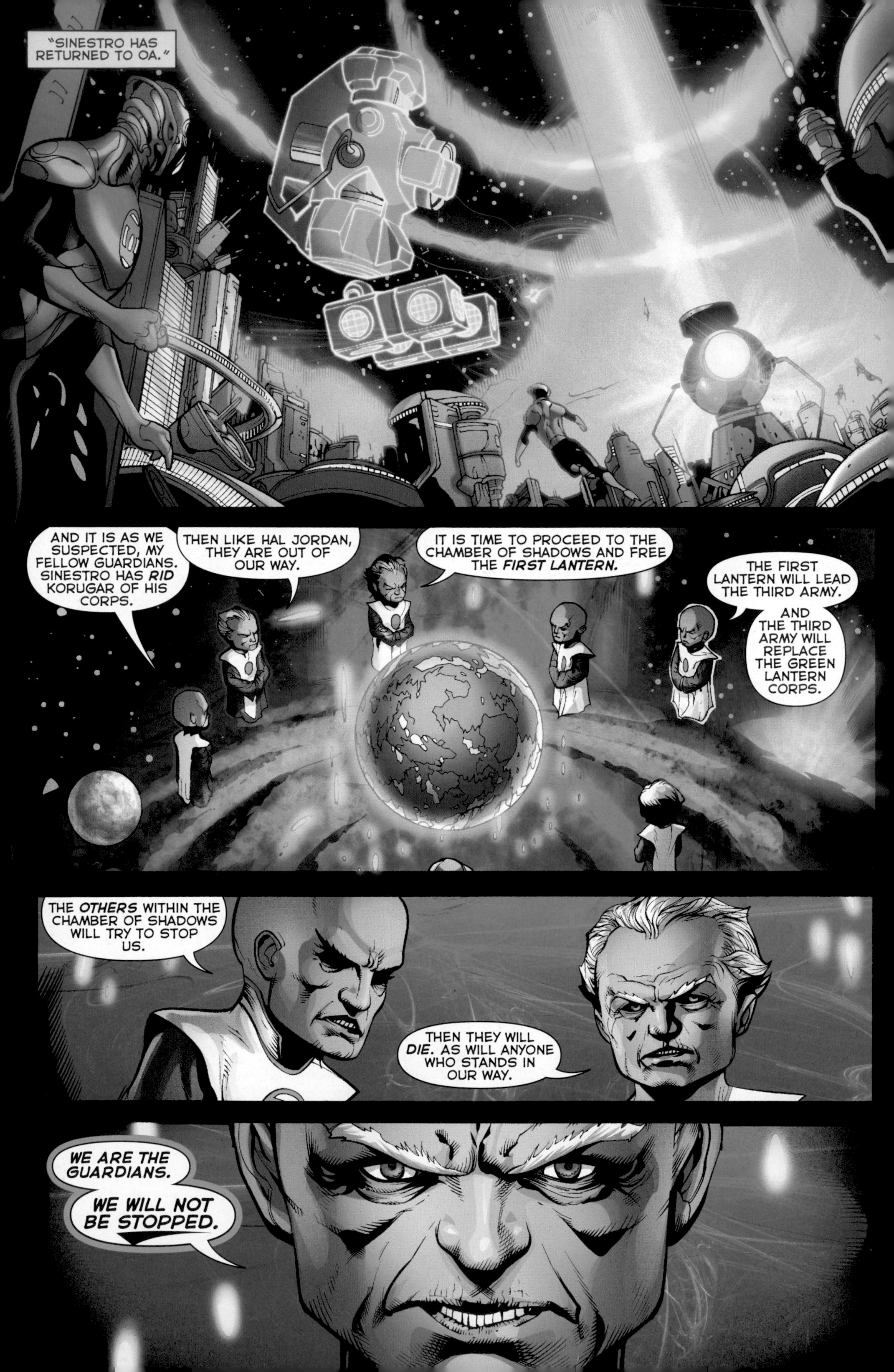
"SINESTRO HAS RETURNED TO OA."
AND IT IS AS WE SUSPECTED, MY FELLOW GUARDIANS. SINESTRO HAS RID KORUGAR OF HIS CORPS.
THEN LIKE HAL JORDAN, THEY ARE OUT OF OUR WAY.
IT IS TIME TO PROCEED TO THE CHAMBER OF SHADOWS AND FREE THE FIRST LANTERN.
THE FIRST LANTERN WILL LEAD THE THIRD ARMY.
AND THE THIRD ARMY WILL REPLACE THE GREEN LANTERN CORPS.
THE OTHERS WITHIN THE CHAMBER OF SHADOWS WILL TRY TO STOP US.
THEN THEY WILL DIE. AS WILL ANYONE WHO STANDS IN OUR WAY.
WE ARE THE GUARDIANS.
WE WILL NOT BE STOPPED.

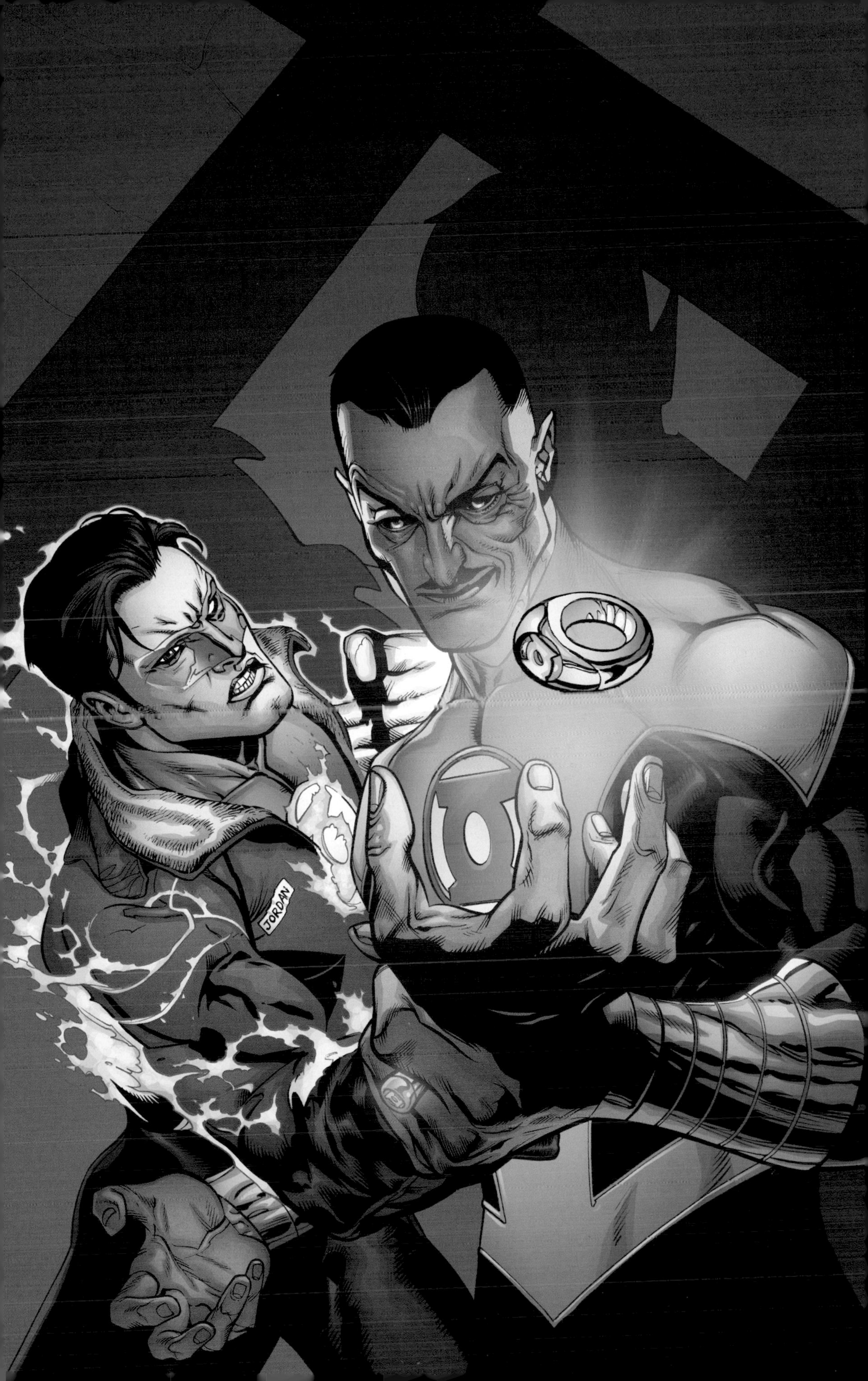
JORDAN

Doug Mahnke, Keith Champagne & David Baron

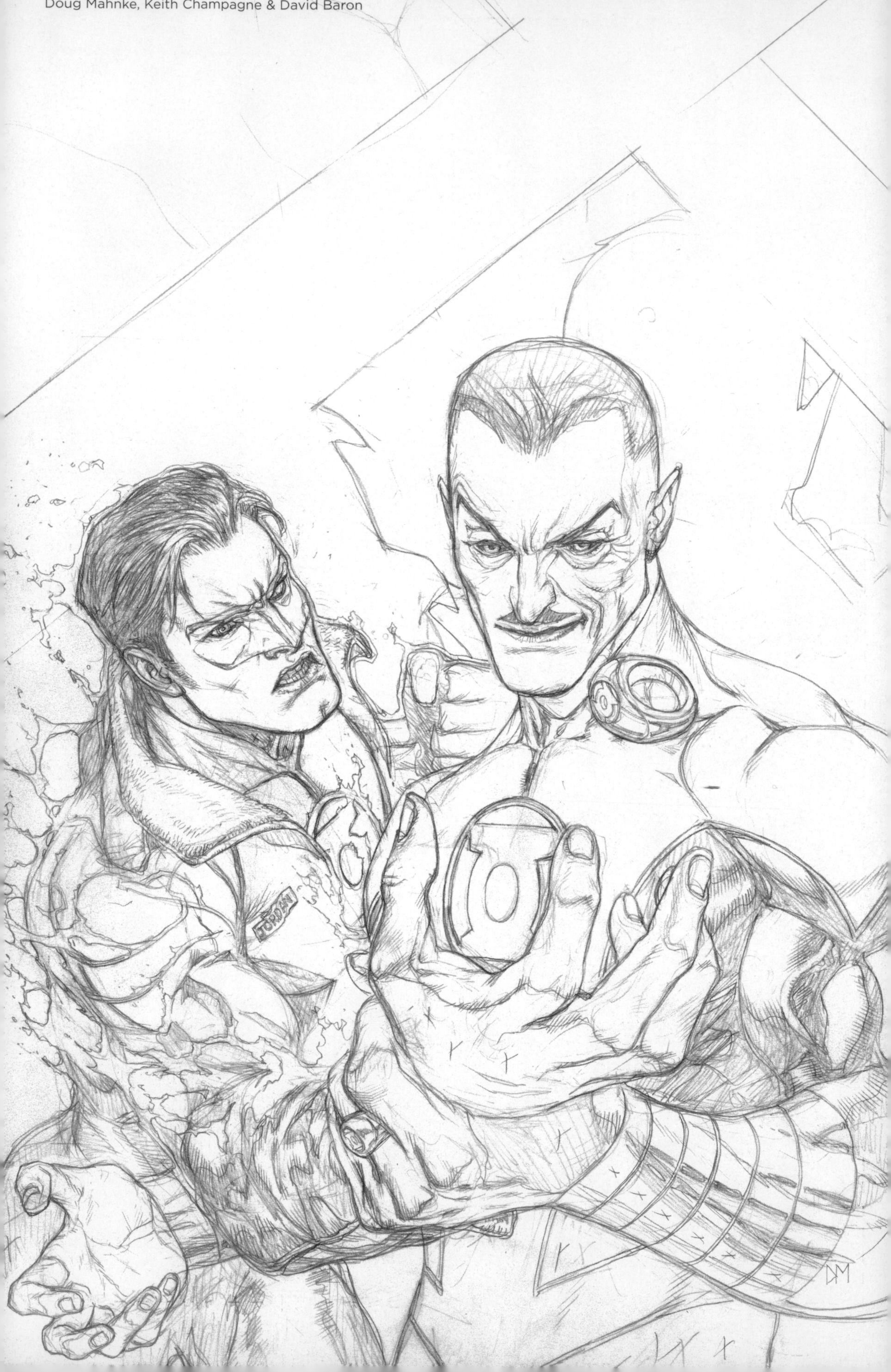

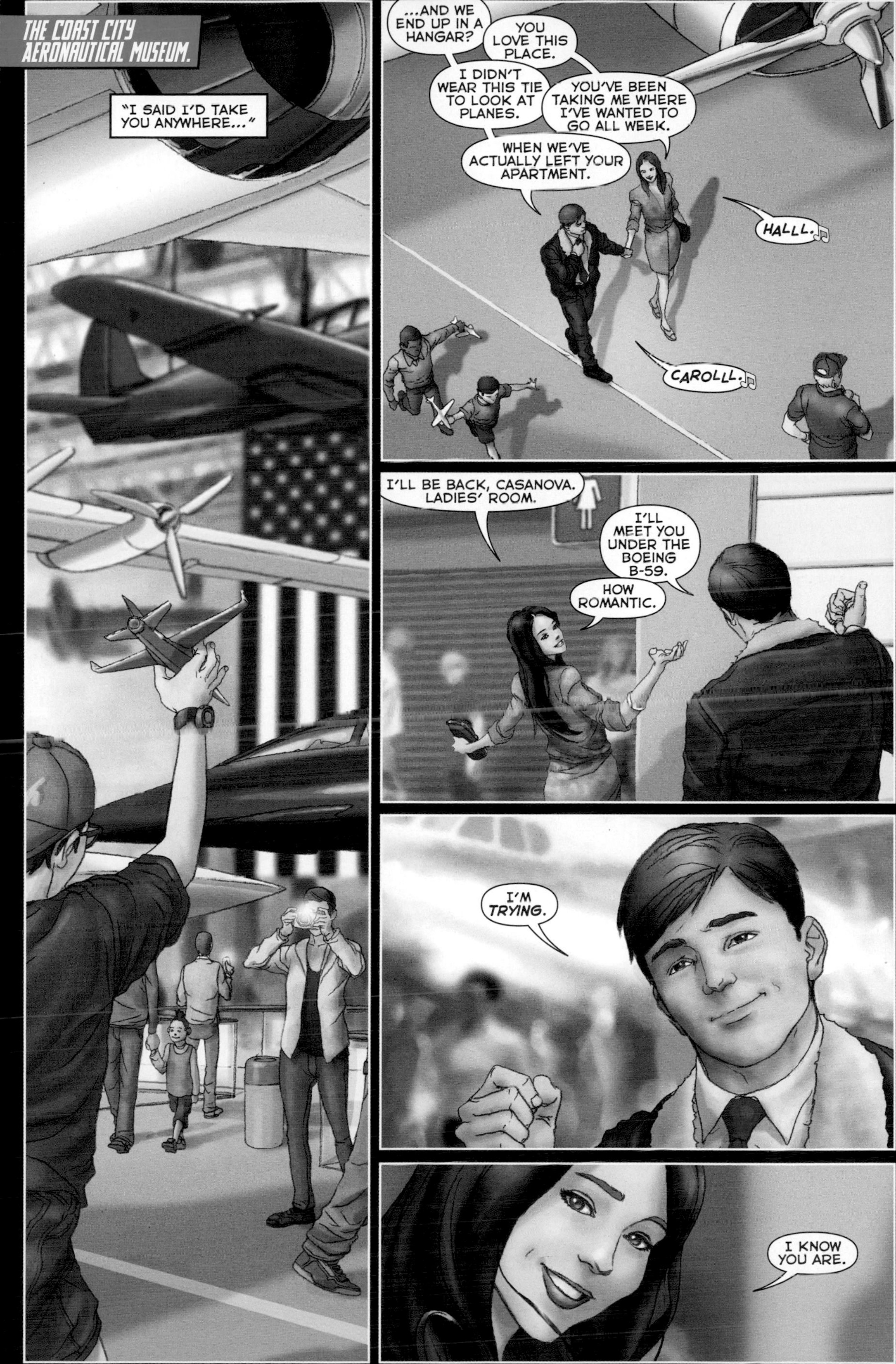

THE COAST CITY AERONAUTICAL MUSEUM.
"I SAID I'D TAKE YOU ANYWHERE..."
...AND WE END UP IN A HANGAR?
YOU LOVE THIS PLACE.
I DIDN'T WEAR THIS TIE TO LOOK AT PLANES.
YOU'VE BEEN TAKING ME WHERE I'VE WANTED TO GO ALL WEEK.
WHEN WE'VE ACTUALLY LEFT YOUR APARTMENT.
HALLL.♫
CAROLLL.♫
I'LL BE BACK, CASANOVA. LADIES' ROOM.
I'LL MEET YOU UNDER THE BOEING B-59.
HOW ROMANTIC.
I'M TRYING.
I KNOW YOU ARE.

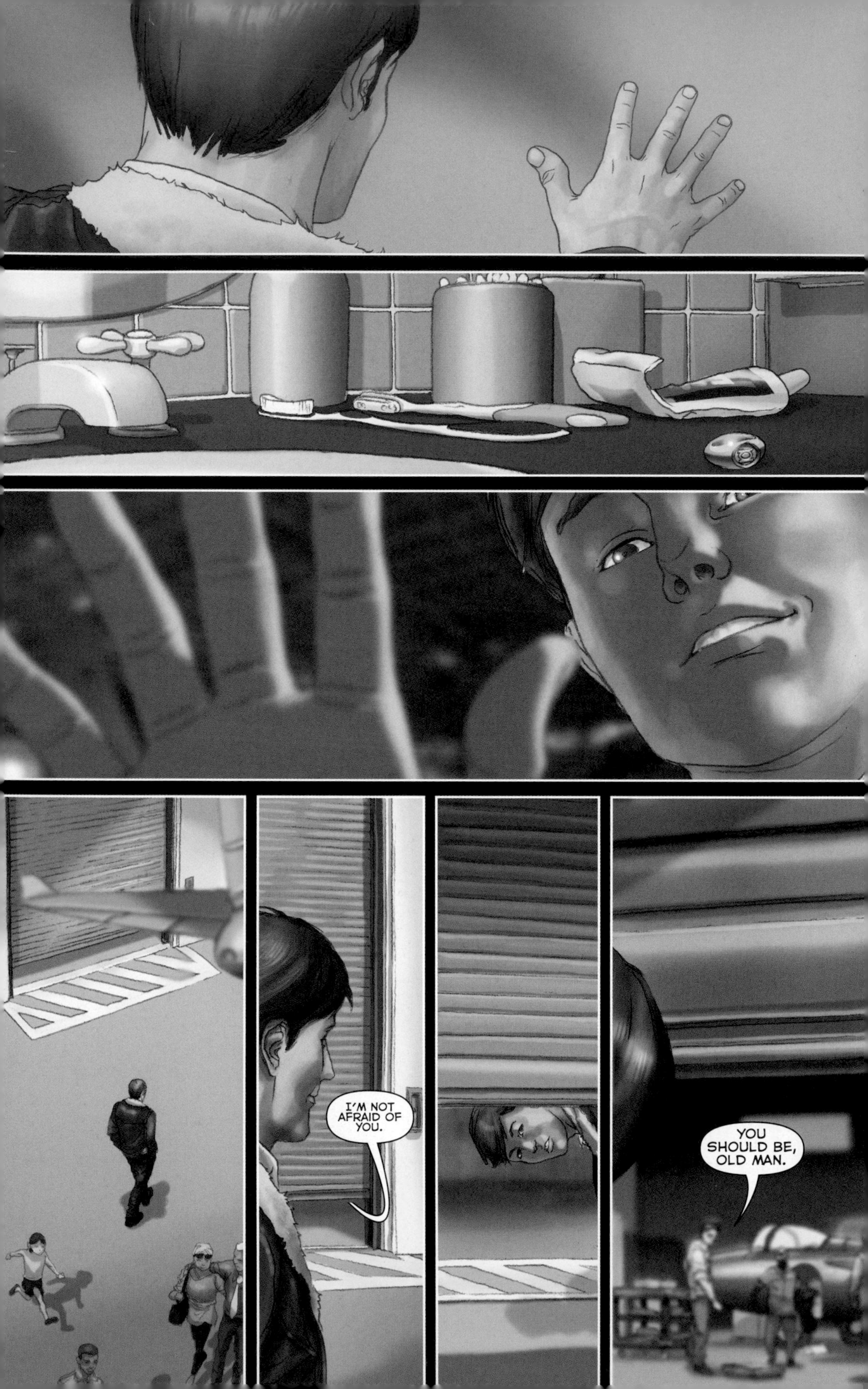
I'M NOT AFRAID OF YOU.
YOU SHOULD BE, OLD MAN.

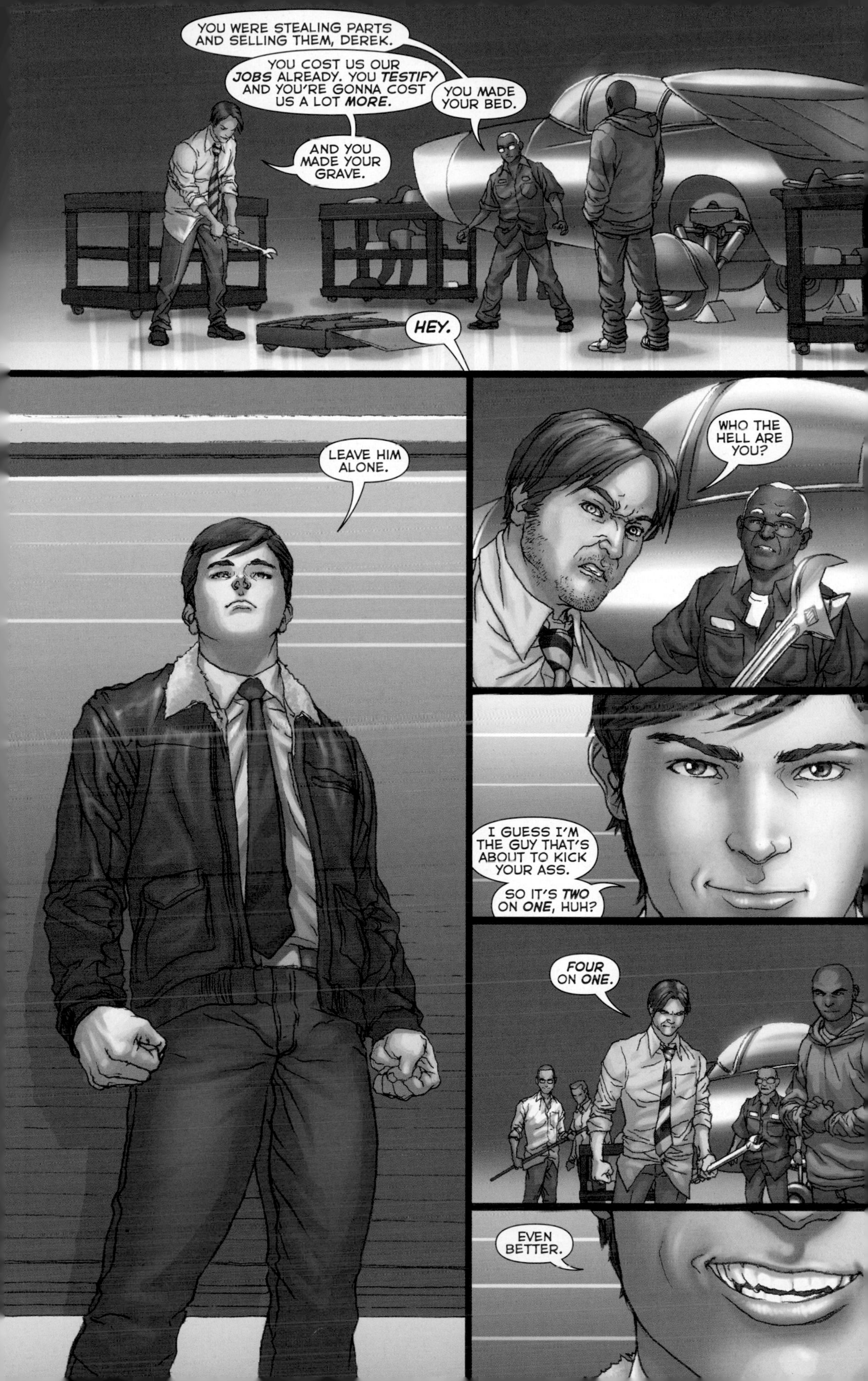
YOU WERE STEALING PARTS AND SELLING THEM, DEREK.
YOU COST US OUR JOBS ALREADY. YOU TESTIFY AND YOU'RE GONNA COST US A LOT MORE.
YOU MADE YOUR BED.
AND YOU MADE YOUR GRAVE.
HEY.
LEAVE HIM ALONE.
WHO THE HELL ARE YOU?
I GUESS I'M THE GUY THAT'S ABOUT TO KICK YOUR ASS.
SO IT'S TWO ON ONE, HUH?
FOUR ON ONE.
EVEN BETTER.

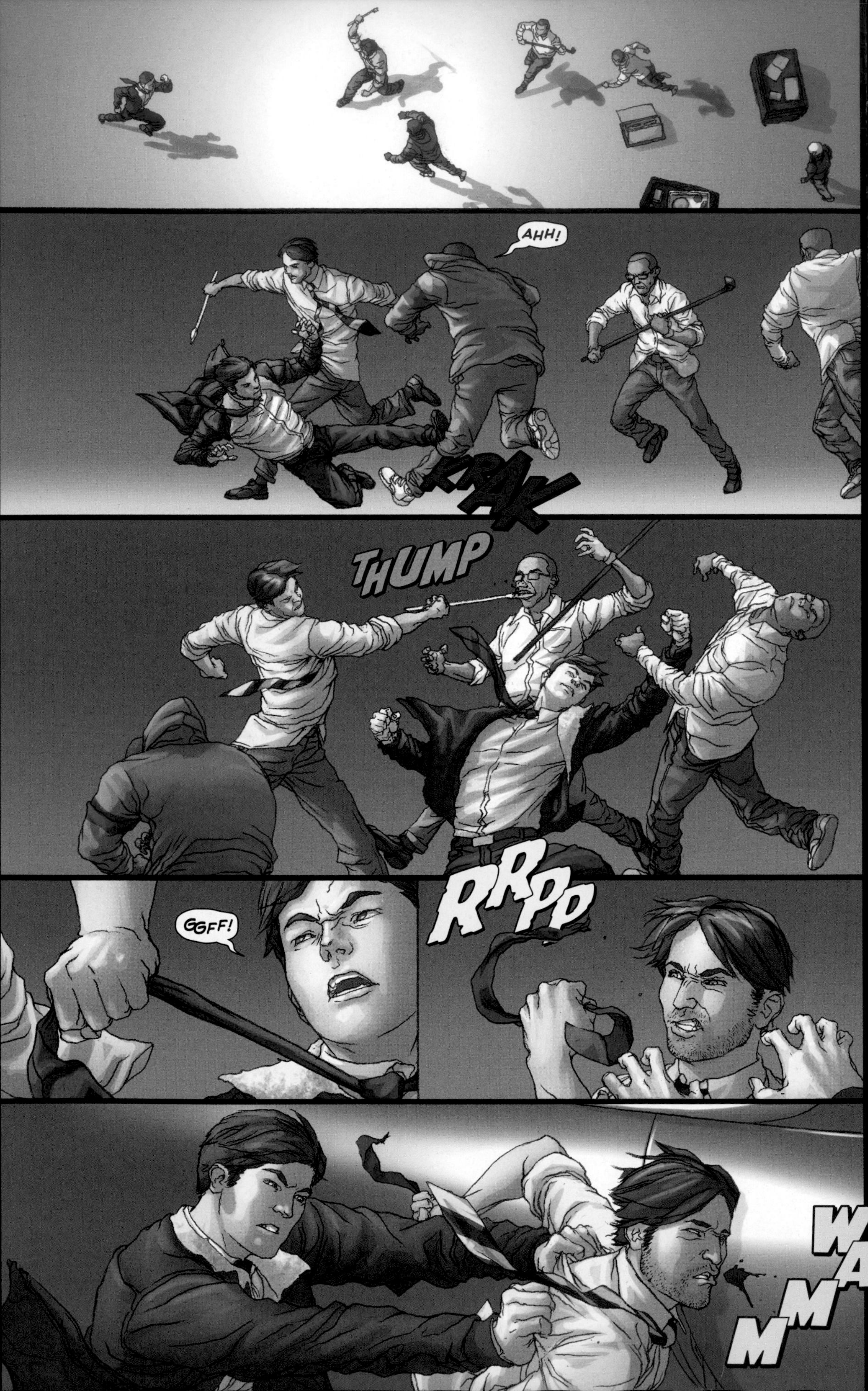
AHH!
KRAK
THUMP
GGFF!
RRPD
WAMMM

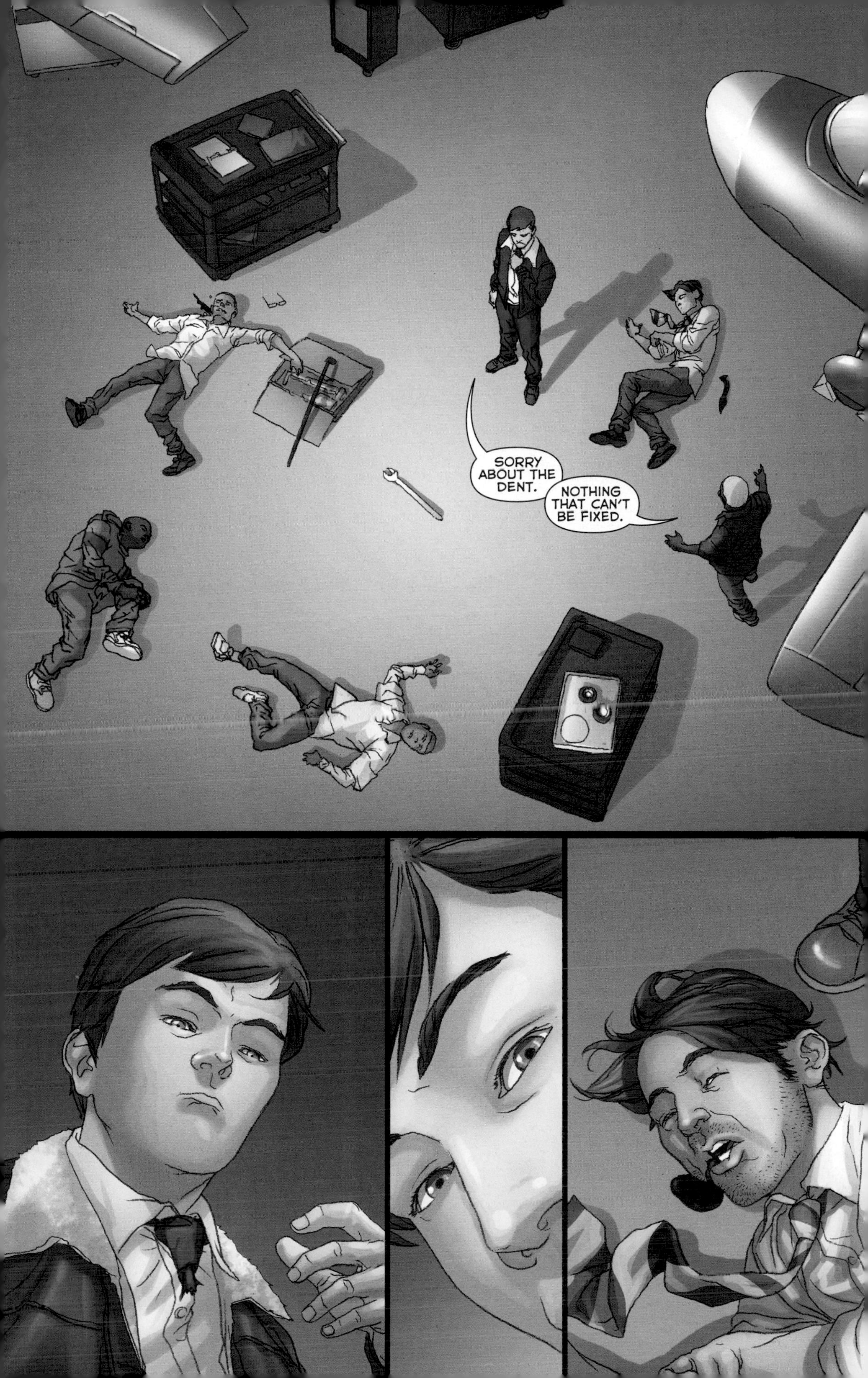
SORRY ABOUT THE DENT.
NOTHING THAT CAN'T BE FIXED.

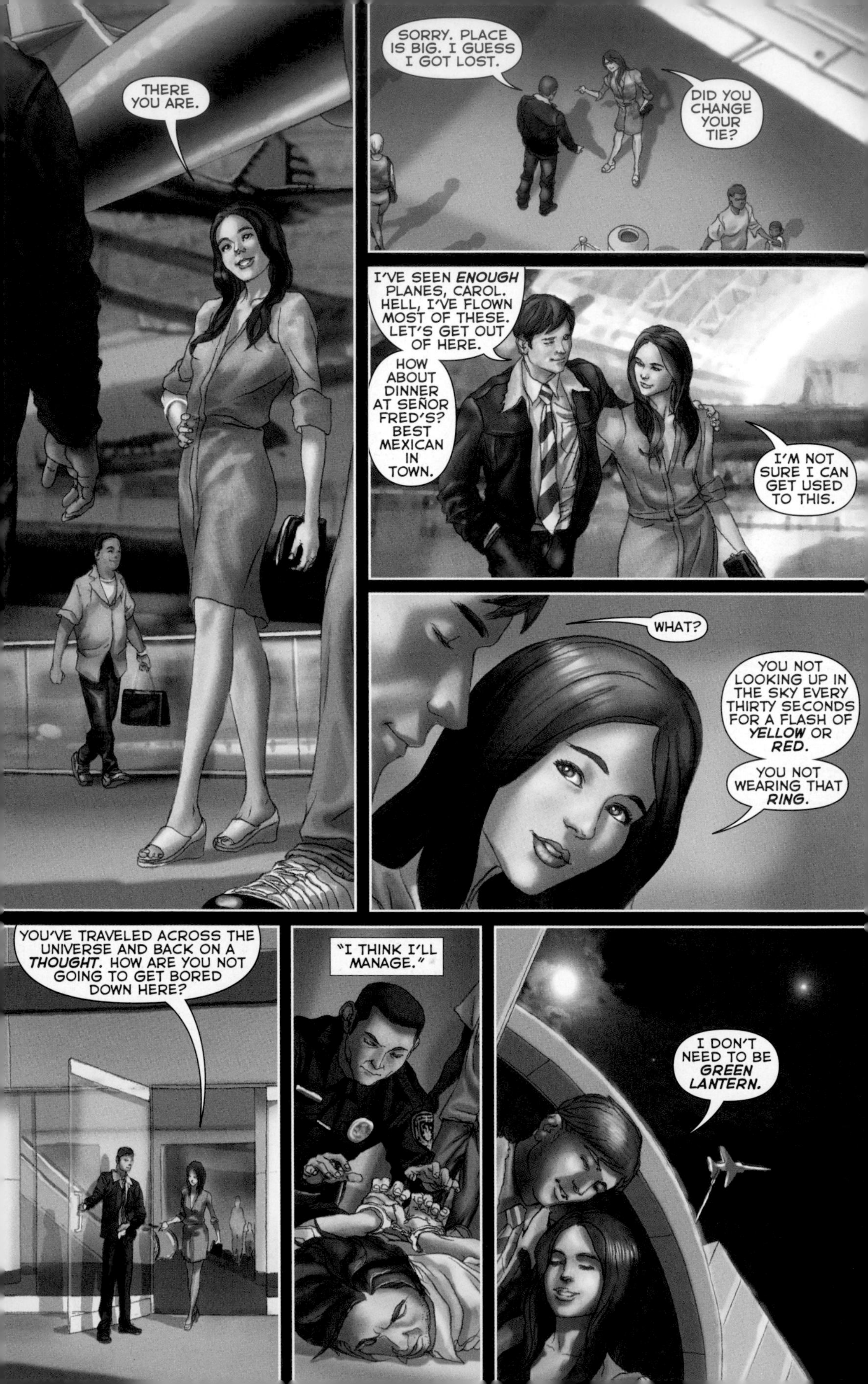
THERE YOU ARE.
SORRY. PLACE IS BIG. I GUESS I GOT LOST.
DID YOU CHANGE YOUR TIE?
I'VE SEEN ENOUGH PLANES, CAROL. HELL, I'VE FLOWN MOST OF THESE. LET'S GET OUT OF HERE.
HOW ABOUT DINNER AT SEÑOR FRED'S? BEST MEXICAN IN TOWN.
I'M NOT SURE I CAN GET USED TO THIS.
WHAT?
YOU NOT LOOKING UP IN THE SKY EVERY THIRTY SECONDS FOR A FLASH OF YELLOW OR RED.
YOU NOT WEARING THAT RING.
YOU'VE TRAVELED ACROSS THE UNIVERSE AND BACK ON A THOUGHT. HOW ARE YOU NOT GOING TO GET BORED DOWN HERE?
"I THINK I'LL MANAGE."
I DON'T NEED TO BE GREEN LANTERN.

"I DON'T NEED TO BE SOME KIND OF 'SUPER HERO' ANYMORE."

SPACE SECTOR 1417. THE PLANET OGORO.

EEEK EEEK EEEK

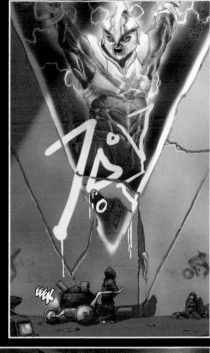

EEEK

EEEK EEEK

WHAT HAPPENED TO YOU?

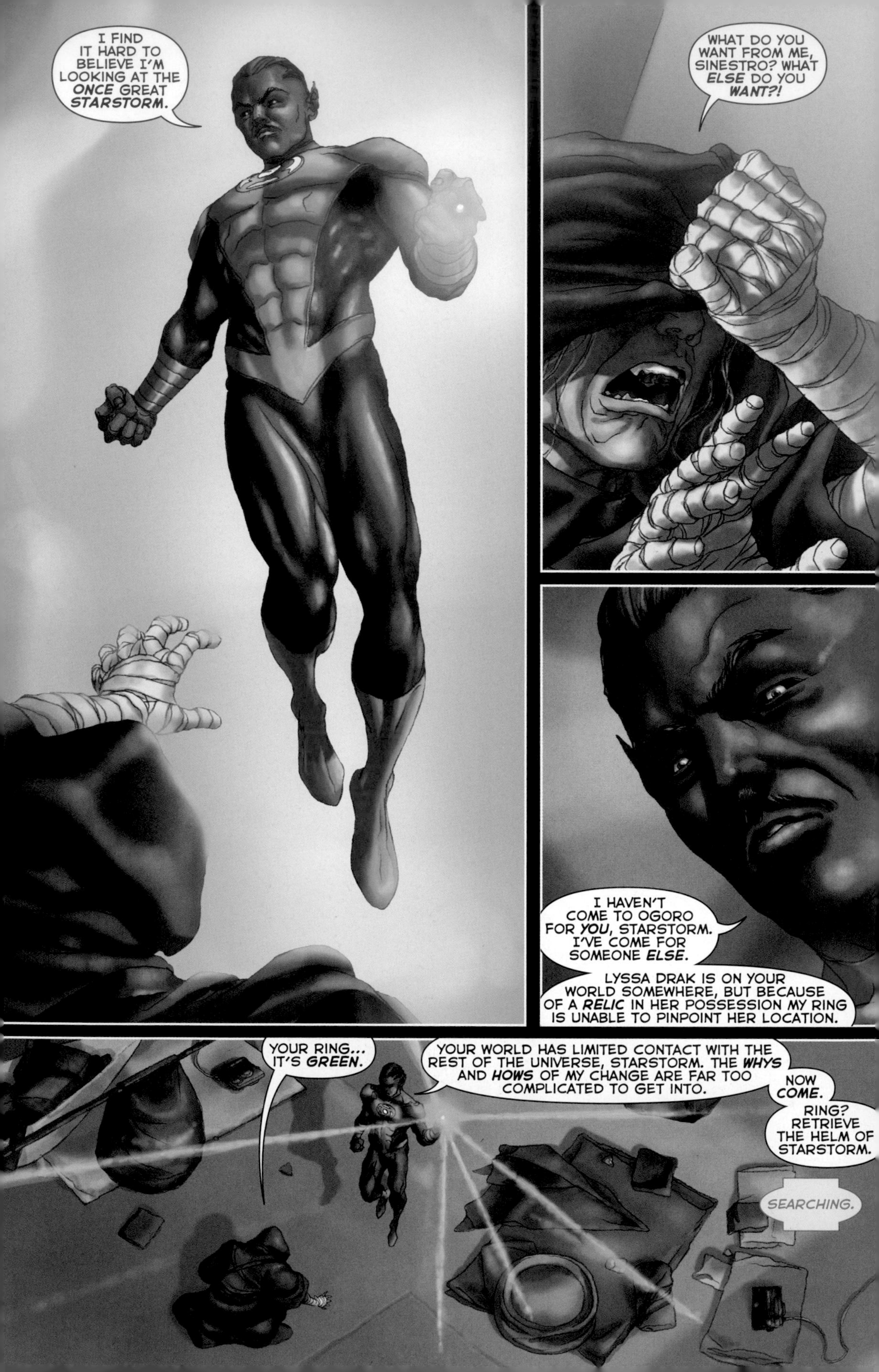
I FIND IT HARD TO BELIEVE I'M LOOKING AT THE ONCE GREAT STARSTORM.
WHAT DO YOU WANT FROM ME, SINESTRO? WHAT ELSE DO YOU WANT?!
I HAVEN'T COME TO OGORO FOR YOU, STARSTORM. I'VE COME FOR SOMEONE ELSE.
LYSSA DRAK IS ON YOUR WORLD SOMEWHERE, BUT BECAUSE OF A RELIC IN HER POSSESSION MY RING IS UNABLE TO PINPOINT HER LOCATION.
YOUR RING... IT'S GREEN.
YOUR WORLD HAS LIMITED CONTACT WITH THE REST OF THE UNIVERSE, STARSTORM. THE WHYS AND HOWS OF MY CHANGE ARE FAR TOO COMPLICATED TO GET INTO.
NOW COME.
RING? RETRIEVE THE HELM OF STARSTORM.
SEARCHING.

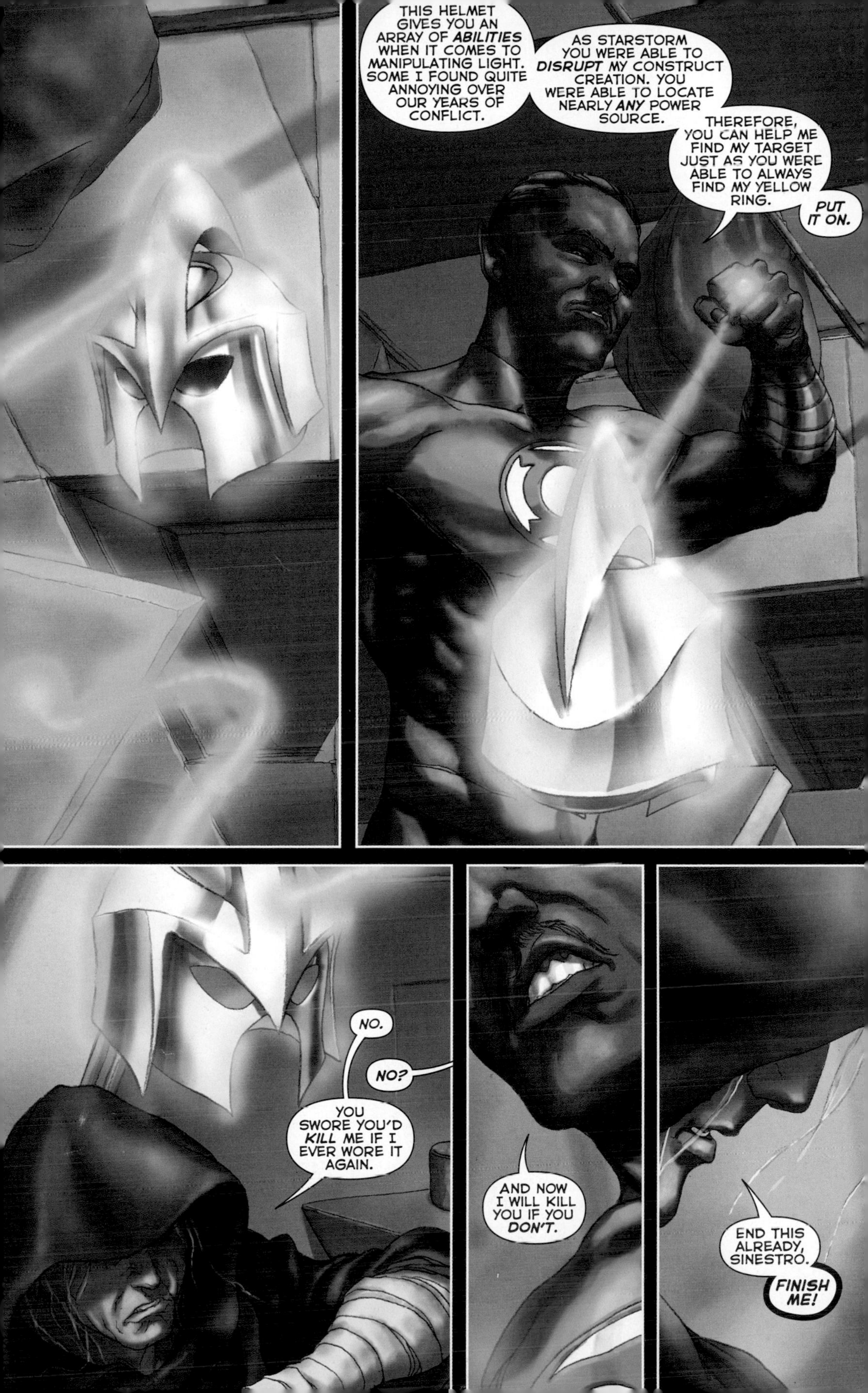
THIS HELMET GIVES YOU AN ARRAY OF ABILITIES WHEN IT COMES TO MANIPULATING LIGHT. SOME I FOUND QUITE ANNOYING OVER OUR YEARS OF CONFLICT.
AS STARSTORM YOU WERE ABLE TO DISRUPT MY CONSTRUCT CREATION. YOU WERE ABLE TO LOCATE NEARLY ANY POWER SOURCE.
THEREFORE, YOU CAN HELP ME FIND MY TARGET JUST AS YOU WERE ABLE TO ALWAYS FIND MY YELLOW RING.
PUT IT ON.
NO.
NO?
YOU SWORE YOU'D KILL ME IF I EVER WORE IT AGAIN.
AND NOW I WILL KILL YOU IF YOU DON'T.
END THIS ALREADY, SINESTRO.
FINISH ME!

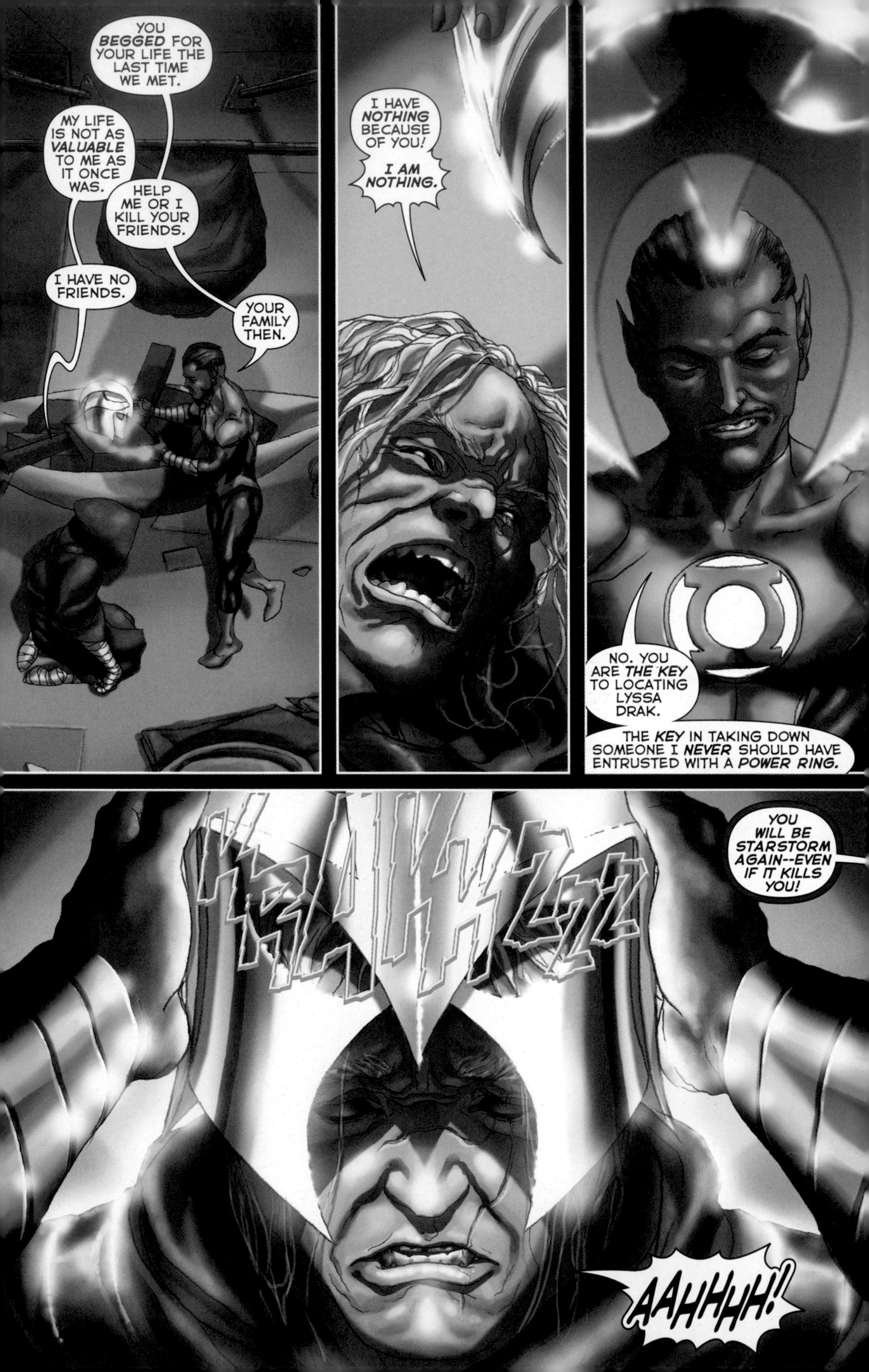
YOU BEGGED FOR YOUR LIFE THE LAST TIME WE MET.
MY LIFE IS NOT AS VALUABLE TO ME AS IT ONCE WAS.
HELP ME OR I KILL YOUR FRIENDS.
I HAVE NO FRIENDS.
YOUR FAMILY THEN.
I HAVE NOTHING BECAUSE OF YOU!
I AM NOTHING.
NO. YOU ARE THE KEY TO LOCATING LYSSA DRAK.
THE KEY IN TAKING DOWN SOMEONE I NEVER SHOULD HAVE ENTRUSTED WITH A POWER RING.
YOU WILL BE STARSTORM AGAIN--EVEN IF IT KILLS YOU!
AAHHHH!

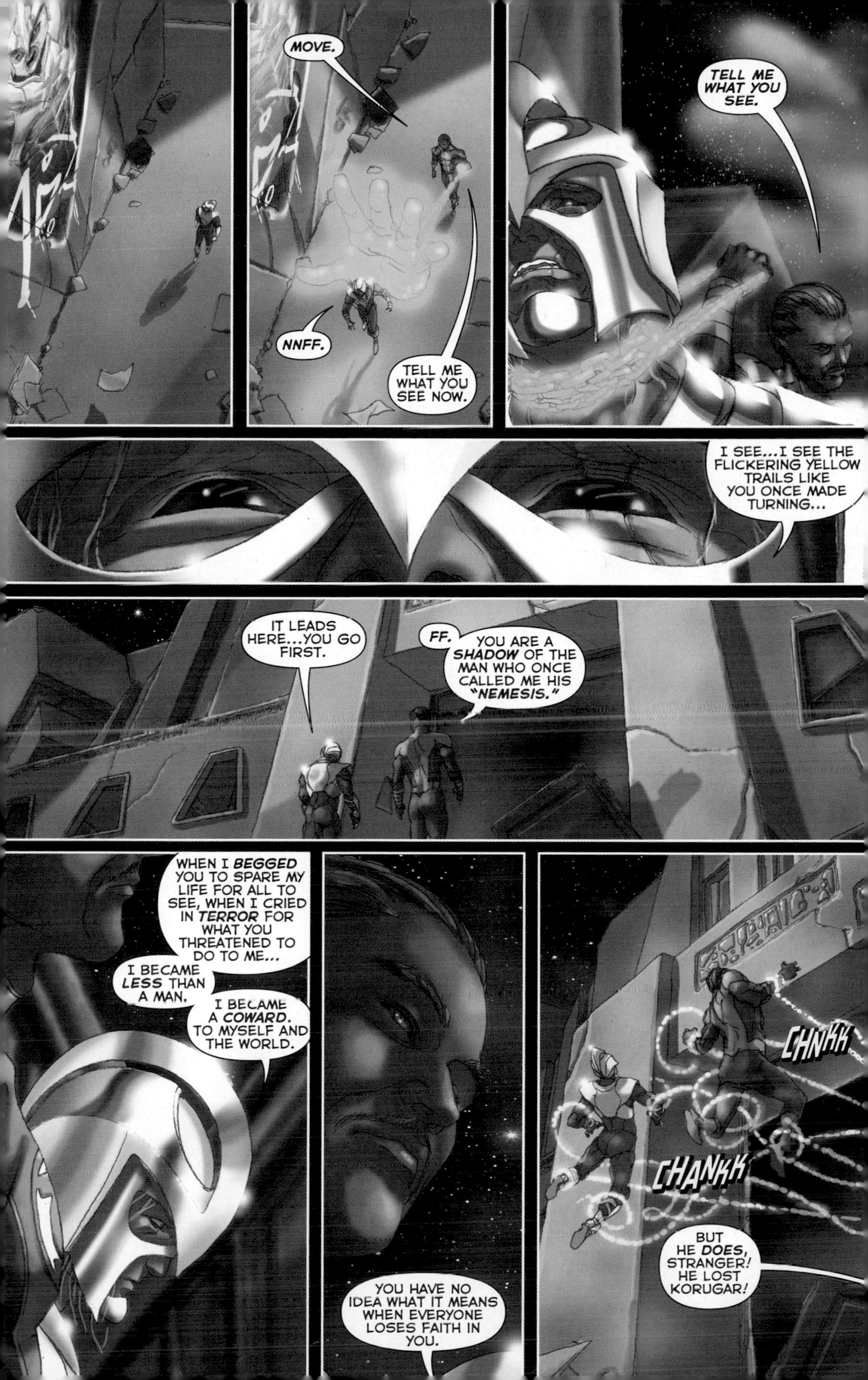
MOVE.
NNFF.
TELL ME WHAT YOU SEE NOW.
TELL ME WHAT YOU SEE.
I SEE...I SEE THE FLICKERING YELLOW TRAILS LIKE YOU ONCE MADE TURNING...
IT LEADS HERE...YOU GO FIRST.
FF.
YOU ARE A SHADOW OF THE MAN WHO ONCE CALLED ME HIS "NEMESIS."
WHEN I BEGGED YOU TO SPARE MY LIFE FOR ALL TO SEE, WHEN I CRIED IN TERROR FOR WHAT YOU THREATENED TO DO TO ME...
I BECAME LESS THAN A MAN.
I BECAME A COWARD. TO MYSELF AND THE WORLD.
YOU HAVE NO IDEA WHAT IT MEANS WHEN EVERYONE LOSES FAITH IN YOU.
CHNKK
CHANKK
BUT HE DOES, STRANGER! HE LOST KORUGAR!

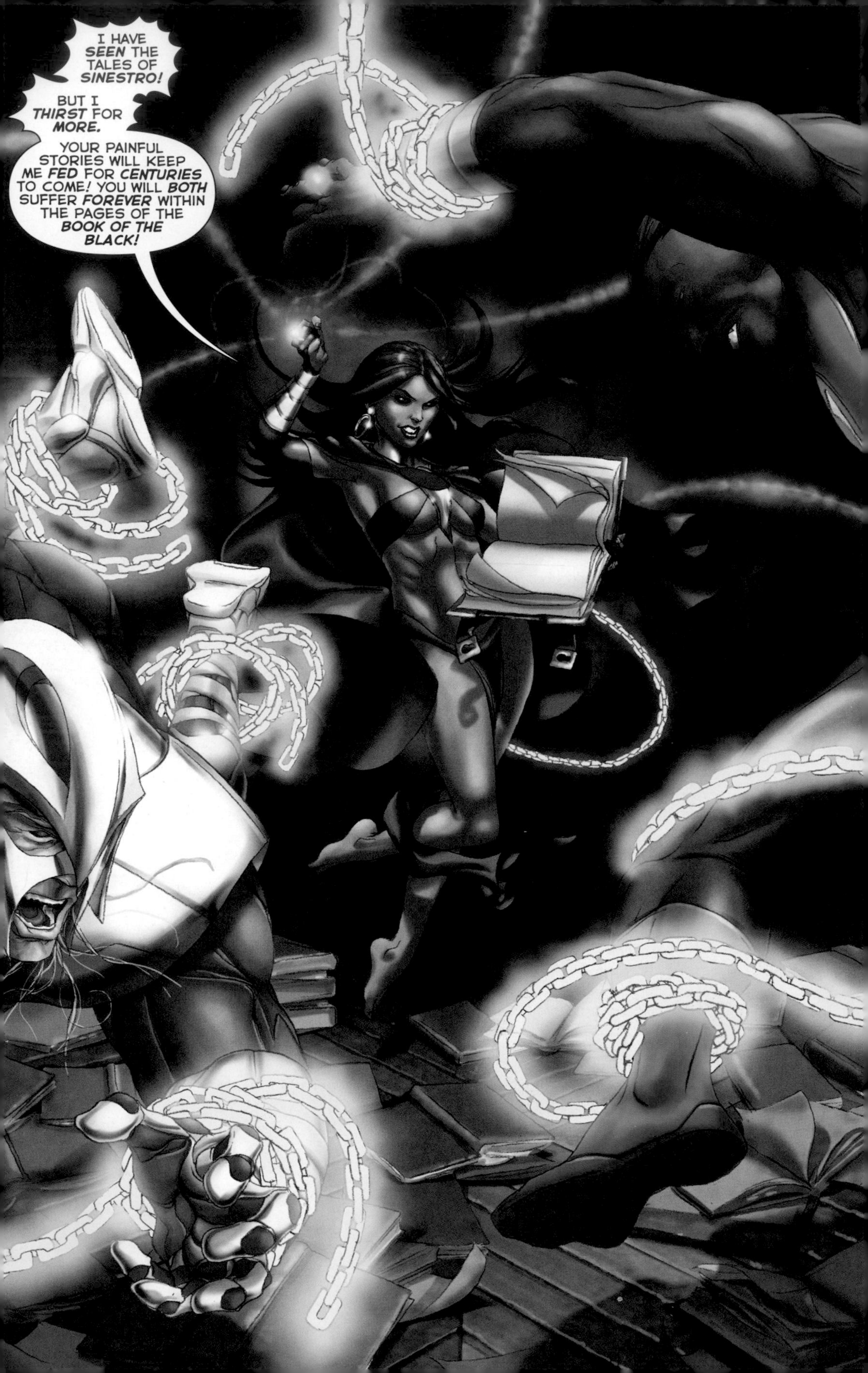
I HAVE SEEN THE TALES OF SINESTRO!
BUT I THIRST FOR MORE.
YOUR PAINFUL STORIES WILL KEEP ME FED FOR CENTURIES TO COME! YOU WILL BOTH SUFFER FOREVER WITHIN THE PAGES OF THE BOOK OF THE BLACK!

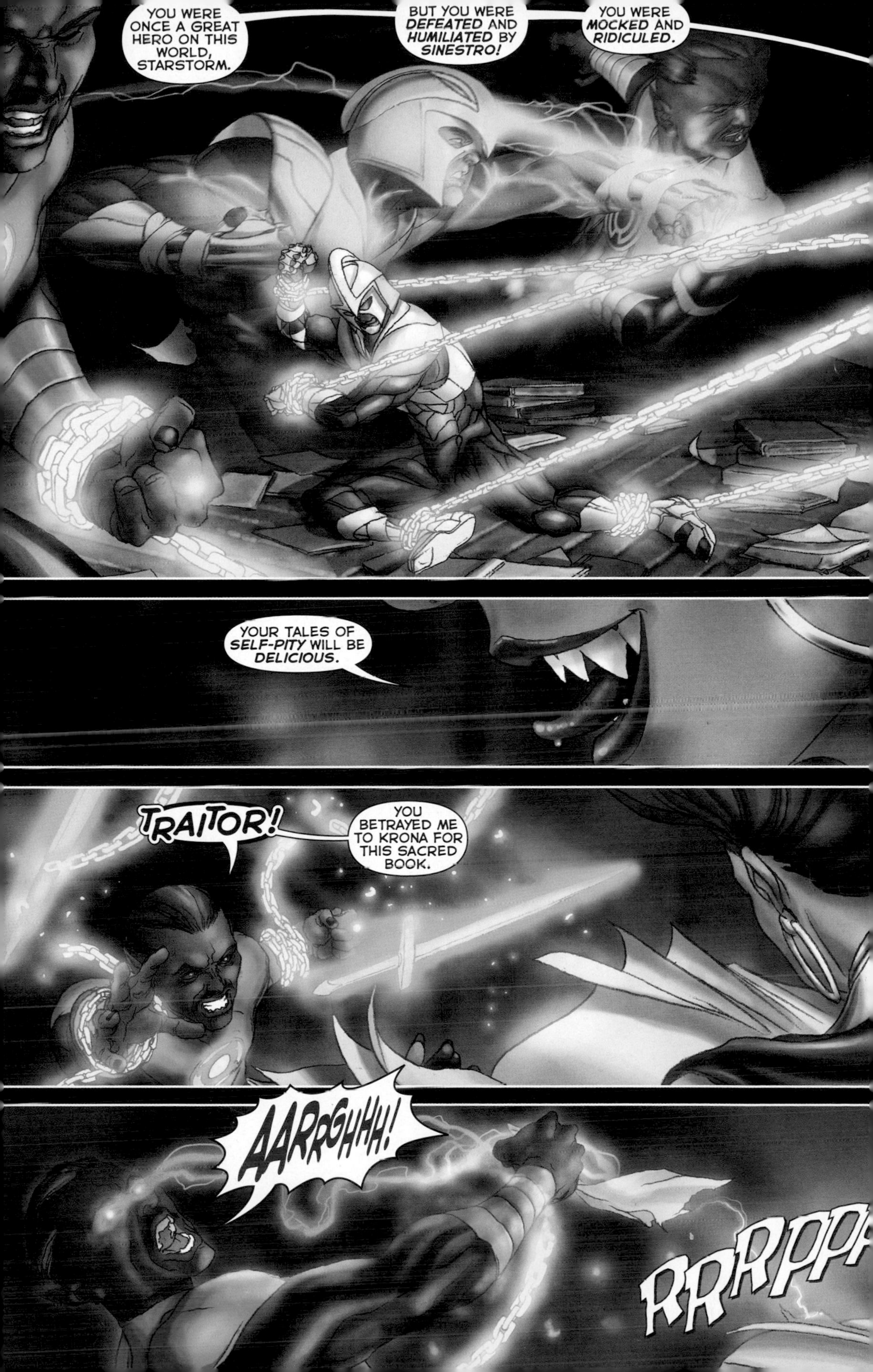

YOU WERE ONCE A GREAT HERO ON THIS WORLD, STARSTORM.
BUT YOU WERE *DEFEATED* AND *HUMILIATED* BY *SINESTRO!*
YOU WERE *MOCKED* AND *RIDICULED.*
YOUR TALES OF *SELF-PITY* WILL BE *DELICIOUS.*
TRAITOR!
YOU BETRAYED ME TO KRONA FOR THIS SACRED BOOK.
AARRGHHH!
RRRPPP

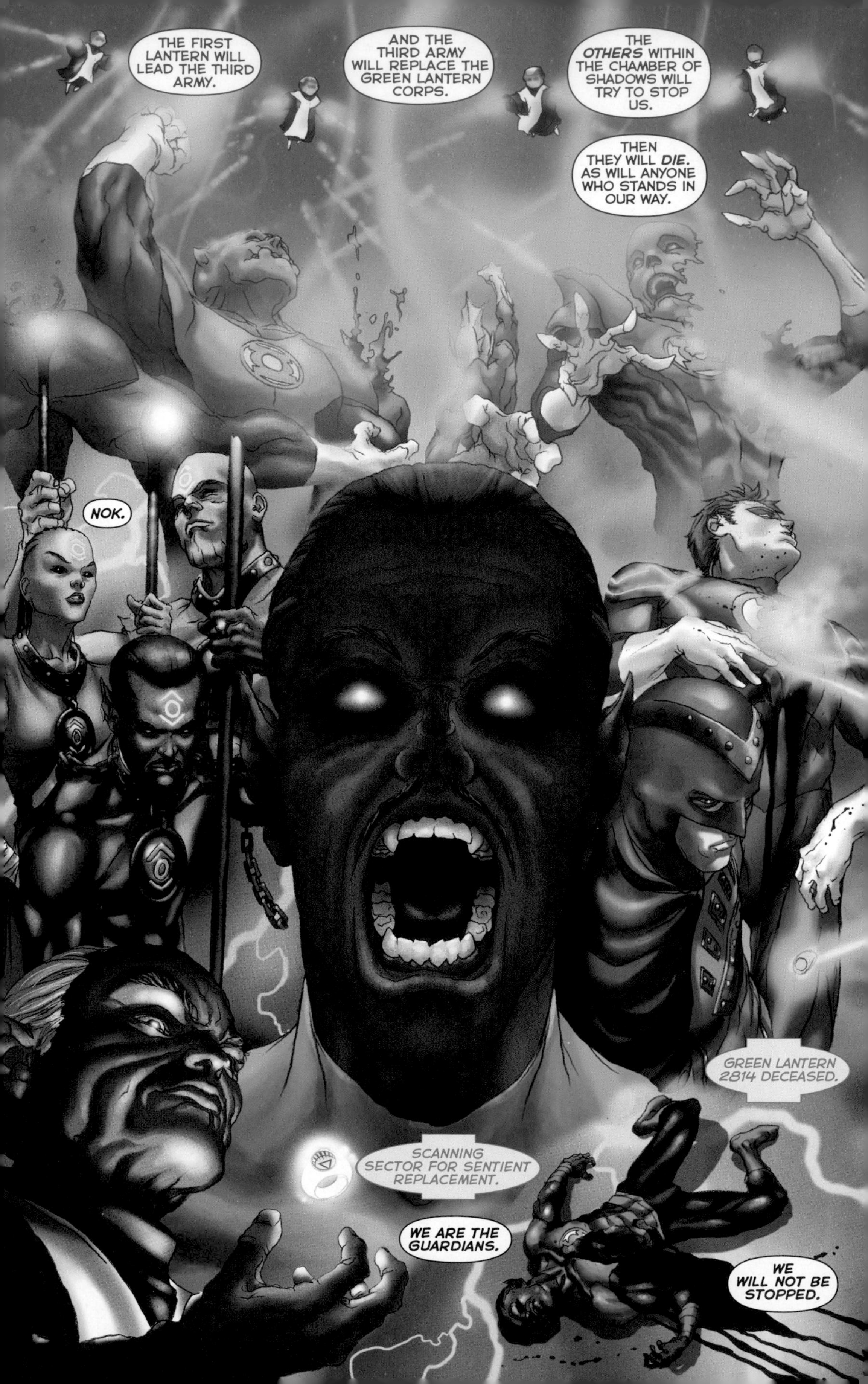
THE FIRST LANTERN WILL LEAD THE THIRD ARMY.
AND THE THIRD ARMY WILL REPLACE THE GREEN LANTERN CORPS.
THE *OTHERS* WITHIN THE CHAMBER OF SHADOWS WILL TRY TO STOP US.
THEN THEY WILL *DIE*. AS WILL ANYONE WHO STANDS IN OUR WAY.
NOK.
GREEN LANTERN 2814 DECEASED.
SCANNING SECTOR FOR SENTIENT REPLACEMENT.
WE ARE THE GUARDIANS.
WE WILL NOT BE STOPPED.

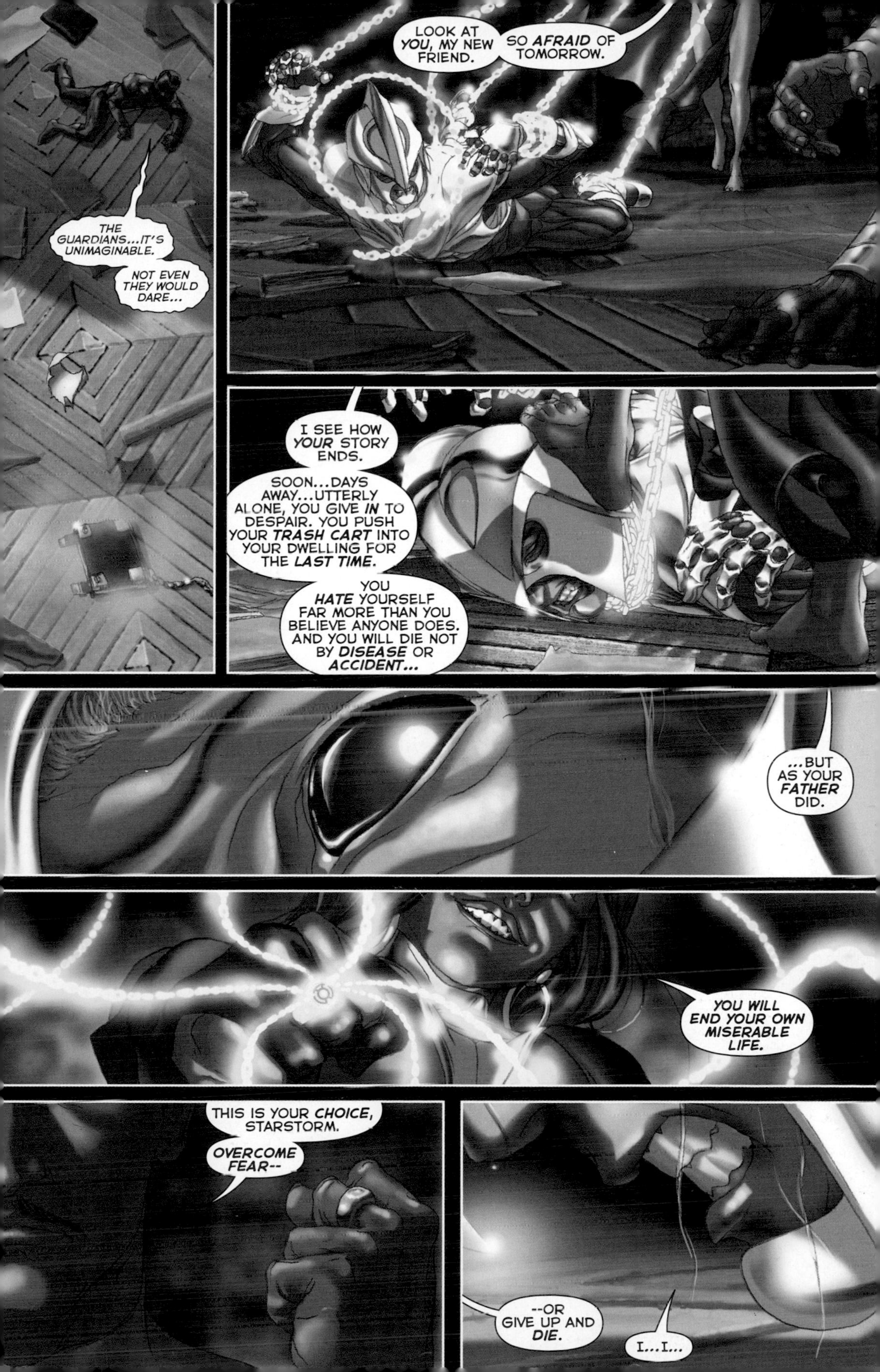

THE GUARDIANS...IT'S UNIMAGINABLE.
NOT EVEN THEY WOULD DARE...
LOOK AT YOU, MY NEW FRIEND.
SO AFRAID OF TOMORROW.
I SEE HOW YOUR STORY ENDS.
SOON...DAYS AWAY...UTTERLY ALONE, YOU GIVE IN TO DESPAIR. YOU PUSH YOUR TRASH CART INTO YOUR DWELLING FOR THE LAST TIME.
YOU HATE YOURSELF FAR MORE THAN YOU BELIEVE ANYONE DOES. AND YOU WILL DIE NOT BY DISEASE OR ACCIDENT...
...BUT AS YOUR FATHER DID.
YOU WILL END YOUR OWN MISERABLE LIFE.
THIS IS YOUR CHOICE, STARSTORM.
OVERCOME FEAR--
--OR GIVE UP AND DIE.
I...I...

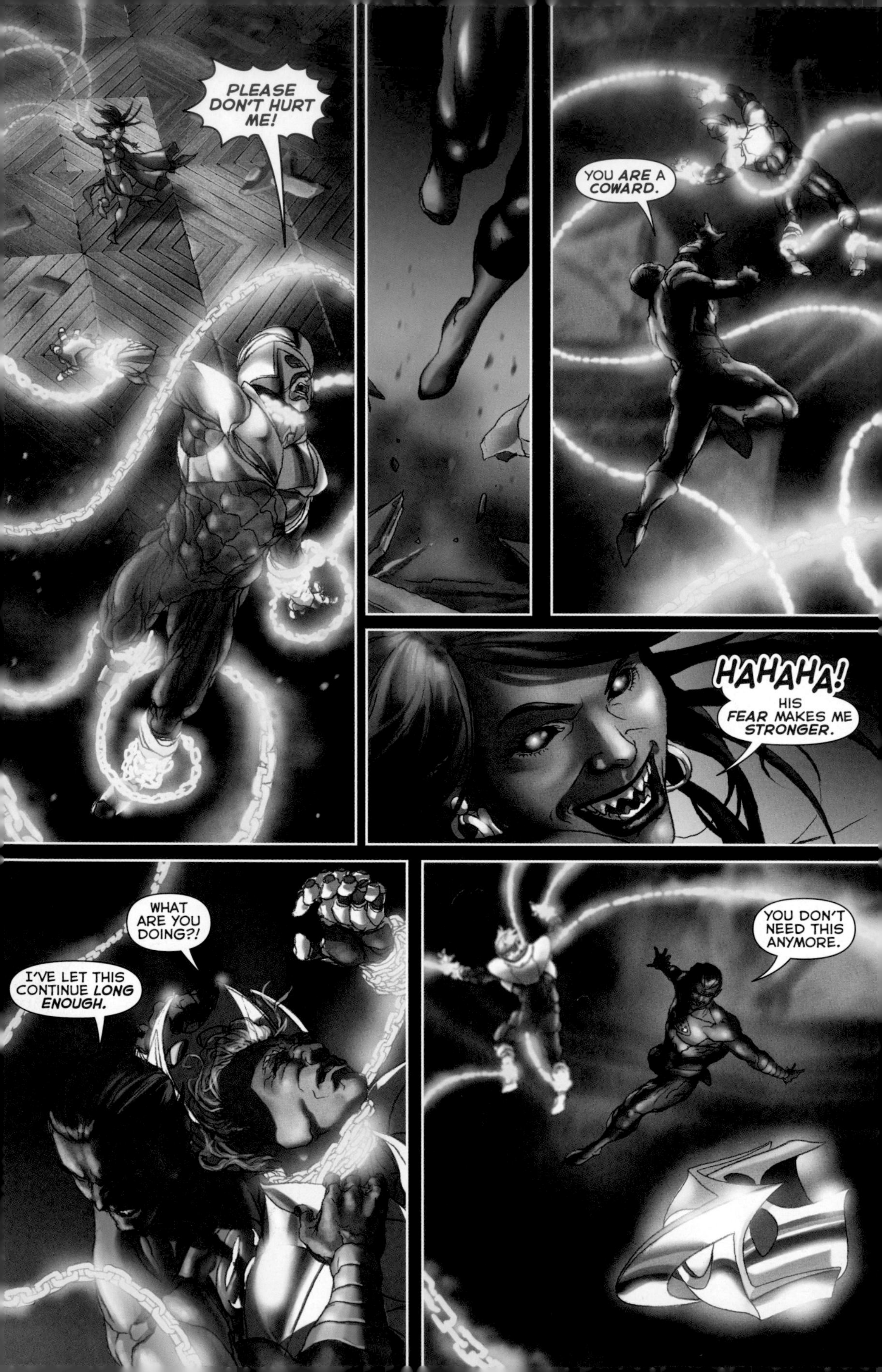
PLEASE DON'T HURT ME!
YOU ARE A COWARD.
HAHAHA!
HIS FEAR MAKES ME STRONGER.
WHAT ARE YOU DOING?!
I'VE LET THIS CONTINUE LONG ENOUGH.
YOU DON'T NEED THIS ANYMORE.

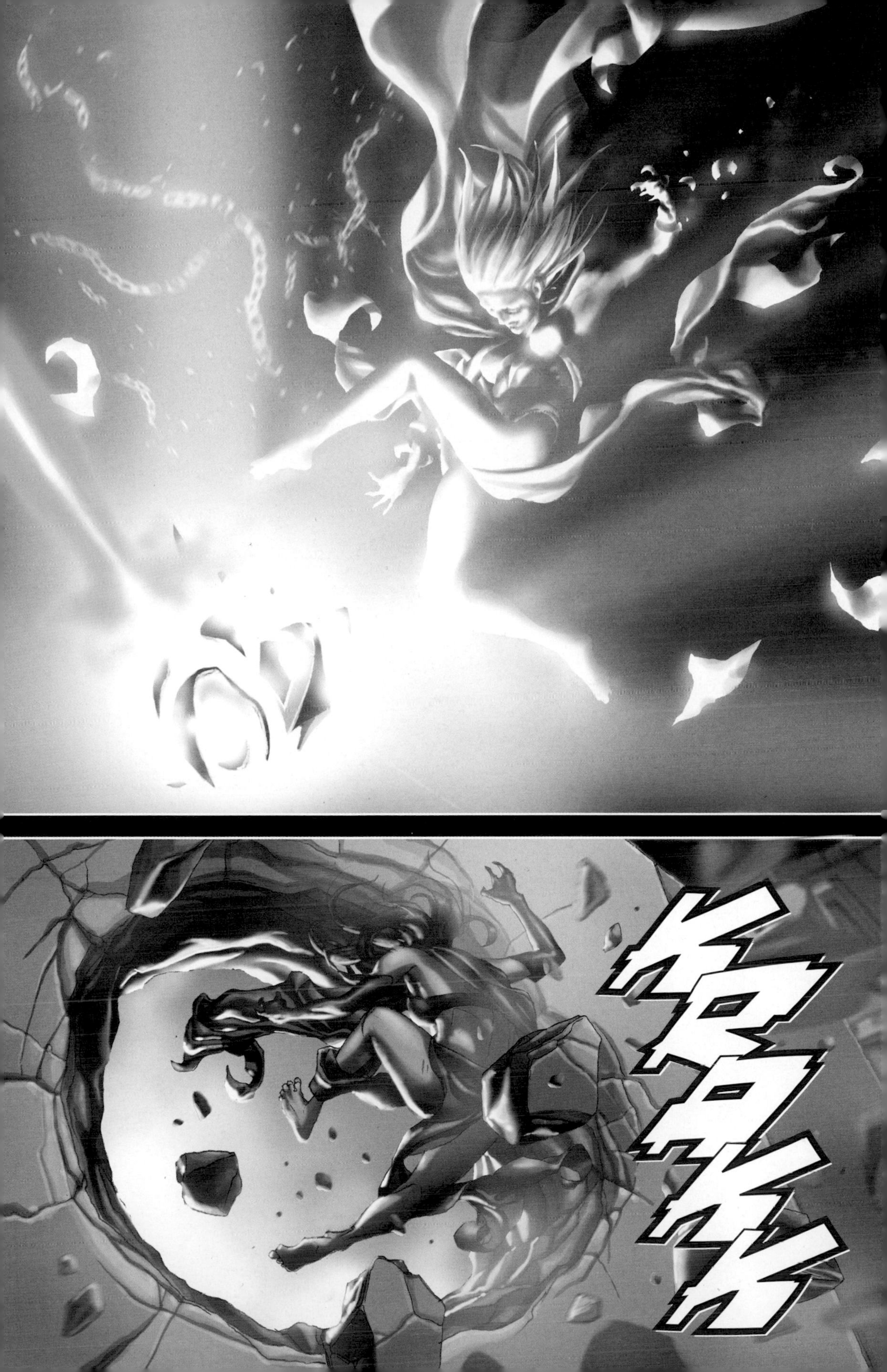
KRAKK

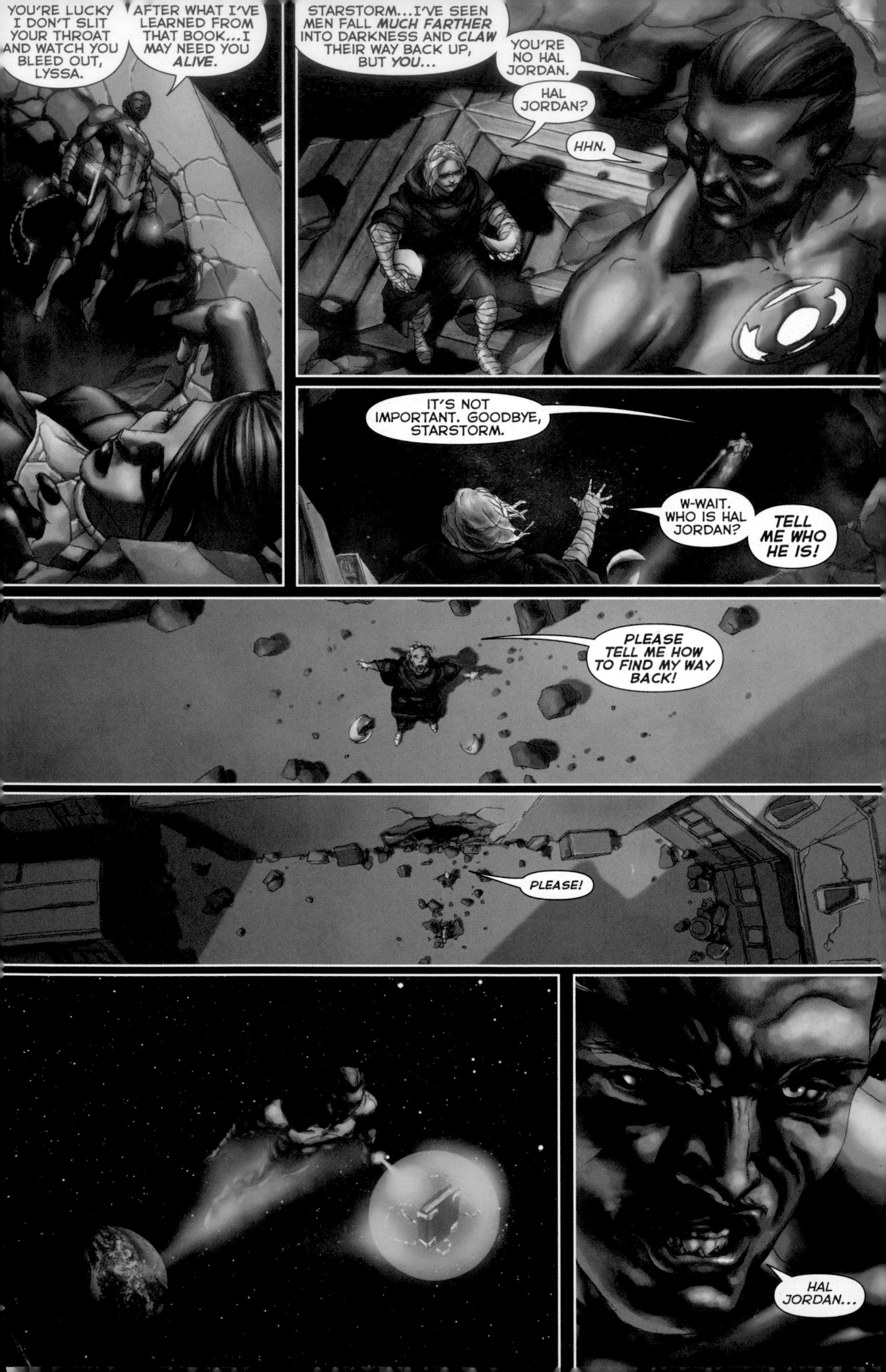
YOU'RE LUCKY I DON'T SLIT YOUR THROAT AND WATCH YOU BLEED OUT, LYSSA.
AFTER WHAT I'VE LEARNED FROM THAT BOOK...I MAY NEED YOU *ALIVE*.
STARSTORM...I'VE SEEN MEN FALL *MUCH FARTHER* INTO DARKNESS AND *CLAW* THEIR WAY BACK UP, BUT *YOU*...
YOU'RE NO HAL JORDAN.
HAL JORDAN?
HHN.
IT'S NOT IMPORTANT. GOODBYE, STARSTORM.
W-WAIT. WHO IS HAL JORDAN?
TELL ME WHO HE IS!
PLEASE TELL ME HOW TO FIND MY WAY BACK!
PLEASE!
HAL JORDAN...

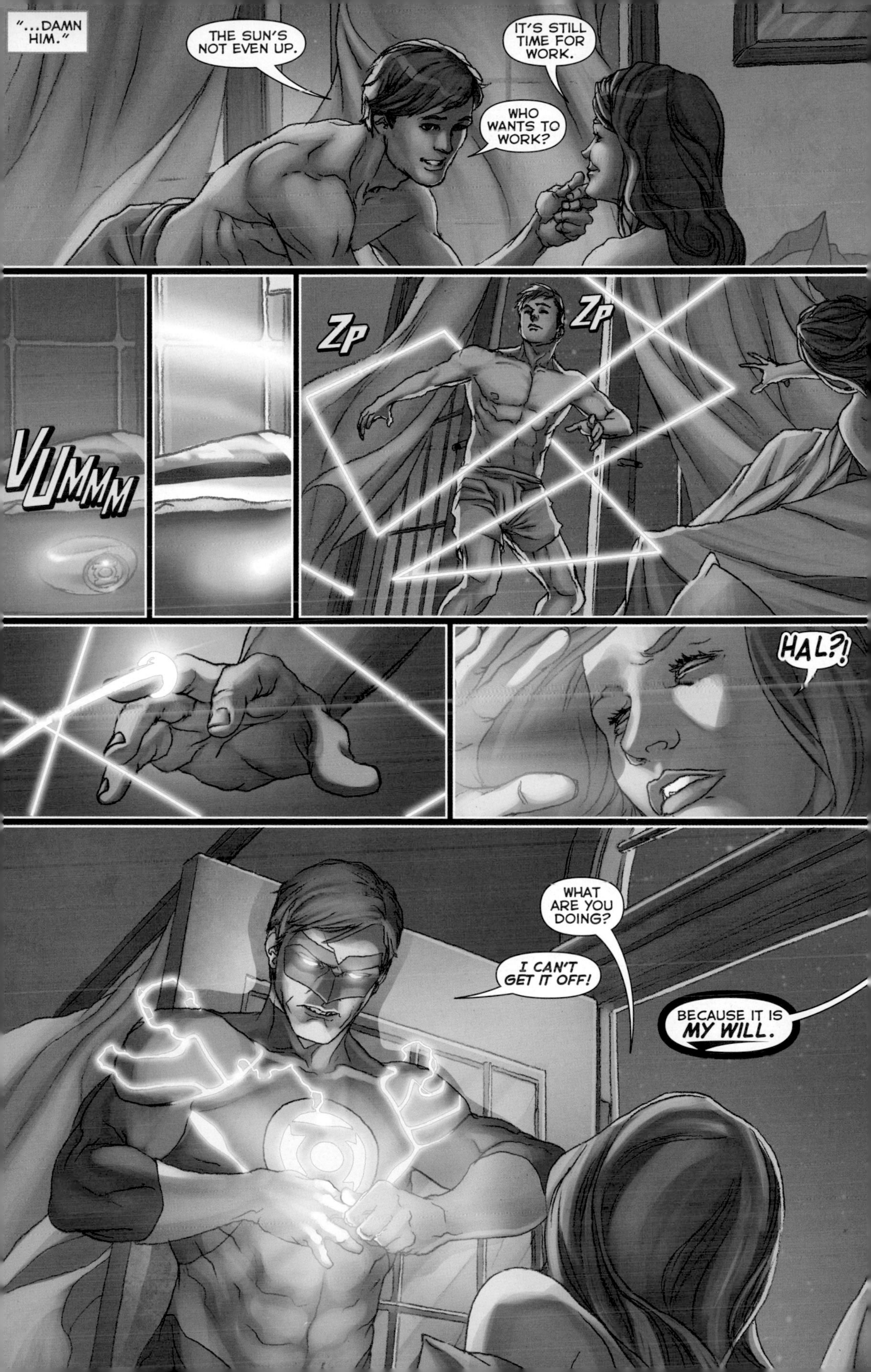
"...DAMN HIM."
THE SUN'S NOT EVEN UP.
IT'S STILL TIME FOR WORK.
WHO WANTS TO WORK?
VUMMM
ZP
ZP
HAL?!
WHAT ARE YOU DOING?
I CAN'T GET IT OFF!
BECAUSE IT IS MY WILL.

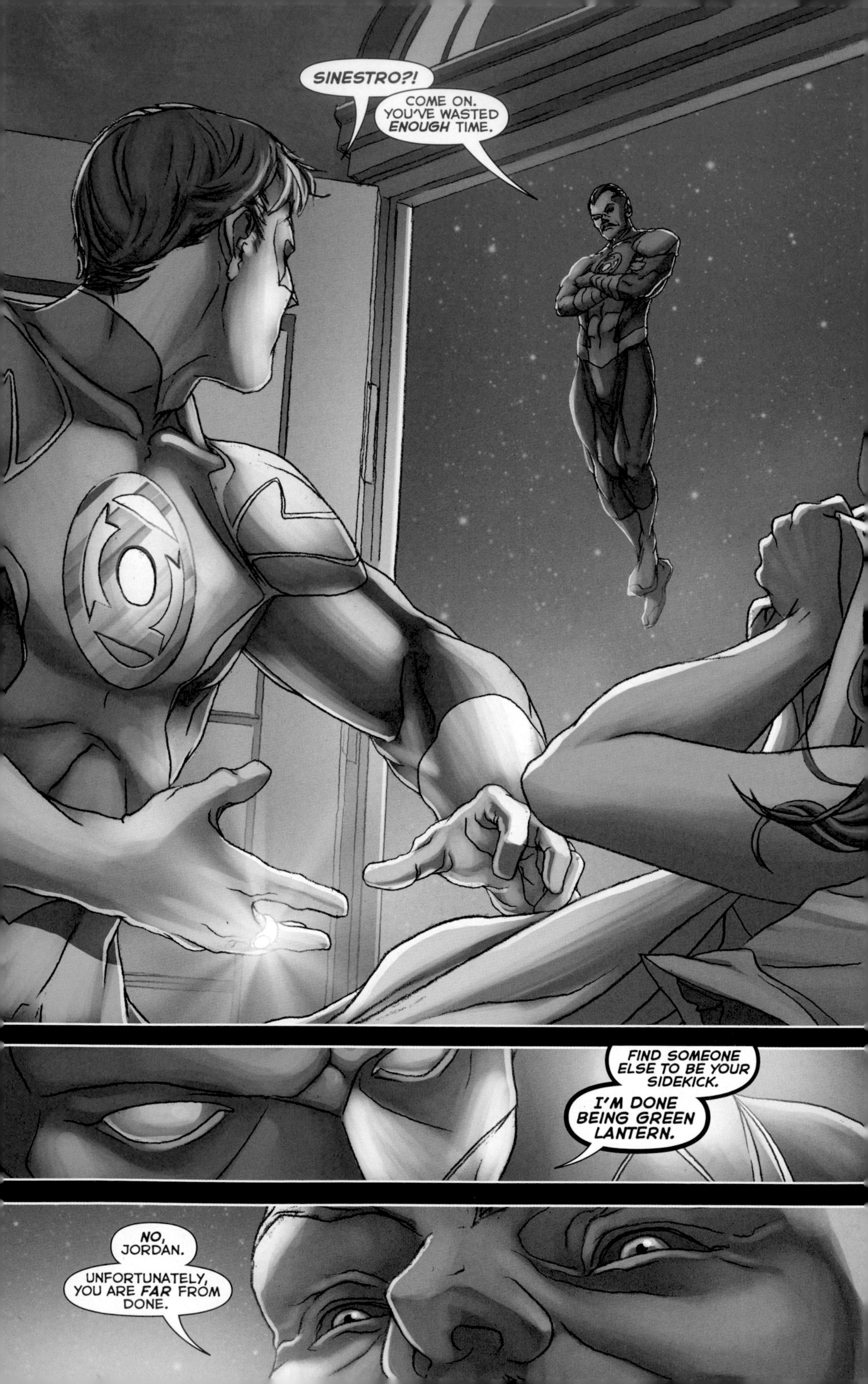
SINESTRO?!
COME ON. YOU'VE WASTED *ENOUGH* TIME.
FIND SOMEONE ELSE TO BE YOUR SIDEKICK.
I'M DONE BEING GREEN LANTERN.
NO, JORDAN.
UNFORTUNATELY, YOU ARE *FAR* FROM DONE.

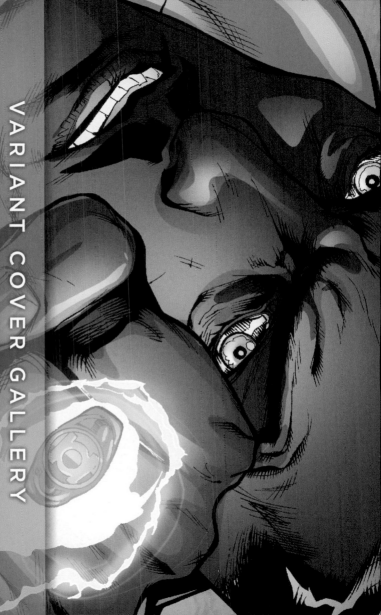

VARIANT COVER GALLERY

GREEN LANTERN 1
by Greg Capullo

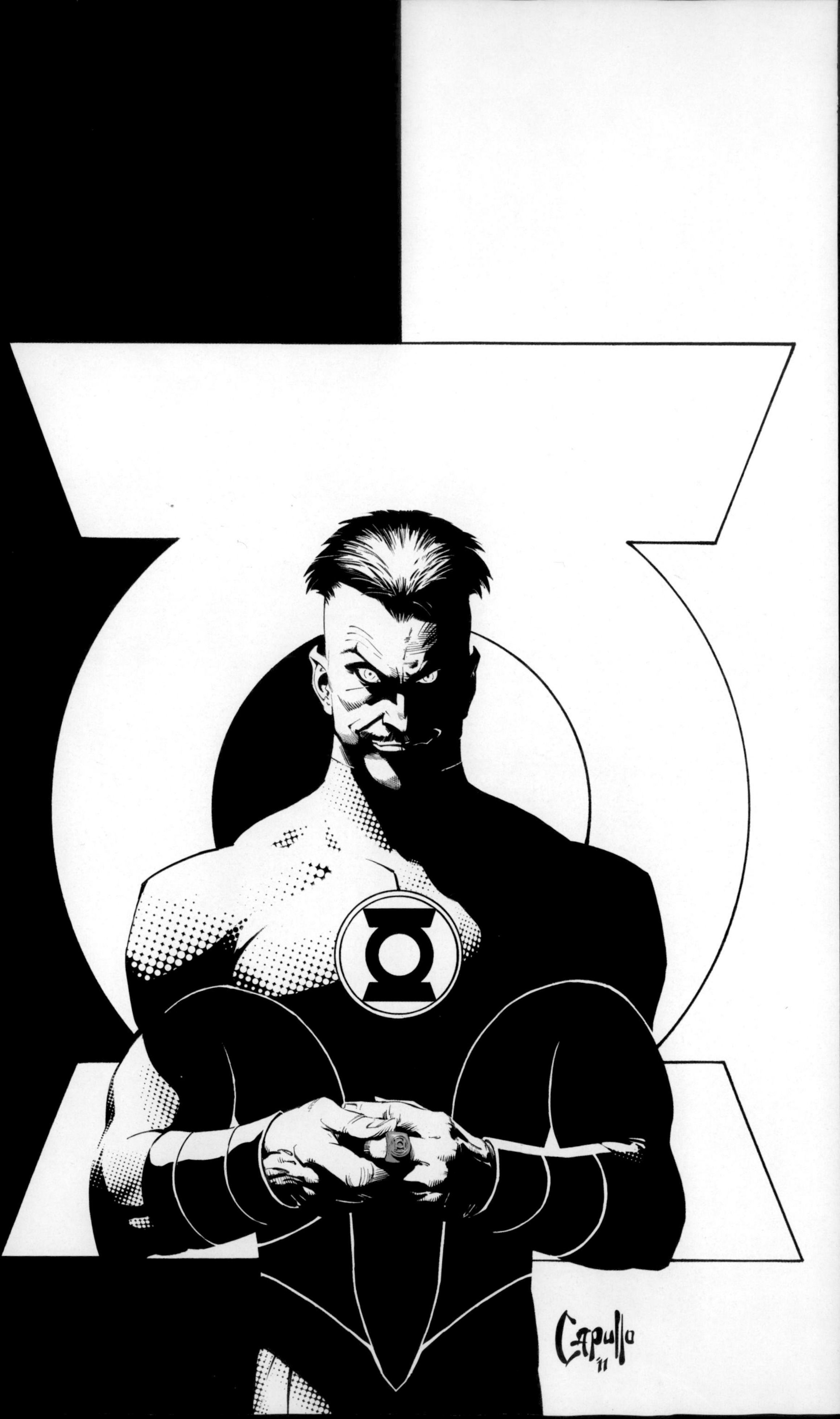
CAPULLO
'11

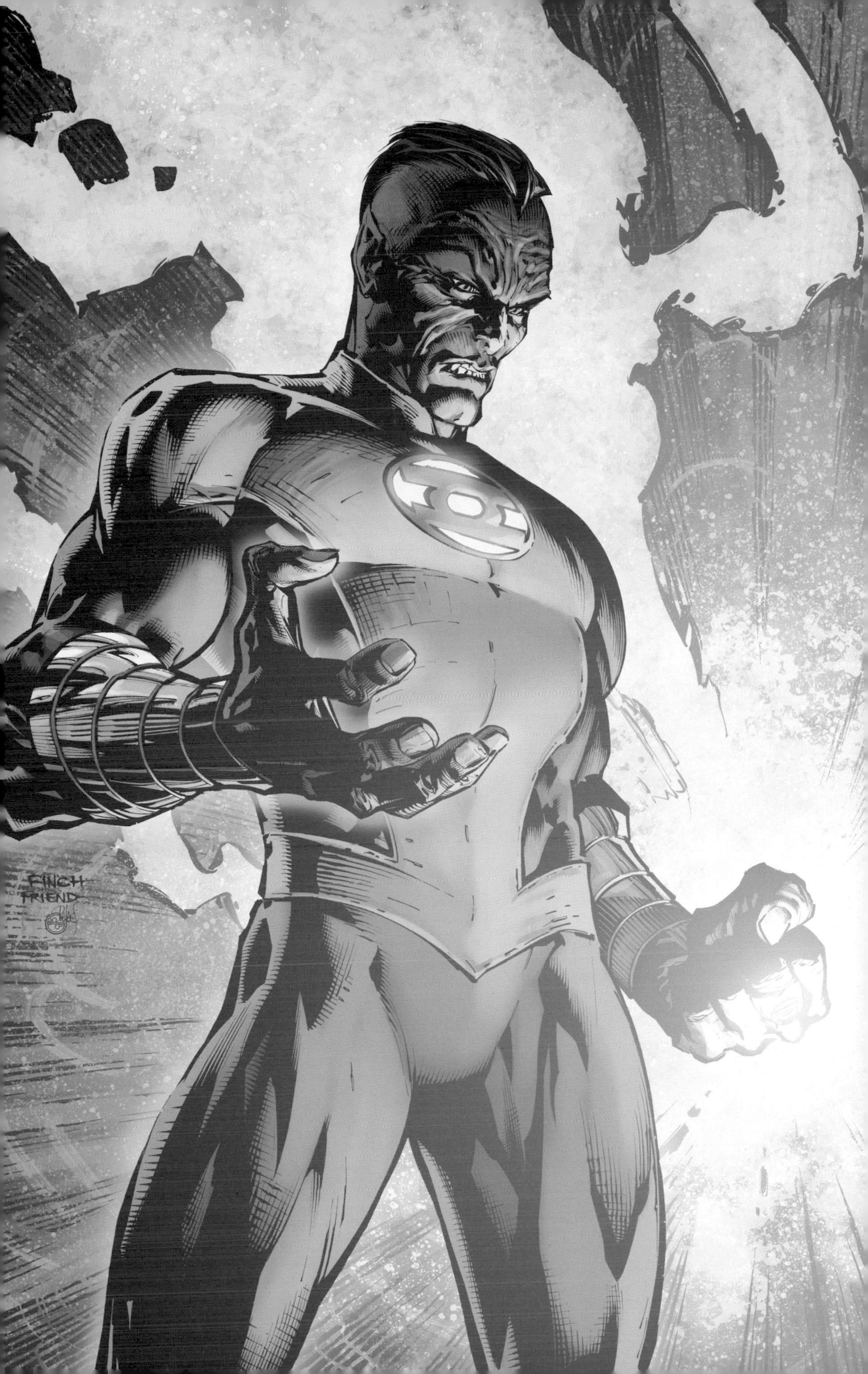
FINCH
FRIEND

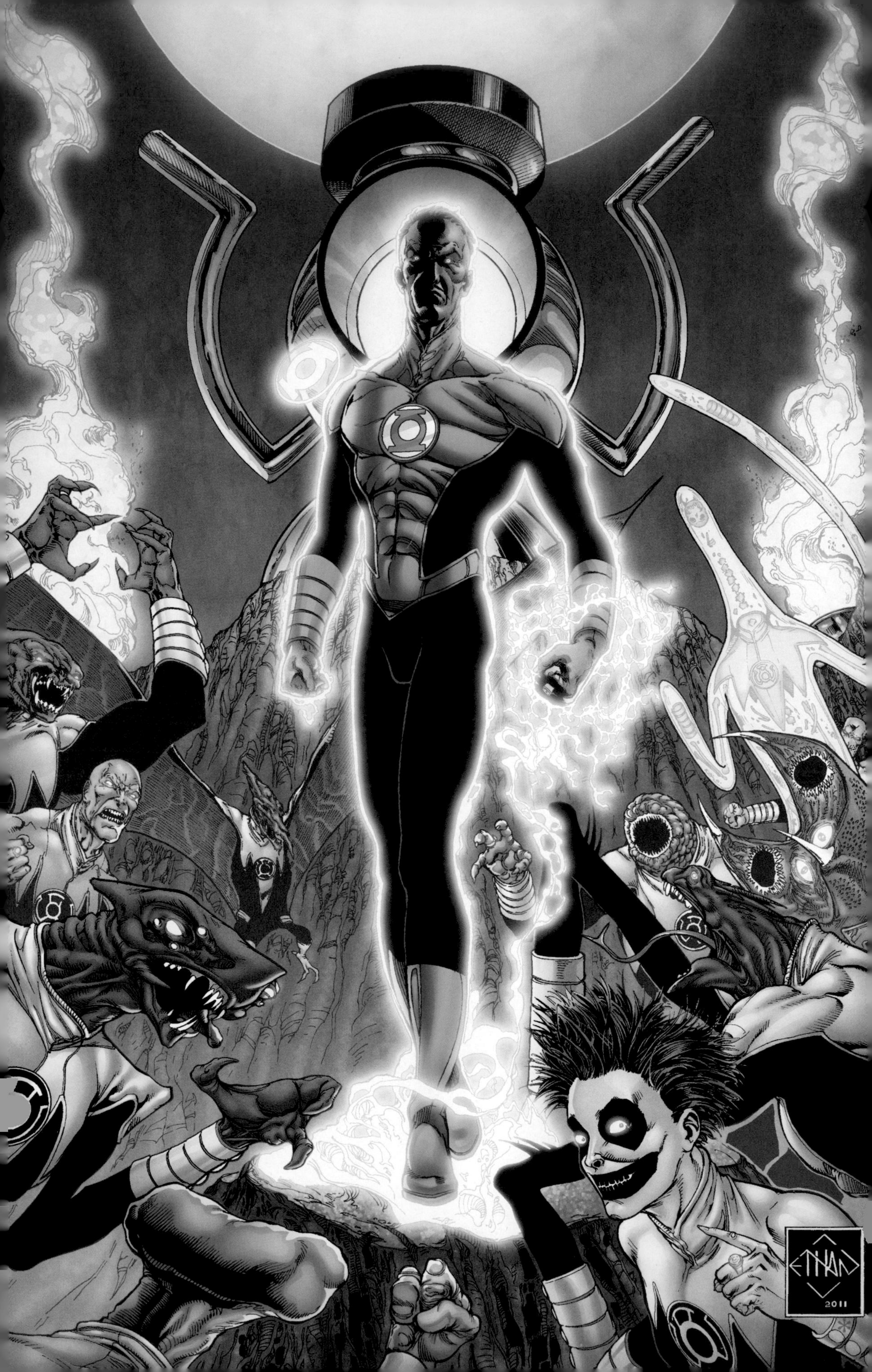
2011

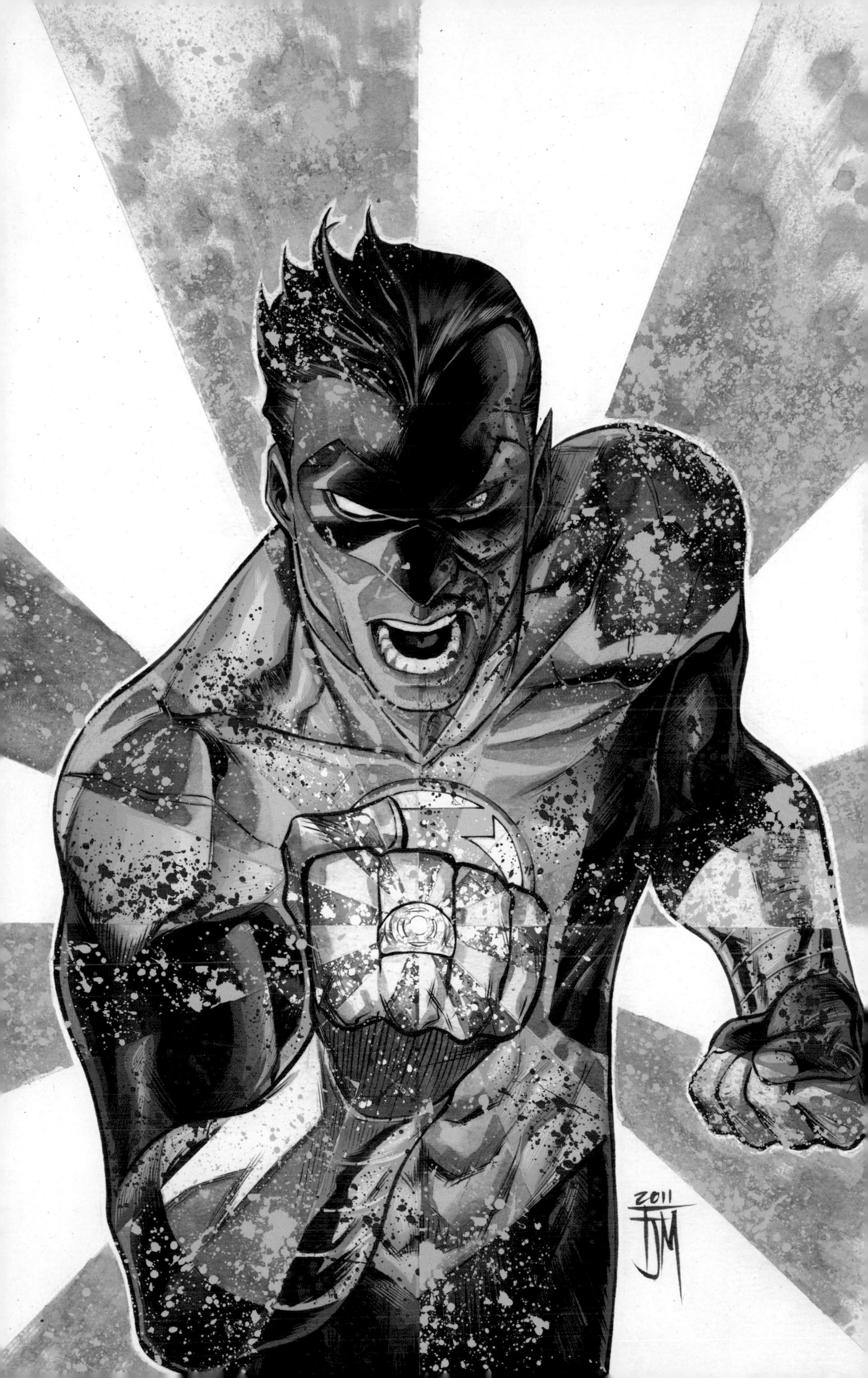
2011
FJM

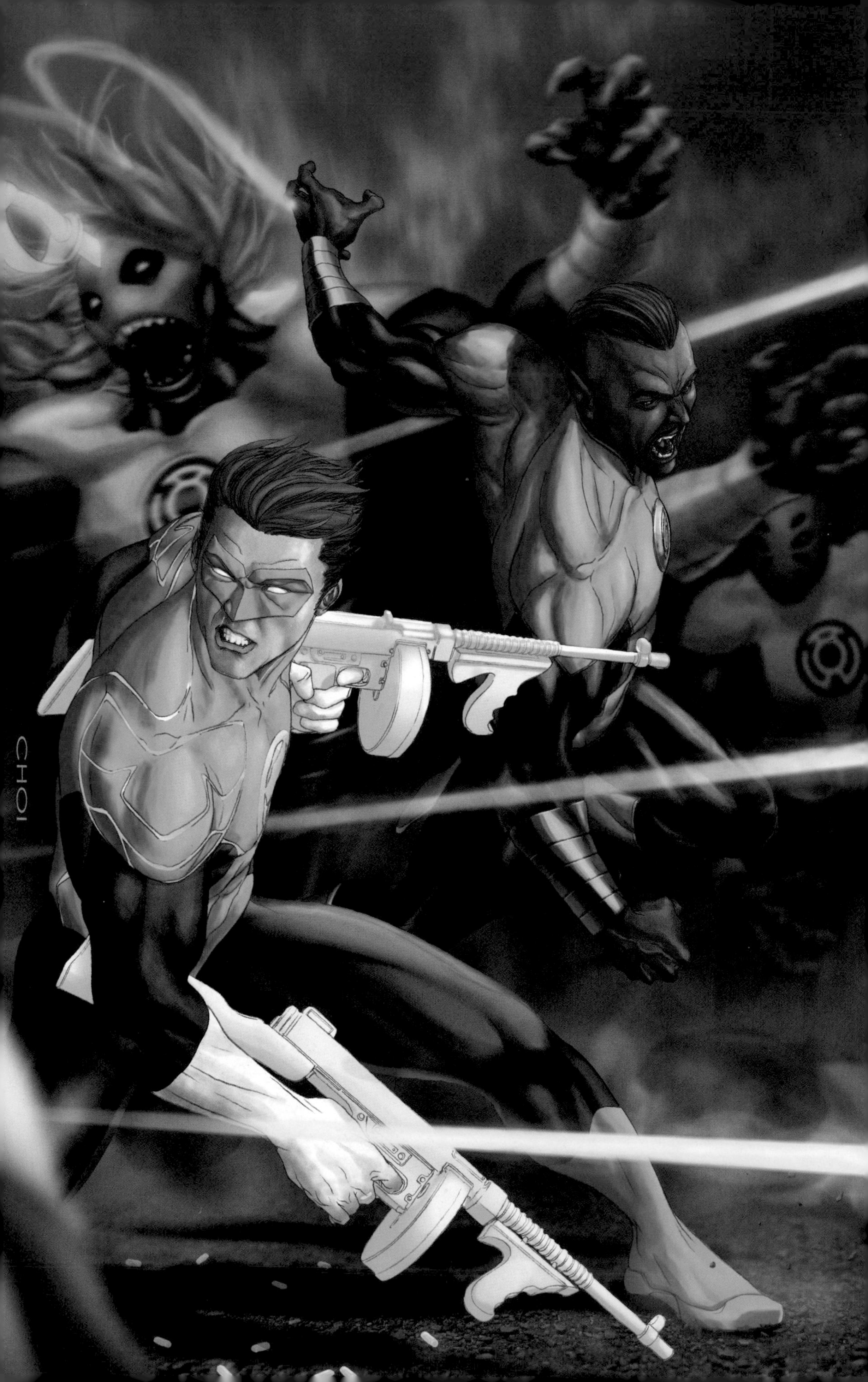
CHOI

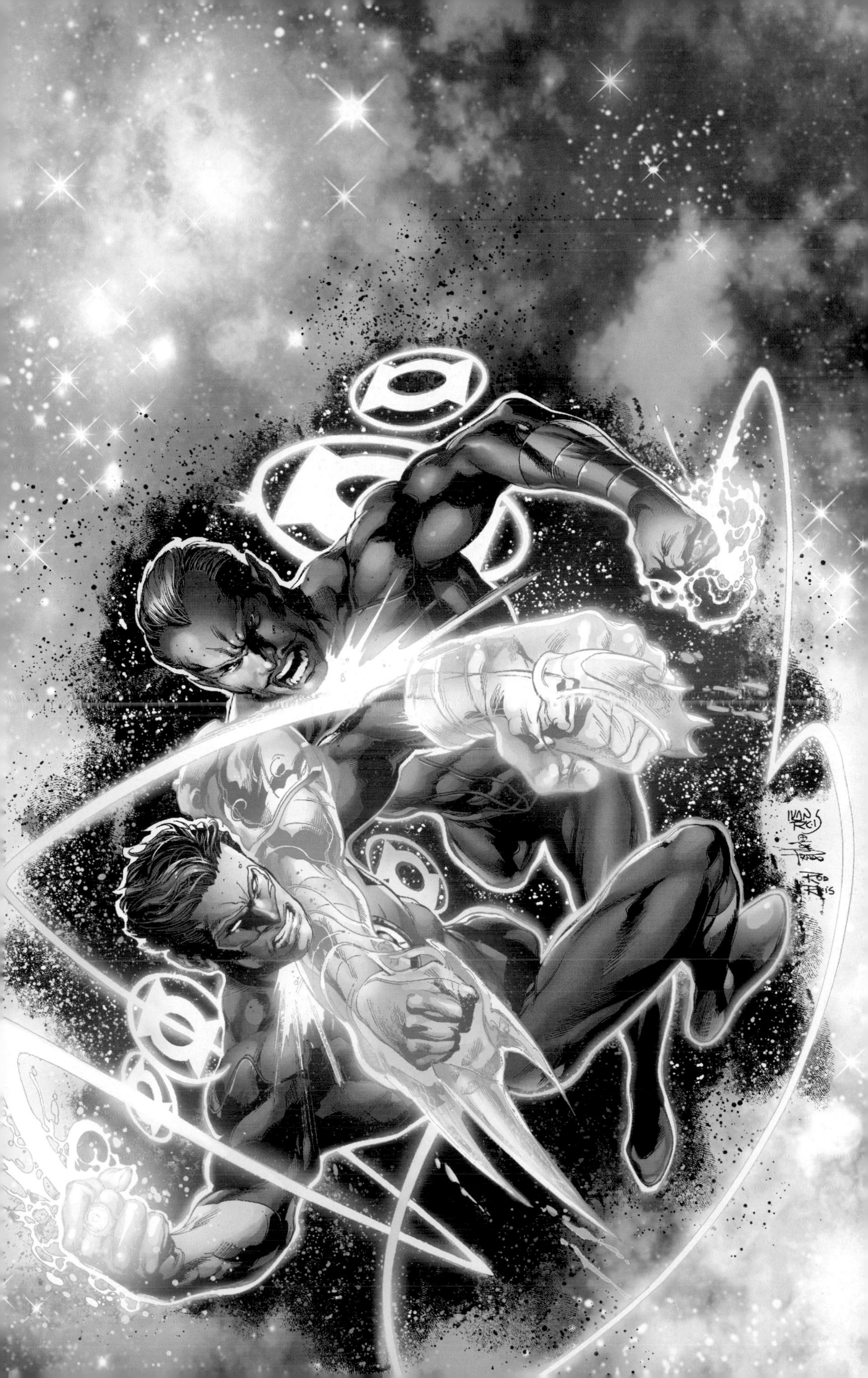

GREEN LANTERN #3

GREEN LANTERN #3

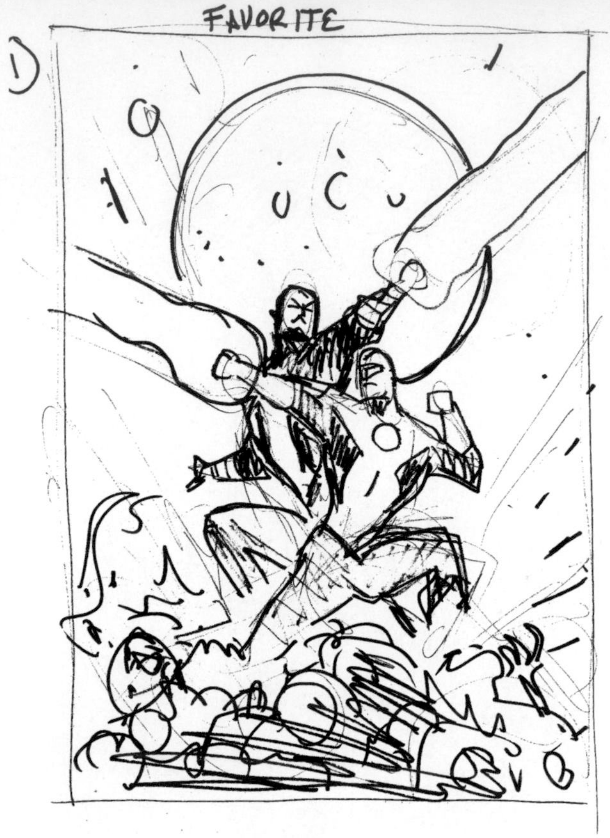
FAVORITE
1

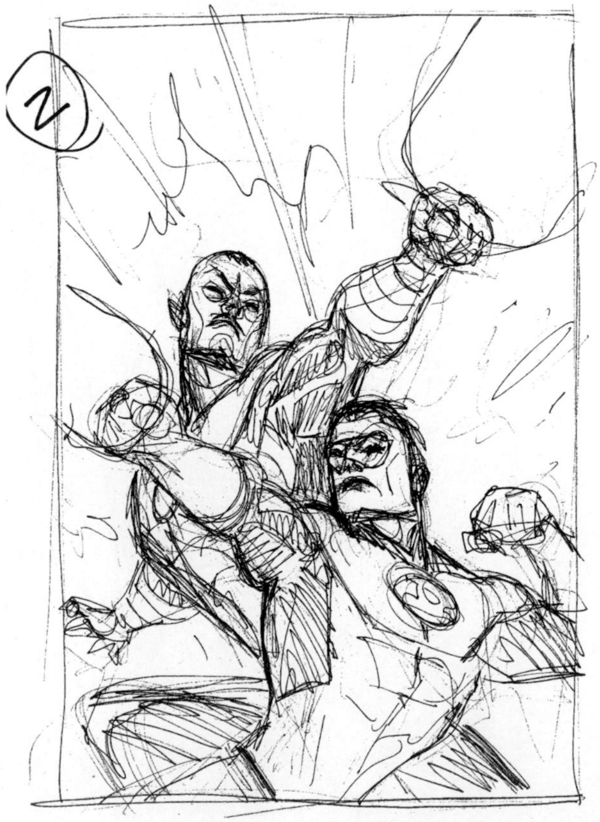
2

GREEN LANTERN #5

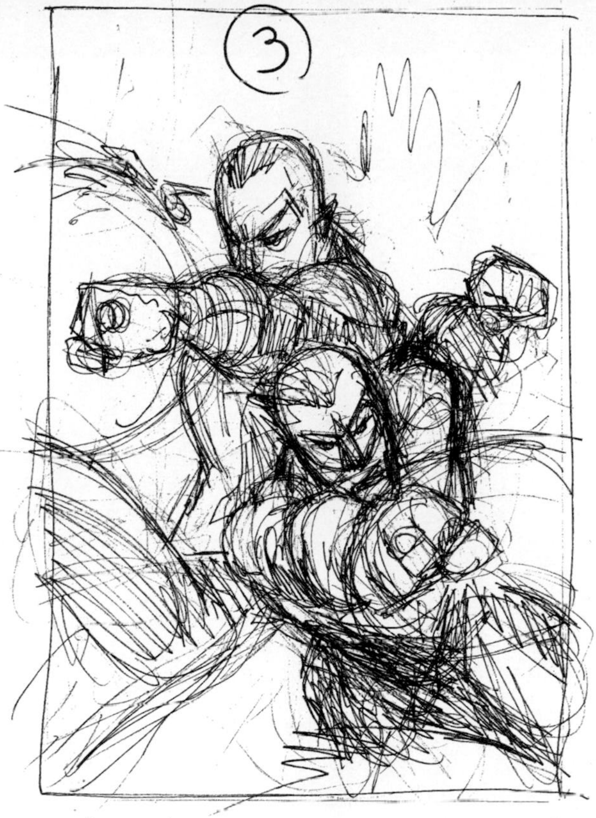
3

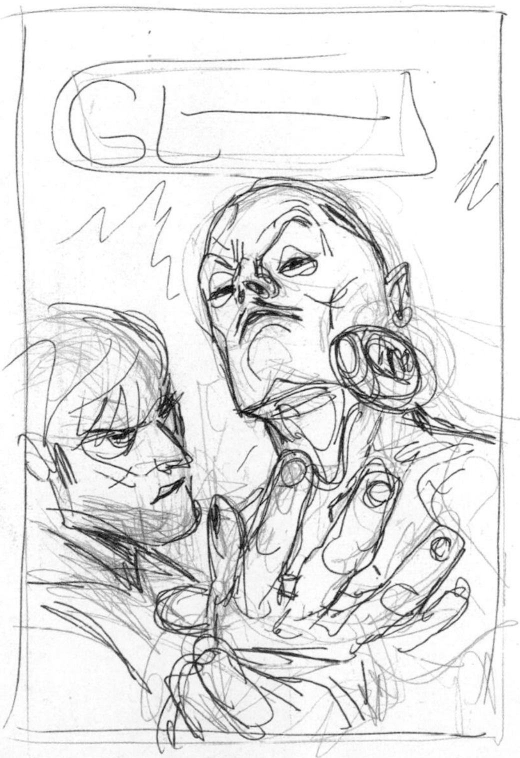
GL

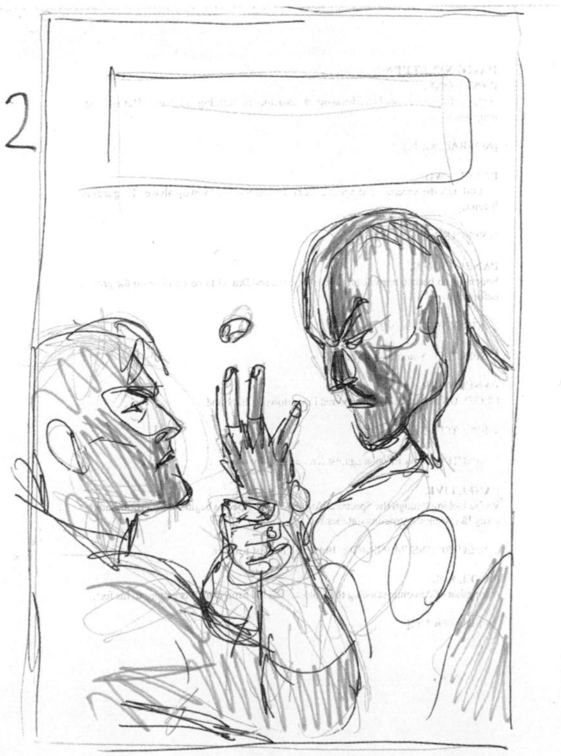
2

GREEN LANTERN #6

GREEN LANTERN

#1 PAGE ROUGHS BY DOUG MAHNKE

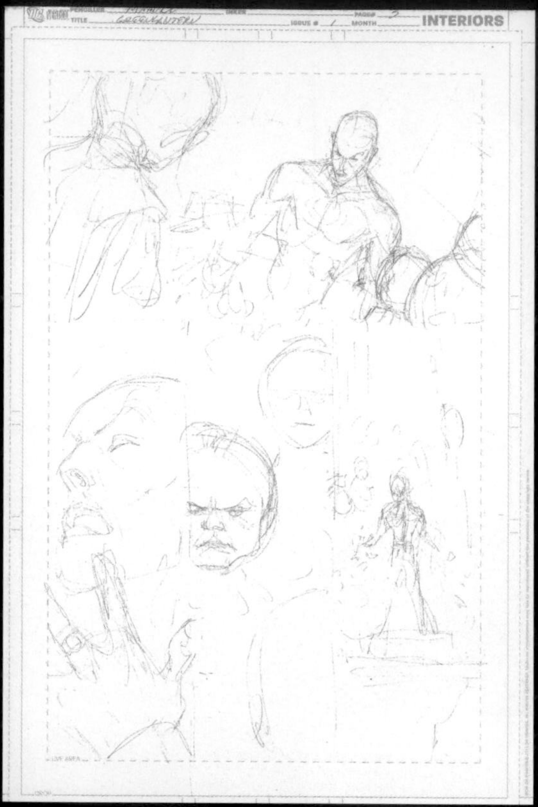
INTERIORS

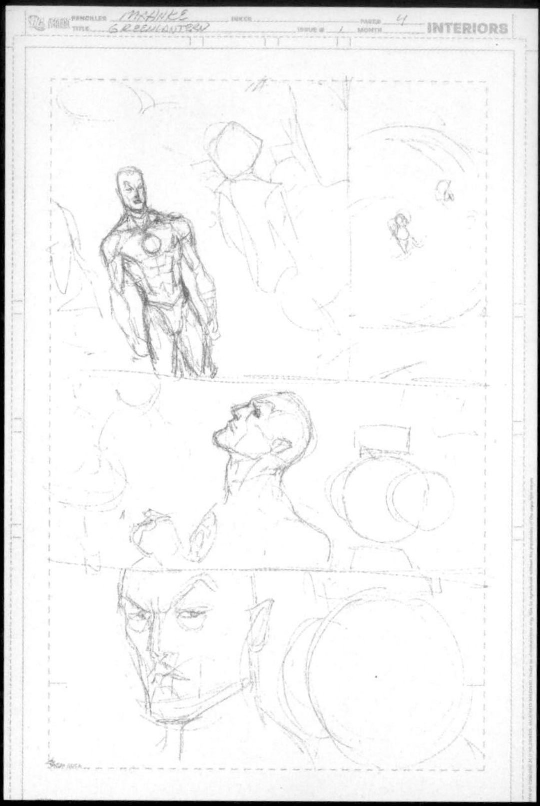
INTERIORS

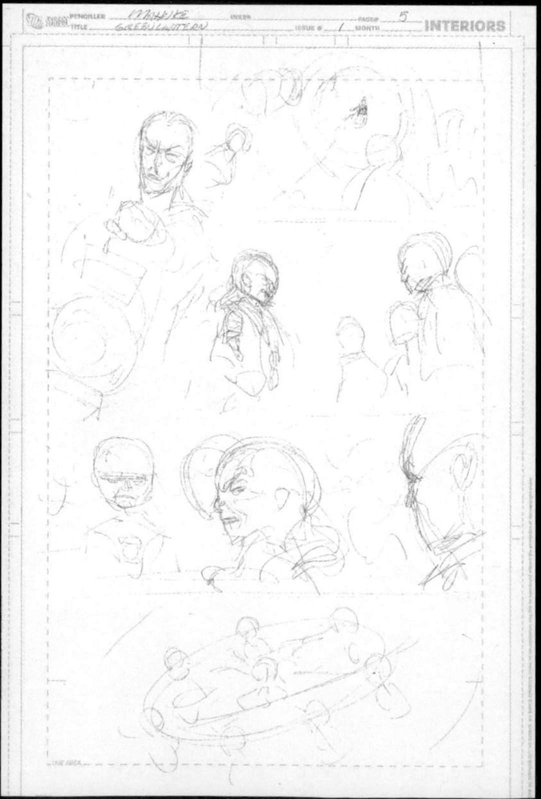
INTERIORS

GREEN LANTERN

#1 PAGE PENCILS BY DOUG MAHNKE

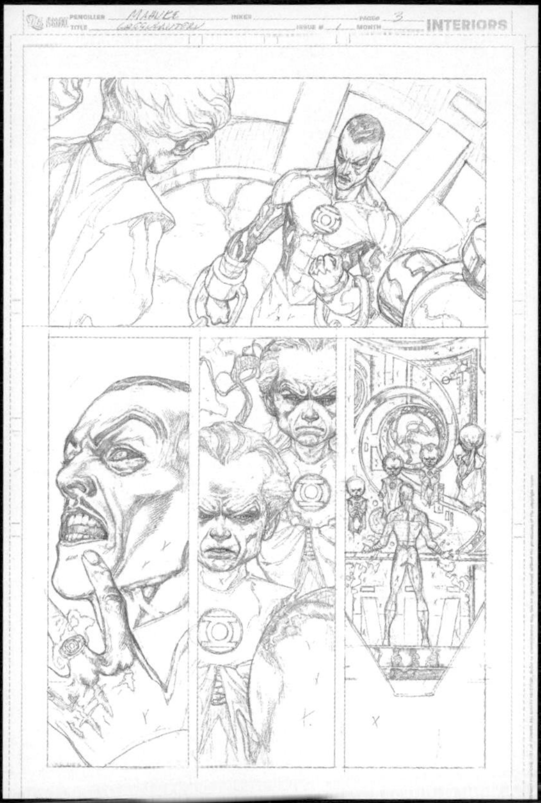
INTERIORS

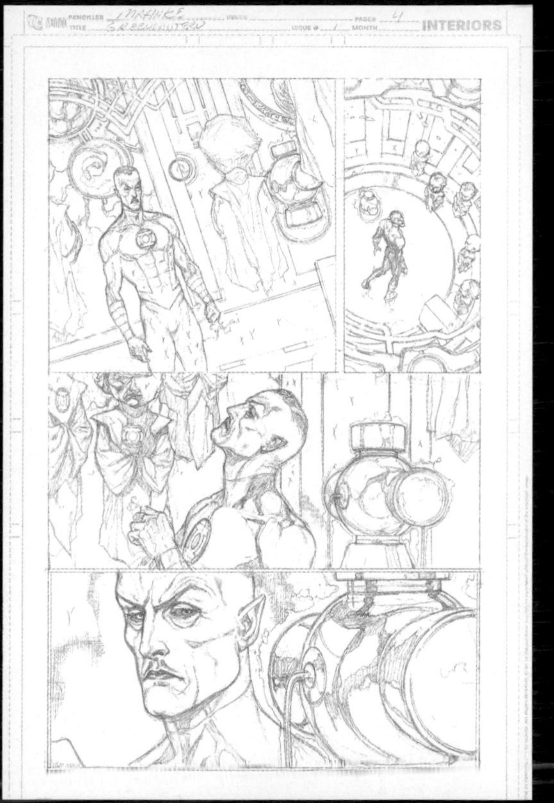
INTERIORS

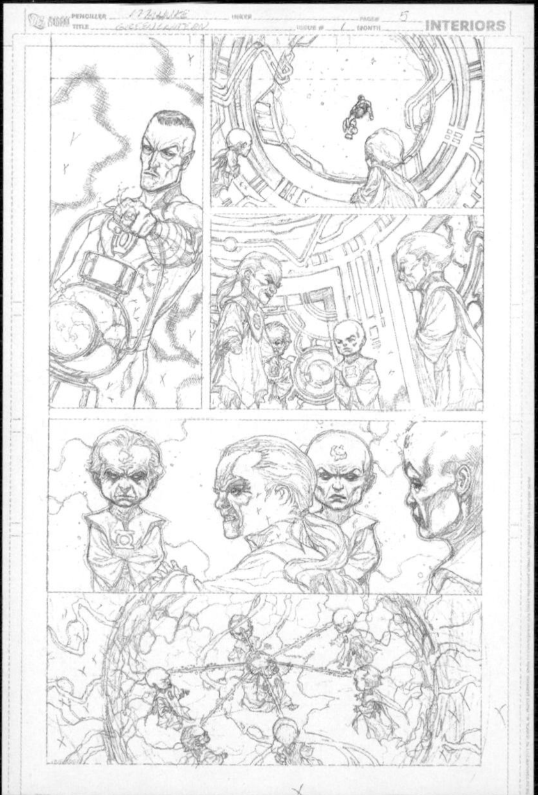
INTERIORS

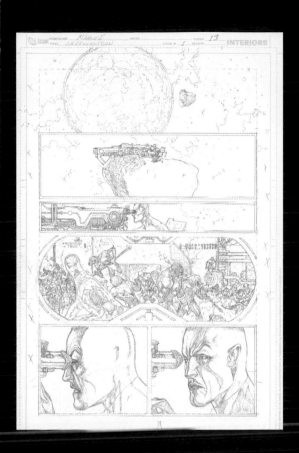

GREEN LANTERN
#2 PAGE ROUGHS BY DOUG MAHNKE

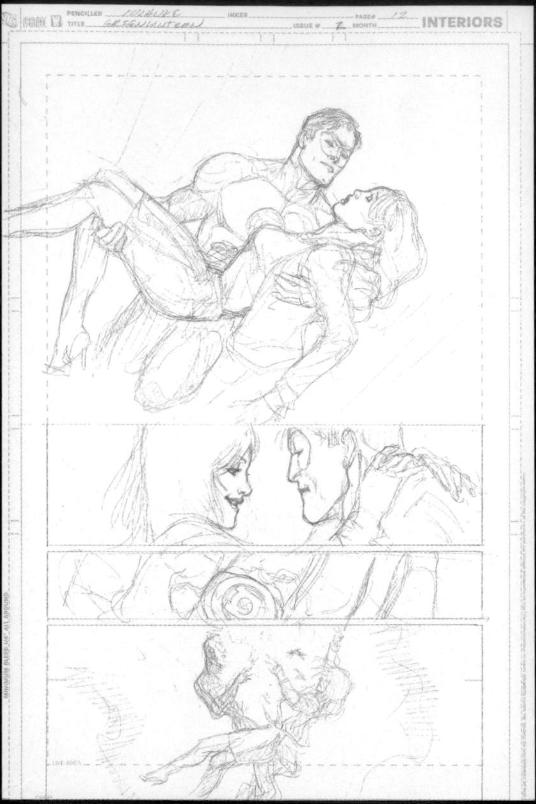
INTERIORS

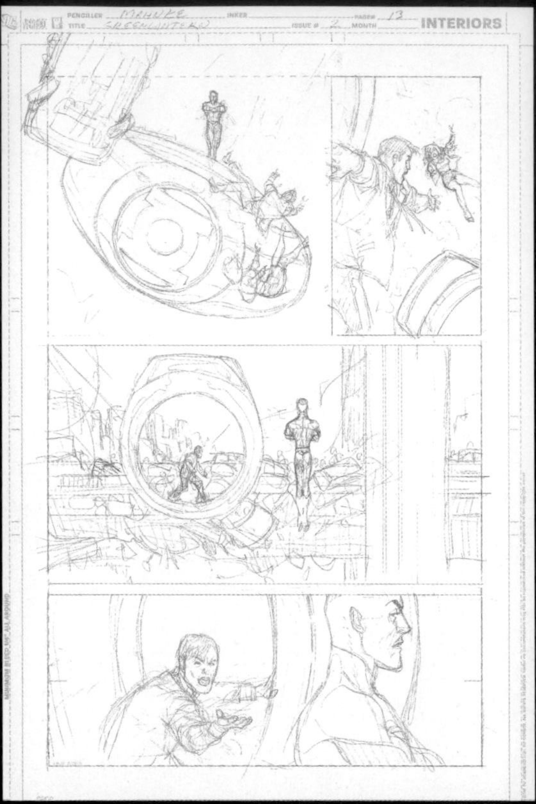
INTERIORS

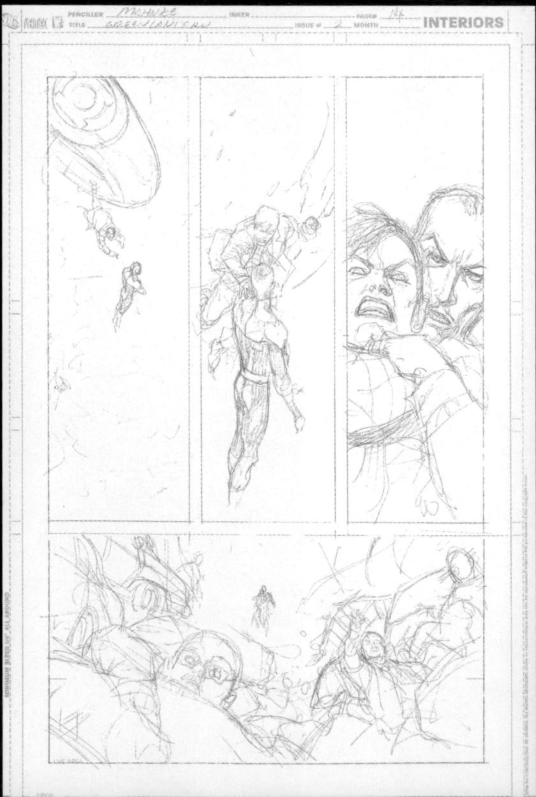
INTERIORS

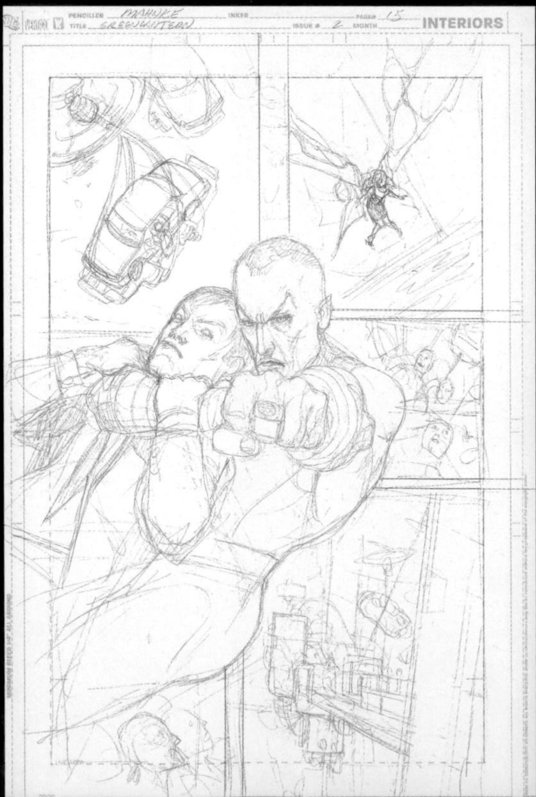
INTERIORS

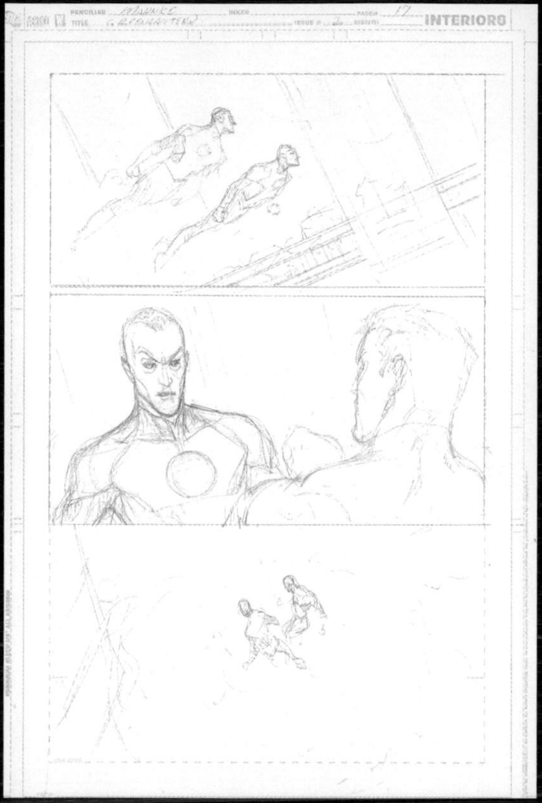

PENCILLER MAHNKE
TITLE GREEN LANTERN
INKER
PAGE# 17
ISSUE # 2
INTERIORS

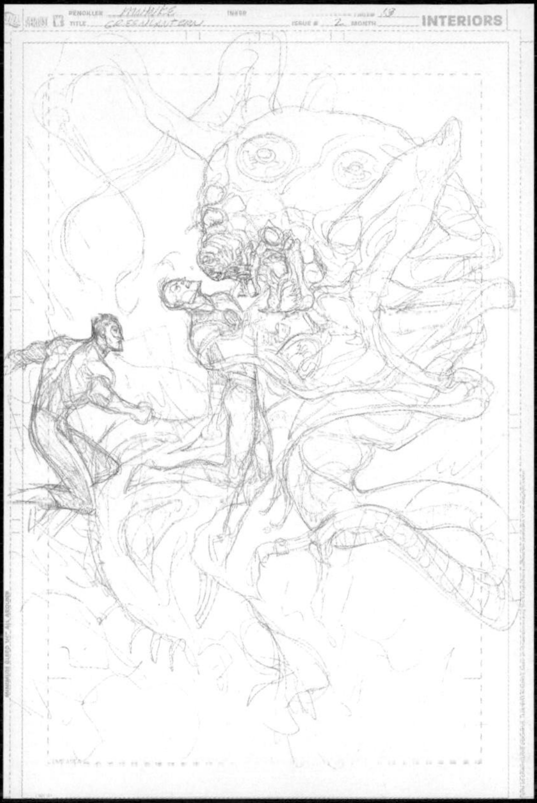

PENCILLER MAHNKE
TITLE GREEN LANTERN
INKER
PAGE# 18
ISSUE # 2
INTERIORS

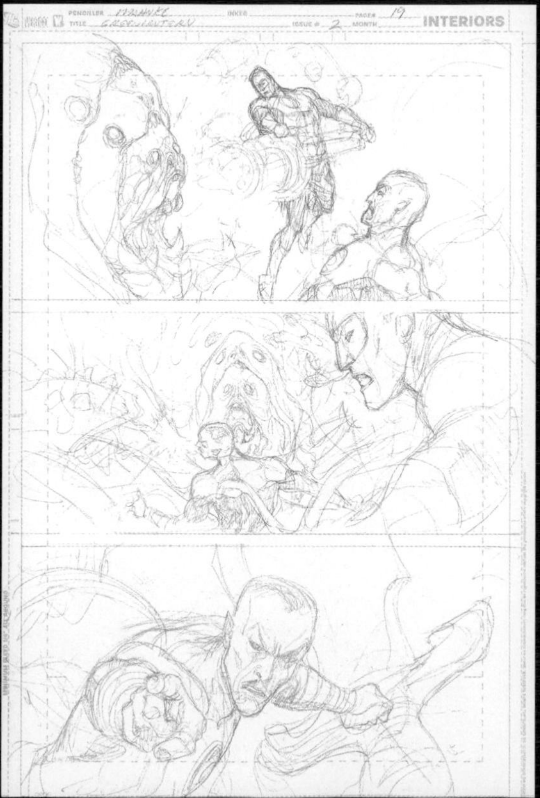

PENCILLER MAHNKE
TITLE GREEN LANTERN
INKER
PAGE# 19
ISSUE # 2
INTERIORS

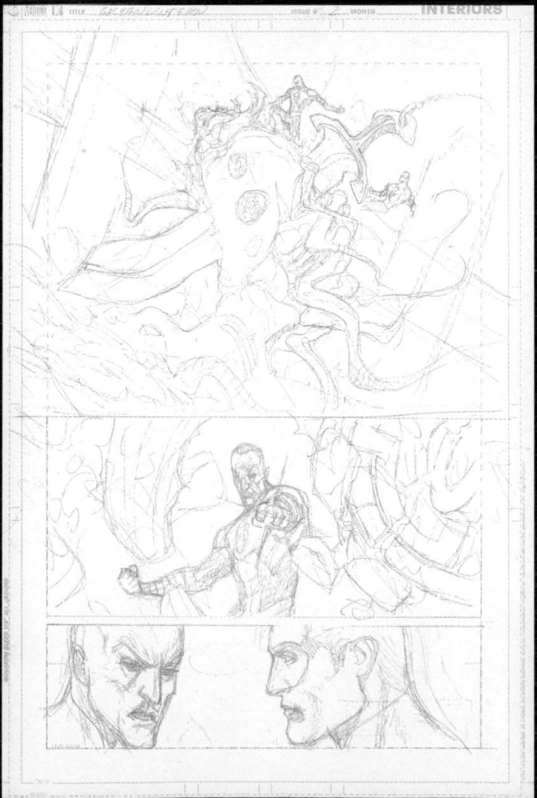

TITLE GREEN LANTERN
ISSUE # 2
INTERIORS

GREEN LANTERN
#3 PAGE PENCILS BY DOUG MAHNKE

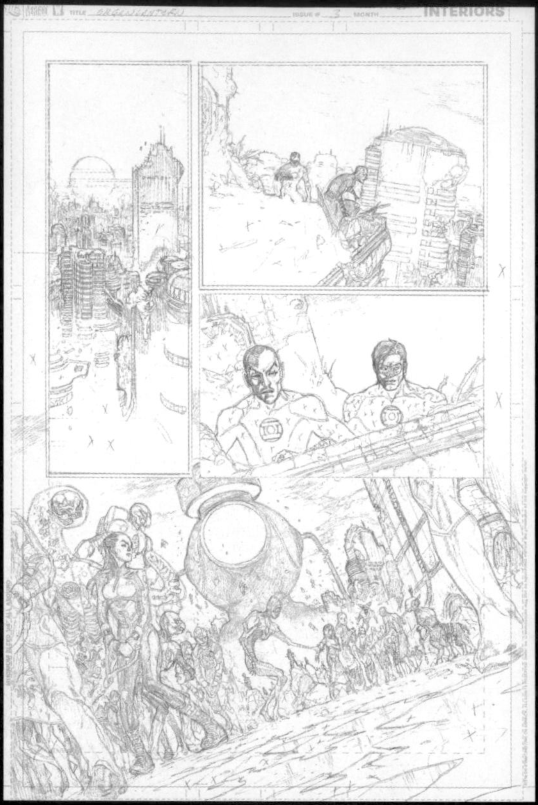
INTERIORS

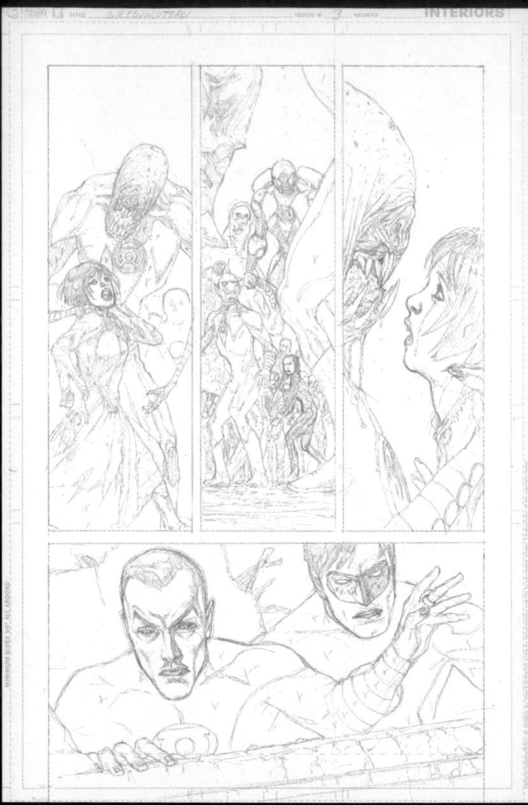
INTERIORS

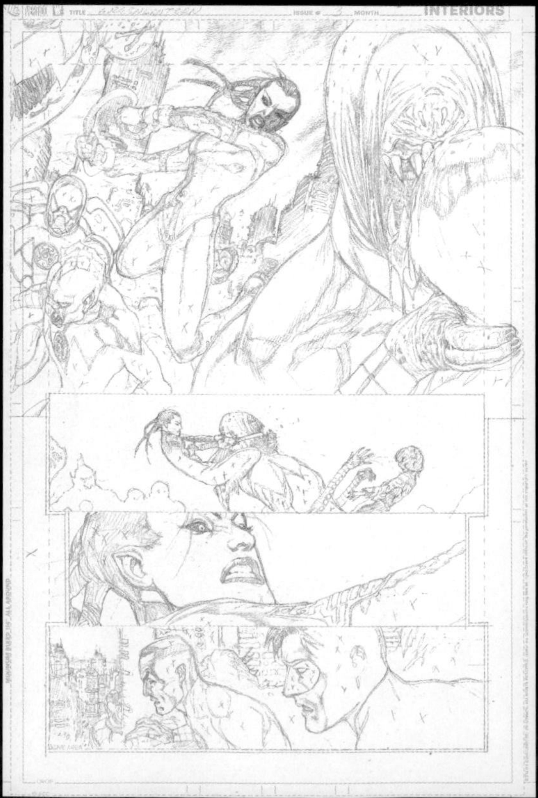
INTERIORS

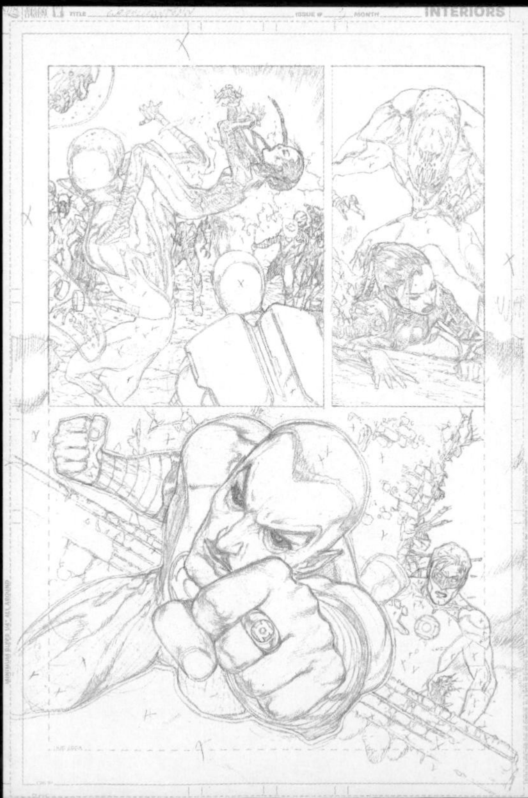
INTERIORS

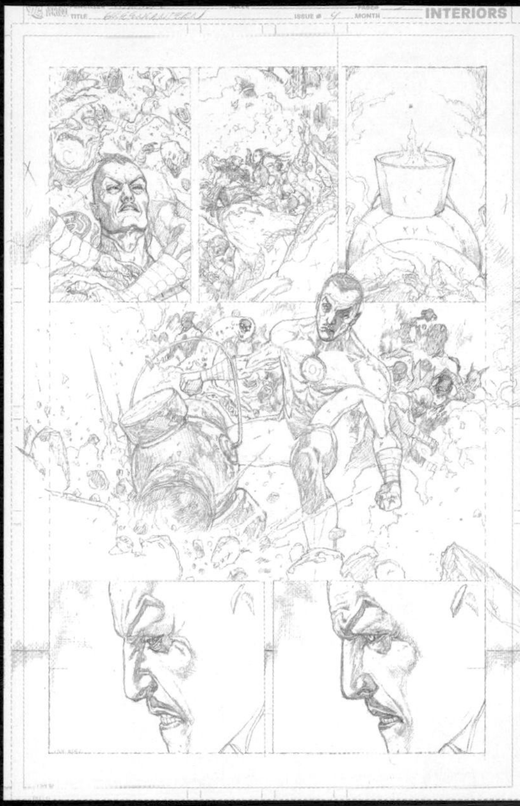
INTERIORS
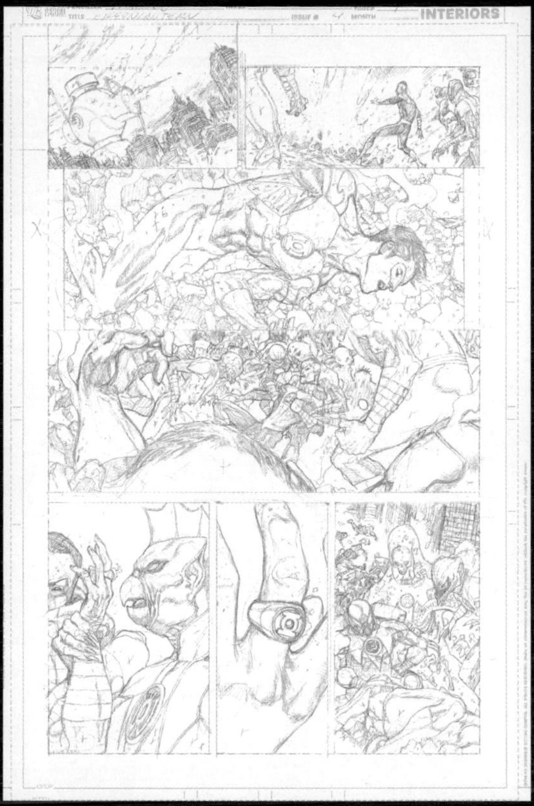
INTERIORS
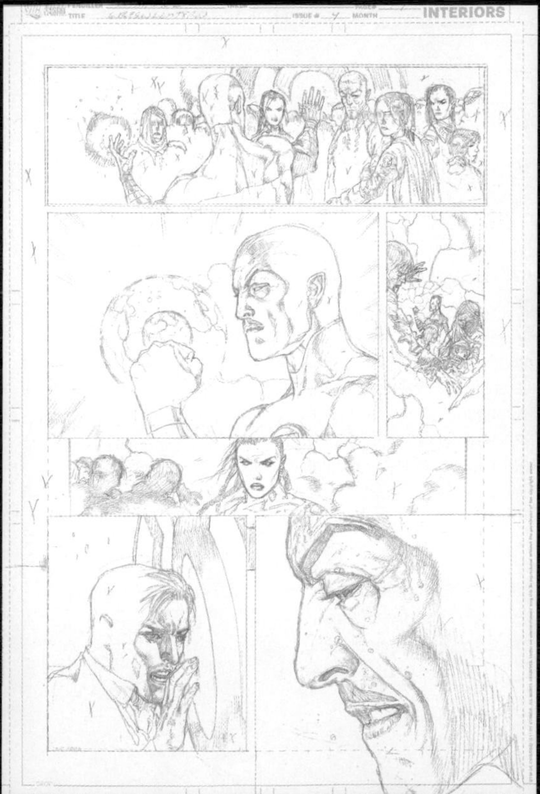
INTERIORS
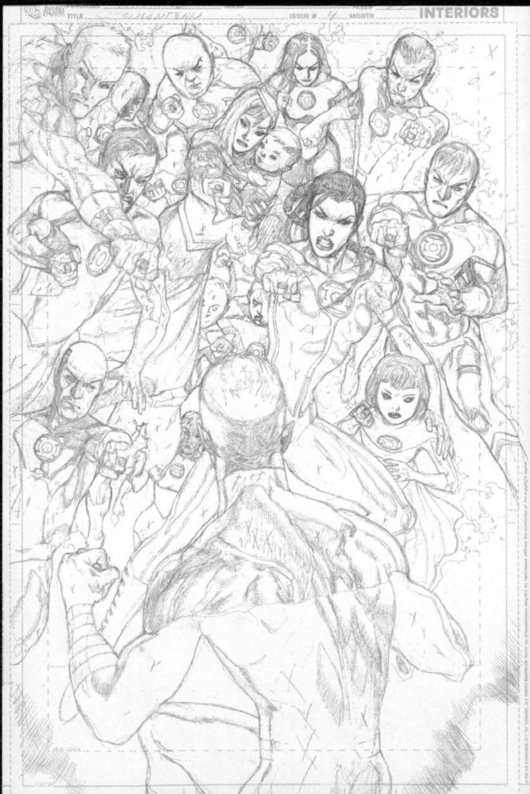
INTERIORS

Character Chest Emblem

Costume Details & Call-Outs

Concept art by Cully Hamner
Based on designs by Jim Lee

Note that on costume, the ring surrounding the emblem is the same thickness as the emblem.

Ring: Negative area in the center of the ring glows continuously and more intensely when active.

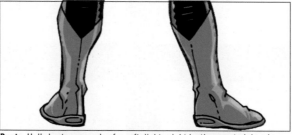

Boots: Hal's boots are made of a soft, lightweight leathery material and feature rubber sneaker-like soles.

Chest Area: The chest emblem on Green Lantern's costume glows continuously even when inactive. It radiates a green plasma-like energy when active or engaging in combat. The lines running through the upper shoulders and the chest also glow like the emblem although with slightly less intensity since there is less surface area. The linear detail maintains a faint glow when Hal's powers are inactive.

Character Name: Green Lantern
Real Name: Hal Jordan
Height: 6' 2"
Weight: 186 lbs.

Eye Color: Brown
Hair Color: Brown
First Appearance:
Justice League #1 (2011)

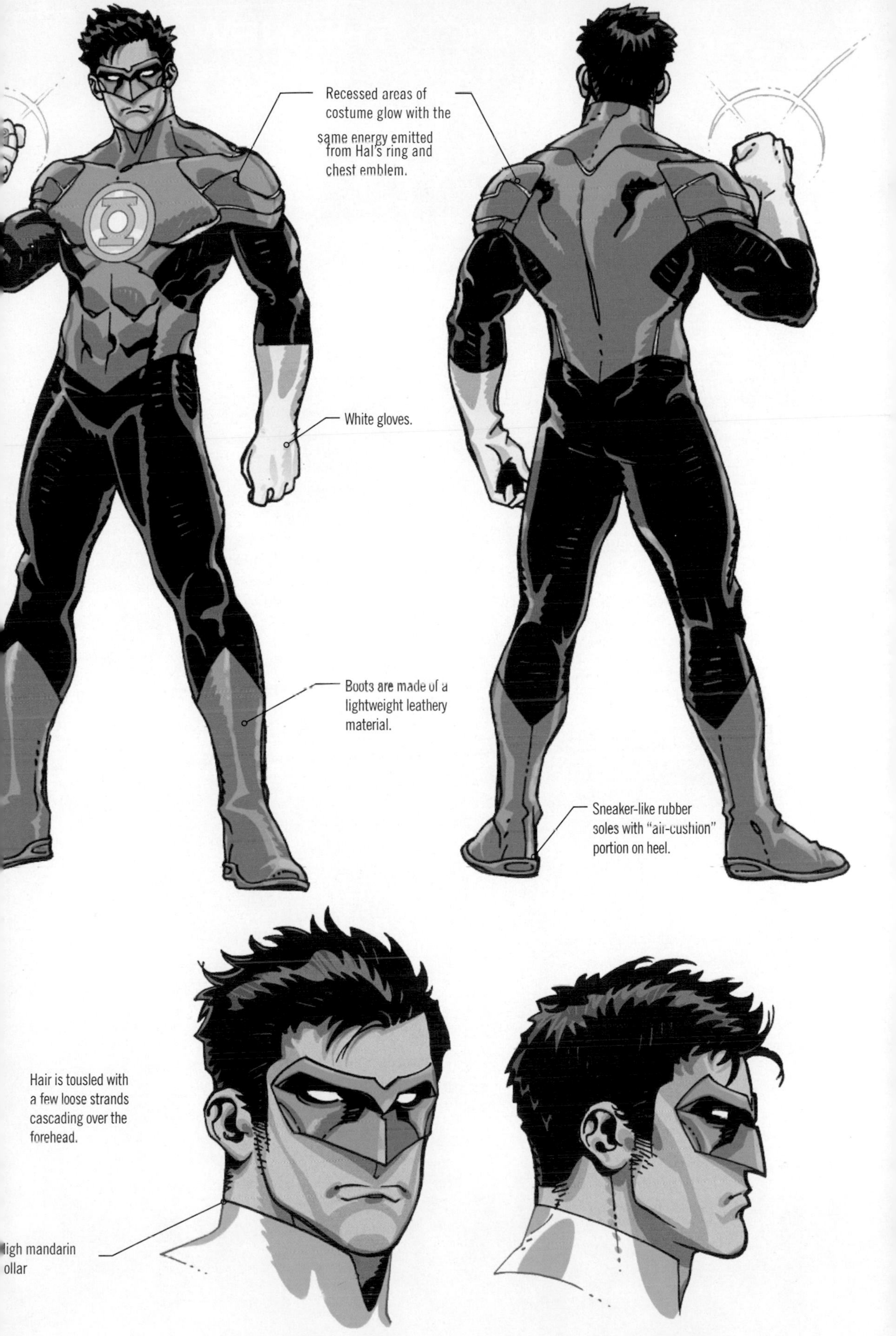
Recessed areas of costume glow with the same energy emitted from Hal's ring and chest emblem.
White gloves.
Boots are made of a lightweight leathery material.
Sneaker-like rubber soles with "air-cushion" portion on heel.
Hair is tousled with a few loose strands cascading over the forehead.
ligh mandarin ollar

DC COMICS-THE NEW 52!

GRAPHIC NOVELS RELEASE SCHEDULE

MAY
- Animal Man Vol 1: The Hunt
- Batman Vol 1: The Court of Owls
- Catwoman Vol 1: The Game
- Green Arrow Vol 1: The Midas Touch
- Green Lantern Vol 1: Sinestro
- Justice League International Vol 1: The Signal Masters
- Justice League Vol 1: Origin
- Stormwatch Vol 1: The Dark Side
- Wonder Woman Vol 1: Blood

JUNE
- Batman: Detective Comics Vol 1: Faces of Death
- Batwoman Vol 1: Hydrology
- Frankenstein Agent of S.H.A.D.E. Vol 1: War of The Monsters
- Legion of Super-Heroes Vol 1: Hostile World
- Mister Terrific Vol 1: Mind Games
- Red Lanterns Vol 1: Blood and Rage
- Static Shock Vol 1: Supercharged

JULY
- Batgirl Vol 1: The Darkest Reflection
- Batwing Vol 1: The Lost Kingdom
- Batman and Robin Vol 1: Born to Kill
- Demon Knights Vol 1: Seven Against the Dark
- Grifter Vol 1: Most Wanted
- Men of War Vol 1: Uneasy Company
- Suicide Squad Vol 1: Kicked in the Teeth

AUGUST
- Deathstroke Vol 1: Legacy
- Hawk and Dove Vol 1: First Strikes
- O.M.A.C. Vol 1: Omactivate!
- Resurrection Man Vol 1: Dead Again
- Superman: Action Comics Vol 1: Superman and The Men of Steel
- Superboy Vol 1: Incubation
- Swamp Thing Vol 1: Raise Them Bones

SEPTEMBER
- Aquaman Vol 1: The Trench
- Birds of Prey Vol 1: Trouble in Mind
- The Fury of Firestorm: The Nuclear Men Vol 1: God Particle
- Green Lantern Corps Vol 1: Fearsome
- Legion Lost Vol 1: Run from Tomorrow
- Teen Titans Vol 1: It's Our Right to Fight
- Voodoo Vol 1: What Lies Beneath

OCTOBER
- All-Star Western Vol 1: Guns and Gotham
- Batman: The Dark Knight Vol 1: Knight Terrors
- Green Lantern: New Guardians Vol 1: The Ring Bearer
- I, Vampire Vol 1: Tainted Love
- Justice League Dark Vol 1: In the Dark
- Nightwing Vol 1: Traps and Trapezes
- The Savage Hawkman Vol 1: Darkness Rising
- Supergirl Vol 1: The Last Daughter of Krypton

NOVEMBER
- Blackhawks Vol 1: The Great Leap Forward
- Blue Beetle Vol 1: Metamorphosis
- Captain Atom Vol 1: Evolution
- DC Universe Presents Vol 1 Featuring Deadman & Challengers of the Unknown
- The Flash Vol 1: Move Forward
- Red Hood and The Outlaws Vol 1: Redemption
- Superman Vol 1: What Price Tomorrow?

The First Volumes of the Decade's Biggest Comics Event

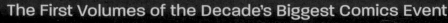

DCCOMICS.COM

DC COMICS